THE
MIGRATION
READER

THE
MIGRATION
READER

Exploring Politics and Policies

edited by
Anthony M. Messina
Gallya Lahav

LYNNE
RIENNER
PUBLISHERS

BOULDER
LONDON

To our students and colleagues, who fueled our efforts;
Strasbourg, where our minds met and the volume was conceived; and
our respective families, large and small, but especially (for Anthony)
Fran and Michael and (for Gallya) Michael, Odeya, and Erez—
whose hearts inspire it all

Published in the United States of America in 2006 by
Lynne Rienner Publishers, Inc.
1800 30th Street, Boulder, Colorado 80301
www.rienner.com

and in the United Kingdom by
Lynne Rienner Publishers, Inc.
3 Henrietta Street, Covent Garden, London WC2E 8LU

Library of Congress Cataloging-in-Publication Data
The migration reader : exploring politics and policy / edited by Anthony M. Messina &
Gallya Lahav.
      p.   cm.
   Includes bibliographical references and index.
   ISBN 978-1-58826-314-8 (hardcover : alk. paper)
   ISBN 978-1-58826-339-1 (pbk. : alk. paper)
   1. Emigration and immigration—Government policy.   2. Emigration and immigration.
3. Transnationalism.   I. Messina, Anthony M.   II. Lahav, Gallya.
JV6038.M5463   2005
325'.1—dc22
                                                                            2005018563

British Cataloguing in Publication Data
A Cataloguing in Publication record for this book
is available from the British Library.

Printed and bound in the United States of America

∞ The paper used in this publication meets the requirements
of the American National Standard for Permanence of
Paper for Printed Library Materials Z39.48-1992.

10   9   8   7   6   5   4

Contents

chapter 1

Introduction

Gallya Lahav & Anthony M. Messina

The phenomenon of migration is rooted in human prehistory, when people routinely traveled over great distances to hunt, fish, establish a livelihood, and secure a home. However, it only became politicized, and hence legally and politically circumscribed, beginning in the nineteenth century, when the modern nation-state arose and erected political-territorial borders around ethnocultural communities. From this point forward the nation was the political community that conferred the state's legitimacy over its territory and transformed the latter into an entity comprising formal citizens. Following from this historical development, the concept of nationality emerged to link all citizens formally to the state. The phenomenon of international migration came to be defined as the movement of persons, that is, nonnationals or foreigners, across national borders for purposes other than travel or short-term residence.

With approximately 175 million people currently residing outside their country of origin, international migration is at its historical zenith. Within this group are more than 17 million asylum seekers, refugees, and other persons of concern to the United Nations High Commissioner for Refugees. Although Australia, Canada, Israel, New Zealand, and the United States are typically considered the classic immigration-receiving countries, these five have been joined by others during the past two decades, including many in Europe, that traditionally have been classified as countries of emigration. On the other side of the immigration divide, Latin America, most prominently Mexico, contributes the largest percentage of foreign-born persons to the major countries of immigrant settlement. Of a current population of 108 million Mexican-born persons, approximately 8 million now reside in the United States.

Although the study of international migration necessarily focuses on individuals or groups of people, it is the role of states, laws, and politics that makes migration an especially complex and controversial phenomenon. In this context, international migration inherently raises a tension between the right of individuals to circulate freely (a right rooted in international human rights law) and the right of states to control their borders (based on the principles of sovereignty and institutionalized in international and domestic constitutional law). Furthermore, although the right to leave one's country of origin is generally recognized as a fundamental human right (United Nations Universal Declaration of Human Rights, 1948: Article 13), a corresponding right of persons to enter countries other than their own has never evolved, in part because no modern state wishes to permit unregulated trespassing. Indeed, the tensions between national and international law pertaining to migration have been reconcilable historically only as long as liberal democracies sought to maintain free markets and open borders. In the current global era, haunted by the specter of unique security concerns and daunting economic challenges, contradictions between the two domains of law have increasingly come to the fore, posing dilemmas for policymakers on every side of the migration equation.

The previously published works and original essays that are collected in this volume represent the many and oftentimes controversial and conflicting voices that reverberate within the contemporary scholarship on migration. In crafting this reader, we have been guided by three central objectives. First, we aim to introduce students to the wide range of issues, trends, and topics that spring from the phenomenon of international migration. Second, we wish to familiarize students with the diverse literatures and disciplinary perspectives on the subject. Finally, we seek to inspire students to consider critically the key questions and practical dilemmas that migration poses for contemporary politics, public policy, society, and international relations. Informing these objectives is our fervent belief that the study of international migration provides an intellectual window through which students can better comprehend the nature and direction of the historic macroeconomic and political changes currently occurring within the international environment and state-society relations within both affluent and less-developed countries. Because the restrictions imposed by states on the movement of persons across their territorial boundaries affect the welfare of both prospective immigrants and citizens, the study of international migration, in our view, necessarily intersects critical questions pertaining to contemporary citizenship, democratic practice, equality, freedom, globalization, and liberalism.

This reader also seeks to fill a pedagogical void. Having analyzed numerous course syllabi from Europe and the United States, we detect two trends in the teaching of international migration and refugee movements. First, given the unavailability of a comprehensive reader on migration, many instructors have compensated by assembling unwieldy course packets comprising seminal articles. Second, the themes and questions that are typically covered in these syllabi and course packets often overlap, thus leading to unhelpful and distracting repetition. In our view, both trends signal a need for an accessible general reader that can facilitate teaching the subject of migration from an international and comparative perspective.

Although *international migration* explicitly refers to the movement (both emigration and immigration) of people across international borders, the formal categories of who is and who is not an "immigrant" have varied over time and place. As we shall see in Chapter 2, some countries consider anyone settled longer than one year an immigrant; others designate a three-year term. Some governments consider people born in their own country migrants, while others automatically recognize them as citizens. These numerous and often fluid practices make comparative analysis difficult, and they account for the imperfect classifications that are created by international organizations and official statistical agencies that collect and aggregate such data.

To complicate matters further, a single country may admit several types of migrants at the same time, which means that some countries that seem especially "generous" to highly skilled workers may have very different and less generous policies toward unskilled laborers. In addition, the traditional classification of the world's countries into "labor-importing countries," "permanent immigration countries," or "migrant-exporting countries" has increasingly become less valid because of the complex and convoluted nature of migration. Countries such as the Philippines that have historically contributed a large percentage of the foreign-born persons to the major countries of immigrant settlement (especially as domestic workers and nurses) have also recently become significant countries of destination, thus making them both immigration-receiving and -sending countries.

The various academic disciplines naturally approach the study of migration in different and sometimes conflicting ways. As a result, a comprehensive understanding of the migration dynamic can seem elusive. As political scientists, our objective in this volume is to provide a comparative and international relations perspective on the broad-based scholarly literature on migration. Because politics is fundamentally about managing conflict, we privilege the numerous conflicts (demographic, economic, security, social, etc.) that migration generates for states through the lenses of comparative politics and international relations, subfields of political science. We are especially interested in the interrelationship between international migration and the nation-state, the latter of which is the central unit organizing the political world. Although we recognize that the demographic, economic, or sociological dimension of migration may top the political agenda at any given moment, our bias is to focus primarily on the controversies that require resolution in the first instance by politics. This is our value added to an anthology of immigration that explores politics and policy from the perspective of political science broadly defined. Adopting politics and policy as our primary reference points allows us to explore the immigration dynamic from the perspective of the multiple actors that are especially central to the immigration process (e.g., immigrants, society, policymakers) as well as the international regimes that influence the transnational flow of immigration (e.g., the Bretton Woods order, the Geneva Refugee regime).

In considering international migration from multiple perspectives and contexts and connecting it to the contemporary world, this reader necessarily touches on issues and questions that should be of interest to more than political scientists. Historians, for example, might ask whether contemporary waves of immigration are unusually large. Anthropologists might ponder whether migration will transform the ethnic composition of a country. Other questions might be economically inspired. For example, are immigrants unusually enterprising? Does immigration depress wages or increase unemployment? Does immigration lead to a more unequal distribution of income? Do immigrants impose an undue welfare burden on domestic economies? Does their labor reduce or increase international competitiveness? In addition to these questions, issues of ethics, national security, and culture are represented within these pages.

Whatever their specific nature, conflicts about immigration almost inevitably generate considerable heat and much popular passion. Although empirical research can inform and perhaps even cool this passion, only rarely does it resolve most controversies. As the collected articles in this volume document, scholars frequently diverge in their thinking on even the most important questions. For example, some econometricians claim that the effects of immigration on the wages of native workers are few and relatively inconsequential, whereas others, informed by alternative and contrary empirical evidence, claim that immigration has especially negative effects. Similarly, some demographers see immigration as a solution to the problems of population decline and demographic aging, whereas others vehemently deny this claim.

One of the reasons that empirical research, however rigorous, does not necessarily resolve the disagreements regarding migration is that, at their root, many of the conflicts are as much about ethics and values as they are about objective facts. For example, what sort of country one wants and how one sees immigrants and their descendants fitting into it are highly subjective questions. If we ultimately conclude, as several of the authors in this volume do, that the heart of the contemporary immigration dilemma centers on values, then we must equally conclude that, whatever immigration's future trajectory or volume, domestic and international conflict over it is likely to endure. Given that politics, according to at least one prominent definition, is about "the authoritative allocation of values," immigration will long be the object of conflict management and politics.

In line with the aforementioned objectives and perspectives, we have organized the volume into four parts. Part 1 introduces the general concepts, issues, and trends associated with international migration and the

paradigms that inform, organize, and inspire the prevailing scholarly literature. This section also explores the various disciplinary accounts of the
"pushes" and "pulls" that govern population movements, approaches that
range from the demographic and economic to the social and political.
Among the important questions raised in this section are: Who are the
migrants? Why do people migrate?

Part 2 traces the historical origins of contemporary migration. Among
the arguments this section introduces is the notion that contemporary patterns of migration are a product of the interrelationship between the forces
of capitalism and the consolidation of nation-states as the latter play out
within the international order. In focusing on its economic, demographic,
and political dimensions, this section locates migration at the crossroads of
the literatures of international political economy and international security.

Part 3 considers the many factors that constrain immigration and immigrant policymaking within the major immigration-receiving countries.
Within this context, the section introduces the range of actors, including
legislatures, courts, bureaucracies, mass publics, political parties, and pressure groups, as well as nonstate actors that influence the formulation and
implementation of public policy. A key question raised in this section is:
How does mass immigration contribute to the growth and proliferation of
extreme-right political parties? This section concludes by assessing the
challenges of transforming immigrants into citizens and incorporating the
new ethnic minorities into the societies and politics of the immigration-
receiving countries.

Part 4 raises three timely questions. First, can migration be effectively
regulated? Second, can states realistically and successfully respond to the
challenges posed by immigration by acting unilaterally? Third, to what
degree do states have a moral obligation to maintain open borders and societies? The section concludes by exploring the changing dynamics of migration in an increasingly global environment and its implications for state
sovereignty. Among the issues raised here are the practices of human smuggling and trafficking, fraudulent asylum seeking, the growth of female
migration, east-west migration flows, and new multilateral responses to
secure national borders.

As the chapters in this volume will attest, the enormous exodus of persons around the world springs from varied circumstances. Moreover, as
many of the chapters show, immigration is driven and sustained by numerous and increasingly complicated causes. With little sign of abating any
time soon, the annual flow of millions of persons across national borders
will continue to pose daunting problems for virtually all contemporary
societies and states.

ing in the host country. In several countries in Western Europe, for example, denizens are permitted to vote in local elections. Although there are numerous denizens in Europe and elsewhere, their numbers are fewer than they might be if it were not for the fact that dual citizenship has become increasingly tolerated within both the economically developed and the underdeveloped countries.

In countries where immigration has been significant and long-lived and has attracted a critical number of persons from societies with very different cultural, religious, and social mores and traditions, one is likely to find significant pressures for *multiculturalism,* specifically multicultural public policies. Although a highly contested concept, multiculturalism generally implies the near equal coexistence of different cultures within a given society. It is inspired by the insight that different cultures represent different interpretations of the good life that are equally deserving of community-wide respect. The central political claim of multiculturalism is that minority groups can be successfully incorporated within the host society only when governments acknowledge through their public policies that the culture of each minority group has a value equal to that of the so-called majority group. By this standard, contemporary Austria, Britain, France, the Netherlands, Norway, and Sweden are multicultural societies.

When multicultural policies fail, and quite often even when they do not, the cause and/or the result can be elevated levels of *xenophobia,* or the popular fear or hatred of strangers or foreigners. Citizens or so-called natives often succumb to xenophobia because immigrants and other foreigners introduce into their environment customs, languages, and/or religious practices that are unfamiliar and therefore threatening. Perhaps even more seriously than xenophobia, *racism* is a full-fledged ideology within which negative qualities are attributed to groups or persons of a particular race or color. Taking different forms in different countries over time, racism promotes the idea that a discernible and stable racial hierarchy exists among the world's populations.

Both xenophobia and racism find particularly fertile ground when immigrants do not successfully integrate or assimilate into the mainstream of the host society. *Assimilation* is the process whereby immigrants and their descendants become increasingly similar to the majority population in their patterns of cultural, economic, or political behaviors and perspectives. A society within which immigrant assimilation is an explicit goal and an ongoing process is often referred to as a *melting pot,* an end state in which the mixing of native and immigrant cultures gradually produces a new and somewhat different national culture. The process of immigrant assimilation can be mostly spontaneous, voluntary, and self-interested or, alternatively, may be encouraged or mandated by government and other major societal actors.

■ Reference

Collinson, Sarah. 1994. *Europe and International Migration*. London: Pinter
    Publishers.

Deutsche Bank Research

International Migration: Who, Where and Why?

Fears have been spreading for quite some time that migration flows, especially in the poor countries, will grow rapidly due to globalisation and that another great migration of peoples will set in. Time and again, people have been forced to leave their traditional home or felt inclined to do so, e.g. because the Huns invaded their country, there was a risk of famine or the Promised Land beckoned. In most cases, such migration flows gave rise to tensions, in some cases even hatred between the domestic population and the new arrivals. The debate on the management of migration continues to be a major issue of concern. However, the need for a solution to the problem is becoming increasingly urgent for most industrial nations as severe changes in the structures of societies are ahead: for quite some time the population of many industrial countries has grown only as a result of a higher life expectancy and immigration. In the next few decades immigration will increasingly be required in order to stabilize population figures. This development is accompanied by a shift in the age structure: the share of older people is growing steadily. This puts particular pressure on social-security systems financed on a pay-as-you-go basis. Furthermore, the business world fears a dramatic lack of skilled labour if no regulations covering managed migration are implemented. As qualified human capital is increasingly becoming a crucial production factor, the importance of appropriate policies to manage migration flows is growing. A hesitant attitude with respect to this issue could have serious repercussions as almost all industrial nations face the same challenge. In the western world, a long-term, fierce "beauty contest" for highly qualified staff is ahead, but much more is at stake. This does not mean that the industrial countries can escape their humanitarian responsibility though. The reception of refugees from crisis areas will continue to be an integral part of immigration policy.

Excerpts from "International Migration: Who, Where and Why?" *Current Issues: Demography Special* (Frankfurt: Deutsche Bank Research, Aug. 1, 2003).

■ Why People Emigrate

On the assumption that people act rationally and on their own responsibility all decisions are—apart from those shaped by political constraints—ultimately attributable to individual considerations. In this sense, the decision for migration is based on people's assumption that a move will improve their living conditions; the net benefits of staying and migrating are offset against each other. The motives for migration are much more complex than pure wage gaps (disposable net income) between the country of origin and the host country. Mass phenomena only occur if many individuals make similar decisions based on rational factors because they are living in the same environment.

Furthermore, differences in the cost of living between the country of origin and the destination country have to be taken into account. For example, gross monthly wages in Poland are more than 70% below Western European levels. If these figures are adjusted for country-specific purchasing power, the wage gap narrows to roughly 50%. Such differences continue to be a major incentive for migration, however. In addition, people in Poland still run a much higher risk of becoming unemployed than in Germany.

As a matter of fact, a simple wage comparison is insufficient as non-work income, the availability of public goods and the required financing contribution also have to be taken into account. Furthermore, it must not be overlooked that a decision to migrate often implies a long-term commitment. Thus, potential migrants will not only look at current wage gaps but also at relative growth prospects. If wages are expected to rise strongly in the country of origin, a wait-and-see attitude becomes more attractive for potential emigrants, it can even make sense for past emigrants to return. For example, very many Spanish people returned to their country after Spain joined the European Community. Then, immigrants usually cannot reach the same wage levels as the domestic population right from the start as they first have to build up society-specific, company-specific and local know-how.

The potential income gains (pull factors) have to be set against the costs of migration. These include direct costs for the job search, the move and the adjustment to the new environment (e.g. need to overcome the language barrier). In addition, social costs—which are hard to quantify—caused by the separation from traditional family, societal and cultural networks are of major importance. The distance between the country of origin and the destination country has a substantial impact on the costs of migration. The greater the distance to the country of destination, the higher the expense of moving; staying in touch with the previous environment also becomes more difficult, i.e., more expensive. Finally, geographic distance is also an indication of cultural proximity. The greater the distance between

public expenditure to enable asylum-seekers to cover their basic economic needs. An evaluation under economic efficiency criteria would be out of place as the principle of humanitarian aid has top priority in such cases. Here, economic considerations can at best contribute to decision-making processes.

An economic analysis becomes more important in cases where the search for better living conditions rather than an actual threat is the motive for migration. For the performance of the economies concerned to be optimised and productivity maximised, workers have to be able to choose the location where they can reach the highest productivity. In this sense, employment migration is the result of an arbitrage process at the end of which more goods and services can be produced with the same quantity of input factors. This means that the freedom to move has the same effect as free trade; the usual integration benefits are expanded from tradable to non-tradable goods. Here, the following two aspects are of major importance: the destination country hopes to achieve an increase in productivity as a result of the brain gain. This would at least maintain competitiveness and offer scope for wage increases. However, the country of origin would suffer a brain drain; especially the catch-up economies could lose the most creative and innovative individuals of their workforce. For the emerging markets, a wide-ranging liberalisation of the international labour market could therefore lead to the loss of valuable human resources.

True, overall prosperity increases as a result of a better allocation of production factors. However, it would be wrong to assume that all people benefit from such a development to the same extent. Similar to the technological progress which leads to structural changes, there is a transition period with clear losers in income distribution. If, for example, mainly low-skilled workers migrate to a particular country, the negotiating position of staff with low skills already working in that country weakens. Wages for this group could come under pressure; in very inflexible labour markets at least wage increases will slow down and/or workers will lose their jobs. At the same time, capital owners, skilled labour and, of course, migrant workers benefit from the situation. Even the workforce staying in the country of origin may post rising incomes in traditional migration models as their wage-negotiating position improves as a result of the move of potential competitors. Actual wage losses for workers when there is scope for substitution by migrants depend on the extent of integration of the respective national economies in the international division of labour. The more open they are, the more likely migration leads to an increase in output and a shift in imports and exports. In such cases, even low-skilled workers can benefit in the destination country. According to studies on employment and wage effects triggered by immigration, the impact has so far been non-existent or limited.[8]

■ Immigration Policy of the Future . . .

The increased integration of the global village has facilitated migration flows in many respects and made people more sensitive to the challenge— both in the countries of origin and the destination countries. For this reason migration is unlikely to decline strongly in the next few decades. Neither has the international community in the last few decades been successful in reducing the number of conflict spots, nor have breakthroughs been achieved in the fight against poverty. Furthermore, the immigration issue is moving to the fore of political debate especially as a result of the ageing of society in most industrial countries. In particular, the recruitment of qualified and highly qualified labour as well as labour in growth sectors, such as nursing care, could become crucial. The already frequently cited war for talents will thus increasingly become an international phenomenon and part of domestic and foreign-policy debate.

Although experts have recognised the benefits of immigration in the societies concerned, much remains to be done in this respect. Consensus has so far been reached only on the principle of selective and managed immigration. Thus, very similar concepts are likely to be worked out across borders. As undesired immigration is to be avoided, the early 21st century will probably be marked by controlled migration. In this sense most OECD countries are advocating more, and stricter, immigration controls.[9] Besides the stronger protection of borders, cooperation with sending countries is being agreed upon, in most cases probably on the basis of development aid (barter), which as a result of economic and political improvements in the sending countries could reduce undesired migration. Furthermore, the selection process for qualified job-seekers and asylum-seekers is to start and be conducted in the home country of the applicant. The motives behind this measure are to reduce the number of unfounded asylum applications and to achieve an improvement in the selection and preparation of skilled emigrant labour.

In the host country itself extended measures on illegal immigration and illegal occupation aim to curb unwanted immigration. Streamlined and effective asylum application and reception processes could help to control illicit immigration while, at the same time, promoting the integration of migrants who satisfy the selection criteria. Successful efforts towards integration could in combination with government-supported measures and information campaigns help to combat discrimination and racism.

■ . . . And Its Implementation

Given the situative adjustments in many countries in the last few decades a revision of immigration legislation seems overdue. Germany is no exception in this respect. Although new bills have been under debate in Germany as well, fundamental issues have not yet been resolved. First, it has to be

number of migrants, followed by the Russian Federation with 13 million and Germany with 7 million.

. . . The four highest [countries with the highest proportion of migrant stock] are in Western Asia: United Arab Emirates (74 percent), Kuwait (58 percent), Jordan (40 percent) and Israel (37 percent).

About 9 percent of the migrants are refugees. At the end of 2000, the number of refugees in the world stood at 16 million, of which 12 million are under the mandate of United Nations High Commissioner for Refugees (UNHCR) and 4 million under the mandate of United Nations Relief and Welfare Agency (UNRWA). The largest number of refugees is found in Asia, 9 million, and in Africa, 4 million. Three million refugees are in developed countries and 13 million in developing countries.

Beginning in the late 1970s, major changes in Governments' views and policies on the level of immigration have been taking place, as a result of growing concerns with the economic, political and social consequences of immigration. By 2001, almost one-quarter of all countries viewed immigration levels as too high. Although developed countries are more inclined towards lowering immigration, developing countries are also moving in a similar direction towards more restrictive policies. In 2001, 44 percent of developed countries had policies aiming to lower immigration levels, as did 39 percent of developing countries. Developed and developing countries are strikingly similar in their views and policies concerning levels of emigration. About three-quarters of both developed and developing countries view their level of emigration as satisfactory. One in five countries have policies in place to lower levels of emigration.

Remittances sent back to the home country by migrants are a major source of foreign exchange earnings for some countries and are an important addition to gross domestic product. For example, in 2000, remittances from abroad were more than 10 percent of the gross domestic product for countries such as Albania, Bosnia and Herzegovina, Cape Verde, El Salvador, Jamaica, Jordan, Nicaragua, Samoa and Yemen. Remittances can be used to import capital goods and provide investment funds for entrepreneurs. Also important, remittances can augment household income and savings and be used for the purchase of consumer products and services.

Since 1951, the international community has adopted a number of conventions and protocols for the protection of migrants. Among the most prominent are the 1951 Convention and 1967 Protocol, which relates to the status of refugees, and the 1990 Convention and 2000 Protocol which considers the protection of migrants and trafficking in persons. The 1951 Convention relating to the Status of Refugees, ratified by 141 countries, establishes legal protections and a clear definition of the status of refugees. It also prohibits the expulsion or forcible return of persons accorded refugee status. The 1967 Protocol relating to the Status of Refugees, ratified by 139 countries, extends the scope of the 1951 Convention, which benefited only persons who became refugees prior to 1 January 1951. It also extends the application of the Convention to persons who became refugees after that date.

The 1990 International Convention on the Protection of the Rights of all Migrant Workers and Members of their Families, ratified by 19 countries, establishes an international definition of the different categories of migrant workers. It formalizes the responsibility of receiving States in regard to upholding the rights of migrants and assuring their protection. The 2000 Protocol to Prevent, Suppress and Punish Trafficking in Persons, Especially Women and Children, supplementing the United Nations Convention against Transnational Organized Crime, ratified by 18 countries, aims to prevent and combat trafficking in persons, particularly women and children; to protect and assist the victims of such trafficking; and to promote cooperation among States parties to meet these objectives. Finally, the 2000 Protocol against the Smuggling of Migrants by Land, Sea and Air, supplementing the United Nations Convention against Transnational Organized Crime, ratified by 17 countries, aims to combat and prevent the smuggling of human cargo, reaffirming that migration in itself is not a crime, and that migrants may be victims in need of protection.

This report provides a wealth of information on international migration levels, trends and policies. Nevertheless, migration information remains incomplete and often inaccurate. Many of the data provided in this report are based on imputation or proxies of the numbers of foreign born; in particular, data on citizenship are used in the absence of data on place of birth. Documenting migration levels, trends and policies remains a major challenge. In many countries, the information is neither available nor produced on a regular basis. Furthermore, responsibility for the formulation, implementation and evaluation of migration data is often diffused among Government bodies as well as among international organizations.

■ The National Response

As a global phenomenon involving a growing number of countries, international migration has been thrust to the forefront of the international policy agenda. When the United Nations Secretariat began systematically tracking international migration policies in the 1970s, following the 1974 World Population Conference in Bucharest, international migration was an issue of secondary interest to most Governments. Major demographic concerns at that time included high levels of population growth, fertility and mortality. Government policies on migration focused mainly on the administrative regulation of national borders.

As concerns with the demographic, economic, social and political contion, only a fragmented set of theories that have developed largely in isolation from one another, sometimes but not always segmented by disciplinary boundaries. Current patterns and trends in immigration, however, suggest that a full understanding of contemporary migratory processes will not be achieved by relying on the tools of one discipline alone, or by focusing on a single level of analysis. Rather, their complex, multifaceted nature requires a sophisticated theory that incorporates a variety of perspectives, levels, and assumptions.

The purpose of this article is to explicate and integrate the leading contemporary theories of international migration. We begin by examining models that describe the initiation of international movement and then consider theories that account for why transnational population flows persist across space and time. Rather than favoring one theory over another a priori, we seek to understand each model on its own terms in order to illuminate key assumptions and hypotheses. Only after each theory has been considered separately do we compare and contrast the different conceptual frameworks to reveal areas of logical inconsistency and substantive disagreement. In undertaking this exercise, we seek to provide a sound basis for evaluating the models empirically, and to lay the groundwork for constructing an accurate and comprehensive theory of international migration for the twenty-first century.

■ The Initiation of International Migration

A variety of theoretical models has been proposed to explain why international migration begins, and although each ultimately seeks to explain the same thing, they employ radically different concepts, assumptions, and frames of reference. Neoclassical economics focuses on differentials in wages and employment conditions between countries, and on migration costs; it generally conceives of movement as an individual decision for income maximization. The "new economics of migration," in contrast, considers conditions in a variety of markets, not just labor markets. It views migration as a household decision taken to minimize risks to family income or to overcome capital constraints on family production activities. Dual labor market theory and world systems theory generally ignore such micro-level decision processes, focusing instead on forces operating at much higher levels of aggregation. The former links immigration to the structural requirements of modern industrial economies, while the latter sees immigration as a natural consequence of economic globalization and market penetration across national boundaries.

Given the fact that theories conceptualize causal processes at such different levels of analysis—the individual, the household, the national, and the international—they cannot be assumed, a priori, to be inherently incompatible. It is quite possible, for example, that individuals act to maximize income while families minimize risk, and that the context within which both decisions are made is shaped by structural forces operating at the national and international levels. Nonetheless, the various models reflect different research objectives, focuses, interests, and ways of decomposing an enormously complex subject into analytically manageable parts; and a firm basis for judging their consistency requires that the inner logic, propositions, assumptions, and hypotheses of each theory be clearly specified and well-understood.

Neoclassical Economics: Macro Theory

Probably the oldest and best-known theory of international migration was developed originally to explain labor migration in the process of economic development (Lewis, 1954; Ranis and Fei, 1961; Harris and Todaro, 1970; Todaro, 1976). According to this theory and its extensions, international migration, like its internal counterpart, is caused by geographic differences in the supply of and demand for labor. Countries with a large endowment of labor relative to capital have a low equilibrium market wage, while countries with a limited endowment of labor relative to capital are characterized by a high market wage, as depicted graphically by the familiar interaction of labor supply and demand curves. The resulting differential in wages causes workers from the low-wage country to move to the high-wage country. As a result of this movement, the supply of labor decreases and wages rise in the capital-poor country, while the supply of labor increases and wages fall in the capital-rich country, leading, at equilibrium, to an international wage differential that reflects only the costs of international movement, pecuniary and psychic.

Mirroring the flow of workers from labor-abundant to labor-scarce countries is a flow of investment capital from capital-rich to capital-poor countries. The relative scarcity of capital in poor countries yields a rate of return that is high by international standards, thereby attracting investment. The movement of capital also includes human capital, with highly skilled workers moving from capital-rich to capital-poor countries in order to reap high returns on their skills in a human capital-scarce environment, leading to a parallel movement of managers, technicians, and other skilled workers. The international flow of labor, therefore, must be kept conceptually distinct from the associated international flow of human capital. Even in the most aggregated macro-level models, the heterogeneity of immigrants along skill lines must be clearly recognized.

The simple and compelling explanation of international migration offered by neoclassical macroeconomics has strongly shaped public thinking and has provided the intellectual basis for much immigration policy. The perspective contains several implicit propositions and assumptions:

1. The international migration of workers is caused by differences in wage rates between countries.

2. The elimination of wage differentials will end the movement of labor, and migration will not occur in the absence of such differentials.

3. International flows of human capital—that is, highly skilled workers—respond to differences in the rate of return to human capital, which may be different from the overall wage rate, yielding a distinct pattern of migration that may be opposite that of unskilled workers.

4. Labor markets are the primary mechanisms by which international flows of labor are induced; other kinds of markets do not have important effects on international migration.

5. The way for governments to control migration flows is to regulate or influence labor markets in sending and/or receiving countries.

Neoclassical Economics: Micro Theory

Corresponding to the macroeconomic model is a microeconomic model of individual choice (Sjaastad, 1962; Todaro, 1969, 1976, 1989; Todaro and Maruszko, 1987). In this scheme, individual rational actors decide to migrate because a cost-benefit calculation leads them to expect a positive net return, usually monetary, from movement. International migration is conceptualized as a form of investment in human capital. People choose to move to where they can be most productive, given their skills; but before they can capture the higher wages associated with greater labor productivity they must undertake certain investments, which include the material costs of traveling, the costs of maintenance while moving and looking for work, the effort involved in learning a new language and culture, the difficulty experienced in adapting to a new labor market, and the psychological costs of cutting old ties and forging new ones.

Potential migrants estimate the costs and benefits of moving to alternative international locations and migrate to where the expected discounted net returns are greatest over some time horizon (Borjas, 1990). Net returns in each future period are estimated by taking the observed earnings corresponding to the individual's skills in the destination country and multiplying these by the probability of obtaining a job there (and for illegal migrants the likelihood of being able to avoid deportation) to obtain "expected destination earnings." These expected earnings are then subtracted from those expected in the community of origin (observed earnings there multiplied by the probability of employment) and the difference is summed over a time horizon from 0 to n, discounted by a factor that reflects the greater utility of money earned in the present than in the future. From this integrated difference the estimated costs are subtracted to yield the expected net return to migration. . . .

In theory, a potential migrant goes to where the expected net returns to migration are greatest, leading to several important conclusions that differ slightly from the earlier macroeconomic formulations:

1. International movement stems from international differentials in both earnings and employment rates, whose product determines expected earnings (the prior model, in contrast, assumed full employment).

2. Individual human capital characteristics that increase the likely rate of remuneration or the probability of employment in the destination relative to the sending country (e.g., education, experience, training, language skills) will increase the likelihood of international movement, other things being equal.

3. Individual characteristics, social conditions, or technologies that lower migration costs increase the net returns to migration and, hence, raise the probability of international movement.

4. Because of 2 and 3, individuals within the same country can display very different proclivities to migrate.

5. Aggregate migration flows between countries are simple sums of individual moves undertaken on the basis of individual cost-benefit calculations.

6. International movement does not occur in the absence of differences in earnings and/or employment rates between countries. Migration occurs until expected earnings (the product of earnings and employment rates) have been equalized internationally (net of the costs of movement), and movement does not stop until this product has been equalized.

7. The size of the differential in expected returns determines the size of the international flow of migrants between countries.

8. Migration decisions stem from disequilibria or discontinuities between labor markets; other markets do not directly influence the decision to migrate.

9. If conditions in receiving countries are psychologically attractive to prospective migrants, migration costs may be negative. In this case, a negative earnings differential may be necessary to halt migration between countries.

10. Governments control immigration primarily through policies that affect expected earnings in sending and/or receiving countries—for example, those that attempt to lower the likelihood of employment or raise the risk of underemployment in the destination area (through employer sanctions), those that seek to raise incomes at the origin (through long-term development programs), or those that aim to increase the costs (both psychological and material) of migration.

The New Economics of Migration

In recent years, a "new economics of migration" has arisen to challenge many of the assumptions and conclusions of neoclassical theory (Stark and

countries to protect investments abroad and to support foreign governments sympathetic to the expansion of the global market, when they fail, produce refugee movements directed to particular core countries, constituting another form of international migration.

6. International migration ultimately has little to do with wage rates or employment differentials between countries; it follows from the dynamics of market creation and the structure of the global economy.

■ The Perpetuation of International Movement

Immigration may begin for a variety of reasons—a desire for individual income gain, an attempt to diversify risks to household income, a program of recruitment to satisfy employer demands for low-wage workers, an international displacement of peasants by market penetration within peripheral regions, or some combination thereof. But the conditions that initiate international movement may be quite different from those that perpetuate it across time and space. Although wage differentials, relative risks, recruitment efforts, and market penetration may continue to cause people to move, new conditions that arise in the course of migration come to function as independent causes themselves: migrant networks spread, institutions supporting transnational movement develop, and the social meaning of work changes in receiving societies. The general thrust of these transformations is to make additional movement more likely, a process known as cumulative causation.

Network Theory

Migrant networks are sets of interpersonal ties that connect migrants, former migrants, and nonmigrants in origin and destination areas through ties of kinship, friendship, and shared community origin. They increase the likelihood of international movement because they lower the costs and risks of movement and increase the expected net returns to migration. Network connections constitute a form of social capital that people can draw upon to gain access to foreign employment. Once the number of migrants reaches a critical threshold, the expansion of networks reduces the costs and risks of movement, which causes the probability of migration to rise, which causes additional movement, which further expands the networks, and so on. Over time migratory behavior spreads outward to encompass broader segments of the sending society (Hugo, 1981; Taylor, 1986; Massey and García España, 1987; Massey, 1990a, 1990b; Gurak and Caces, 1992).

Declining costs. The first migrants who leave for a new destination have no social ties to draw upon, and for them migration is costly, particularly if it involves entering another country without documents. After the first migrants have left, however, the potential costs of migration are substantially lowered for friends and relatives left behind. Because of the nature of kinship and friendship structures, each new migrant creates a set of people with social ties to the destination area. Migrants are inevitably linked to nonmigrants, and the latter draw upon obligations implicit in relationships such as kinship and friendship to gain access to employment and assistance at the point of destination.

Once the number of network connections in an origin area reaches a critical threshold, migration becomes self-perpetuating because each act of migration itself creates the social structure needed to sustain it. Every new migrant reduces the costs of subsequent migration for a set of friends and relatives, and some of these people are thereby induced to migrate, which further expands the set of people with ties abroad, which, in turn, reduces costs for a new set of people, causing some of them to migrate, and so on.

Declining risks. Networks also make international migration extremely attractive as a strategy for risk diversification. When migrant networks are well-developed, they put a destination job within easy reach of most community members and make emigration a reliable and secure source of income. Thus, the self-sustaining growth of networks that occurs through the progressive reduction of costs may also be explained theoretically by the progressive reduction of risks. Every new migrant expands the network and reduces the risks of movement for all those to whom he or she is related, eventually making it virtually risk-free and costless to diversify household labor allocations through emigration.

This dynamic theory accepts the view of international migration as an individual or household decision process, but argues that acts of migration at one point in time systematically alter the context within which future migration decisions are made, greatly increasing the likelihood that later decisionmakers will choose to migrate. The conceptualization of migration as a self-sustaining diffusion process has implications and corollaries that are quite different from those derived from the general equilibrium analyses typically employed to study migration:

1. Once begun, international migration tends to expand over time until network connections have diffused so widely in a sending region that all people who wish to migrate can do so without difficulty; then migration begins to decelerate.

2. The size of the migratory flow between two countries is not strongly correlated to wage differentials or employment rates, because whatever effects these variables have in promoting or inhibiting migration are pro-

wages are flexible downward, but not upward. Over time, therefore, fluctuations in wage rates in jobs filled by immigrants should not be strongly related to fluctuations in labor supply and demand. During periods of low labor immigration and high labor demand, wages in receiving countries should not rise to attract native workers because of institutional rigidities, but during periods of high immigration and low demand there is nothing to prevent wages from falling in response to competitive pressure. We thus expect an interaction between changes in wage rates and whether or not immigration was contracting or expanding during the period: the effect is expected to be zero in the former case and negative in the latter. We also expect a widening wage gap between these jobs and those held by native workers over time.

Although world systems theory constitutes a complex and at times diffuse conceptual structure, it yields several relatively straightforward and testable propositions, the first of which is that international flows of labor follow international flows of capital, only in the opposite direction. According to Sassen and others, emigrants are created by direct foreign investment in developing countries and the disruptions that such investment brings. Thus, we should observe that streams of foreign capital going into peripheral regions are accompanied by corresponding outflows of emigrants.

This basic migratory process should be augmented by the existence of ideological and material ties created by prior colonization as well as ongoing processes of market penetration. If one were to specify a model of international migration flows to test world systems theory, therefore, one would want to include indicators of prior colonial relationships, the prevalence of common languages, the intensity of trade relations, the existence of transportation and communication links, and the relative frequency of communications and travel between the countries.

Finally, world systems theory specifies not only that international migration should flow from periphery to core along paths of capital investment, but also that it is directed to certain "global cities" that channel and control foreign investment. Although the theory does not provide specific criteria for defining a "global city," a set of operational criteria might be developed from information about capital assets and corporate headquarters. One could then examine the relative frequency of movement to global cities, as opposed to other places within the developed or developing world.

Network theory leads to a series of eminently testable propositions. According to Piore, Massey, and others, once someone has migrated internationally, he or she is very likely to do so again, leading to repeated movements over time. Thus the likelihood of an additional trip should increase with each trip taken; the probability of transnational migration should be greater among those with prior international experience than among those without it; and the likelihood of additional migration should increase as the amount of foreign experience rises.

A second proposition is that controlling for a person's individual migrant experience, the probability of international migration should be greater for individuals who are related to someone who has prior international experience, or for individuals connected to someone who is actually living abroad. Moreover, the likelihood of movement should increase with the closeness of the relationship (i.e., having a brother in Germany is more likely to induce a Turk to migrate there than having a cousin, a neighbor, or a friend); and it should also rise with the quality of the social capital embodied in the relationship (having a brother who has lived in Germany for ten years is more valuable to a potential emigrant than having one who has just arrived, and having one who is a legal resident is better than having one who lacks residence documents).

Another hypothesis stems from the recognition that international movement requires migrants to overcome more barriers than does internal movement. In addition to the normal costs of travel and searching for work are the costs of learning and adapting to a new culture, the costs of acquiring appropriate documentation, and, if acquiring legal papers is impossible, of evading arrest and deportation. In general, the greater the barriers to movement, the more important should network ties become in promoting migration, since they reduce the costs and risks of movement. We should thus observe that network connections are systematically more powerful in predicting international migration than internal migration. Taylor (1986) finds this differentiated effect of migration networks for a sample of Mexican households.

Within households, we should also be able to detect the effect of social capital on individual migration behavior. In general, members of households in which someone has already migrated abroad should display higher probabilities of movement than those from households that lack migratory experience. If network theory is correct, for example, a common vector by which migratory behavior is transmitted is from fathers to sons (Massey et al., 1987). Dependent sons whose fathers are active or former international migrants should be more likely to emigrate than those whose fathers lack foreign experience.

Finally, at the community level, one should be able to observe the effect of the prevalence of network ties. People should be more likely to migrate abroad if they come from a community where many people have migrated and where a large stock of foreign experience has accumulated than if they come from a place where international migration is relatively uncommon (Massey and García España, 1987). Moreover, as the stock of social ties and international migrant experience grows over time, migration should become progressively less selective and spread from the middle to

termed statist societies, whose social boundaries coincide, by and large, with the frontiers delineated by international law as those of the state. As the occurrence of human migrations indicates that these several entities do not constitute closed systems, it is evident that they interact as parts of some larger whole. The perspective adopted thus requires that its characteristics be specified as well.

Second, the emphasis on transfer of jurisdiction as the constitutive element of international migrations is not to be taken as an exercise in juridical formalism, nor as an argument on behalf of the adoption of a statist point of view in evaluating costs and benefits. From the point of view of the individuals involved, the transfer is coupled with a concomitant process whereby they cease being members of one society and become instead members of another. These changes can be initiated by the individual or by the state, a distinction which does not quite coincide with the traditional categories of voluntary and forced migrations; and it is evident that these initiatives can be motivated on a variety of grounds. Although international frontiers delineate mutually exclusive sovereignties, the changes under consideration are not necessarily an all-or-nothing affair, as the jurisdiction that states exercise over individuals is divisible, and membership in societies can be segmental as well. These processes can, therefore, be thought of as continuous, ranging from the partial and/or temporary to the all-encompassing and/or permanent.

The third and most important point for clarification is that the adoption of a political perspective reveals an elusive, yet crucial, social attribute of the overall subject under consideration: international migration constitutes a deviance from the prevailing norm of social organization at the world level. That norm is reflected not only in the popular conception of a world consisting of reified countries considered as nearly natural entities, but also in the conceptual apparatus common to all the social sciences, predicated on a model of society as a territorially-based, self-reproducing cultural and social system, whose human population is assumed, tacitly or explicitly, to renew itself endogenously over an indefinite period. How axiomatic this model has become can be grasped by the difficulty encountered in conceptualizing alternative models of holistic social organization, an exercise which brings to the fore the notion of diaspora, and thereby draws attention to the disturbing character of international migration in a world of societies (Armstrong, 1976).

From a different perspective, a view of international migration as deviance arises, somewhat paradoxically, from a consideration of current discussions concerning freedom of international movement. Recent efforts in this sphere have focused largely on the implementation of Article 13(2) of the Universal Declaration of Human Rights, which restates the principle originally enunciated by the French Revolution, "Everyone has the right to leave any country, including his own, and to return to his country" (Plender, 1972:41). Albeit somewhat short of the "right of expatriation" militantly advocated by the United States a century ago, and however inadequately implemented, the principle of freedom of exit has come to be generally acknowledged as a desirable norm so that the states who violate it are, so to speak, on the defensive in relation to the international community. It is therefore startling that one cannot conceive of a similar consensus arising from what appears to be a concomitant principle: "Everyone has the right to enter any country." On the contrary, there exists a universal and unambiguous concensus on the very opposite principle, namely, that every state has the right to restrict the entry of foreigners.

Such a right, widely acknowledged in classical jurisprudence and so much taken for granted that it does not appear in national constitutions, cannot be attributed simply to the prevalence of xenophobia.[3] It is an essential attribute of political sovereignty, without which that concept would have little significance; and it can be thought of in sociological terms as a necessary mechanism whereby societies maintain their integrity. Indeed, were the right of individuals to enter any country other than their own to be generalized, the world would thereby undergo a more radical transformation than any it has experienced since the beginnings of modern times.[4] It is the absence of such a right which demonstrates most dramatically the sense in which international migration is fundamentally at odds with the world.

These considerations suggest that the analysis of international migration must be approached by way of a framework which takes its perturbing aspect as a point of departure rather than as the merely incidental feature of an otherwise normal social process. This can be approximated if we conceive of a world which consists, on the one hand, of individuals seeking to maximize their welfare by exercising a variety of choices, including among them that of transferring from one political jurisdiction to another; and which simultaneously consists, on the other hand, of mutually exclusive societies, acting as organized states to maximize collective goals by controlling the exit or entry of individuals. The deviant character of international migration is thus seen to be related to a fundamental tension between the interests of individuals and the interests of societies.

Evocative of the social contract convention devised by philosophers with respect to the foundations of social and political life, the present representation of the world is much less fictional as a large number of individuals do in fact change their societal affiliation by way of physical relocation. In practice, individuals "vote with their feet," *i.e.*, they express their preferences by staying or leaving (including, of course, by attempting to stay or to leave), or by moving temporarily rather than permanently.[5] On the societal side, the notion that exit and entry are controlled in accordance with certain collective interests must be understood in a very broad sense. Control includes not only the erection of more or less restrictive barriers to free movement across state boundaries but also a policy of permissive indifference or benign neglect, as is the case with respect to exit in most liberal regimes during peacetime. To basic policy orientations must be added incentives or sanctions devised to induce or prevent certain movements. On the entry side, control also includes all aspects governing naturalization and legal provisions concerning nationality in general.[6] Collective interests do not refer to some abstraction such as the public good, but rather to the social forces governing the processes of decision-making in the sphere under consideration, whether it be by fiat or in a pluralist manner. What matters is that the resulting regulations are binding on individuals and affect their lives even if they themselves are not involved in the migration process.

The emphasis on political tension does not preclude the possibility that individual and collective interests will coincide in particular instances, as for example with respect to the freedom to stay or to leave, and to return to one's own country, which prevails in liberal democracies. However, the heuristic value of that notion is that it forces reflection on the theoretical issues involved to ascertain under what circumstances individual preferences and societal interests concur, and under what others they are more or less antagonistic. One should not lose sight, finally, of the fact that international migration conceptualized in this manner entails not only a tension between individuals and societies at each end of the trajectory, but also involves a tension in the same sense between sending and receiving states or societies, each of which regulates migration in accordance with goals of its own.

■ World System: A Multidimensional Approach

Unlike the behaviors that are of ordinary concern to social scientists, the preferences of individuals concerning political jurisdiction and societal affiliation, as well as the policy orientations of statist societies with respect to the movement of individuals across their boundaries, entail some orientation toward a larger world of which societies themselves are subordinate units. This can be conceptualized as a set of structures and concomitant processes which are the constitutive elements of an international social system, an entity that is something more than a mere aggregate of autonomous national components but less than a society.

Albeit long familiar in certain forms to political scientists specializing in international relations (*e.g.*, the balance of power system), to economists specializing in international trade, and, at least implicitly, to some global historians, the concept of a global social system remained, until recently, rather marginal among the social sciences. Although a full discussion of this subject would take us too far afield, because a particular version of the international social system has rapidly gained currency in the field of migration theory, it is necessary at this point to indicate its limitations and to adumbrate an alternative model.

I am referring here to Wallerstein's well-known analysis of the modern world system as an entity generated by the birth of capitalism in Western Europe and its subsequent expansion on a global scale (Wallerstein, 1974a and 1974b). Within the system, processes of uneven exchange between geographical regions determined, over the long term, the emergence of a differentiated structure, consisting of a core, a semiperiphery and a periphery. Albeit quite heuristic for the analysis of some aspects of past and present migrations, and particularly for contemporary patterns of temporary labor migrations from the periphery toward the core, Wallerstein's undimensional model cannot account for certain features of the world system that are equally significant from the point of view of international migrations and that often determine trends which contradict, or at least substantially modify, the tendencies generated by the economic structure alone.

In Wallerstein's view, the world system is, by and large, devoid of any overarching political structure, and states are mere instrumentations of the capitalist dynamic (Zolberg, 1980). Moreover, it is the location of societies in each of the segments which determines the form of their political organization: the state is strongest in the core, weakest in the periphery. Yet it is evident that such a conceptualization is fallacious, in that from the beginning of European expansion to the present, international political processes generated by the organization of the world into states have interacted with the forces generated by capitalism in such a way as to determine complex configurations in which economic and political determinants are inextricably linked. In particular, the ability of societies to muster strategic force, which is as much a function of their political organization as of other factors, plays a major role in determining their location in one or the other segment of the modern world system, or even permitting them to remain outside of its domain altogether. This is still true today, as it is force which enables some societies to resist incorporation into the capitalist system or to remove themselves from it, and hence accounts for the coexistence of a world capitalist economy with several noncapitalist world systems. As to the relationship between a given society's position in the modern world system and its regime form, the problem is more complex than Wallerstein allows. For example, if strength and weakness refer to the state as a concrete form of political organization, then within the world system with which Wallerstein is concerned the countries of the core have always varied considerably in the respect that: 1) in the contemporary period, the degree of stateness tends to increase as one moves from the core toward the periphery; and 2) nowhere in the capitalist world system does the state achieve a degree of strength such as is encountered in noncapitalistic ones.

These are by no means incidental matters to the analysis of international migrations, since variations in regime form are directly related to exit and entry policies, and hence contribute to the determination of global patterns of international migration. It is the lack of attention to this aspect of things which mars, for example, the global system of international migration put forth by Richmond and Verma (1978). It is therefore necessary to go beyond Wallerstein and to conceptualize an international social system on a phenomenologically sounder basis in terms of at least two distinct but interacting structures, the one largely economic and the other largely political.

Leaving aside the question of regime variation already mentioned, in contrast with what occurs in the economic sphere the world's political structure does not consist of component units that can be arrayed along a single continuum. On the other hand, formally independent states are distributed along a scale of strategic power which determines more acute inequalities than any other social hierarchy in that ultimately a few can literally obliterate all the others. On the other hand, however, these same states are fundamentally equal as sovereignties. A very recent development, this equality cannot be dismissed out of hand as legal formalism. However much their interactions are shaped by processes of uneven economic exchange and by the inequalities of strategic power, states definitely acknowledge each other as equals in their aspect of societies, self-contained human aggregates with distinct cultures, except when at war. Far from being subordinate to economic processes, the world's peculiar political structure determines an international social system of sorts, of which the capitalist world system and the others are themselves mere components. Most important, it is out of the formal equality among states, which demonstrates why the conceptualization of the international social system cannot be founded on a mere extrapolation of societal ontology, that each derives the right to maintain its integrity by controlling entry.

Without elaborating the model further, it can be suggested that in a world which is differentiated in such a complex manner, individual preferences for living here or there are likely to be determined not only by considerations of economic welfare, but also by political concerns which are in every way rational. Concomitantly, from the vantage point of the states, the concerns that enter into play in the determination of exit and entry policies are likely to be founded on two distinct perspectives as well. Populations are viewed as actors in markets (producers and consumers), but they are also inevitably considered as actors in the political sphere, with all the implications this perspective entails. They constitute, most obviously, assets and liabilities in relation to the mustering of military power. To the extent that the international social system is also differentiated into regime types forming one or more axes of ideological cleavage, their strategic value is assessed as well in terms of a more diffuse criterion related to loyalty, an attribute which may be operationalized in a variety of ways ranging from cultural characteristics (religious affiliation, ethnic descent) to class background and political attitudes.

In practice, however, specific strategic calculations are indistinguishable from those evoked by a more generic concern to maintain the society's integrity, as that is defined politically at any given time, or to achieve a more desirable state of affairs in this respect. Viewed in this light, the perennial intrusion of racial and ethnic considerations in the determination of immigration policies is not merely the consequence of prejudice, conceived as an attribute of individuals, but the effect of systemic mechanisms whereby societies seek to preserve their boundaries in a world populated by others, some of whom are deemed particularly threatening in light of prevailing cultural orientations (Barth, 1969).[7] Similar considerations often underlie the processes whereby certain indigenous groups come to be designated as undesirables who should be eliminated from the body politic. However morally abhorrent, the exercise of such forms of discrimination constitutes instrumentally rational behavior in relation to the universal striving toward a world of statist societies.

How distinctive perspectives on population are formed in a given state at a particular time, which concerns prevail, how they are operationalized and transformed into migration policy, is also a function of general internal social processes, as is the case in other spheres of decision-making. Moreover, the complex structure of the international social system suggests that certain groups or categories of population, or migrants in general, can be assets from one perspective while liabilities from another. Yet, although we should therefore not expect migration policies to be mechanistically determined by a state's position in the international social system, the overall structural configuration of the latter does provide an approximate analytic matrix from which broad tendencies can be hypothesized to unravel the complexity of migration policies. Their contradictions and inconsistencies notwithstanding, these can be thought of as more or less adequate solutions to both the interests a state seeks to maximize in each of its distinct roles, and the perennial confrontation between individuals and societies. How the framework might guide in the task will be illustrated by considering two topics of current concern: labor migrations from the Third World to the industrial democracies; and the recrudescence of refugees from the new nations.

■ Workers and Refugees

Marxist analysts are quite correct in pointing out that international migrant labor (as against immigrants) represents the most extreme form of proletarianization in the contemporary world. It is not merely the conditions to which the workers are subjected which make them so archetypical, but the very process underlying those conditions. Whereas within most industrial societies the market processes tending to reduce human beings to their essential economic role generated at an early stage various forms of protective or antimarket institutions, as analyzed for example by Polanyi (1957:77–102), no such institutions have arisen internationally precisely because society does not exist at that level. Between slavery, the earliest form of labor importation, and the present lie the various forms of bondage and indenture that prevailed until well into the twentieth century. The coercive element that is coupled with economic unidimensionality to produce these forms arises largely as a consequence of the investment employers (or the state acting on their behalf, or intermediaries) must make in order to transport that labor over long distances. Although the more extreme forms of coercion have been largely eliminated from the legal market, they continue to prevail in the illegal segment; and in the legal market, imported labor remains subjected to contracts even in societies where such practices have been rejected as abhorrent with respect to indigenous labor.

The literature on the economic aspects of the subject is so abundant and the dynamics of interests governing it sufficiently well understood so that there is no need to review it here (Piore, 1979). I should merely like to point out that most of the contemporary importing countries have been doing so for a very long time, generally before they reached a stage that might be identified as postindustrial or organized-capitalism. Britain, including both England and Scotland, has relied on the Irish from the very beginning of its industrialization in the late eighteenth century to the present. Its West Indian colonies began to import Asian labor under indenture as soon as slavery was abolished in the 1830s until the flow ebbed after World War I as a consequence of political protest in India. Beginning its development while it was beyond the reach of Europe, the West Coast of the United States resorted to Chinese coolies; the *padrone* system arose on the East Coast shortly after the Civil War; and by the turn of the century, a majority of those other than Jews who entered the United States came as migrant labor rather than as immigrants. When the flow from Europe ebbed with the onset of World War I, the United States, which had already recruited Barbadians to dig the Panama Canal, imported labor from Mexico, the Caribbean and French-speaking Canada. In Europe, Germany institutionalized a guestworker program in response to the sort of criticism voiced by Weber while France began importing Polish agricultural workers shortly after the turn of the century (Dibble, 1968:95-109). The extraordinary Italian contribution to Swiss manpower is long standing as well. Suspended during the Great Depression and World War II, European recruitment resumed during the period of postwar reconstruction in such countries as France and Belgium, whereas the process was less visible in West Germany during the period of the economic miracle only because it largely relied on migration from the East until the Berlin Wall was erected in 1961. In the Africa of the 1950s, the use of migrant labor was visible not only in the mining regions of the south but also among relatively affluent West African countries such as Ghana and the Ivory Coast whose African-owned cocoa and coffee farms were largely worked by migrants from Upper Volta and Niger.

Considered over the longer term, however, a remarkable feature of the migrant labor pattern is its instability, in the sense that the unidimensionality on which it is founded cannot be maintained for very long. Sooner or later, any foreign worker comes to be conceived of not only as an economic actor, but also as a cultural, social or political actor—I shall use the term "moral actor" to refer to these roles—and hence as a potential member of the society.

What makes for this instability appears to be a conjunction of two sets of considerations arising from very different perspectives. The first of these might be termed integrative concern within the receiving country which focuses sharply on the moral dimension of the immigration process. This pertains most often to the religious or ethnic character of the migrants; but this is itself only the most obvious indicator and summary of their moral character evaluated on conventional scales of cultural distance. True conservatives, who may in terms of their class position rank among those who benefit most from an abundant supply of imported labor, nevertheless insist on regarding them as full-fledged human beings whose presence is undesirable as such. As with other aspects of ethnic relations, tensions may be exacerbated by extraneous factors such as conflict at the international level, whereby groups come to be evaluated as well in terms of their putative loyalty.

One of the reasons why integrative concerns intrude repeatedly into the process of policymaking stems from the systemics of labor recruitment. It can be taken as a given that cultural heterogeneity—from the point of view of a given society—increases with physical distance (the exceptions, incidentally, are often the result of earlier labor migrations such as slavery or can be associated with a colonial past). Most receiving societies that recruited labor started to do so internally, usually bringing to the poles of industrial development domestic peripherals who were culturally distinct, such as the Irish to Britain, or Bretons and Auvergnats to the Paris region, and then moved toward recruitment of foreigners located in adjacent countries of cognate cultural character (*e.g.*, Belgians and Italians to France in the 1860s, Northwestern Europeans to the United States until approximately the Civil War). Exceptions were attributable to special circumstances (*e.g.*, Asians to the Pacific coast of the United States and Canada) and evoked integrative concerns much earlier than in most other cases.

In the long run, internal or nearby pools became exhausted, or underwent transformations that made their populations no longer suitable to the role. A major result has been the extension of recruitment to more distant pools: American recruitment efforts in the post–Civil War period reached Northern Europe (Scandinavia), as well as southern and eastern regions (Austro-Hungarian Empire, Italy, the Balkans, and even the Ottoman Empire). The same sort of phenomenon has prevailed more recently in postwar Europe: Italians and Spaniards have for the most part given way to more distant Mediterraneans, as well as in some cases to black Africans and Asians. This constant extension of the area of recruitment tends to have as its general consequence an exacerbation of concern with the cultural character of the migrant labor. No sooner has the receiving society become somewhat tolerant of the old immigrant than new immigrants begin to arrive. In the United States, the old immigrants, who appeared to be preferred in the 1880s to the new, had themselves once been new, as the anti-Catholic agitation of the 1830s and 1840s directed toward the Irish and the Germans attests; in Britain, the Eastern European Jews arriving in the last two decades of the 19th century were deemed worse than the Irish, and the latest wave constituted, so to speak, the straw that broke the camel's back; in contemporary France, black Africans are considered as more of a threat than Algerians.

Generally speaking, it is the very qualities (real or imputed) that make certain groups particularly suitable for their role as workers that make them unsuitable for membership in the receiving society. Shared by all classes and strata in the receiving society, these integrative concerns, whether expressed in manifestly xenophobic ideologies or by way of euphemistic codes, universally impinge upon the determination of immigration policy. The conflicting interests of industrial societies—to maximize the labor supply and to protect cultural integrity—can be thought of as a dilemma to which a limited number of solutions are possible.

The most common solution is to confine migrants strictly to their economic role by reinforcing the barrier against citizenship, a legal device which can be translated sociologically as the erection of a boundary within the territorial confines of the receiving society to offset the consequences of physical entry. Its most notorious forms are, of course, slavery and extreme segregation, as in modern apartheid, as well as the outright exclusion of a category of immigrants from citizenship, as practised by the United States with respect to Asians for more than half a century.[8] In less extreme form, a similar solution has prevailed in Western Europe with respect to the naturalization of foreign workers throughout the 20th century, most explicitly in Switzerland and Germany (Empire and Federal Republic) and somewhat less so in France, where natalist concerns exacerbated by strategic considerations sometimes dictated a more permissive naturalization policy.

Throughout Europe, maintenance of the societal boundary is further facilitated by a legal tradition which does not automatically grant citizenship to
native-born children of foreign parents. With respect to white immigrants,
the United States maintained a policy of easy naturalization, congruent
with its advocacy of the right of expatriation, in spite of perennial nativist
efforts to the contrary; and the *jus soli* tradition prevailed as well. As the
internal boundary solution was impracticable, the same sorts of concerns
that led to its adoption in Europe, or in the U.S. with respect to Asians,
were projected instead upon immigration regulation, where they were eventually institutionalized in the form of the National Origins Quota System. It
is noteworthy that the abandonment of that system was coupled with the
imposition of an unprecedented numerical limitation on immigrants from
the Western Hemisphere, a measure whose legislative history reveals the
importance of explicit apprehensions concerning the entry of Caribbean
blacks and Hispanics, and whose effect was to create a category of illegal
immigrants whose very status insures that they will work but not become
incorporated (Zolberg, 1978a).

In at least one case, the prominence of this integrative dimension probably led one advanced industrial society (Japan) to refrain from importing
labor altogether. Having imported Korean workers when it exercised imperial hegemony over that country in the interwar period, in its post–World
War II period of renewed capitalist expansion Japan resorted instead to a
policy of capital export to the low-wage areas within its region, an alternative solution now increasingly attractive to Europeans as well, precisely on
the grounds that the labor-importing strategy is unstable or counterproductive. Britain has inclined toward a similar avoidance since the beginning of
the 20th century and affirmed it forcefully after a brief exceptional inter-
lude in the 1950s.

Because the concern with identity-maintenance or integration has so
often been expressed in acute form and has rested on abhorrent racialist
ideologies—often crystallized in the very process of reaction-formation
triggered by the arrival of immigrants—it is difficult to conceive of it otherwise than as a form of psychopathology. As such, little is known about
the dynamics of the boundary-maintenance mechanism. Yet there is no
gainsaying that no society can tolerate sudden and large-scale threats to its
institutionalized culture, and that the question is therefore always one of
how much of a challenge it believes it can handle at a given time. Given an
equal challenge, the degree of tolerance of cultural diversity may vary as a
function of the character of the receiving society. A highly homogeneous
culture, such as may be found in an ethnically undiversified nation with a
dominant religion, and which as a consequence of its insularity has experienced little immigration in the recent past, may have a lower threshold of
tolerance than a more heterogeneous one, whose identity may have come to

be founded on political rather than ethnic criteria. Societies that are guilt-ridden, or at least must present a clean outlook because of their past record, may compensate by leaning toward greater tolerance at a later date; societies that pride themselves on the universalism of their culture and on their assimilationist capacity may also gravitate toward the tolerant side of the continuum.

If this concern is thought of as normal, then what is surprising is how generally unsuccessful the guardians of the conventional moral order are in defending the existing culture against external intrusions. Their long-term weakness is due, of course, to the supremacy in most capitalist industrial societies of business interests that insist on maintaining an open door to insure a steady flow of manpower in all but the most acute depressions. If the main gate is shut, others—often even less desirable than those who have been excluded—are brought in through the back door. It is also the case that over the long run, it is nearly impossible to treat workers as "shirts," so that the most virulent xenophobes are quite correct in pointing out that labor migration serves as a vehicle whereby individuals transfer permanently from one society into another.

Once they occur, labor migrations nearly always generate a permanent residue because the costs to the receiving societies of preventing this from occurring tend to be very high. An extreme illustration is that of the United States, where under *jus soli* all the native born obtain automatic citizenship, regardless of the legal status of their progenitors. France began to depart from the continental European norm with respect to naturalization to acquire military manpower in the late 19th century and has, until recently, maintained more permeable boundaries than its neighbors. This policy has also improved its bidding position vis-à-vis others in periods of economic expansion when recruiting countries compete with one another in the labor market. Characteristically, as a concomitant of their general posture, both the U.S. and France have erected fewer barriers to the entry of families of workers. Under U.S. law, of course, relatives are given the very highest immigration priority; and the French government's abrupt attempt to depart from this tradition in 1977 was decisively invalidated by the Council of State on constitutional grounds. Competition between Germany and Switzerland in the late 1960s and early 1970s led both to relent from their rigid posture against family reunion.

Once dependents begin to arrive, however, the process of permanent transfer gets underway. The very negation of a purely economic migration, family reunion is an earmark of the fundamental instability of the pattern under consideration. Once it begins to occur, the advantages of imported labor to capital in the receiving country rapidly wane; and at the same time, cultural concerns are exacerbated. It is precisely at the moment when workers are no longer treated as "shirts" that those who object to them as human beings are likely to raise their voice. The solutions that arise at this point include prohibition against further immigration (and refoulement of those already there), or alternatively, the exercise of considerable pressure for assimilation. The two postures are not necessarily mutually exclusive; groups may be treated differently, as France appears to be doing at present by pressing for the assimilation of Portuguese migrant workers who are allowed or even encouraged to bring families, restricting the arrival of North African families, and resorting to refoulement with respect to black Africans and Asians.

Turning briefly to the specifics of the contemporary configuration, it is evident that additional factors contribute to undermine the postwar European pattern. The present emphasis on the tension between the pursuit of economic advantages and the concern with integration should not be taken as a minimization of the importance of variation on the economic side itself since the general function of imported labor, as Piore (1979) and others have shown, is to cushion the effects of cyclical fluctuations in the receiving economy. Rather, it can be suggested that it is precisely when economic expansion grinds to a halt that the other concerns are likely to have a greater impact on policymaking. Under such conditions, not only do the economic interests of employers move them closer to the position normally advocated by the guardians of the moral order, but within the economic dimension alone the usually antagonistic interests of capitalists and indigenous labor in relation to immigration become more congruent as well.

Not to be ignored in the analysis of long-term trends, however, is the growing importance of what might be termed liberal humanistic objections to a purely market-oriented policy. It is somewhat paradoxical that the evolution of advanced industrial societies toward a postindustrial phase, which generates a tendency toward the structuring of economic tasks into a dual labor market, also gives rise to a heightened sensitivity to the human condition which makes the confinement of foreign workers (or certain indigenous groups) to the lower stratum of such markets generally less tolerable to certain segments of the public, who are usually found in the upper stratum. The carriers of this sensitivity are not only intellectuals, a characteristic group of postindustrial societies, but also organizations which have a clientelist interest in migrants: churches (as with Slovenian or Croatian Catholics in Germany, or Latin Catholics in the United States) and certain labor unions which, when faced with the inevitability of immigration, may opt for the incorporation of foreign workers into their own ranks.[9] Arising largely in the wake of the movements of the 1960s in Western Europe and in the United States, this sensitivity has produced a general rise of consciousness which constrained the exercise of rational economic behavior on the part of the receiving countries even in the neoconservative and

matched without regard to international boundaries, might very well be an economically more efficient world. But it would no longer be a world of sovereign states.

Thus, even the most ardent neoclassical economists recognize that with respect to the movement of people there are other considerations than the efficient use of resources. In the absence of state controls over immigration, one country could peacefully invade another through colonization. If 35 million hardworking Chinese were allowed to settle in Burma, the Burmese economy might very well prosper, and the Burmese themselves might be economically better off. But for the Burmese their country would no longer be Burma. The Burmese would no longer be able to control the central cultural symbols of their national life; and, of course, the Burmese would have lost political control over their own state.

A concern by government policymakers and by their citizens for the preservation of a particular national identity (or identities) and widely shared values, and a concern for maintaining control over political institutions preclude a policy of open entry. Countries often do offer open entry to those with whom their population shares a close ethnic affinity. Thus, the People's Republic of China was the primary haven for Vietnamese refugees of Chinese extraction; India has readily accepted Hindus from Pakistan and Bangladesh; Israel admits Jews from anywhere in the world under its Law of Return; France opened its doors to the *pieds-noirs* from Algeria, including those who had never lived in France; members of the Gulf Cooperation Council (consisting of the Arab states on the western shore of the Persian Gulf) permit their citizens to move freely from one state to another; and in the 1920s Greece opened its doors to all ethnic Greeks seeking to relocate from Turkey.

Countries have also selectively permitted entry by members from another people with whom they have had historic ties or in cases in which a sense of obligation or guilt exists. Hence, the United States admitted refugees from Vietnam, the Dutch admitted people from Timor, the United Kingdom admitted Indians from East Africa and, for a while, citizens of other Commonwealth nations.

The decision of the European Economic Community to permit citizens of member nations to move freely about represented a historic step toward the elimination of full member state sovereignty; it also represented a major step toward the redefinition and an enlargement of national identities to encompass a European nationality.

The United States is among a small number of countries in which national origins and ethnicity have been superseded by educational and occupational considerations as determinants of entry. It is true, of course, that the countries of Western Europe and of the Persian Gulf have made entry by foreigners into the labor force easier, but unlike the United States they sharply distinguish between the rules of entry for employment and the rules for becoming a citizen.[1]

What these comments suggest is that entry rules are only marginally shaped by economic considerations even for those countries that are relatively open to the flow of trade, capital, and technology. How a people define their national identity and their receptivity to other peoples with different identities shape the entry rules set by governments and condition the way governments respond to changes in the demand for labor.

■ Rules of Entry

States differ markedly on their rules of entry. In broad terms we can suggest five types of rules.

1. Unrestricted entry rules. Although no country freely permits entry to everyone, some countries grant virtually unrestricted entry to citizens of neighboring countries. A transborder ethnic group, for example, may be allowed to move freely back and forth across the borders, as has historically been the case for Pashtun-speaking tribals traversing the Afghanistan-Pakistan borders. Similarly, West Germany freely admits anyone from East Germany, and members of the European Common Market allow their citizens to move freely from one member country to another.

2. Promotional entry rules. Countries may actively promote entry in an effort to increase their population (e.g., countries of the Western Hemisphere, Australia, and New Zealand in the nineteenth and early twentieth centuries) or to fill a temporary demand for labor. In the 1950s and 1960s Western European countries actively sought migrant labor from Turkey, Greece, North Africa, and Iberia. And in the 1970s and early 1980s the oil-producing Persian Gulf states actively recruited labor from other Arab states and from Asia. Israel, in fulfillment of its nationalist ideology to create a homeland for Jews, promotes immigration of Jews irrespective of their country of origin.

3. Selective entry rules. Many governments selectively admit but do not actively promote the entrance of migrants. They may permit family unification, selectively allow some to enter the labor force, or admit refugees, although there may be limitations as to their characteristics and numbers.

4. Unwanted entry rules. Some governments that legally restrict or prohibit entry are unable or unwilling to prevent illegal entry. The result is an illegal migrant population often unprotected or even harassed by legal authorities.

5. Prohibition entry rules. While all countries restrict immigration, a few (Japan, for example) effectively ban virtually all long-term entries and make it almost impossible for foreigners to become citizens.

■ Rules of Exit
We can specify five sets of exit rules as well.

1. Prohibition exit rules. While all sovereign states have rules of entry, and all states recognize the right of other states to have such rules, governments have quite dissimilar views on the relevance of the concept of sovereignty to the rules of exit. Democratic states subscribe to the notion that citizenship implies the right to leave. But totalitarian states do not grant their citizens this right, since the mechanisms of political control that characterize totalitarian states would be eroded were such a right granted. For this reason the Helsinki Declaration and the United Nations Declaration of Human Rights concerning the rights of citizens to leave their country are de facto violated by totalitarian regimes.

Communist states ordinarily prohibit citizens from leaving to seek employment abroad or to change their citizenship. From time to time, however, they have relaxed the prohibition to selectively permit citizens to leave, most recently when the East German government permitted some of its citizens to migrate to West Germany, and earlier when the Soviet Union selectively permitted Jews to leave for Israel.

2. Selective exit rules. Governments may selectively allow citizens with some characteristics to leave, but not others. They may restrict the emigration of individuals possessing certain skills: at one time Egypt restricted the emigration of physicians. Or they may give exit permits to some ethnic groups, but not to others.

3. Permissive exit rules. Some governments freely permit citizens to leave as long as they have performed the obligations of citizens (i.e., they have paid their taxes, have not broken the law, etc.). Western democracies ordinarily treat the freedom to leave as a fundamental right of citizenship, although in practice such rights can be circumscribed by currency regulations.

4. Promotional exit rules. Governments may encourage citizens to seek employment abroad in order to relieve unemployment or to increase remittances. Some governments have developed educational programs to provide citizens with skills that could enhance their opportunities for finding employment abroad. Sri Lanka, Pakistan, Bangladesh, and India all promote emigration to the Middle East. Earlier, the government of Turkey promoted emigration to Germany, and the Algerian government promoted emigration to France.

5. Expulsion exit rules. Governments may expel individual citizens; they may also induce entire groups of people to leave by threatening their safety and income if they remain. The group may be a dissident or threatening social class (e.g., the middle class in Cuba after the Castro revolution) or it may be an ethnic minority (Indians in East Africa, Chinese in

Vietnam). Many refugee movements widely seen as an unintended consequence of internal political upheavals or unexpected famines are often quite
deliberate consequences of state policies, ways in which regimes choose to
deal with class enemies or dissident ethnic minorities.

■ Access Rules and Theories of International Migration

The rules of entry and of exit are important variables influencing the magnitude, the composition, and the directionality of international migration. There
are four "clusters" of variables that shape international migration. One "cluster" can be characterized as differential variables, such as wage differentials,
differences in employment rates, differences in land prices, and even differences in degree days! A second group of variables are spatial, such as distance and transportation costs. A third group can be characterized as affinity
variables, such as religion, culture, language, and kinship networks. And the
fourth are the access variables, the rules for exit and for entry. Differential
and spatial variables are usually the concern of economists; spatial variables
are of particular interest to geographers; affinity variables attract the interest
of sociologists and anthropologists; and access variables are the concern of
political scientists and students of international relations.

High on a list of priorities for future research should be the study of the
determinants of exit and entry rules. While the policies of some individual
countries have been studied, except for the recent work by Aristide
Zolberg, Astri Suhrke, and Michael Teitelbaum[2] there is little systematic
comparative and theoretical work on such issues as how and why states
make their access rules, the interplay between domestic and international
considerations, the relationship between regime types and access rules, and
how the rules are affected by internal political transformations.

Regrettably, the theoretical literature on international migration tends to
treat the access variables as exogenous, as a kind of interference or noise in a
"process." The tendency, especially by economists, is to assume the primacy
of differential, distance, and affinity variables, leaving access variables outside their analysis. In fact, the rules of access influence other variables affecting migration, and in turn the other variables influence the rules of access.
Where, for example, differentials are high, affinities are close, and distances
are small, a country is usually faced with difficult decisions about its access
rules (e.g., the United States in relation to Mexico, and India in relation to
Bangladesh), but where differentials and affinities are low, even though distances are small neighboring countries often need not be concerned about
their rules of entry (e.g., France and Germany prior to World War II).

Individual decisions by migrants are obviously influenced by the rules
of entry. What is less obvious is that migrants also consider the exit rules of

countries to which they contemplate migration. Migrants are usually reluctant to seek entry into countries that have restricted exit rules. Countries that restrict exit are less attractive than countries with similar economic opportunities that freely permit exit. Similarly, migrants may consider whether their decision leaves open or precludes subsequent migration. Jewish emigrants from the Soviet Union, for example, considering whether to migrate to either the United States or Israel, may choose the United States, knowing that the option of moving to Israel remains open, while the alternative decision may preclude further migration.

The access rules adopted by a government are also likely to have significant consequences both for the movement of capital and for the adoption of technology. Governments are generally better able to control the exit and entry of people than they are of the flow of capital. By restricting the entry of people when the demand for labor has risen, a government may thereby have unintentionally adopted a policy that induces an outflow of capital. Thus, the Japanese government policy of prohibiting Japanese firms from recruiting labor abroad (a decision made for cultural and political, not economic reasons) was a factor in the decision of some Japanese firms to relocate plants abroad. In contrast, the decision of the French and German governments to import Algerian and Turkish workers may have slowed the relocation of industrial plants abroad. Similarly, a decision to employ or not to employ imported labor has an impact on the pace of technological innovation; firms that can cut costs by using low-wage immigrants are less likely to adopt labor-saving technologies. An important area for future research is precisely how a change in the access rules affects the other factors of production.

■ International Migration and International Relations

Understanding access rules is important from another perspective. They affect not only international migration, but also international relations. The congruence or incongruence of rules between states will influence the patterns of international conflict and cooperation. A brief consideration of emigration/immigration intersections may suggest some of these patterns:

• Where one state promotes entry and another state promotes exit—where, for example, one country wants to import labor from a country that is willing to export labor—the two countries have compatible objectives that enable them to negotiate such matters as wages, conditions of employment, rules for expatriation, arrangements for remittances, and so on. The French-Algerian arrangements are an example.[3] Bilateral arrangements become possible; and where several countries are involved in the exchange, multilateral arrangements are also possible, as is the case among the Persian Gulf states. One country may also want to promote the exodus of an ethnic minority, while another country in which the concerned ethnic group is the majority may want to promote its entry. There may be a formal agreement (as took place among several countries in the Balkans in the 1920s) or there may be a tacit understanding.

• Where one state permits, promotes, or compels emigration to a state that prohibits entry, the situation carries a high potential for conflict.[4] Migration from Bangladesh to northeastern India has been a source of conflict between the two countries; so has the migration of refugees from Afghanistan to Pakistan. Illegal migrations from Mexico to the United States have been an issue between the two countries, although thus far it has not been as conflictual as have been the unwanted population movements in South Asia.

• Where one country restricts emigration that another country seeks to promote, migration policies may become a "bargaining chip" in a large negotiation package. Both the United States and Israel promote the entry of Jews from the Soviet Union, while the Soviet Union no longer permits the exit of significant numbers of Jews; the result has been a concerted effort, particularly by the United States, to influence Soviet migration policies.

• Countries with strained relations may effectively seal their borders to population movements in order to avoid further conflicts. The People's Republic of China, for example, prohibits exit and the Soviet Union prohibits entry, with the result that the border between these two countries, the longest border in the world, is one in which population movements do not take place in spite of the very substantial income and employment differentials between the two countries.

• Expulsions need not be a source of international conflict if another country is concerned with the promotion of immigration; hence the forcible exit of Jews from North Africa to Israel in the 1950s was not a source of international tension. In contrast, of course, the forcible exit of many Arabs from Israel in 1948 has been followed by an interminable conflict between Israel and its Arab neighbors.

These are merely examples of the interplay of various combinations of entry and exit rules. Precise operational definition of the rules would be useful, while a filling in of a matrix of exit and entry combinations would be suggestive of different configurations of international relations.

■ International Relations and the Rules of Access

It is not simply that the rules of access and entry affect international migration and international relations. In examining the second proposition, it becomes clear that the rules themselves are often shaped by relations between states. The rules may be a matter of international negotiations, as is the case of the EEC rules concerning population movements within the Common Market. There are also conventions established by the International Labour Organization, although their effect on the rules set by governments seems to be negligible. Often the entry rules set by one country are shaped by the exit rules set by another. Thus, West Germany permits free access to individuals coming from East Germany, a rule set in the context of an East German policy that restricts people from exiting. (East Germany permits citizens over age 65 to exit if they forgo state-provided social security benefits.) But now that the East Germans permit Turks, Sri Lankans, and Pakistanis to enter and to freely exit through Berlin, the West German government is concerned with the growing number of non-German migrants seeking status as political refugees.

Similarly, the Austrian government permits refugees to enter from the Soviet bloc, but it does so because of the willingness of third countries to permit permanent entry; its rules of entry are thus conditional upon the entry rules of others.

Once again it should be emphasized that access rules are not merely the political expression of economic forces, however important these may be. Global economic changes may induce governments to change their access rules: the oil price rise led to a labor shortage in oil-producing countries while inducing other countries to export labor so as to improve their balance of payments through remittances. Moreover, particular agricultural and industrial policies may lead to an increase in the demand for labor, or to a large surplus, putting pressure on a government to ease its entry or its exit rules. But it would be a mistake to think that the choices governments make are necessarily dictated by economic considerations.[5] Indeed, governments often choose entry and exit rules that economists would regard as inefficient, because the government seeks to maximize values other than economic efficiency. A productive minority may be expelled in order to improve the status of a politically dominant ethnic group. Or a government may fear the political consequences of an unwanted immigration even as it recognizes that the migrants might contribute to national wealth.

Access rules should be understood as more than the formally prescribed legal norms and the procedures and mechanisms for enforcement of these norms. Rules include administrative capacity and the willingness of states to enforce legal norms; they also include the expectations states have of one another, their reputations for behaving in a particular manner.[6] Consider, for example, the reputation of states toward expulsions. Any country can expel illegals, but such expulsion is obviously politically easier for authoritarian countries than for democracies. It is also easier for a government to expel a minority group with which the dominant ethnic group has no affinity than to expel one where the affinities are close. It was not difficult for Uganda to expel its Indian population, and it would not be difficult for the Persian Gulf monarchies to expel their Asian migrants, but it is politically more difficult for India to expel illegal Bangladeshi migrants, for the United States to expel illegal Mexican migrants, or for the Gulf states to expel Arab migrants. Communist regimes have a reputation for expelling dissident social classes, or for creating conditions that induce large numbers of people to flee: large numbers of Cubans after the Castro revolution; the Chinese from Vietnam; refugees from Kampuchea and Laos; Tibetans after the Chinese communist occupation; Hungarians and Czechs after their government crackdown on dissidents; and Afghans after the communist coup and in even larger numbers after the Soviet invasion. A communist revolution or takeover is likely to result in a substantial unwanted population exodus to neighboring countries. For this reason, a government may be alarmed by the prospects of a communist takeover in a neighboring state because it expects such a change of regime to provoke a large population flight. More broadly, it should be noted that other kinds of regime changes may also affect the rules of exit in ways that shape the security of a neighboring country.[7]

The foregoing analysis suggests that an important subject for future research is precisely how states make their access and entry rules, how states influence one another in shaping these rules, and how these rules in turn affect relations between states. We need some rigorous case studies. Focusing on particular regions would be useful since considerations of proximity are often crucial in setting entry and exit rules.[8]

One might, for example, take a closer took at South Asia, where international migrations between the countries of the region are largely unwanted by receiving countries. In this region there are unwanted movements from Bangladesh to India, Afghanistan to Pakistan, India to Nepal, Sri Lanka to India, Nepal to Bhutan, and a proposed (and unwanted) migration from Bangladesh to Pakistan. The result is that conflicts over population movements tend to be great, and a "high" politics over population movements emerges involving heads of state and high officials. The region has had one war resulting from unwanted migration—India's decision to invade Pakistan in large part because of the massive influx of refugees from East Pakistan. India's present involvement in Sri Lanka is partly guided by India's concern over the possibility of a large-scale refugee movement of Tamils from Sri Lanka. A number of the actions pursued by states in the region (Pakistan toward Afghanistan and toward the Soviet Union, and India toward both Bangladesh and Sri Lanka) can in part be understood in the context of the efforts of these states to prevent unwanted population movements or to mitigate their effects.

Another but quite different example would be interregional movements in the Middle East, where the population flows have, in the main, been approved by both sending and receiving countries. Negotiations between states on migration matters have, therefore, been of a "low" politics, involving bureaucrats in the ministries of the respective countries, and it has also been possible to deal with migration issues at a multilateral level through the Gulf Regional Council. In this context governments have attempted to adjust their manpower policies on the basis of assumptions concerning future population movements. And there have been discussions between states in the region about integrating some of their development policies, taking into account the relationship of these policies to migration.

One goal of such regional case studies would be to increase our understanding of the factors that shape wanted and unwanted migrations and to better understand the ways in which conflicts can be reduced and cooperation increased in the management of international population movements.

■ International Migrants as Links

The third and last proposition is that international migrants are becoming important political actors influencing both the political process of the country in which they reside and the relationship between their country of residence and their country of origin. I shall briefly suggest some of the dimensions of this complex and increasingly important phenomenon.

Migrants, or their descendants, have sought to influence migration policies in their country of residence; they have sometimes promoted policies intended to benefit the economic or foreign policy interests of their country of origin; and alternatively they have been critics of their country of origin and pressured their host government to influence the domestic politics of their country of origin. In short, migrants may attempt to promote many types of political interventions. Just to refer to a few groups that have been politically active is to demonstrate these variations: Sikh secessionists in the United Kingdom; immigrant Filipino opponents of President Marcos in the United States; anti-Turkish Armenian terrorists in the United States and in Western Europe; Turkish fundamentalists in West Germany; Polish immigrants and their descendants in Chicago; Cuban refugees in Florida; Nicaraguan refugees in the United States; immigrants from Timor in Holland; Yemenites in Saudi Arabia.

Diasporas are not necessarily politically good news for the government of a sending country; nor are they necessarily good news for the home ministry or the foreign affairs ministry of the government of the country in which they reside. They have become a political factor that governments of both sending and receiving countries need to take into account.[9]

Migrants invariably seek to recreate their own religious, social, and cultural institutions. Where permitted they often develop their own media, schools for their children, religious institutions, and political organizations. The initial concern of migrants is often to preserve their cultural heritage (and to transmit that heritage to their children), and to protect the interests of the community. Community members may turn to their country of origin to assist them in both objectives; and in turn, they may attempt to influence the policies of their host country toward their country of origin.

The precise linkage sought by the migrant community is a complicated one. It depends in part on why migrants left their country of origin, and how their political attitudes toward both host and home country have developed. The migrant community itself may be divided in its attitude toward the government of the home country, as were Iranians during the Islamic revolution, overseas Indians during the Emergency, and overseas Chinese since the Chinese communist revolution. Ethnic divisions within the migrant community may also shape the relationship of particular nationals with their home country: the attitudes of Tamils from Sri Lanka, Sikhs from India, and Chinese from Malaysia may differ from attitudes of other nationals from these countries. Finally, one should note that, other things being equal, migrants from a country that permits its citizens to travel abroad to visit relatives are more likely to be friendly (or at least not hostile) to their country of origin than when the country restricts its citizens from traveling. Compare, for example, the attitude toward their home country of Hungarians in the United States (Hungary has relatively liberal rules of travel) with that of Russian emigrants to the United States.

If sections of the migrant community are opposed to the government of their country of origin, strains may be created between the sending and receiving countries. The position taken by Third World governments toward their migrant populations is also a complicated and changing one. They may view cultural and religious linkages with satisfaction (as is the attitude of the Indian government toward institutions promoting Indian culture among overseas Indians) or with concern (as is the attitude of the Turkish government toward the growth of Islamic fundamentalism among Turkish migrants in Germany). Third World countries initially concerned primarily with the flow of remittances have become increasingly interested in the role that migrant businessmen and professionals play in investment and in the transfer of technology. The governments of China and India, for example, now actively work with their overseas communities to promote investment and technology transfers. It should be noted that the links that develop between migrants and their country of origin may not only shape relations between migrants and their homeland, but may also influence the patterns of cultural pluralism within the countries in which the migrants have settled.[10]

The environment for political participation in the host country will affect the role migrants can play. In the labor-importing countries of the

Middle East, Arab and Asian migrants have quite different linkages to indigenous forces; and in Western Europe migrant workers have political rights not accorded to migrant workers in the Middle East. The opportunities for coalition-building between migrants and groups within the host society also vary greatly.

The changing role or status of transborder peoples is still another important development. Porous borders enable members of an ethnic group divided by an international boundary to move freely back and forth and to maintain their social cohesion; yet one or both governments may regard this free movement as threatening to their security, to their capacity to control trade, and especially to what they regard as measures for achieving national integration. Thus, population movements across international boundaries once regarded as benign are increasingly regarded as a problem.[11]

These are merely illustrations of some of the new domestic and foreign policy issues that have arisen as a consequence of the emergence of new diasporas and the transformation of old ones. What needs to be emphasized is how these diasporas link internal and international politics. A government that is host to a migrant population must now anticipate the political reactions among its migrants to changes in foreign policy. The foreign minister of the Federal Republic of Germany must consider the reaction of Germany's Turkish population to changes in policies toward either Turkey or Greece; the British Broadcasting Corporation must now consider how Indo-British relations would be affected by giving television time to Sikh secessionist migrants; the Pakistan government must consider the reactions of its Pashtun-speaking population, and its many Pashtun refugees, to a decision to close the borders to further refugees, or to prevent armed Pashtuns from returning to Afghanistan; and just as American politicians earlier had to consider the effects of US policies toward Europe on European immigrants, now consideration must be given to the effects of US policies toward many developing countries on Asian and Latin American immigrants.

■ The Emerging Policy Process

We return, then, to the venerable notion of sovereignty and how it is being transformed under the new international realities. It is, of course, an old story that states are becoming interdependent, that there are more and more international constraints on domestic policies, that global trends in transportation, in technologies, in weapons, and in the very structure of the world economy have eroded earlier notions of sovereignty. What is unique about international migration, however, is that it changes the very composition of one's population and therefore potentially one's domestic policies; it brings the outside in, as it were, and it involves sending a piece of one's nation into another society. The result is not merely an impersonal interaction involving monetary systems, trade flows, or acid rain, but the deeper, affective interactions involving human beings.

As international migration has become more salient among policymakers, and as policymakers have become more aware of the international-relations aspects of decisions involving migrants, new bureaucratic agencies become involved in the decisionmaking process. If the issue of migration becomes a matter for bilateral or regional negotiations, then a shift in power will take place from ministries and departments concerned with labor and home affairs to those concerned with external affairs and defense. The bilateralization of migration may also become linked to other bilateral issues—trade, investment, aid, water resources, and environment—involving therefore a variety of bureaucratic agencies hitherto not involved in considerations of migration. Any examination of the internationalization of migration issues must entail a close study of the changing intra-bureaucratic relationships within both sending and receiving countries.

Moreover, the issues now raised by international migration are no longer matters for the national government alone, as any state official in Assam or Texas will affirm. Indeed, as one looks at both sending and receiving countries, it is striking to see how many actors have entered into the political struggles over migration. Perhaps we should end, then, with a fourth proposition, that the internationalization of migration issues is changing intra-bureaucratic relationships, and introducing new and often conflicting interests into considerations of policies affecting migration in both sending and receiving countries.

Here, then, is another area of research, for if scholars are to have any useful input into policy they must be cognizant of the policymaking process within which decisions are made, the actors who participate in that process, and the political constraints on policies.

■ Notes

This paper was initially prepared for a seminar convened by the Population Council and funded by the Ford Foundation. I am grateful to Charles Keely, organizer of the seminar, and to seminar participants for their comments.

I am also grateful to the members of the Harvard-MIT Research Seminar on Migration and Development, to Oded Stark, co-chairman of the seminar, to my colleagues Hayward Alker, Gene Skolnikoff, and Nazli Choucri, to Peter Katzenstein and Sharon Russell, and to the graduate students in my seminar on the political economy of international migration for criticisms and suggestions.

1. The relationship between migration and citizenship in the Middle East is analyzed by George Dib, "Migration and naturalization laws in Egypt, Lebanon, Syria, Jordan, Kuwait and the United Arab Emirates, Part II: Naturalization laws," *Population Bulletin*, no. 16 (June 1979).

2. Aristide Zolberg and Astri Suhrke, "Social conflict and refugees in the Third World: The cases of Ethiopia and Afghanistan," paper presented at the annual meeting of the American Political Science Association, Washington, D.C., 1984. See also Aristide Zolberg, "International migrations in political perspective," in Mary M. Kritz, Charles B. Keely, and Silvano M. Tomasi (eds.), *Global Trends in Migration: Theory and Research on International Population Movements* (New York: Center for Migration Studies, 1981); and Michael S. Teitelbaum, "Immigration, refugees, and foreign policy," *International Organization* 38, no. 3 (1984): 429–450.

3. For an examination of how migration affected French-Algerian relations see Mark Miller, "Reluctant partnership: Foreign workers in Franco-Algerian relations, 1962–1979," *Journal of International Affairs* 33, no. 2 (1979): 219–237; and Stephen Adler, *International Migration and Dependence* (Hampshire, England: Cower Publishing Company, 1979).

4. For an account of forced migration as an instrument of both domestic and foreign policy, see Michael S. Teitelbaum, "Forced migration: The tragedy of mass expulsions," in Nathan Glazer (ed.), *Clamor at the Gates: The New American Migration* (San Francisco: ICS Press, 1985); on the law of asylum see Michael S. Teitelbaum, "Political asylum in theory and practice," in *The Public Interest*, no. 76 (Summer 1984): 74–86. See also Guy S. Goodwin-Gill, *International Law and the Movement of Persons Between States* (Oxford: Clarendon Press, 1978).

5. Neoclassical economists and Marxists share a tendency to explain international migration primarily in terms of changes in the global economy or by particular patterns of capitalist development in both sending and receiving countries. For an analysis of Mexico-US migration using this latter perspective see Alejandro Portes, "Illegal immigration and the international system: Lessons from recent Mexican immigration to the United States," *Social Problems* 26, no. 44 (April 1979). See also W. R. Böhning, "Elements of a theory of international economic migration to industrial nation states," in *Global Trends in Migration*, cited in note 2.

6. For a discussion of the ways in which reputations of states affect their relations with one another see Robert O. Keohane, *Beyond Hegemony* (Cambridge: Harvard University Press, 1984).

7. The policy of inducing certain categories of unwanted people to leave is not, of course, confined to communist regimes, nor is it a recent development. In the nineteenth century the British pursued a policy of inducing indigents to emigrate in order to relieve the state of the costs of having to provide for the poor. See H. J. M. Jonston, *British Emigration Policy 1815–1830, Shovelling Out Paupers* (Oxford: Clarendon Press, 1972). The British also had a policy of "shovelling out" prisoners. The crowding of jails in Britain in the 1770s and 1780s led the Crown to send convicts to Australia. Cuba followed a similar policy when it sent some of its prison population on boats to the United States in 1980 from the port of Mariel. For a discussion of induced or forced emigration from Third World countries based on internal political factors or as a means of exerting political pressure on neighboring states, see Myron Weiner, "International emigration: A political and economic assessment," paper presented to the Conference on Population Interactions Between Poor and Rich Countries, sponsored by the Harvard University Center for Population Studies and the Draeger Foundation, Cambridge, Massachusetts, 6–7 October 1983, pp. 39ff.

8. For a comparative review of European policies on entry and exit see W. R. Böhning, "Immigration policies of Western European countries," *International Migration Review* 8, no. 2 (1979): 155–164; and Ray C. Rist, "The European

Economic Community and manpower migrations: Policies and prospects," *Journal of International Affairs* 33, no. 2 (1979): 201–218.

9. For a study of the role played by diasporas in international relations see Gabi Sheffer (ed.), *Diasporas* (London: Croom Heim, 1985).

10. On pluralism in Europe as it is being shaped by the presence of migrant workers, see Gary P. Freeman, *Immigrant Labor and Racial Conflict in Industrial Societies: The French and British Experience, 1945–1975* (Princeton: Princeton University Press, 1979); and Ray C. Rist, *Guestworkers in Germany: The Prospects of Pluralism* (New York: Praeger, 1978).

11. See Myron Weiner, "Transborder peoples," in Walker Connor (ed.), *Mexican Americans in Comparative Perspective* (Washington, D.C.: The Urban Institute, 1985). See also Frederik Barth (ed.), *Ethnic Groups and Boundaries* (Boston: Little, Brown, 1969). "Boundaries" is a term used by Barth in the dual sense of a community's self-definition in relation to others, as well as in the juridical/geographic sense.

part 2

The Historical Origins of Contemporary Migration

ance by the state of violence directed against target groups; (b) policies include public inaction (i.e., laissez-faire or benign neglect); and (c) on the receiving side, the relevant sphere of policy includes naturalization as well as immigration stricto sensu.

It is assumed further that the goals the groups under consideration seek to achieve by securing such policies can be understood in terms of some instrumental calculation, on the basis of existing beliefs and available information, of how certain interests are likely to be affected by the population movements the policy is designed to prevent or to bring about. The determinants of such policy are multifaceted because the human beings involved are simultaneously assessed in two very different ways: as market actors, and within this most prominently as workers, and as actors within political institutions and cultural arenas. Each of these perspectives, which may be referred to as the "economic" and the "moral," determines a distinct structure of interest alignments with respect to policy alternatives. Most familiarly, assessment of the economic impact of the flow on the country of origin or of destination links migration policy to more general economic strategies; and the interest alignments that come into play are closely related to the general configuration of class relations in the relevant country. On the receiving side, for example, a given group of immigrants can be viewed simultaneously by employers as a welcome addition to the labor pool, by indigenous workers as unwelcome competition, and by welfare agencies or local taxpayers as "free riders" who constitute a burden on welfare facilities; and similar considerations arise in the country of origin as well. Moreover, the economic perspective on international migrations also entails assessments of the value of a particular flow from the respective points of view of the sending and receiving country.

But migrants are never viewed exclusively from an economic perspective. They are also seen as members of racial, ethnic, religious, and linguistic groups, as well as persons imbued with distinctive political dispositions and preferences. Concomitantly, the actual or potential role of the migrants as members of society evokes their assessment on a scale of moral value, referring to their impact on regime-maintenance and national integration. There is no gainsaying that, if it is difficult to assess with precision the economic effects produced by given population movements, it is well-nigh impossible to do so in the sphere presently under consideration. Nevertheless, it is very much the case that all established migration policies and all attempts to change them are predicated on some such assessment. How do the scales on the basis of which groups are judged to be assets or liabilities arise? "Prejudice," "xenophobia," and other individual-level explanations only go halfway.

An alternative starting point is the observation that constituted societies commonly strive to achieve and maintain a certain degree of cultural homogeneity, and that the codes which delineate the preferred culture often take the form of an emphasis on distinctions between "us" and "others," whereby the latter function as a negative anti-cultural model to be avoided. The "others" are always mythical; but the myth is often thought to be incarnated by actual groups, whose known attributes may in fact have contributed to shaping the myth in the first place. If such groups happen to be physically located within the state, they may be confined, segregated, or even expelled; should they be outside, little action is required unless, by some play of circumstances, they start flowing across the border; the most obvious response is then to keep them out altogether. But, paradoxically, situations have repeatedly arisen whereby an immigrant population is simultaneously highly desirable from an economic point of view, and highly undesirable from the perspective presently under discussion. This is so because, by and large, "cheap labor" comes from the periphery. As will be demonstrated below, the ensuing dilemma has been resolved variously in different historical epochs.

■ The Age of Absolutism and Mercantilism

From the middle of the fifteenth century on, as a consequence of internal transformations within Europe and its outward expansion, "for the first time, the world began to be one migratory network dominated by a single group of technologically advanced and culturally similar states" ((3), p. 96). This is also when international migration, properly speaking, emerged as a distinctive phenomenon, since its distinctiveness is predicated on the organization of global space into territories controlled by sovereign states that have the right to control the movement of people across their borders. Such migration was almost entirely controlled by sending and receiving states. Migration from one European state to another (including to foreign colonies) was very limited. Since population was considered a scarce economic and military asset, rulers deployed considerable efforts to police their territorial boundaries and to confine subjects within them. This process was acknowledged in, and reinforced by, the formation of international law in the seventeenth century ((7), pp. 91–96; (11)).

As I have documented in previous publications, the three largest components of the Western network during this period were: (a) the importation of an estimated 7.5 million West African slaves to work plantations, initially in Europe or its outlying islands, and then in the New World; (b) the relocation of two to three million Europeans in the New World colonies, mostly under some form of bondage; and (c) the expulsion or flight of approximately one million persons from the newly-forming European states in the XVIth and XVIIth centuries (17).

Coercion was probably a necessary concomitant of labor importation under prevailing colonial conditions. On the one hand, transportation costs were very high in relation to the workers' potential output and were usually assumed by the employer in advance; similarly, the employer (or intermediaries, such as brokers) must pay in advance for a substantial share of the estimated labor output. Under such circumstances, it was imperative to secure control over the actual performance of the labor. This was particularly difficult to achieve under colonial conditions, since the abundance of open land normally afforded any person the possibility of engaging in subsistence agriculture as an alternative to working for others. Bondage, in one form or another, thus arose as a solution to prevent workers from taking advantage of the labor-scarcity conditions that prompted their importation in the first place. For Europeans, initially mostly Spaniards and later mostly British, the typical arrangement was indenture, under which the prospective employer or a colonial labor agent bore the costs of transfer and settlement in exchange for a seven-year contract. Imperial authorities sought to regulate such movements to avoid a counterproductive drain of valuable population from home and the autonomous development of colonies in competition with the metropole; but if they leaned too far in this direction, as was the case with France in the XVIIth century, then the very development of the colonies was jeopardized.

Cultural considerations came into play early on. For example, France prohibited the settlement of its own Protestant subjects in its North American possession, Acadia and New France, probably out of fear they might be disloyal in the event of a conflict with Britain and the Netherlands; similarly, Britain in practice prohibited the settlement of its own Catholic subjects in the New England colonies exposed to the possibility of conflict with France; Protestant dissenters, however, were not ruled out as their bitter anti-Catholicism insured they would function as reliable guardians of empire. With respect to Africans, debate still rages as to whether white racism was a precondition for the emergence of chattel slavery, or whether slavery fostered racism as a rationalization. What matters most, for the present purpose, is that the extreme segregation associated with the Northwest European form of slavery (British and Dutch) can be thought of as a rational (in the sense of instrumental) solution to the problem of importing economically valuable but culturally undesirable labor. What such segregation entails, institutionally, is the erection of an internal boundary which prevents the group under consideration from becoming incorporated into the receiving society.

The contradictory dictates of economic and political considerations also came into play within Europe itself, where the cultural dynamics associated with the process of state-formation sometimes led rulers to willfully divest themselves of otherwise valuable population groups or to persecute them to the point of driving them into flight. In a competitive international setting, state-building entailed strenuous efforts to render populations more homogeneous within, so as to emphasize national differences and thus promote identification among subjects with the interests of their rulers. The main cultural instrument to that effect was religion. It is noteworthy, in this respect, that official expulsion of Jews living in England and France—as against local attacks on them—coincided with the take-off of their respective monarchies in the late XIIIth century. From such a perspective, it stands to reason that by expelling the unconverted Jews in 1492, the newly united Spanish monarchy was merely trying to "europeanize" Iberian society. A similar fate was subsequently meted out to the Iberian population of Arab descent (the *moriscos*) who not only were considered "unassimilable," like the Jews, but thought to constitute a strategic liability because of their location on the Mediterranean coast vulnerable to attack by Spain's Moslem enemies—a situation akin to the one which arose with respect to U.S. citizens of Japanese descent on the West Coast in World War II. In the same manner, in the late XVIth century Spanish authorities knowingly jeopardized the economic viability of their valuable Netherlandish possession (approximately present-day Belgium) by driving Protestants, who figured prominently in that region's manufacturing and commerce, out of the country. Numerous forced population exchanges occurred during the Thirty Years' War and in its aftermath, when the principle of conformity to the prince's religion was generalized throughout German Europe. The last massive wave of refugees were the Protestants who fled France when Louis XIV revoked the Edict of Nantes (1685), another major instance of a compulsive striving for cultural homogeneity in the name of raison d'état, with little or no regard for the economic consequences—let alone the human costs—of such action.

The immigration policy of European states during this period was generally governed by acquisitiveness. Sovereigns aspiring to economic development welcomed foreign artisans and often sought out valuable population groups, sometimes to the point of conceding to such foreigners a significant degree of religious toleration. A similar orientation prevailed with respect to the importation of mercenaries who were in some sense the original guestworkers. In the XVIIth century, the generous asylum policy of the newly independent Netherlands toward foreign Protestants and toward Jews contributed significantly to bringing about its spectacular economic development; and this example, widely broadcast by contemporary thinkers, in turn fostered the emergence of greater religious tolerance throughout the region in the XVIIIth century.

■ The Liberal Epoch

In retrospect, the nineteenth century constituted a deviant episode in the history of international migrations, when a group of states in one part of the

■ Contemporary Patterns

The contrast between the policy patterns of the liberal age and those of our own time is very sharp. Starting around the turn of the XXth century, one after the other the states of destination began to close their gates, restricting access to relatively small numbers of people of the receivers' choosing, and with some minor modifications and occasional but temporary exceptions, this still remains the basic stance of the affluent liberal states today. At the same time, the world began to produce refugees on a hitherto unprecedented scale, while a number of states, containing a substantial proportion of the world's population, erected more effective barriers than ever devised before against exit. Our interest in international migration should not blind us to the fact that it is an exceptional phenomenon, which occurs against a background of enforced immobility. Most human beings alive today are confined in the country of their birth as a consequence of restrictive exit or entry policies, or of some combination of both. It is also the case that among the migrations that have occurred in the XXth century, refugees outnumber voluntary migrants (1).

These trends emerged rapidly in the last decades in the XIXth century, when the market and the state became truly worldwide forms of social organization, and the globe was linked for the first time into a single network of rapid mass transportation (steamship and railroad) and telecommunications. The unevenness of world conditions was accentuated by a growing gap between a small number of capital-rich, technologically advanced, and strategically powerful countries, European or of European origin plus Japan, and the rest, whose internal conditions the leading countries affected more than ever by way of colonial control and of the transnational economic, social, cultural, and political processes they generated. In the demographic sphere, completing the revolution they had begun to experience in the XVIIIth century, the industrialized countries entered into a phase of much slower growth; whereas in the previous century and a half they had grown at a more rapid rate than the rest, the difference was now reversed; Europe reached its historical maximum proportion of world population around World War I, and the United States and Japan did so around 1950 ((16), p. 205). Whereas the achievement of peak rates of population growth by Western countries generally coincided with a rate of economic growth sufficient to absorb additional manpower and to foster a secular increase in per capita income—taking into account the redistribution of population among them by way of overseas migration in the XIXth century—this combination rarely occurred in other parts of the world. Hence, as world population mounted in the XXth century, an ever-larger proportion of them were poor.

Given the way in which the world is structured, the work any person is capable of performing will bring much higher returns in an affluent than in a poor country, especially if "collective goods" as well as individual ones are taken into account. It is therefore quite reasonable for many people living in poor countries—even if they are themselves not among the poorest—to aspire to relocate. The availability of such a vast reserve of cheap labor located abroad provides obvious opportunities for capitalists in the industrial countries, most prominently the possibility of cushioning the effects of the business cycle by procuring labor when it is needed and divesting themselves of it when it no longer is, without bearing the costs of maintaining it when unproductive. But the potential number of candidates to fill the ranks of cheap labor is much vaster than any conceivable demand in receiving countries, and for obvious reasons, many workers admitted on a temporary basis end up wanting to stay. It is evident that as ordinary residents, however, they become less valuable economically, and in the face of a tendency to settle, objections are also raised concerning their cultural impact on the receiving country.

The escalation of refugees is attributable in the first instance to the breakdown of empires and their concomitant replacement with a plethora of new states whose founders tend to adopt the national model fostered by earlier developers. As noted earlier, state building in Europe resulted in the formation of target groups whose elimination was thought to be necessary in order to achieve political integration; unleashed in highly populated and culturally more heterogenous regions in the XXth century this process has resulted in a proliferation of religious, racial, or ethnic minorities subjected to the most extreme forms of persecution, including not only expulsion but also immobilization and mass murder. Paradoxically, those who in fact become refugees—as a result of expulsion or flight—sometimes turn out to be the more fortunate members of the original victim groups. Because state-formation commonly encompasses an entire region, it also tends to generate international tensions and conflicts which interact with the process delineated earlier to produce further flows. The political transformations under consideration are sometimes accompanied by attempts to restructure society as a whole, and in the course of social revolutions or counterrevolutions entire classes are cast in the role of victim-groups.

In recent decades, the international community has come to acknowledge special obligations toward refugees, but the number of claimants is much greater than states are collectively willing to admit as permanent residents, so that some form of triage must come into play. Moreover, the circumstances under which people become refugees often involve a mix of political oppression and economic distress, which makes determination of the validity of individual claims difficult. And finally, once refugees are admitted, their impact is indistinguishable from that of other newcomers, so that the issues mentioned earlier move to the fore in this case as well.

The economic and political processes outlined may be considered as the global givens in relation to which the world's more affluent and liberal countries have determined their immigration policies in the XXth century. One very striking outcome has been a steady reduction of the long-standing distinctiveness of the "nations of immigrants," as these countries took steps to reduce the role of immigration in their societal development. This is well illustrated by the experience of the largest of them, the United States, where from the 1890s on, pressures mounted to drastically reduce the entry of "new immigrants" from southern and eastern Europe. Expressed with respect to the undesirability of specific nationalities and ethnic groups, the new restrictionism in fact represented growing opposition to mass immigration of any kind.

Political alignments were much as before; to the restrictionist camp was now added organized labor, and resistance to it came mostly from the business community and from the ranks of recent immigrants. Under the impact of World War I and ensuing upheavals, including the Soviet revolution, the restrictionists gained a succession of victories in 1917–24, as the result of which annual U.S. immigration from Europe was reduced, in relation to population size, to below the pre-1830 level. Few concessions were made to the plight of refugees in the interwar period. United States business adjusted to the exclusion of Asians and to the reduction in European immigration by turning to cheap labor from Mexico and the Caribbean; beginning in World War I, and again in World War II, government assistance was provided to insure a flow of temporary labor. In this manner, U.S. policy came to be divided into a segment pertaining to immigration by way of the main gate, and another governing labor procurement through the back door.

In 1952, the United States reaffirmed a very restrictive stance with respect to the main gate; however, many ad hoc enactments in effect implemented a somewhat more generous policy toward European refugees and family reunion in the post–World War II period. These reforms were formalized in 1965, when all traces of racial and ethnic discrimination were removed; however, quantitative limitations were maintained and extended to include the Western hemisphere, hitherto unrestricted in this respect. At about the same time, the long-standing temporary workers program, involving several hundred thousand annual entries from Mexico, was eliminated; instead, back door policy drifted toward benign neglect of the southern border, allowing for a massive flow of undocumented workers. Notwithstanding mounting concern with the latter in the 1970s exacerbated by high unemployment and fear of "hispanization," proposals to effectively restrict their entry by imposing sanctions on employers of illegal aliens have been resisted by the employers themselves as well as by U.S. citizens and residents of hispanic culture, so far (early 1983) successfully. In keeping with its foreign policy interests, since the 1950s the United States has been especially generous toward refugees from Communist regimes, most recently with respect to Indochinese and Cubans; concomitantly, there is considerable official reluctance to accord refugee status to persons originating in states considered friendly. Refugee admissions are likely to be curtailed because of mounting objections from local communities to the escalating welfare costs the settlement of large numbers of Cubans and Indochinese has entailed.

In the XXth century, the European states hitherto concerned mostly with emigration came to be countries of destination and were faced with the need to devise an immigration policy. For many of them, the issue first arose in earnest with the arrival of Jews from eastern Europe beginning in the 1880s. Germany reacted forcefully by resorting to administrative refoulement; Britain, hitherto more liberal than the others with respect to foreigners, devised a restrictive Aliens Act (1906). In contrast with these, France maintained an open door—not because of an absence of anti-Semitism, but because the state looked upon immigration in general as a device for increasing its demographic weight in the face of a declining rate of natural reproduction. For those same reasons, rendered more urgent by population losses in World War I, France continued to welcome immigrants in large numbers in the 1920s and absorbed much of the flow deflected from the United States by the new restrictive legislation; as of 1930, approximately 7% of the population was foreign-born, a much higher level than found elsewhere in Europe. Massive refugee flows were triggered off by the breakdown of liberal democracies in the interwar period, particularly in Germany; but when wartime conditions and the refusal of liberal countries to open their doors made it impossible for the Nazis to expel undesirables, they turned to a form of forced emigration that produces no refugees.

To a remarkable extent, the national orientations established in Europe before World War I guided policy-making after the region recovered from World War II (5,8). The situation differed somewhat in each of the principal cases. The United Kingdom remained inhospitable to general immigration while continuing to rely on the Irish; however, in the course of the negotiations leading to the establishment of the Commonwealth (1948), Britain extended to the citizens of its various member states a status that was tantamount to British nationality, which allowed them to settle freely in the British isles. Within a decade, the ensuing flows of West Indian blacks and of Asians from the Indian subcontinent, albeit welcomed by some employers, had propelled immigration to the forefront of political controversy. In 1961, a Conservative government began to undo the permissive effects of the 1948 arrangements, so as to transform "new Commonwealth" populations into ordinary aliens, whose entry might be restricted; Labour subsequently joined in, and the task was finally completed in 1981. However, in the intervening period a sizeable nonwhite minority had become permanently established in Britain.

The German economy benefited in the immediate postwar period from the additional supply of labor provided by a steady flow of refugees and returnees from the East, but even before this ebbed, the Federal Republic revived the guestworker pattern by negotiating bilateral agreements with less developed European countries (Italy, Spain, Greece) and later with Turkey and Yugoslavia. By the early 1970s, foreign workers constituted about one-tenth of the country's labor force. Contrary to original intent, however, some of them were beginning to turn into permanent residents; Turks, who constitute only about one-third of the foreign total, have been singled out as a source of special concern. The energy crisis of 1973 brought an end to new labor immigration, but the question of whether established workers and their families will be allowed to stay—i.e., whether Germany will become an immigration country—is not yet settled. With relatively minor variations, German experience was replicated in Switzerland, Belgium, Luxemburg, and later the Netherlands, Sweden, and Norway. French exceptionalism prevailed until about 1972, after which policy shifted toward the continental norm; similar tensions have surfaced there, particularly with respect to Algerians. The socialist regime which came into power in 1981 has moved toward allowing established foreign workers to settle permanently, while erecting more rigorous barriers against new arrivals.

■ Conclusion

In the permanent face of a large mass of external population propelled into the migration stream by economic distress or brutal force, the countries of putative destination have steadily moved in recent times toward the adoption of extremely restrictive entry policies, for which Japan might serve as a model. The trend has been accelerated by the economic crisis of the past decade, but was already in the making before this occurred, and it is likely that the new restrictionism will outlast the current depression. As it appears impossible to operate guestworker programs without incurring permanent settlement, entrepreneurs are henceforth much more likely to relocate their capital in cheap labor regions than to import workers from the Third World. Immigration into the affluent societies is thus likely to remain limited to a small stream of family reunion and a cautious intake of refugees. It is obviously rational for affluent societies to erect walls in order to protect the desirable economic, cultural, and political conditions they have achieved, and there is no gainsaying that these states owe it to their own populations to provide them with such protection. But one should understand these policies for what they are: a collective device to prevent the redistribution of existing world resources to the benefit of the disadvantaged.

Notwithstanding their exploitative character, policies designed to procure cheap labor have been the source of one of the few openings in an otherwise impenetrable wall. Minimal justice requires that the foreign workers who contributed to the affluence of the receivers be allowed to stay and have an opportunity, if they wish, to bring in their immediate families so as to complete the process of relocation and begin that of integration into a new society. Such integration requires mutual adjustment by the newcomers and the host society, but nowhere are the numbers involved so overwhelming, nor the people involved so incapable of change as to make accommodation impossible.

Beyond this, in the worldwide process of triage, the highest priority must be granted to political refugees. Liberal states should, of course, wherever possible avoid engaging in actions that contribute to the generation of refugees, and they might be able to contribute, by way of diplomacy and assistance, to alleviate somewhat refugee-producing tensions in certain parts of the world. However, the flow of victims is certain to continue in the foreseeable future, and the refugee camp is rapidly emerging as one of the major images of the age.

Refugee policy consists of two very different components, the one involving aid and assistance to refugees in "third countries," the other involving their admission to one's own country, together with assistance for doing so. Both are vital, but international relief should not be viewed as a substitute for asylum. To take in the victims of willful persecution, regardless of whether the persecutor is friend or foe, is one of the fundamental obligations of states founded on justice; and given the paucity of such states on the world scene, each of them must assume an equitable share of the common burden.

■ References
(1) Beijer, G.J. 1969. Modern patterns of international migratory movements. In *Migration*, ed. J.A. Jackson. Cambridge: Cambridge University Press.
(2) Davis, D.B. 1975. The Problem of Slavery in the Age of Revolution, 1770–1823. Ithaca: Cornell University Press.
(3) Davis, K. 1974. The migrations of human populations. Sci. Am. 231:92–105.
(4) Dibble, V. 1968. Social science and political commitments in the young Max Weber. Eur. J. Soc. 7: 95–110.
(5) Freeman, G. 1979. Immigrant Labor and Racial Conflict in Industrial Societies: The French and British Experience, 1945–1975. Princeton: Princeton University Press.
(6) Furnivall, J.S. 1948. Colonial Policy and Practice. London: Cambridge University Press.
(7) Glass, D.V. 1967. Population: Policies and Movements in Europe. London: Frank Cass and Co.
(8) Kubat, D., ed. 1979. The Politics of Migration Policies. New York: Center for Migration Studies.

(9) Kuznets, S. 1966. Modern Economic Growth: Rate, Structure, and Spread. New Haven: Yale University Press.
(10) Piore, M. 1979. Birds of Passage: Migrant Labor and Industrial Societies. Cambridge: Cambridge University Press.
(11) Plender, R. 1972. International Migration Law. Leiden: A.W. Sijthoff.
(12) Potter, D. 1976. The Impending Crisis, 1848-1861. New York: Harper.
(13) Smith, M.G. 1965. The Plural Society in the British West Indies. Berkeley: University of California Press.
(14) Thomas, B. 1973. Migration and Economic Growth: A Study of Great Britain and the Atlantic Economy. Cambridge: Cambridge University Press.
(15) Tinker, H. 1974. A New System of Slavery: The Export of Indian Labor Overseas, 1830–1920. London: Oxford University Press.
(16) Wrigley, E.A. 1969. Population and History. New York: McGraw-Hill.
(17) Zolberg, A.R. 1978. International migration policies in a changing world system. In Human Migrations: Patterns and Policies, eds. W. McNeill and R. Adams, pp. 241–286. Bloomington: Indiana University Press.
(18) Zolberg, A.R. 1981. International migrations in political perspective. In Global Trends in Migration: Theory and Research on International Population Movements, eds. M. Kritz, C.B. Keely, and S.M. Tomasi, pp. 3–27. New York: Center for Migration Studies.
(19) Zolberg, A.R. 1983. Contemporary transnational migrations in historical perspective: patterns and dilemmas. In U.S. Immigration and Refugee Policy: Global and Domestic Issues, ed. M.M. Kritz, pp. 15–51. Lexington: D.C. Heath.

Migration in Modern European History

■ What Is Migration?

. . . The concept of migration faces . . . difficulties. From the continuous locomotion of human beings, to pick out some moves as more definitive than others reflects the concern of bureaucrats to attach people to domiciles where they can be registered, enumerated, taxed, drafted and watched. A vagrant—a person without a domicile—gives trouble not only to the police but also to definitions of migration. Are gypsies migrants? The crisp definitions and statistics essential to an answer emerged with the consolidation of national states and state bureaucracies.

With rare exceptions, both practical definitions and available evidence concerning migration state the answers to some combination of these three questions:

1. Who lives here *now*?
2. Where did they live *then*?
3. Who else lived *here* then?

A single enumeration of the population can produce answers to the first two questions. The third question requires enumerations at more than one point in time. But all three can be answered within a single administrative unit. Only rarely do we find an answer to a fourth obvious question in the series: Where do they live *now*? That requires two difficult operations: looking in several places, and tracing people forward in time. Counts of migration therefore consist mainly of comparisons, one place at a time, (a) between the answers to questions 1 and 2; (b) among the answers to questions 1, 2, and 3.

All the elements—who, where, when—are problematic. All are quite vulnerable to the administrative vagaries that vexed Oskar Morgenstern. "Who" may refer to heads of households, workers, citizens, legal residents, or everyone on hand. "Where" may mean in some particular dwelling, in

---

Charles Tilly, "Migration in Modern European History," in W. H. McNeil and R. S. Adams, eds., *Human Migration* (Bloomington: Indiana University Press, 1978), pp. 48–72.

tance. Circular migration may do the same thing, but it is somewhat more likely to disperse the available workers among a number of opportunities. Local migration involves many destinations within a circumscribed range. Career migration, finally, tends to spread people far and wide. The geographic differences suggest the following grouping of the migration patterns:

| | | Supply of Relevant Skills | |
		General	Special
Cost of Information About Opportunities	High	chain	circular
	Low	local	career

Chain and circular migration are ways of combatting high costs of information about opportunities for employment, proprietorship, and other desired ends. Circular and career migration respond to situations in which the skills the migrants exercise are not generally available—because they are hard to learn, because the migrants have monopolized them, or because other people are unwilling to work at them. Thus as the cost of information about job opportunities declines, chain and circular migration give way to local and career migration. But to the extent that all job skills are unevenly distributed, circular and career migration tend to supplant chain and local migration.

The rough classification of migration into local, circular, chain, and career does not exhaust the significant distinctions one might make. For example, it catches quite imperfectly the important difference between individual and collective migration; although on the whole chain and circular migration involve single individuals less frequently than do local and career migration, there are individual and collective versions of all four types. . . . The classification into local, circular, chain, and career migrations separates some significantly different social arrangements from each other, but it does not make all the distinctions one might wish to employ.

The sorts of administratively produced evidence we have concerning European migration do not permit us to distinguish easily among local, circular, chain, and career migration. To do so, one needs life histories, detailed accounts of intentions and social relations at the time of moves, or both. Records of official changes of domicile yield the former with great difficulty, and the latter not at all. On the basis of the scattered evidence available, nevertheless, it seems safe to say that in the age of industrialization the general character of European migration shifted from the lower left to the upper right of our diagram: away from local and short-distance circular migration, toward longer-distance, more definitive chain and career migration. It also seems safe to say that the *pace* of migration changed much less than its *character*. The history of Europe shows us not so much periods of immobility and mobility as decisive shifts among types of mobility.

■ The Great Flows

William McNeill has portrayed the repeated sweeps of conquering bands across the continent. He has also recounted the less dramatic, but no less momentous, flows of agricultural settlers into the continent's emptier spaces. Before the last millennium, large-scale movements of armed men and tribute-takers set the rhythm of European political history. Armed men and tribute-takers have thrived into our own time, but on the whole they have fixed themselves in space, reduced the scale and duration of their movements, and worked harder and harder at controlling the flows of people and goods into and out of their own fixed territories. Within Europe, long-distance flows of agricultural settlers continued, although their relative volume seems to have declined irregularly with the approach of our own time.

The last massive migration of agricultural workers within Europe was the Medieval flow of German-speakers into the East and South of the continent. That flow continued past 1500. But by then its volume had greatly diminished. By that time German-speaking migrants consisted mainly of one variety or another of conqueror: officials, managers, merchants, and landlords. The seventeenth- and eighteenth-century expansion of the Prussian state formally incorporated a number of eastern German enclaves and took in a good deal of predominantly Slavic population. It did not, however, produce movements of population comparable to those of three or four centuries earlier. Despite Frederick the Great's strenuous efforts at settlement, for example, Silesia remained predominantly Polish-speaking. Further south, the Austrians also sought to settle German speakers to their east by such straightforward devices as dispossessing the Czech landlords of Moravia. Although such planned migrations were of the greatest political importance, the numbers involved were relatively small. Indeed, they bucked the long-range trend, which was for Slavic-speakers, given weight by their generally higher levels of natural increase, to push westward into areas earlier occupied by Finns, Swedes, and Germans. On either side of the linguistic frontier, massive long-distance rural-to-rural migration became less prevalent after 1500.

Long-distance moves of workers into nonagricultural employment are a different matter. They accelerated some two hundred years ago, and have remained important since then. The migration of Poles into the mining areas of western Germany and eastern France and the rush of Irishmen to

Liverpool and London illustrate the importance of long-distance migration within industrial Europe. Contrary to first impressions, few of these long-distance migrants moved directly from farm to factory. For the most part, the farmers who moved to cities found low-level employment in services and commerce. The apparent exceptions were commonly small-town artisans or rural industrial workers rather than peasants or farm laborers. Indeed, over the last two centuries the most important single category of urban employment for rural-to-urban migrants within Europe has most likely been domestic service. Only an undue concentration on males and on manufacturing has obscured that fact.

During the period of swift natural increase from the mid-eighteenth century to the end of the nineteenth, Europe also sent millions of its residents to the agricultural and industrial areas of the Americas and of Oceania. The great flows of the nineteenth and twentieth centuries followed smaller but still important migratory movements which accompanied European colonial expansion during the three previous centuries. In this great overseas migration, millions of rural Europeans *did* migrate to farms. French migrants peopled rural Quebec as well as Quebec City and Montreal. Portuguese emigrants became Brazilian farmers as well as residents of São Paulo and Rio de Janeiro. Later, more than two million Germans and Scandinavians sailed to America. There, many of them settled on frontier farms.

Altogether, Europe's net migration from 1800 to World War I was on the order of fifty million persons. Given the frequent returns of chain migrants, a much larger number must have made the trip at one time or another. Since a return rate of 30 percent is plausible, the true number could easily be 65 million sometime emigrants. Over half of all European emigrants in that period went to the United States.

The British Isles—especially Ireland—were the champion exporters of humankind, and the chief purveyors to America. About three-quarters of nineteenth-century emigrants from Britain went to North America. As a result, at least a third of all American immigrants in that century were native speakers of English. Nevertheless, Germany, Greece, Italy, and the Scandinavian countries all became major sources of overseas migrants at some time during the nineteenth century.

One of the best-documented cases is Denmark. With a total population in the range of two million, Denmark sent over 300,000 migrants overseas between 1840 and 1914 (Hvidt, 1975, p. 9). Over 90 percent went to North America. Within that small country, rates of emigration differed dramatically from one district to another. On the whole, they were much higher in the southeast than elsewhere. More generally, urban areas sent migrants at a significantly higher pace than rural areas did. Yet where urban growth and industrialization were vigorous, relatively little emigration occurred.

The ideal origin for Danish emigrants seems to have been the stagnant town in which underemployed long-term migrants from nearby rural areas were accumulating. Landless laborers and servants were especially good prospects for emigration. Kristian Hvidt quotes a letter describing the situation on the high-migration island of Bornholm . . . (Hvidt, 1975, p. 129). Chain migration was the predominant pattern among the 300,000 Danes who left Denmark. Toward the end of the nineteenth century, around a quarter of all Danish migrants to the United States came on steamship tickets prepaid by migrants already in America. (The comparable figures for Norway and Sweden run from 40 to 50 percent.) "Letters, money, and prepaid tickets came in a constant stream, the volume of which would quite likely surprise most people," writes Hvidt,

> since the emigrants were generally believed to have formed the poorest part of the population and to have been characterized by intellectual narrowness and insufficient education. Improved economic conditions in the United States combined with the emotional longings inherent in emigration furthered both letter writing and sending tickets home. These personal contacts with the Old Country may well be sufficient explanation of why mass emigration accelerated whenever economic conditions permitted. (Hvidt, 1975, p. 194)

Indeed, it was partly *because* they were poor and uneducated that the Danish emigrants relied on their compatriots for aid, encouragement, and information in the long migration to America.

In the period after World War I, with declining European rates of natural increase and rising American resistance to immigration, the pace of European emigration diminished. Nevertheless, Canada, Argentina, Brazil, Australia, and New Zealand continued to receive large numbers of European migrants. In that period, as Table 4.3.1 shows, the British Isles regained the predominance they had lost to Italy during the period 1891 to 1920. Poorer areas of the British Isles, such as the declining Welsh mining region, sent their surplus labor overseas in the company of a smaller number of highly educated people from all over Britain. Since the table deals only with the total number of overseas emigrants, it conceals an important countercurrent: while the poor areas of northwestern Europe continued to send migrants overseas, the more prosperous areas began to bring in migrants from elsewhere in Europe.

Since World War II, northwestern Europe has become an even more active importer of migrants. Yugoslavia, Spain, Portugal, Italy, Ireland, and Turkey became major suppliers to the highly industrialized regions of Europe. This last shift has its ironies: we see the nations which peopled the rest of the western world with their poor now drawing their unskilled labor from poor immigrants, and fretting about the disruption such migrations

Table 4.3.1   **Percentage of All European Overseas Emigrants Leaving from Selected Countries, 1846–1963**

Countries	Period			
	1846–90	1891–1920	1921–39	1946–63
British Isles	47.9	17.7	29.0	27.7
Germany	20.2	3.4	9.8	15.7
Sweden, Denmark, Norway	6.9	3.8	3.8	2.1
France, Switzerland, Netherlands	4.2	1.5	2.5	14.9
Italy	8.2	27.0	18.6	19.0
Austria, Hungary, Czechoslovakia	3.7	15.9	4.1	?
Russia, Poland, Lithuania, Estonia, Finland	2.1	13.0	12.0	?
Spain, Portugal	6.9	15.3	15.0	12.1
Total emigrants from Europe per year (x 1,000)	376	910	366	585

Source: Calculated from Kosínski 1970: 57.

The figures describe gross migration, not net loss through migration. Boundaries as of the 1960s apply to all periods.

may cause. Switzerland, which long disposed of its surplus men as mercenaries in European armies, now has a sixth of its population foreign-born. Great Britain, which flooded America with English-speaking families, now debates the desirability of its 5 percent born elsewhere. According to Stephen Castles and Godula Kosack, France, West Germany, Switzerland, and Great Britain, among others, have come to rely almost entirely on foreigners to do their dirty work. Yet they have proved quite hostile to granting the newcomers a permanent stake in their host countries. Xenophobia is nothing new. But the backing it has received from West European states in recent years is unusual.

■ The Impacts of War and Politics

The most dramatic twentieth-century change in European migration patterns was not the northwest's shift from export to import of migrants. It was the expanding role of political pressures and political controls. Politics impinged on migration in three distinct ways: through war, through deliberate relocation of ethnic minorities, and through stringent national controls over immigration and emigration.

During the twentieth century, in more senses than one, war became the prime mover. Earlier, such continental conflicts as the Thirty Years' War and the Napoleonic Wars had produced hordes of refugees. They also produced some long-term displacement of population away from the war zones. But World Wars I and II produced incomparably greater migratory currents in Europe. According to Eugene Kulischer's compilation

(Kulischer, 1948, pp. 248–49), the largest flows within Europe and the adjacent sections of Asia from 1918 to 1939 were:

1.2 million Greeks to Greece from Turkey (1922–1923)

1.15 million Russians to Europe outside the Soviet Union (1918–1922)

1.1 million repatriated from Russia to Poland (1918–1925)

900 thousand Poles from former Russian and Austrian Poland to former German Poland (1918–1921)

700 thousand Germans from Western Poland, Danzig and Memel to Germany (1918–1925)

Only then do we arrive at migratory streams in which the war and the peace settlement did not play a large, direct part: the estimated 650 thousand Italians who went from Italy to France over the 21 years from 1919 to 1939, and the estimated 450 thousand Poles who made the move to France over the same period. (These are net figures; according to Polish statistics, for example, 622 thousand Poles went to France from 1919 through 1939, but 200 thousand returned to Poland, for a net of 422 thousand migrants: Kosínski, 1970, pp. 79–80.)

These numbers are large. They are, however, modest compared to the figures for World War II and its aftermath. To take again the leaders in Kulischer's compilation (Kulischer, 1948, pp. 302–4):

6 million Reich Germans from New Poland to Germany (1944–1947)

5 million Jews from Germany to extermination camps in Poland and elsewhere (1940–1944)

4 million Reich Germans from the Soviet Zone to the U.S. and British Zones (1945–1946)

3 million Poles from Old Poland to New Poland (1945–1947)

2.7 million ethnic Germans from Czechoslovakia to Germany and Austria (1945–1946)

1.8 million Czechs and Slovaks from Inner Czechoslovakia to the former Sudetenland (1946–1947)

1 million ethnic Germans from Old Poland to Germany (1944–1945)

The list goes on. However approximate these figures are, and however much double-counting they include, they portray World War II and—especially—the postwar settlement as one of the greatest demographic whirlwinds ever to sweep the earth.

Some of these migrants fled from war zones. Many more of them moved at the behest of governments. On the whole, the refugees contributed to the diversity of population at their destinations. When states deliberately relocated people, however, they tended to homogenize the language and culture of the people within any particular set of national boundaries. The net effect of the migrations surrounding the two world wars was therefore to homogenize nation-states and probably to increase their capacity for nationalism.

Heightened nationalism and the recurrent labor shortages of the richer European countries have combined to produce a contradictory situation. On the one hand, such countries as Switzerland, West Germany, and France have become sorely dependent on poorer countries for supplies of unskilled labor. On the other hand, those same countries and their neighbors have greatly increased their controls over immigration and emigration. There is, to be sure, a sharp difference between eastern and western Europe in those regards. On the whole, the richer western European countries have encouraged circular migration of low-wage workers from elsewhere but have made it difficult for them to become long-time residents and, especially, to acquire citizenship. The Soviet Union and other Communist states have simply made all forms of entry and exit difficult.

The last five centuries of European long-distance migration show us three major factors at work: (1) a changing geographic distribution of opportunities for employment; (2) alterations of regional differentials in natural increase; (3) actions and policies of national states—notably making war, controlling migration and deliberately recruiting, expelling, or relocating specific ethnic and religious groups. The first two factors have shaped migration throughout the five hundred years. To explain why and how they worked is to trace out the expansion of capitalism, the proletarianization of the European population as a whole, the march of urbanization and industrialization. The third factor—actions and policies of national states—gained importance as the five centuries wore on. By the twentieth century, wars and their settlements rivaled the interplay of employment and natural increase as incentives to long-distance migration.

■ The Local Flows

No one has given us a comprehensive statistical atlas of long-distance migration within, from, and to the European continent. That would be a useful enterprise. But at least the existence and broad directions of the long-distance flows are well known. In the present state of our knowledge, local migration provides more puzzles.

Recent work on the historical demography of Europe has experienced a nice dialectic. The fastidious methods for reconstructing precensus demographic characteristics developed by such scholars as Louis Henry and E. A. Wrigley sometimes assume, and always apply more easily to, relatively immobile populations. Yet one of the most impressive and consistent findings of the historical demographers has been the high level of local mobility among preindustrial European people. In studies of eighteenth-century agricultural villages, it is not unusual to find over a tenth of the population making a significant change of residence each year. If the sheer frequency of moves (rather than the distance moved) is the criterion, it is not at all clear that industrialization produced a major increase in the European population's mobility.

The findings coming in jar our preconceptions concerning the settled peasant world that industrialization is supposed to have broken up. Still, the idea of a settled peasant world is not so much wrong as incomplete. Let us consider "peasants" to be members of households whose major activity is farming, households which produce a major share of the goods and services they consume, which exercise substantial control over the land they farm, and which supply the major part of their labor requirements from their own energies. If that is what we mean by peasants, a majority of the European population was probably peasant until late in the eighteenth century. The true peasant population was, so far as we know, relatively immobile.

But the extrapolation of peasant immobility to the European population as a whole errs in several ways. A substantial minority of the population was *not* peasant. From the later eighteenth century, the nonpeasants were probably a majority. Among the nonpeasants were significant groups of traders and artisans for whom movement was a way of life. Less obvious among them was a large, growing mass of landless laborers. (To take one of the extreme cases, Gregory King estimated for the England of 1688 that only 350 thousand of the 1.2 million families in agriculture lived from their own land: Pollard and Crossley, 1968, p. 154.)

The landless and land-poor moved frequently, sometimes seasonally, in response to the demand for wage-labor. As Paul Slack points out, the seventeenth-century English local authorities regularly whipped the "vagrants" who were multiplying in the countryside and sent them back to their parishes of origin. But those "vagrants" were only a minority of the many landless laborers then on the roads. They were the ones who had failed to find work. As enclosures and population growth swelled the numbers of people who had no place on the land in their home villages, many migrated in search of employment elsewhere. Local authorities treated them ambivalently: welcoming their labor if the parish needed it and could control it, but striving to make sure the wanderers gained no claims on parish welfare funds. Hence the whip.

Contrary to ideas linking high mobility to industrialization, however, the spread of rural industry seems to have helped the landless to settle down. It meant they could piece together starvation wages from industrial and agricultural work in their own villages. In his rich study of the Zurich uplands during early industrialization, Rudolf Braun shows us exactly this fixing of the proletarian population in place via cottage industry. Whereas the surplus hands of previous generations had walked off to military careers, domestic service, or another kind of unskilled work elsewhere, the villagers of the eighteenth century began to stay on the land, spinning and weaving . . . (Levine, 1977, p. 40). . . .

As opportunities for industrial employment expanded in Shepshed, more people lived out their lives in the parish, and saw their children do the same.

Some true peasant households were also quite mobile. It is doubtful that the majority of European peasant households owned the bulk of the land they farmed before some time in the nineteenth century. Most were tenants of one type or another. Tenancy meant turnover. Annual, quinquennial, or even nine-year leases brought the significant possibility of a move when the lease expired. The scattered studies in historical demography that have been able to make the essential distinctions with respect to control of land have found tenants migrating to and from villages in significant numbers. During the nineteenth- and twentieth-century "rural exodus," landless laborers were generally the first to leave the countryside, tenants next, and owners quite slow to depart.

■ Demographic Stimuli to Migration

In addition to the effects of tenancy and employment, old-regime demographic conditions provided their own spurs to migration. The best-known of those demographic conditions was the enormous death rate in cities. The rates were high enough that before the nineteenth century large cities could maintain their populations only through substantial in-migration, and could grow only through massive recruitment of outsiders. For example, in the little North Sea port of Husum from 1765 to 1804 the crude birth rate was about 26.6 and the crude death rate about 28.9, for a natural *decrease* of about 2.3 persons per thousand per year. That was true despite an age structure favorable to low mortality. In the forty years after 1804, by contrast, the crude birth rate rose a trifle to 27.1, while the crude death rate declined to 24.8. That produced a natural *increase* of about 2.3 per thousand (computed from Momsen, 1969, pp. 58, 66). In actual numbers, the breakdown of Husum's growth in the two periods ran like this:

Period	Population Change	Births-Deaths	Net Migration
1769–1802	+165	-345	+510
1803–1844	+249	+358	-110

Thus in the early nineteenth century natural increase more than supplied Husum's need for new hands and a surplus migrated elsewhere. But in the eighteenth century the city had to bring in migrants simply to maintain its population.

Husum and other small cities generally drew the bulk of their migrants from their immediate hinterlands. In most cases, a small city's radius of intensive attraction was no more than ten or fifteen miles (see Patten, 1973). Before the rising natural increase of the eighteenth and nineteenth centuries, the supply of migrants behaved a good deal like the supply of food: cities consumed more than they produced; they drew the hard-won surplus from many surrounding communities, and thus affected those communities deeply; they drew more specialized supplies from greater distances via other cities; when they grew fast, that growth generated a demand which reverberated through more and more of the hinterland.

Large cities drew on correspondingly larger areas of supply. In times of relatively rapid urban growth, such as significant parts of the sixteenth and eighteenth centuries, major cities drew their increments from vast hinterlands. London grew from about 400 thousand in 1650 to about 650 thousand a century later. That growth had a large impact on the food production of southern England. It also altered English migration systems, despite the fact that they were already centered in London. E. A. Wrigley speculates that in the high-growth century from 1650 to 1750 a sixth of the entire adult population of England spent some part of their lives in London (Wrigley, 1967, p. 49). The high-mortality metropolis stuffed itself with an entire country's demographic surplus.

Urban natural decrease was not the only important demographic condition. In a time of high, fluctuating fertility and high, unstable mortality, households that had relatively inelastic labor requirements often found their supply and demand badly matched. Artisans with an expensive stock in trade and peasants with fixed allotments of land, for instance, tended to develop a well-defined household division of labor by age, sex, and marital status. They could absorb an extra hand or do without one of the standard household members only at great strain. Either the death of a mother or the survival of an extra child jostled a delicate equilibrium. In the short run, such households used migration to adjust the supply to the demand. Extra children migrated, temporarily or definitively, into domestic service, armies, peddling. The household made up shortages by bringing in servants and/or kinsmen from elsewhere. A very high proportion of all individual migration before the twentieth century consisted of these transfers of labor among households.

In quantitative terms, however, marriage and the termination of marriage were probably the most significant demographic spurs to migration. Throughout the centuries, almost every European marriage has required at least one spouse to make a definitive change of residence. With some lags and exceptions due to co-residence with parents, the great majority have led to the formation of a new household in a new location. As nuptiality rose in the nineteenth century, the frequency of marriage-linked migration rose as well. The termination of marriages through divorce or death played a smaller part, but not a negligible one, in causing migration. To know whether its importance increased or decreased, we need not only to grasp the trends in the divorce rates, but also to balance off the migration-inducing effects of remarriages against the changing likelihood that a bereaved spouse will remain in the household she or he already occupies. We do not now have the necessary evidence. My speculation is that the termination of marriages became a less important occasion for migration in Europe after the eighteenth century.

■ Qualifications and Conclusions

Over the five centuries or so we have been reviewing, most migrants have moved short distances. Most moves have responded to demographic imbalances and changing employment opportunities. Both conditions remained true during the nineteenth century with its massive overseas migration and during the twentieth century with its major displacements by war. Furthermore, local systems of migration often provided the bases of subsequent longer-range migration. That happened in circular migration systems which included cities; if opportunity rose in the city and declined in the countryside, the system started depositing a permanent residue of migrants in the city. It also happened in some essentially rural systems of labor migration to which an overseas destination became available: mobile agricultural workers in Denmark or Portugal found themselves working, in the company of their compatriots, in New York or Toronto. The long-run trend of European migration ran from local and circular migration to chain and career migration. The average distances moved and the definitiveness of breaks with the place of origin both increased. But the continuities between the older and newer forms of migration were impressive.

I have stressed the high mobility of European populations before the nineteenth century because it requires us to rethink the relationship between industrialization and mobility. If I have given the impression that nothing changed in the nineteenth and twentieth centuries, however, that is wrong. The average distances of migration rose dramatically with large-scale industrialization. The unprecedented concentration of opportunities for employment in large cities oriented migration to those cities as never before. The growing power of national states impinged on twentieth-century migration through war and through deliberate controls over entries and exits. Those are novelties of the modern world.

The high mobility of the preindustrial world also requires some qualification. In general, the distances involved in rural migration or in migration to small cities were small. The bulk of the migrants to any locality typically came from within five or ten miles. Only larger cities regularly escaped from that rule. If we were to set a local labor market as the limit within which a move counts as "mobility" instead of "migration," we would eliminate many of the extremely high rates of migration now coming in from demographic studies of preindustrial European populations. The generalization would then read: before large-scale industrialization, rural labor markets were typically larger than a single village; they were often very active, especially where tenancy and/or wage labor prevailed; people moved frequently within those labor markets in response to demographic imbalances and shifting opportunities for livelihood.

We might speculate, in fact, that despite all the reverence for the village, the parish, or the commune which European historians have developed, the fundamental local unit was larger than any of them. The area served by a single market has turned out to be the basic building block of traditional China (Skinner, 1964, 1965). It defined the familiar world, the world of labor exchange, marriage, social mobility, local solidarity. Perhaps local market areas played a similar role in traditional Europe. The village, parish, or commune then may have acquired importance only when national states required mutually exclusive administrative units which they could hold collectively responsible for taxation, conscription, road labor, the provision of food and the maintenance of public order.

To the degree that we expand the definition of local mobility and become more stringent in our definition of migration, the era of large-scale industrialization and massive expansion of national states separates from the previous era. Long-distance, definitive migration did increase with industrialization and statemaking. Gross and net flows of migrants from rural to urban areas came to dominate the migration map as never before. As urban mortality declined, large rural-urban flows increasingly meant rapid urban growth. As rural natural increase declined, large rural-urban flows increasingly meant a depletion of the rural population. As national states grew, wars, peace settlements, and national policies acted more and more powerfully as spurs and checks to migration. In the same era, local mobility did not increase significantly; in rural areas and small towns, it probably declined.

The study of migration, then, gets us into the homely adjustments ordinary Europeans made among their own life plans and the labor requirements of the various organizations which had claims on them, or on which they had claims. Organizational structure, life plans, demography: changes in any of these three large elements eventually affect the character of the other two. Every major change in European organizational structure, life plans, and demography has produced a durable transformation of European migration patterns. As time has gone on, national states have increasingly shaped and reshaped those patterns—by deliberately controlling the possibilities of migration, by intentionally relocating ethnic minorities, and by destructively making war. The history of European migration is the history of European social life. . . .

■ References

Anderson, Grace. 1974. *Networks of Contact: The Portuguese and Toronto.* Waterloo, Ontario: Wilfred Laurier University Press.

Aymard, Maurice. 1974. "La Sicile, Terre d'Immigration," in M. Aymard et al., *Les migrations dans les pays méditerranéens au XVIIIe et au début du XIXème.* Nice: Centre de la Méditerranée Moderne et Contemporaine.

Banks, J. A. 1968. "Population Change and the Victorian City." *Victorian Studies*, 11, pp. 277–89.

Beijer, G. 1963. *Rural Migrants in Urban Setting: An Analysis of the Literature on the Problem Consequent on the Internal Migration from Rural to Urban Places in European Countries (1945-1961).* The Hague: Nijhoff.

Blaschke, Karlheinz. 1967. *Bevölkerungsgeschichte von Sachsen bis zur industriellen Revolution.* Weimar: Böhlhaus.

Brandes, Stanley H. 1975. *Migration, Kinship, and Community: Tradition and Transition in a Spanish Village.* New York: Academic Press.

Braun, Rudolf. 1960. *Industrialisierung und Volksleben: Die Veränderung der Lebensformen in einem landlichen Industriegebiet vor 1800 (Züricher Oberland).* Zürich: Rentsch.

————. 1970. *Sozio-kulturelle Probleme der Eingliederung italienischer Arbeitskräfte in der Schweiz.* Zürich: Rentsch.

Buckatzsch, C. J. 1949–1950. "Places of Origin of a Group of Immigrants into Sheffield, 1624–1799." *Economic History Review*, second series, 2, pp. 303–6.

————. 1951. "The Constancy of Local Populations and Migration in England before 1800." *Population Studies*, pp. 62–69.

Butcher, A. F. 1974. "The Origins of Romney Freemen, 1433-1523," *Economic History Review*, second series, 27, pp. 16–27.

Castles, Stephen, and Kosack, Godula. 1973. *Immigrant Workers and Class Structure in Western Europe.* London: Oxford University Press.

Chambers, J. D. 1963. "Three Essays on the Population and Economy of the Midlands." In D. V. Glass and D. E. C. Eversley (eds.), *Population in History: Essays in Historical Demography.* Chicago: Aldine.

Charbonneau, Hubert. 1970. *Tourouvre-au-Perche aux XVIIe et XVIIIe siècles.* Paris: Presses Universitaires de France. Institut National d'Etudes Démographiques, Travaux et Documents, Cahier 55.

Chevalier, Louis. 1950. *La formation de la population parisienne au XIXe siècle.* Paris: Presses Universitaires de France.

Clark, Peter. 1972. "The Migrant in Kentish Towns 1580-1640." In Peter Clark and Paul Slack (eds.), *Crisis and Order in English Towns, 1500–1700.* London: Routledge & Kegan Paul.

Corbin, Alain. 1975. *Archaisme et modernité en Limousin au XIXe siècle.* Paris: Marcel Rivière. 2 vols.

Cornwall, Julian. 1967. "Evidence of Population Mobility in the Seventeenth Century." *Bulletin of the Institute of Historical Research*, 40, pp. 143–52.

Delumeau, Jean. 1957. *Vie économique et sociale de Rome dans la seconde moitié du XVIe siècle*. Paris: Boccard. 2 vols.

Eriksson, Ingrid, and Rogers, John. 1973. "Mobility in an Agrarian Community. Practical and Methodological Considerations." In Kurt Agren et al., *Aristocrats, Farmers, Proletarians. Essays in Swedish Demographic History*. Uppsala: Scandinavian University Books. Studia Historica Upsaliensa, 47.

Friedl, Ernestine. 1976. "Kinship, Class and Selective Migration." In J. G. Peristiany (ed.), *Mediterranean Family Structures*. Cambridge: Cambridge University Press.

Goreux, L. M. 1956. "Les migrations agricoles en France depuis un siècle et leur relation avec certains facteurs économiques." *Etudes et Conjoncture*, 11, pp. 327–76.

Hammer, Carl. 1976. "The Mobility of Skilled Labour in Late Medieval England. Some Oxford Evidence." *Vierteljahrschrift für Sozial- and Wirtschaftsgeschichte*, 63, pp. 194–210.

Hannan, Damian. 1970. *Rural Exodus*. London: Geoffrey Chapman.

Henry, Louis. 1967. *Manuel de démographie historique*. Geneva & Paris: Droz.

———. 1972. *Démographie, analyse et modèles*. Paris: Larousse.

Hesse, Sharlene. 1975. "Migrants as Actors: A Case Study of Life-Cycle and Geographical Mobility in Sweden." Doctoral dissertation, Department of Sociology, University of Michigan.

Hollingsworth, T. H. 1971. "Historical Studies of Migration." *Annales de Démographie Historique 1970*, pp. 87–96.

Hvidt, Kristian. 1975. *Flight to America: The Social Background of 300,000 Danish Emigrants*. New York: Academic Press.

Iatsounski, V. K. 1971. "Le rôle des migrations et de l'accroissement naturel dans la colonisation des nouvelles régions de la Russie." *Annales de Démographie Historique 1970*, pp. 302–8.

Kasdan, Leonard. 1965. "Family Structure, Migration and the Entrepreneur," *Comparative Studies in Society and History*, 7, pp. 345–57.

Kollmann, Wolfgang. 1959. "Industrialisierung, Binnenwanderung, und 'Soziale Frage,'" *Vierteljahrschrift für Sozial- and Wirtschaftsgeschichte*, 46, pp. 45–70.

Kosínski, Leszek A. 1970. *The Population of Europe: A Geographic Perspective*. London: Longman.

Kulischer, Eugene M. 1948. *Europe on the Move: War and Population Changes, 1917–47*. New York: Columbia University Press.

Laslett, Peter. 1968. "Le brassage de la population en France et en Angleterre aux XVIIe et XVIIIe siècles." *Annales de Démographie Historique 1968*, pp. 99–109.

Levi, Giovanni. 1971. "Migrazioni e popolazione nella Francia del XVII e XVIII secolo." *Rivista Storica Italiana*, 83, pp. 95–123.

———. 1974. "Sviluppo urbano e flussi migratori nel Piemonte nel 1600." In M. Aymard et al. (eds.), *Les migrations dans les pays méditerranéens au XVIIIème et au début du XIXème*. Nice: Centre de la Méditerranée Moderne et Contemporaine.

Levine, David. 1977. *Family Formation in an Age of Nascent Capitalism*. New York: Academic Press.

Liang, Hsi-Huey. 1970. "Lower-Class Immigrants in Wilhelmine Berlin," *Central European History*. 3, pp. 94–111.

Lopreato, Joseph. 1962. "Economic Development and Cultural Change: The Role of Emigration." *Human Organization*, 21, pp. 182–86.

MacDonald, John S., and MacDonald, Leatrice D. 1964. "Chain Migration, Ethnic Neighborhood Formation, and Social Networks." *Milbank Memorial Fund Quarterly*, 42, pp. 82–97.

McNeill, William H. 1963. *The Rise of the West: A History of the Human Community*. Chicago: University of Chicago Press.

Merlin, Pierre, et al. 1971. *L'exode rural, suivi de deux études sur les migrations*. Paris: Presses Universitaires de France. Institut National d'Etudes Démographiques, Travaux et Documents, Cahier 39.

Momsen, Ingwer Ernst. 1969. Die Bevölkerung der Stadt Husum von 1769 bis 1860. Kiel: Selbstverlag des Geographischen Instituts der UniversiOt Keil.

Morgenstern, Oskar, 1963. *On the Accuracy of Economic Observations*. Princeton: Princeton University Press. 2d ed.

Morrill, Richard L. 1965. *Migration and the Spread and Growth of Urban Settlement*. Lund: Gleerup. Lund Studies in Geography, Series B, no. 26.

Norberg, Anders, and Åkerman, Sune. 1973. "Migration and the Building of Families: Studies on the Rise of the Lumber Industry in Sweden." In Kurt Ågren et al. (eds.), *Aristocrats, Farmers, Proletarians: Essays in Swedish Demographic History*. Uppsala: Scandinavian University Books. Studia Historica Upsaliensia, 47.

Öhngren, Bo. 1974. *Folk i rörelse. Samhallsutveckling, flyttningsmönster och folkrörelser i Eskilstuna 1870-1900*. Uppsala: Almqvist and Wiksell. Studia Historica Upsaliensia, 55.

Pasigli, Stefano. 1969. *Emigrazione e compartamento politico*. Bologna: Il Mulino.

Patten, John. 1973. *Rural-Urban Migration in Pre-Industrial England*. Oxford: School of Geography. Research Papers No. 6.

———. 1976. "Patterns of Migration and Movement of Labour to 3 Pre-Industrial East Anglian Towns." *Journal of Historical Geography*, 2, pp. 111–19.

Perez Díaz, Victor. 1971. *Emigración y cambio social: Procesos migratorios y vida rural en Castilla*. Barcelona: Ariel. 2d ed.

Perrenoud, Alfred. 1971. "Les migrations en Suisse sous l'Ancien Régime: Quelques problèmes." *Annales de Démographie Historique 1970*, pp. 251–59.

Pitié, Jean. 1971. *Exode rural et migrations intérieures en France: L'exemple de la Vienne et du Poitou-Charentes*. Poitiers: Norois.

Pollard, Sidney, and Crossley, David W. 1968. *The Wealth of Britain*. London: Batsford.

Pourcher, Guy. 1964. *Le peuplement de Paris*. Paris: Presses Universitaires de France. Institut National d'Etudes Démographiques, Travaux et Documents, Cahier 43.

Poussou, Jean-Pierre. 1971. "Les mouvements migratoires en France et à partir de la France de la fin du XVe siècle au début du XIXe siècle: Approches pour une synthèse." *Annales de Démographie Historique 1970*, pp. 111–78.

———. 1974. "Introduction à l'étude des mouvements migratoires en Espagne, Italie et France méditerranéenne au XVIIIe siècle." In M. Aymard et al. (eds.), *Les migrations dans les pays méditerranéens au XVIIIème et au début du XIXème*. Nice: Centre de la Méditerranée Moderne et Contemporaine.

Pred, Allen. 1961. *The External Relations of Cities During 'Industrial Revolution.'* Chicago: Department of Geography, University of Chicago.

Redford, Arthur. 1964. *Labor Migration in England, 1800-1850*. W. H. Chaloner (ed.). Manchester: Manchester University Press. 2d ed.

Reinhard, Marcel R., Armengaud, André, and Dupâquier, Jacques. 1968. *Histoire générale de la population mondiale*. Paris: Montchrestien.

Roof, Michael K. and Leedy, Frederick A. 1959. "Population Redistribution in the Soviet Union, 1939–1956." *Geographical Review*, 49, pp. 208–21.

Russell, J. C. 1959. "Medieval Midland and Northern Migration to London, 1100–1365." *Speculum*, 34, 641–45.

Sabean, David. 1971. "Household Formation and Geographic Mobility: A Family Register Study in a Wurttemberg Village 1760–1900." *Annales de Démographie Historique 1970*, pp. 275–94.

Saville, John. 1957. *Rural Depopulation in England and Wales, 1851-1951.* London: Routledge and Kegan Paul.

Schofield, R. S. 1971. "Age-Specific Mobility in an Eighteenth-Century Rural English Parish." *Annales de Démographie Historique 1970*, pp. 261–74.

Schon, Lennart. 1972. "Västernorrland in the Middle of the Nineteenth Century: A Study in the Transition from Small-Scale to Capitalistic Production." *Economy and History*, 15, pp. 83–111.

Shaw, R. Paul. 1975. *Migration Theory and Fact: A Review and Bibliography of Current Literature.* Philadelphia: Regional Science Research Institute. Bibliography Series, No. 5.

Skinner, G. William. 1964–1965. "Marketing and Social Structure in Rural China," Parts I, II, III. *Journal of Asian Studies*, 24, pp. 3–43, 195–228, 363–99.

Slack, Paul A. 1974. "Vagrants and Vagrancy in England, 1598–1664." *Economic History Review*, 2d series, 27, pp. 360–79.

Smith, C. T. 1968. *An Historical Geography of Western Europe before 1800.* London: Longmans.

Tauriaienen, Juhani, and Koivula, Samuli. 1973. *The Conditions in and Problems of Rural Depopulation Areas.* Helsinki: Department for Social Research, Ministry of Social Affairs and Health. Official Statistics of Finland, Series 32, no. 33.

Willcox, Walter F. 1929–1931. Ed., *International Migrations.* New York: National Bureau of Economic Research. 2 vols. Publications of the National Bureau of Economic Research, nos. 14 & 18.

Wrigley, E. A. 1966. Ed., *An Introduction to English Historical Demography.* London: Weidenfeld & Nicholson.

———. 1967. "A Simple Model of London's Importance in Changing English Society and Economy, 1650–1750." *Past and Present*, 37, pp. 44–70.

———. 1969. *Population and History.* New York: McGraw-Hill.

chapter 5
Post–World War II
Labor Migrations

5.1 *the Editors*

Introduction

The post–World War II era witnessed an enormous shift in the distribution of international economic, political, and military power and, concomitant with this shift, one of the greatest experiments with labor and other types of mass migration (see also Chapter 6). Punctuated by the dissolution of the British and French empires and the emergence of the United States as a superpower, today's advanced capitalist societies were forged in the context of Europe's diminishing political influence in the world and the refocusing of the major European countries on economic and moral renewal.

It was in the aftermath of the devastation of World War II that the Bretton Woods system was born. This 1944 Anglo-American agreement to promote free trade, nondiscrimination, and stable exchange rates established a set of multilateral institutions (the International Trade Organization, the General Agreement on Tariffs and Trade, the International Monetary Fund, and the World Bank) as the foundation of a new international economic regime. Although these institutions did not deal explicitly with freedom of movement for peoples, they implicitly provided a normative context for post–World War II migration to the advanced capitalist societies.

The creation of the Bretton Woods institutional economic regime had several implications for migration. First, as James Hollifield in Chapter 5.3 makes clear, it established a liberal institutional international order, one comprising new types of exchange and the appearance of numerous transnational actors that were ultimately successful in fundamentally altering the basis of international relations. Second, in promoting economic growth and reconstruction, it heightened the need for manpower in Europe,

147

thus precipitating the entrance of new workers, including women, youth, and migrants, into the domestic labor market. As Gary Freeman in Chapter 5.2 reveals, once policymakers determined that migration was acting as an accelerator of postwar economic growth, an abundant supply of foreign labor was seen as critical not only for the purposes of reconstruction but also to facilitate further economic expansion. Finally, it prompted greater international economic competition, ironically pitting European countries against one another in a competition for foreign labor. Portending the political challenges embedded in today's immigration-related conflicts, this competition in turn inspired European countries to grant immigrants expansive social rights, such as the right of family reunification, in order to attract new foreign workers to the host countries.

The Western industrialized countries structured their competition for foreign labor in different ways. Some initially relied upon spontaneous migration, but most of these countries soon discovered that migrant workers were needed in numbers that far outstripped their "natural" supply. Other countries, particularly those with colonial traditions, such as Britain, France, and the Netherlands, actively recruited foreign workers from the beginning of the postwar period. Finally, a third set of countries lacking former colonies (principally Germany and Switzerland) executed a so-called guestworker system in which foreign workers were to be rotated in and out of the host society as the need for their labor and the business cycle demanded. Whatever their starting assumptions, each of the aforementioned national traditions failed to consider fully the domestic social repercussions of migration, perhaps naively assuming that most migrant workers would return home once the demand for their labor slackened.

In the face of economic recession, growing unemployment and the reality of permanent immigrant settlement, the course of the politics of immigration evolved quite dramatically in Europe during the 1970s and 1980s. By the 1990s, when it was evident to all that Europe's "guests had come to stay" permanently, migration evolved from a mostly economic into a social and political phenomenon.[1] Moreover, as globalization wrought new changes in global investment patterns, accompanied by increased capital investment in new industrialized areas and, into these areas, the introduction of new technologies, high-skilled workers were needed. Globalization also brought new countries in Africa, Latin America, the oil-rich OPEC countries of the Middle East, and the newly industrialized countries (NICs) in Asia, such as Taiwan and Singapore, into the migration dynamic. Everywhere migration was inextricably linked to rapid industrialization and social change.

Theoretical questions about the costs and benefits of migration for capitalist societies were initially raised by scholars in the context of the post–World War II experiences of the Western European countries and have been posed again in the context of more recent developments. Inspired by Karl Marx's thesis that the expansion of capitalism depends upon the availability of a large pool of unemployed and highly mobile workers, scholars such as Gary Freeman tentatively applied the label "industrial reserve army" to the legions of foreign workers migrating to postwar Western Europe during the 1960s and 1970s. Like Marx, Freeman depicted mass migrants as a surplus labor population that could be mobilized during periods of economic growth and potentially dismissed, albeit not without considerable difficulty, during periods of crisis, thus suggesting that migrant workers were integral to the capitalist division of labor and an essential feature of the advanced capitalist societies.

Whatever the merits of the industrial-reserve-army thesis for the 1960s and 1970s, it had become abundantly clear by the 1990s that foreign workers and other categories of migrants, including noncitizens, were not without social and political rights. Partly on the basis of these rights, according to Hollifield, the volume of migration is greater and the socioeconomic position of immigrants more deeply entrenched than any set of national policymakers would prefer.

■ Note

1. Rosemary Rogers, ed. *Guests Come to Stay: The Effects of European Labor Migration on Sending and Receiving Countries* (Boulder, CO: Westview, 1985).

5.2 Gary Freeman*
Immigrant Labour and Working-Class Politics: The French and British Experience

The entrance of large numbers of foreign workers into the countries of Western Europe has challenged the ingenuity of trade unions and socialist parties by complicating social and economic stratification. Horizontally, it has added an underlayer, or subproletariat, of immigrants below the manual workers of the indigenous working-class. Vertically, it has divided the working class into white/non-white, citizen/noncitizen, and Western/Third World components.[1] This article examines the way in which the governments, parties, and unions of France and Britain have responded to immigration. After discussing the size and character of immigration into the two countries and the role immigrant labor plays in advanced, capitalist economies, it turns to an examination of the manner in which governments have managed immigration policy since 1945 and the role of trade unions and working-class based parties in criticizing and shaping that policy. The article addresses the issues which immigration poses for these institutions and, drawing on the French and British experience, explores the possibility of developing a socialist policy on immigration which capitalizes on foreign workers as an instrument of reform.[2]

■ Immigrant Labor in Britain and France
It has been estimated that by mid-1971 there were 1.5 million persons of New Commonwealth ethnic origin in the United Kingdom, or 2.5 percent of the total home population. About one-half of these had been born in Britain. In France, in January 1976, there were 4,196,000 foreigners who comprised over 7 percent of the total population.[3] From 1946 until 1972 France received approximately 47,000 immigrants annually, but in 1962 the figure leaped to 113,069 and had not dropped below 100,000 by 1974. These figures underestimate the total number of foreigners since they do not include clandestine and illegal immigration which reached very high

Gary Freeman, "Immigrant Labour and Working-Class Politics: The French and British Experience," *Comparative Politics* 11, no. 1 (Oct. 1978): 25–41.

levels in the late 1960s. In the early postwar period, Italians were the major source of this labor. In 1962, 36 percent of the immigrants to France came from EEC [European Economic Community] countries, and an additional 32 percent were drawn from Spain, Portugal, Yugoslavia, and Poland. By 1970 the Italian proportion of the immigrant community had fallen to 592,787 or 18 percent, while North Africans (primarily Algerians) made up 28 percent of the total.[4]

Before 1962, the dominant source of migration to Britain was the West Indies, and total immigration from the West Indies, India, and Pakistan fluctuated between 25,000 and 37,000 until 1961. After the introduction of controls through the Commonwealth Immigrants Act, the nature of immigration changed dramatically. West Indian migration declined progressively as did that from India and Pakistan, though these countries still furnished the bulk of the migrants. The total number of immigrants did not clearly reflect new controls because of the practice of allowing dependents to enter. By 1972, the annual entry of dependents had yet to fall below the 10,000 level although in that year only 348 Ministry of Labour voucher-holders were admitted. After the introduction of the Immigration Act of 1971, official entries became negligible, but the actual number of new immigrants was a continuing source of controversy.[5]

Workers were drawn to the industrial centers of Europe through the interaction of massive unemployment in their homelands and chronic labor shortages in the West.[6] They have generally arrived with little education and few skills. Consequently, they have tended to be concentrated in the manual occupational strata and in certain heavy industrial sectors. In Britain, in 1966, 94 percent of Jamaicans, 87 percent of Pakistanis, and 61 percent of Indians held manual positions. In France, in 1968, 38 percent of foreign workers held unskilled, 31 percent semiskilled, and 25 percent skilled positions, compared to the 14 percent of Frenchmen who held unskilled, 34 percent semiskilled, and 37 percent skilled positions.[7] In Britain immigrants have gravitated toward certain types of industrial activity. For example, of the total number of Commonwealth immigrants in the country in 1966, 12 percent of the Jamaicans, 15 percent of the Indians, and 11 percent of the Pakistanis were working in the engineering and electrical goods industries. The percentages for the transport and communications industries for the three nationality groups were 14, 12, and 7, respectively. Furthermore, 14 percent of Jamaicans were in construction jobs. In France in 1973, foreign workers made up 9 percent of the labor force in mining, 23 percent in the production of metals, 18 percent in the glass, ceramics, and chemical industries, 32 percent of the construction industry, and 27 percent of the sanitation industry.[8]

Immigration has generated important economic and political benefits for the host societies because foreign workers have taken on the character of an industrial reserve army.[9] They constitute a large, highly mobile, relatively unskilled labor supply which can be called upon to fill the most physically demanding, dangerous, and undesirable tasks in an increasingly technological society. The manner in which immigrants have arrived in Europe—in largely "spontaneous" and unregulated movements—has enhanced these conditions since it has made it nearly impossible to guarantee adequate working or living arrangements. Nevertheless, the actual contribution of immigrant labor to the economic health of particular countries depends on a variety of specific conditions. Generally, the evidence available indicates that France has reaped sizable benefits from her foreign workers, while the British situation is greatly complicated because the movement into the country has nearly been cancelled out by a massive emigration.[10] In the absence of major immigration, Britain's economic woes would have been even more serious.

In the long run, however, it may be the political advantages of foreign labor that are the most important and the least easily measured. Immigrants, because they often come from agricultural and politically authoritarian backgrounds and because of language and cultural barriers, are much less likely to be politically militant or to participate actively in trade unions than are indigenous workers.[11] Nor are they free to take part in labor disputes since they are vulnerable to deportation if they run afoul of the law or lose their jobs. The very presence of a sizable foreign population constitutes a denationalization of a portion of the working-class, because foreigners cannot vote or participate fully in political activities, and also contributes to the embourgeoisement of a sector of the work force that is pushed up into nonmanual and supervisory positions. Finally, because foreign workers absorb much of the burden of rising unemployment, they serve as a vehicle for the defusion of working-class unrest. Ironically, immigrants may make their greatest contribution to the stability of European regimes, not through their productive activities in the factory, but through their silent departure during hard times.[12]

But immigration is not without its costs for capital and these have increased with the passage of time. Economically, foreign labor has turned out to be a mixed blessing. The easy availability of comparatively cheap manpower has served as a disincentive for industry to modernize plants and equipment, especially among the least progressive and most marginal firms. Furthermore, there can be significant infrastructure costs associated with the presence of immigrant workers—schools, hospitals, and housing must be made available—and these are greater if immigration tends to be for longer periods of time or to include families rather than single workers only.[13]

Perhaps the most serious economic consequence of immigration, however, is the tendency for economies which rely extensively upon it to become structurally dependent on it. In such a situation, migrants are no longer a temporary expedient but a necessity of advanced capitalism. This can occur because foreigners permit the expansion of the industrial apparatus beyond the natural capacity of the indigenous labor force and because a sizable population of foreigners can itself generate increased demand which can be satisfied only by the importation of still more immigrants. Governments cannot easily find a substitute for them, either by the introduction of labor extensive technology or through active manpower policies designed to utilize all available workers as efficiently as possible. Europeans, having been artificially promoted to nonmanual jobs, are loath to return to less desirable tasks, and owners cannot operate profitably and pay high enough salaries for the most unpleasant positions to attract Europeans to them. André Gorz, for example, argues that this is a basic contradiction of European capitalism which foreign workers highlight. He suggests that the prosperity which the majority of workers have enjoyed in Europe since the war has been brought about by and cannot be maintained without excluding a portion of the population from the enjoyment of those standards. Gorz believes that to pay significantly higher wages to native workers to perform the jobs migrants now hold is "incompatible within its [the capitalist system's] pattern of consumption, its economic, social, and political equilibrium, and its scale of ideological values."[14]

The structural dependence of European economics on alien labor is a source of serious management problems for political decision makers. These relate first to the erosion of the regime's legitimacy which is due to a frank and open exploitation of migrants and secondly, to the constraints on the government's flexibility which develop when immigrant/working-class conflict exceeds acceptable bounds. The presence of migrant workers in highly visible and clearly inferior social and economic positions contradicts the liberal ethos which claims that all individuals are equal under the law. Governments are, then, on the horns of a dilemma. If, on the one hand, they actively pursue the exploitation of migrants and allow the wretched conditions to develop which guarantee that immigration will be profitable, they expose the hollowness of their rhetoric about equality and heighten their own legitimation crisis in the eyes of intellectuals and leftist critics. If, on the other hand, they move toward the eradication of the inequalities between foreign and indigenous workers, they diminish the utility of immigration since it is no longer as profitable and arouse working-class and nativist resentment. But the absolute necessity of foreign labor means that they must do one or the other.[15] In the early years of migration, governments could pursue the first course with relative impunity, but as the Left (especially in France) has increasingly demonstrated an ability to mobilize around the immigration issue, governments have been forced to grant equality of conditions. This has made immigration much less desirable from the point of view of economic managers, but nonetheless unavoidable.

Barring the political mobilization of the foreign population by the Left, the emergence of intense immigrant/working-class conflict spells danger to government planners. The creation of racial minorities in countries largely homogeneous in the past has been, in retrospect, a process entered into with remarkably little discussion or hesitation.[16] The full ramifications of this decision are becoming increasingly apparent. Racial conflict may divide and weaken the working-class movement and it may deflect attention from the shortcomings of capitalist regimes, but it also creates disorder and embarrassment for governments which fail to deal with it. It becomes a ticklish political problem to balance the demands of liberals for more forthright action on behalf of foreigners against the more and more insistent clamor of antiimmigrant forces for harsh and repressive policies. Mass resistance to free or large-scale immigration seriously hampers a flexible and vigorous manpower strategy. The history of government policy on immigration can be read as a more or less conscious attempt to balance the advantages of immigration against its growing costs.

Immigration has posed problems of a different order for trade unions and working-class based political parties. It is first a problem of theory— how to understand the causes and consequences of the phenomenon. But it is also a problem of practice—what action to take at minimum to defend the working-class against the abuse of foreign labor and at best to turn immigration into a tool for social democratic or more radical reform. There are essentially four issues which working-class institutions must resolve in order to deal effectively with immigration: (1) the possible conflict of interests between the two groups of workers; (2) the question of whether immigrants fall heir to special disabilities and hardships which require remedies outside trade union and socialist programs; (3) the racism which is widespread in the working class and which threatens not only the solidarity of immigrant and national workers but also the cohesion and stability of unions and parties which defend immigrants; and (4) the integration of immigration policy into a more general attempt to reform capitalist society.

The performance of socialist parties and trade unions on these four issues of immigration policy must be evaluated against the background of British and French governmental policies for the regulation, control, and use of foreign labor.

■ Immigration Policy and Working-Class Politics

Whatever the differences in the contexts and nuances of French and British policy, the most striking aspect of the record is the convergence of policy in the 1970s. Starting from the position of principally free immigration or a laissez faire system of limited controls after World War II, both govern-

many more immigrants would come anyway, that few were arriving as it was, that they were not harmful, that they did not have abnormally high birth rates, and that they should be welcomed. There is nothing wrong in all this, of course, and most of what they said was true. But by taking upon themselves the task of justifying immigration, they were put in the position of attacking the British working man, who was perceived to be the staunchest and most prejudiced critic of immigration. And, perhaps because they sensed the weakness of their position, they would not admit that there was any legitimate cause for concern about the creation of a racial minority in the country. They thought in terms of a colored minority, besieged by the dominant white majority. They were left to appeal to the good faith and sense of fair play of the members of that majority. This sort of appeal is inherently weaker than one based on direct class interests. The latter is the type of argument the French socialists were able to make and explains why they could handle the immigration question with less trauma than their British counterparts.

France

Both the Communist party–dominated *Confédération Général du Travail* (CGT) and the socialist-oriented *Confédération Française Démocratique du Travail* (CFDT) have fluctuated in their attitudes toward immigration controls. They originally favored restrictions in order to protect the domestic employment market, but since the early 1960s they have concentrated less on that aspect of policy than on dealing with immigrants already in France. The CGT and the CFDT have increasingly shared a common perspective on immigration. In 1966 the two federations signed a joint accord as the basis for common political action. This was followed in 1971 with a *joint communiqué* on immigration policy which calls for planned and regulated immigration.[28]

The federations see immigration as a consequence of the failure of capitalist regimes. They have adopted what is essentially a classic reserve army thesis: that foreign workers are a means by which capitalists ensure a plentiful supply of cheap and relatively docile workers. They emphasize the political and social aspects and consequences of government policy—the use of foreigners to divide the working-class, the artificial promotion of indigenous workers into nonmanual and supervisory positions, the dilution of working-class political power because foreigners are disenfranchised. The federations have pursued a formal policy of solidarity with immigrants and have attempted to integrate their immigrant-related activities into their political program. The joint statement issued in 1971 said:

> We believe that immigrant workers are an integral part of the working-class and are not competitive with French workers. We intend to locate

our actions with and for immigrant workers within the general framework of the struggle for all workers.[29]

The CGT/CFDT position, on its surface inconsistent with their reserve army analysis, is advanced in the context of major proposals for the reform of immigration policy. Bringing about the conditions under which immigration could "conform to the interests of all workers"[30] is the goal of the union policy on immigration. The core of this policy is the demand for the equality of rights and status between national and foreign workers.

Both the CGT and the CFDT believe that the demand for absolute equality for immigrants in the social, economic, and union spheres is a means of avoiding the impasse created by rivalries between national and foreign workers and by the contradiction between the unions' restrictive critique of the government's immigration policy and their strategy of solidarity with migrants. The key to this reasoning is their analysis of the function of immigration planning and regulation, the costs of a truly equal foreign labor to the employer, and the necessity of labor participation in the management of immigration.

The basic premise of the unions with regard to immigration regulation is that a failure of planning and adequate controls has caused present French policy to be extremely exploitative. Only a carefully planned policy which guarantees each worker a job, adequate housing, and equal working conditions can ensure that migrants will not be used to weaken the position of indigenous workers. Toward that end, both confederations endorse the principle of restoring the National Immigration Office to its monopoly over-all immigration into France.

The call for a uniform legal status for all foreign workers is a direct attack on the primary tool of French immigration policy—the bilateral accord. This device recommends itself to the policymaker because of flexibility, allowing particular conditions to be set for one group of workers that do not apply to others. But according to the unions this discrimination is one of the basic causes for the exploitation of workers and a prime instrument of division. Since each nationality group is in France under separate agreements, conditions, and regulations, it is difficult for those trying to organize them to create a coherent and unified program. The general confusion over exactly which groups enjoy which rights contributes to the insecurity and precarious nature of the migrants' status.

The unions believe that if an absolute equality of rights were guaranteed for all foreign workers recruited to come to France, the need for labor movements to concern themselves with controls over the numbers entering the country would be greatly reduced. Without the discrimination and inequality that accompany migrant workers, the compelling economic motives for their presence would disappear. Being no cheaper than native labor, foreign workers would seem less and less attractive to employers and immigration would become self-regulated, and that which did occur would not entail economically harmful outcomes. The government, which is inextricably linked to business interests, cannot establish such a policy on its own, however, and for this reason the unions demand a greatly expanded role for the labor movement in the formulation of policy.[31]

Neither the Socialists (PS) nor the Communists (PCF) have said much about immigrants until relatively recently. In general they have limited their activity to rhetorical attacks on government policy, protestations of solidarity with migrants, and condemnations of racism. The reasons for this are clear—migrants pose difficult problems and they do not necessarily or easily fit into traditional categories of analysis. They lack the essential political privileges that would allow them to be recruited and organized by parties for electoral or agitational purposes. Besides, many migrants are apolitical or petit-bourgeois in their orientation. Given the essential electoral strategy of the PS-PCF coalition, a strong defense of the rights of immigrants might have reduced its support among the working-class. All of this has led the established parties to tread lightly in this area and forfeit the immigration issue to the revolutionary Left and counterrevolutionary Right.

The stance of the PCF and the PS must be interpreted in light of the rapprochement which developed between the Communist and non-Communist elements in the late 1960s and which culminated in 1972 in the Union of the Left, and the growing seriousness of attempts by the Left to come to power through elections. The official program which was agreed upon by the union and which served as the platform of its candidate, François Mitterrand, in the 1974 presidential election actually had little to say explicitly about immigrants. The common program promised that the "plan will forecast the number of immigrant *workers* to be received each year in order to clarify the social and economic measures to be taken. Immigrant workers will benefit from the same rights as French workers. The law will guarantee their political, social, and syndical rights."[32] Elsewhere the document said that "all discrimination affecting young people, women, older workers, immigrants, or whatever kind of wage earner will be suppressed."[33] These cryptic remarks need to be understood, however, in the context of a more general analysis of immigration which has been developed by the members of the Union of the Left.

The Communist-Socialist interpretation of immigration flows from an essentially Marxist analysis couched in terms of class and political power, not in the language of "social problems" as is often the case in Britain. The critique of government policy involves an assessment of the uses of migration for the bourgeoisie. The nineteenth Congress of the PCF in 1966 condemned:

the immigration policy of the authorities which results in a scandalous overexploitation [*surexploitation*] of foreign workers and in inhuman living conditions for them. This policy theorizes about xenophobia and racism in order to divide the working-class. At the same time it permits the *patronat* to increase its profits and to hold down the salaries of French workers.[34]

French policy is seen as a transparent effort to create a reserve army. In 1966 the PCF and the Italian Communist party released a joint statement which concluded that:

despite the appearance of appreciable unemployment, the Gaullist regime intensifies its policy of immigration in hopes of putting cheap manpower at the disposal of the monopoly capitalists, thus assuring a maximum of profit and favoring the creation of a reserve of unemployed workers to hold down the salaries of all workers.[35]

It is the potential division of the workers that most disturbs the PCF. Their response is to affirm the need for solidarity, to deny that immigrant workers either hurt or promote the status of French workers, to refute the theory that migrants constitute a subproletariat, and to excoriate those "trotskyists" who seek to organize them into separate unions, parties, or groups outside the CGT and the PCF.[36] There is obviously something here besides a fine appreciation of the theoretical need for unity—the PCF is intent on maintaining its own hegemony among working-class movements and the efforts to organize migrants separately are a clear threat to its position. Georges Marchais highlighted this concern as early as 1963 when he concluded in a report on immigration to the political bureau of the PCF that the "problem is to know how we are going to work so that the activity of the party with respect to immigration is integrated with our general work."[37] In the debate over the special needs of immigrants versus their primary status as workers like any others, then, the PCF firmly believes that the commonalities outweigh the differences. While the party admits that migrants are exploited to a degree that French workers normally do not experience and although there is a compelling need for special demands oriented around the migrants' requirements, these must be tightly integrated within the total program and clearly should not develop any autonomy.

As was the case with the unions, the signatories of the joint program believe that the achievement of equality of rights between foreign and French workers would end the abuses which immigration often creates and also end immigration for all practical purposes.[38] Meantime, however, the common program does not blush at frankly proposing a controlled immigration. There is no feeling that regulation of immigration is in itself morally repugnant or ideologically suspect. On the contrary, it is an essential tool of economic planning. The common program is, after all, a document about planning for a socialist France.[39] To forfeit the conscious manipulation of immigration to the vagaries of the market would be foolhardy, especially since control will be a part of an elaborate system of economic cooperation between France and the developing nations. This is what might be called a state planning approach to immigration. Gaston Deferre, the leader of the Socialist group in the National Assembly, elaborated on this outlook in 1973. He called for a temporary, strictly limited migration with guaranteed equality of conditions. These would be paid for by increasing the assessments made on employers who used migrants. In return for the use of their workers, the exporting countries would receive a greatly enlarged economic aid contribution from France, especially in the form of the construction of factories and the other forms of industrial infrastructure. The goal would be the accelerated economic development of the sending countries so that the workers, having been trained for industrial tasks in France, could return to their homeland.[40] Except for the demand for equality of rights and conditions and the marginally greater financial burden on the employer, and granting the different motivations at work, one must still remark at the essential similarity between the immigration policy of the common program (and that offered by Deferre) and the official governmental proposals already discussed. The means toward the realization of these policies would have to be different, however, since the PS-PCF plan precludes the bilateral arrangements which would continue to be the heart of the government policy. Clearly, the major differences would emerge in the manner in which controls were actually carried out, in the degree to which equality of conditions was actually achieved, and in the extent to which other reforms were undertaken.

The track record of the PS and the PCF on the subject of immigration is not very good. They have often failed to speak up, or rather to do more than that. To what extent this was out of a crude electoral calculation is difficult to say, though it certainly figured into the parties' calculations. Still, one must admit that the parties of the Left in France never catered directly to racist sentiment, never hinted that they would use opposition to immigration for political purposes, never threatened to succumb to grass roots prejudice as the Labour party did. It is equally true that they were never in power, and thus escaped the inevitably compromising responsibilities of governing. Partly as a result of this, they were impervious to insinuations that they were not the legitimate representatives of working-class opinion and they consistently lay the responsibility for the resurgence of racism and xenophobia at the feet of those who were responsible for the failure of French immigration policy.

■ Conclusion

Several observations can be drawn from this abbreviated account. First, both governments moved reluctantly to interfere with the relatively free movement of labor and they moved for different reasons. French officials finally clamped down on spontaneous immigration in response to unemployment, inflation, and reduced growth.[41] The British moved much earlier on this front, not primarily out of economic motives, but in an attempt to squash domestic political restiveness over the rising immigration figures. The results, in any case, were the same—the creation of a temporary, contract-labor system and the removal of the special privileges once enjoyed by ex-colonials. The French and British cases are examples of systems in which the contradictions of migrant labor have worked themselves out in different ways. In France, the government has taken steps in a recessionary period to halt the tide of immigration and to provide incentives both for French managers to find alternatives to alien labor and for French workers to return to manual positions. This policy does not prove false the argument that advanced economies are structurally dependent on foreign labor. On the contrary, the French moves are a chilling confirmation of the government's determination to carry through the logic of a reserve army policy—namely, sending the foreigners home during periods of high unemployment. One can only speculate how much this has reduced class tensions by shifting the burden of the recession onto the alien labor force.

The British record derives from different sources. Although the threat of political unrest, and especially the possibility of a resurgent Left taking advantage of the masses of foreigners, played a role in French calculations,[42] it was the *reality* of mass resistance to immigration that led the British to move from a generous policy of settlement with full citizenship rights for Commonwealth immigrants to a racially exclusive, temporary contract system.[43] The social costs of migration were much more salient in Britain than economic disadvantages. The high rates of emigration, which in fact made immigration all the more vital, served to mask the contribution the newcomers were making to the economy and also reduced the possibility that an oversupplied labor market could have deleterious effects on management decisions.

The question whether socialists have successfully grappled with immigration has two parts. One must first deal with the experience of socialist *governments* in making immigration policy and secondly with the efforts of socialist *oppositions* to mount credible campaigns on behalf of immigrants. No Marxist party has held the reins of power in either country during the period under discussion and therefore, it is impossible to argue that socialism cannot *in theory* overcome the contradictions of the immigration phenomenon. What is clear is that the only socialist party that has held office failed to do so. The policies of the Labour party have differed only marginally from those of the Conservatives. It has usually ratified rather than initiated control legislation (the draconian 1968 Kenyan Asians Act is a sad exception) and it has taken the lead in passing race relations legislation. But the party's efforts can hardly be deemed a success. The Left has become disenchanted and the immigrants have become hostile and suspicious. Labour has failed to deal with immigration in economic, let alone class, terms and its immigration policy is a shambles.

The French Socialist-Communist alliance, on the other hand, arrived at an analysis of immigration in terms of its functions in a capitalist economy. Along with the unions, it has stressed the political uses to which foreign workers could be put by the government and the bourgeoisie. But the alliance has been in perpetual opposition, and it is far from certain that once in power these parties could in fact reconcile the rights and needs of immigrant workers with the demands of the national working-class, the requirements of the French economy, and the welfare of the sending countries. In any case, a successful policy would be feasible only if it were part of fundamental changes in planning, the ownership of capital, the distribution of wealth and power, and French–Third World relations. Within the context of the capitalist system as it presently exists, the parties would be compelled to choose between the interests of the migrants or the indigenous workers, because a program designed to help both would lead to economic disaster.

When one considers the record of socialist parties and the trade unions in defending the interests of national and immigrant workers, regardless of who is in office, it is no longer necessary to speculate. Though no organization's record is unblemished, it is clear that the French unions and parties were better equipped to defend themselves against the corrosive effects of intraclass conflict and were more adept at criticizing government policy and developing alternatives to it. It is not, of course, obvious that the Left has played a major role in molding the government's decisions, but it has increasingly kept the pressure on and has, at least, stoutly refused to blame migrants for the failures of French capitalism. What is more, it has managed to prevent the French working class from being swept up in antialien hysteria. This the British Left has at times seemed incapable of doing.[44] Only an analysis that locates migration in a general interpretation of the capitalist system can serve to unify the working class and defuse racial tensions. The diffusion of such theories among workers in Britain may be one way to combat nativism by providing an outlet and focus for the fears and anxieties which it expresses. This is especially urgent because the institutional representatives of the working class, the trade unions, and working-class oriented parties may be the only institutions in Europe which are capable of negotiating even an uneasy and fragile truce between the races.

■ Notes

*This paper is based on research funded in part by grants from the Graduate School and the Center for the Study of Post-industrial Society, University of Wisconsin, Madison, and the University Research Institute, University of Texas. I would like to acknowledge Leon Epstein, Charles Anderson, James Scott, Lawrence Dodd, Patricia Giles Leeds, and the editors of this issue for their comments on earlier versions of this article.

1. On the position of immigrants in the class structure, see Stephen Castles and Godula Kosack, *Immigrant Workers and Class Structure in Western Europe* (London, 1973); Ira Katznelson, *Black Men, White Cities: Race, Politics, and Migration in the United States 1900–30 and Britain 1948–68* (London, 1973); and Bernard Granotier, *Les travailleurs immigrés en France*, (Paris, 1973, rev. ed.).

2. Socialism has become an extremely slippery concept in Western Europe. Rather than impose a particular definition which could serve to label the parties and trade unions under consideration, I will employ the term very loosely to cover both the Labour party and the Union of the Left. The use of the modifier "oriented" should alert the reader to the weakness of my claims on this point. The wide range of ideology and strategy one finds among the institutions of the Left in Britain and France is, in fact, a major variable in the analysis. Due to space limitations I deal only with the central organizations—the TUC, and the Labour party in Britain; the CGT, CFDT, PS, and PCF in France. For the role of other groups see Gary Freeman, *Immigrant Labor and Racial Conflict in Industrial Societies: The French and British Experience, 1945–1975* (Princeton, forthcoming).

3. Statistics on immigration are not always reliable, especially as they pertain to racial or nationality groups. The British, for example, refuse in principle to collect statistics by race. Furthermore, in British political discourse, the term immigrant is reserved for nonwhites regardless of birthplace. The present figures are from John Simons, "Great Britain," in Bernard Berelson, ed. *Population Policies in Developed Countries* (New York, 1974), p. 612; on France, OECD, *Rapport 1976* (Paris, 1977), cited in Martin Stater, "International Migration and French Foreign Relations" (paper delivered at the Annual Meeting of the International Studies Association, Washington, D.C., 1978), p. 16.

4. Pierre Bideberry, "Bilan de vingt années d'immigration, 1946–1966," *Revue Française des Affaires Sociales*, XXI (April-June 1967), 14; Conseil National du Patronat Français, *Notes et Arguments*, no. 40 (December 1973).

5. See Commonwealth Immigrants Act, Statistics, Cmd. 2397, 2658, 3258, 3594, 4327, 4620, 4951; Immigration Statistics, Cmd. 5603, 6064, 6504.

6. W.R. Böhning, *The Migration of Workers in the United Kingdom and the European Community* (London, 1972); Ceri Peach, *West Indian Migration to Britain* (London, 1968); Marios Nickolinakos, "Notes Toward a General Theory of Migration in Late Capitalism," *Race and Class*, XVII (1975).

7. On Britain, consult Castles and Kosack, pp. 88–90; for France, Rapports des Commissions du Sixième Plan, 1971–75, *Emploi*, II, p. 48.

8. Castles and Kosack, pp. 76–77; Conseil National du Patronat Français, *Notes et Arguments*, no. 40 (December 1973).

9. For the original argument by Marx, see *Capital* (Chicago, 1909), Vol. I, p. 699. For contemporary variants of the thesis, see Charles P. Kindleberger, *Europe's Post-War Growth: The Role of Labor Supply* (Cambridge, [Mass.], 1967); and Antony Ward, "European Capitalism's Reserve Army," *Monthly Review*, XXVII (November 1965).

10. For an extended discussion of the economic impact of immigration see

states into a more open world economy. Constant political battles are fought to prevent and defeat isolationist and protectionist coalitions. Why do states (and their political leaders) do this? Simply put, because they recognize the enormous advantages of free trade and open investment regimes. . . .

But if the logic of trade and finance is one of openness, the logic of migration is one of closure. From a political standpoint, international migration is the mirror image of international trade and finance. The wealthier states push hard to keep the lines of trade and investment open, while the poorer states are more skeptical, fearing dependency. With migration, it is the opposite: By and large, the wealthier states push hard to keep foreigners out, usually for reasons of national security or identity; whereas many poorer states want to export people, in order to reap the benefit of remittances or simply to maintain a social safety valve.

From an economic standpoint, it is difficult to separate trade and investment from migration. The movement of goods, services, and capital necessarily entails the movement of labor and people. Conventional economic wisdom has it that in the long run, trade can substitute for migration through a process of factor-price equalization.[5] But in the short run, historical and empirical studies demonstrate that free trade can lead to increased migration, especially when disparities in wages and incomes are very high, as between the U.S. and Mexico.[6] Although paradoxical, the reasons for this are simple: When backward economies are exposed to strong exogenous competitive pressures, the agricultural sector can collapse and lead to a rural exodus, swelling the population of cities and increasing pressures to emigrate. Likewise, increased trade in services leads to high-end migration, because technical and professional staff are integral parts of those services.

Sorting out winners and losers from migration is at least as complicated in the case of migration as in the case of trade. We can start from the basic premise that migration is heavily dependent on factor proportions and intensities, and that groups will support or oppose migration depending upon whether they represent scarce or abundant factors. This is the political corollary of economic, push-pull arguments, which hold that cross-border movements of people have a strong economic dimension and that such movements are basically a function of demand-pull and supply-push factors.[7] There is little doubt that people move in search of better opportunities—however defined—and that the existence of markets, and information or kinship networks is a necessary condition for migration to occur. But the sufficient conditions for migration are political. States must be willing to open their borders for exit and entry; such openness is not simply a function of interest group politics or cost-benefit analysis. Ideas and institutions play a crucial role in determining openness and closure.

. . . [S]ince 1945 there has been a continuous increase in the world migrant population, both in developed and developing countries and across regions. This increase parallels similar increases in the volume of world trade and foreign investment,[8] despite the absence of an international migration regime. It would be tempting to conclude that migration is simply a part of the inexorable process of globalization and that states have little control over the movements of people.[9] The corollary of the globalization thesis (see below) is that migration will continue so long as there are economic imbalances in the international economy, or until the process of factor-price equalization is complete. But I shall argue that such conclusion is not only simple and premature, but wrong. We must look more closely at political, institutional, and structural factors that govern international migration, ever mindful of the fact that economic pressures for migration are strong and will remain so for the foreseeable future. . . .

A. Neorealism and National Security Arguments

The oldest and most venerable theory of international relations is political realism. Robert Keohane succinctly summarizes the assumptions of this theory as follows: "(1) states (or city-states) are the key units of action; (2) they seek power, either as an end in itself or as a means to other ends; and (3) they behave in ways that are, by and large, rational, and therefore comprehensible to outsiders in rational terms."[10] At first blush, political realism seems to tell us little about international migration, other than that states are sovereign, power-seeking units which act in their own self interest. As such, one would expect states to protect their sovereignty and maximize their power by opening or closing their borders when it is in their national interest to do so. But this argument is not only dangerously close to being a tautology, it also begs the question of why states (at certain points in time) open or close their borders.

As is often the case with (pure) realist arguments, we are thrown back onto an ad hoc analysis of state rationality, seeking to determine, for example, when it is in a state's national interest to open its borders and when it is not, or whether out- or in-migration will enhance the state's power and contribute to its national security. Neorealist theory, which builds upon the basic assumptions of political realism, is somewhat more sophisticated and may offer us more insights into international migration. The father of neorealism, Kenneth Waltz, places great emphasis on the systemic nature of international politics, and the fact that the system is structured by anarchy and that state behavior is conditioned by the distribution of power within this anarchic system.[11] States, according to Waltz, are caught in an inescapable security dilemma. Any policy which has a national security dimension must be made in response to the structure of the international system, if a state is to survive in a world characterized by anarchy and the "war of all against all." Taking a neorealist perspective on international migration, we must ask (1) whether or not international migration has a national security dimension, and (2) to what extent migration and migration

is another economist (like the late Julian Simon) who argues in favor of increased immigration.[16] Like any public policy in a democracy, immigration policy is largely interest driven. One political scientist, Gary Freeman, has constructed a rational-choice/pluralist framework for explaining the difficulties that liberal democracies encounter in their attempts to restrict immigration. He argues that even though it may be in the national interest to restrict low-skilled immigration, restrictions have been difficult because powerful business interests, ethnic lobbies, intellectuals, and others have captured the state; it is thus virtually impossible for governments to carry out what is (in Freeman's view) clearly in the interest of the nation and society as a whole, and what is demanded by the electorate and by public opinion.[17]

All of these interest-based arguments (Borjas, Simon, Freeman) point to the difficulties of reducing migration to a national security issue. They also indicate the extent to which national security itself is a social or cultural construct. In the "constructivist" perspective, the interests and identities of states are heavily influenced by a range of cultural factors,[18] and are constructed by the actors involved. They are not—as realists would have us believe—purely a function of international systemic or structural factors, such as the distribution power within the system. This would be doubly true for international migration, as compared to issues of trade and finance, because migration involves the movement of animate rather than inanimate commodities. Unlike goods and capital, people/foreigners have the potential to immediately and radically transform the culture and politics of societies in which they arrive.[19] Hence, as Myron Weiner has pointed out, migration *can* threaten the national identity, sovereignty, and autonomy of the nation-state itself. It is therefore not surprising that political debates over defining the national interest with respect to migration can be intense. But, no matter how hard we try, it is impossible to remove cultural and social factors from these debates, or to reduce their terms to a cost-benefit calculation. As Max Weber and Claude Lèvi-Strauss remind us, all actions are not strictly economic or instrumental.[20] Subjective and normative elements figure heavily in the construction of interests and national security.
. . .

B. The Globalization Thesis

The globalization thesis stems largely from works in economic sociology and the sociology of international relations, though some economists subscribe to this theory.[21] It stands at the other extreme from neorealist arguments, which stress the role of the nation-state as the primary decision-making unit in international relations. Globalization arguments come in a variety of shapes and sizes, but they all share a common assumption: the regulatory power (and sovereignty) of the national state has been weakened by transnational, social, and economic forces. These forces range from the internationalization of capital, to the rise of transnational communities, to the increasing importance of human rights in international relations. The nation-state is no longer the sole, legitimate actor in international relations, if it ever was. Rather, the tables have been turned against the state, which is unable to control either transnational corporations—especially banks which move vast sums of capital around the globe—or migrants, who move in search of employment opportunities. The internationalization of capital, we are told, has provoked a radical restructuring of production as national economies move up (or down) in the international product cycle. Production itself has been decentralized with the rise of new centers of power and wealth, which Saskia Sassen has dubbed "the global city."[22]

According to Sassen and others, the rise of transnational economies has resulted in the creation of transnational communities, as workers are forced to move from one state to another in search of employment and often leave family members behind. Such communities can be found at both the high and low end of the labor market, as individuals move with more or less ease from one national society to another. A great deal of research has been done to document this practice among Mexican immigrants to the U.S. Douglas Massey was one of the first to point out the importance of transnational social networks in linking communities in the country of origin to those in the country of destination. These kinship and informational networks helped to instill confidence in potential migrants, thus raising their propensity to migrate and, in effect, lowering transaction costs for international migration.[23] Alejandro Portes argues that migrants have learned to use this "transnational space" as a way to get around national, regulatory obstacles to their social mobility. He goes on to point out that changes in Mexican law to permit dual nationality may reinforce this type of behavior, leading to ever larger transnational communities.[24]

The rapid decline in transaction costs and the ease of communication and transportation have combined to render national migration policies obsolete. Indeed, the entire regulatory framework of the state with respect to labor and business has been shaken by the process of globalization. To compete in the new international marketplace, business and governments in Organization for Economic Cooperation and Development (OECD) countries have been forced to deregulate and liberalize labor and capital markets. Less developed states, on the other hand, have been thrown into debt crises, leading to the imposition of painful policies of structural adjustment which in turn cause more migration from poor to rich states.[25] A case in point is the financial crisis in Mexico in the mid-1990s, which led to the devaluation of the peso and a surge in emigration to the U.S. in the latter part of the decade.[26]

Politics and the state have been factored out of international relations in these types of globalization arguments, most of which are inspired by world systems theory.[27] Following on this apolitical logic, both trade and migration (which are closely linked) are largely a function of changes in the international division of labor, and states play at best only a marginal role in determining economic and social outcomes. The prime agents of globalization are transnational corporations and transnational communities, if not individual migrants themselves.[28] If states have such a minor role to play, any discussion of national interests, national security, sovereignty, or even citizenship would seem to be beside the point. But at least one group of sociologists has tried to bring politics and law, if not the nation-state, back into the picture.

Recent works by Yasemin Soysal and David Jacobson focus on the evolution of rights for immigrants and foreigners. Both authors posit the rise of a kind of postnational regime for human rights which remains grounded in the logic of the nation-state,[29] wherein migrants are able to attain a legal status that somehow surpasses citizenship. Jacobson, more so than Soysal, argues that individual migrants have achieved an international legal personality by virtue of various human rights conventions, and both authors view these developments as presenting a distinctive challenge to traditional definitions of sovereignty and citizenship. But Soysal in particular is careful not to use the term "postnational" or "transnational" citizenship, opting instead for the expression "postnational membership." Wrestling with the contradictory nature of her argument, Soysal writes: "Incongruously, inasmuch as the ascription and codification of rights move beyond national frames of reference, post-national rights remain organized at the national level . . . the exercise of universalistic rights is tied to specific states and their institutions."[30]

Another sociologist, Rainer Bauböck, is less circumspect. He argues simply that, given the dynamics of economic globalization, a new transnational/political citizenship is necessary and inevitable.[31] Bauböck draws heavily on political and moral philosophy, especially Kant, in making his argument in favor of transnational citizenship. Like Soysal, he relies heavily on the recent history of international migration in Europe and the experience of the European Union (EU) to demonstrate that migration has accompanied the process of economic growth and integration in Europe; these migrants, many of whom were guest workers, have achieved a rather unique status as transnational citizens. All three of these authors (Soysal, Jacobson, and Bauböck) are attempting to give some type of political and legal content to world systems and globalization arguments. But like Saskia Sassen, they see the nation-state as essentially outmoded and incapable of keeping pace with changes in the world economy.

What do these theories tell us about migration policy (the opening and closing of societies) and the more or less continuous rise in international migration in the postwar period . . . ? At first blush, they would seem to account rather well for the rise in migration. Even though many of the globalization arguments, which draw heavily upon world systems theory, are neo-Marxist in orientation, they share many assumptions with conventional, neoclassical (push-pull) theories of migration. The first and most obvious assumption is that migration is caused primarily by dualities in the international economy. So long as these dualities persist, there will be pressures for individuals to move across national boundaries in search of better opportunities. But whereas many neoclassical economists (like the late Julian Simon) see this as pareto optimal—creating a rising tide that will lift all boats—many globalization theorists (like Sassen and Portes) view migration as further exacerbating dualities both in the international economy and in national labor markets. This variant of the globalization thesis is very close to the old Marxist argument that capitalism needs an industrial reserve army to surmount periodic crises in the process of accumulation.[32] As migration networks become more sophisticated and transnational communities grow in scope and complexity, migration should continue to increase, barring some unforeseen and dramatic fall in the demand for immigrant labor. Even then, some globalization theorists, like Wayne Cornelius, would argue that the demand for foreign labor is "structurally embedded" in the more advanced industrial societies; these societies cannot function without access to a cheap and pliable foreign work force.[33]

The second (crucial) assumption that globalization theorists share with neoclassical economists is the relatively marginal role of the state in governing and structuring international migration. States can act to distort or delay the development of international markets (for goods, services, capital, and labor), but they cannot stop it. With respect to migration, national regulatory regimes and municipal law in general simply must accommodate the development of international markets for skilled and unskilled workers. Talking about the opening and closing of societies is simply a nonstarter in a "global village." Likewise, citizenship and rights can no longer be understood in their traditional national contexts. If we take the example of postwar West Germany, nationality and citizenship laws date from 1913 and (despite efforts at reform) have retained kinship or blood (*jus sanguinis*) as the principal criterion for naturalization.[34] But this very restrictionist citizenship regime has not prevented Germany from becoming the largest immigration country in Europe. Globalization theorists, like Portes, Soysal, and Cornelius can explain this anomaly by reference to the structural demand for foreign labor in advanced industrial societies, the growth of networks and transnational communities, and the rise in postnational membership (which is closely tied to human rights regimes—what Soysal calls universal personhood). National citizenship and regulatory regimes would seem to explain little in the variation of migration flows or the openness (or closure) of German society.

A more fully developed critique of these arguments will be provided in the conclusion. But what can we retain at this point from globalization, as opposed to neorealist, arguments? The biggest shortcoming of the globalization thesis—in contrast to realism—is the weakness, or in some cases the absence of any political explanation. The locus of power and change is in society and the economy. There is no place for states and national regulation in this framework. Almost everything is socially and economically determined. . . .

C. Neoliberalism and Coalitional Arguments

Neoliberal arguments, often referred to among international relations theorists as liberal institutionalism, are heavily rationalist and have some things in common with neorealism. Both schools of thought stress the primacy of interests, the major difference being that neoliberals want to disaggregate the "national interest" and to look at the multiplicity of social and economic groups which compete to influence the state. For neoliberals, both national and international politics can be reduced to an economic game, and ultimately to a problem of collective action. To understand this (means-ends) game, all that is needed is to correctly identify the interests and preferences of social, economic, and political actors.[35] Not surprisingly, neoliberal theorists focus almost exclusively on politics and policy in liberal states, where the competition among groups is relatively open and unfettered by authoritarianism and corruption. Studying competition among groups at the domestic level, as well as the allocational and distributional consequences of policy, presents a clearer picture of why states behave the way they do in the international arena, whether in the areas of trade, finance, or migration.

Since this approach incorporates both economic and political analysis, it has come to be called international political economy (IPE). IPE theorists are very interested in the connections between domestic and international politics. In addition to focusing on domestic interests, they also stress the importance of institutions in determining policy outcomes. For one of the original IPE theorists, Robert Keohane, international institutions hold the key to explaining the puzzle of conflict and cooperation in world politics, especially with the weakening of American hegemony in the last decades of the 20th century. Along with Joseph Nye, Keohane argued that increases in economic interdependence in the postwar period have had a profound impact on world politics, altering the way states behave and the way in which they think about and use power.[36] In the nuclear age and with growing interdependence, it became increasingly difficult for states to rely on traditional military power to guarantee their security, because security was increasingly tied to economic power, and nuclear weapons fundamentally altered the nature of warfare. The challenge for states (especially liberal states) was how to construct a new world order to promote national interests that were tied ever more closely to international trade and investment, if not to migration.

In the first two decades after World War II, this problem was solved essentially by the U.S., which took it upon itself to reflate the world economy and to provide liquidity for problems of structure adjustment. This approach was dubbed hegemonic stability.[37] But with the gradual decline of American economic dominance in the 1970s, the problem arose of how to organize world markets in the absence of a hegemon. The answer would be found, according to Keohane and others, in multilateralism and the building of international institutions and regimes (like GATT and the IMF) to solve the problems of international cooperation and collective action.[38] As the Cold War waned in the 1980s, the entire field of international relations shifted dramatically away from the study of national security towards the study of international economics, especially with respect to trade and finance. In the last decades of the 20th century, even domestic politics, according to IPE theorists, has been thoroughly internationalized.[39]

Despite the fact that international migration would seem to lend itself to neoliberal/IPE arguments (migration has a strong political-economic dimension and it clearly contributes to the internationalization of domestic politics), very little has been written about it from this perspective.[40] The reasons are fairly simple: Until recently, there was little demand for international cooperation (or policy) in the area of migration, with the major exception of refugees, noted above. Even for the refugee regime, the numbers were relatively modest until the 1980s, and the incentives for cooperation among liberal states were closely linked to the Cold War and the bipolar structure of the international system. From the late 1940s through the 1970s, liberal states had little incentive to cooperate or build regimes for managing labor migration; there was an unlimited supply of (unskilled) labor available, which could be recruited through bilateral agreements with the sending countries. . . .

The situation has not changed much in the 1980s and 1990s, despite the end of the Cold War. There is still an unlimited and rapidly growing supply of cheap labor available in developing countries. What has changed, however, are the goals of immigration and refugee policies among the OECD states. The demand now is for policies to control, manage, or stop migration and refugee flows. The Cold War refugee regime, specifically the United Nations High Commissioner for Refugees (UNHCR), has come under enormous pressure to manage various refugee crises, from the Cambodians in Thailand, to the Kurds in Iraq, to the Hutus in Zaire (now the Republic of Congo), to the Albanians in Italy. . . .

What can neoliberal or IPE arguments tell us about the development of international migration during the postwar period and the willingness of states to risk exposing their economies to the exogenous pressures of trade and migration? The first major hypothesis that we can derive from neoliberal theory is that states are more willing to risk opening their economies to trade (and by extension migration) if there is some type of international regime (or hegemonic power) that can regulate these flows and solve collective action and free rider problems. However, as I have pointed out above, there is no regime for regulating migration that comes close to the type of regime that exists (GATT and WTO) for trade, or for international finance (IMF and World Bank). Yet we know that migration has increased steadily throughout the postwar period, in the absence of a regime or any type of effective multilateral process. The EU and Schengen are exceptions. If we accept the neorealist assumptions that states are unitary, sovereign actors, capable of closing as well as opening their economies, then other (political) factors must be at work which drive the increases in migration and maintain a degree of openness to migration, at least among the advanced industrial democracies.

A second (powerful) hypothesis can be derived from neoliberal theory. The maintenance of a relatively open (non-mercantilist) world economy is heavily dependent on coalitions of powerful interests in the most dominant, liberal states. In *Resisting Protectionism*, Helen Milner—a prominent neoliberal theorist—demonstrates how advanced industrial states in the 1970s were able to resist the kind of beggar-thy-neighbor policies that were adopted in the 1920s and 1930s. She argues that growing interdependence (multinationality and export dependence) helped to solidify free trade coalitions among the OECD states in the postwar period, thus preventing a retreat into protectionism following the economic downturns of the 1970s and 1980s.[41] Government leaders in a range of industrial nations were willing (and able) to resist strong political pressures for protectionism in the 1970s, in large part because a powerful constellation of business interests contributed to a substantial realignment within these societies; in some cases polities themselves were (creatively) redesigned by political entrepreneurs to facilitate the maintenance and strengthening of these new (free trade) coalitions.[42] . . .

From a neoliberal/IPE perspective, the central question with respect to migration is how pro-immigration coalitions in the key OECD states formed, and whether they could maintain legal immigration regimes with the end of the Cold War and in the absence of a strong international migration regime. We cannot discount the importance of international systemic constraints, like the end of the Cold War, which clearly has had an impact on political coalitions and alignments in all of the liberal democracies. The end of the Cold War has had a profound impact on coalitions supporting open migration policies, even more so than in the area of trade. The major difference between trade and migration is in the nature and types of coalitions that form to support or oppose them. Although related, in the sense that strong economic liberals tend to support both free trade and more open migration policies,[43] there is a much stronger legal, ideational, and cultural dimension involved in the making of pro-migration coalitions than with free trade coalitions, which tend to be based more narrowly on economic interests. Free trade policies clearly have important political and social effects, but the arguments about comparative advantage and tariff policies tend to be heavily economic, and the interests are organized along sectoral or class lines. With respect to trade, individuals and groups tend to follow their market interests; but in the making of migration policies, this is not always the case. If a state can be sure of reciprocity, e.g. that other states will abide by the Most Favored Nation (MFN) principle, then it is easier to convince a skeptical public to support free trade. With migration, on the other hand, economic arguments (about the costs and benefits of migration) tend to be overshadowed by political, cultural, and ideological arguments. National identities and founding myths, what I have elsewhere called "national models," come into play in the making and unmaking of coalitions for admissionist or restrictionist migration policies.[44] Debates about migration in the liberal-democratic (OECD) states revolve as much if not more so around issues of rights (see below) and national identity than around issues of markets. The coalitions that form to support more open migration policies are often rights-markets coalitions. Debates about sovereignty and control of borders are reduced to debates about national identity—a fungible concept that reflects values, morality, and culture, rather than a strictly instrumental, economic calculus.

If we take a coalitional/IPE/neoliberal approach to understanding the rise of migration in the postwar era, we are thrown back onto an analysis of three factors, which together drive national migration policies. The first of these factors is ideational, historical, and cultural. Migration policy, especially in the big three liberal republics (the U.S., France, and Germany), is heavily influenced by national (or founding) myths, which are codified in citizenship and nationality laws.[45] As I stated above, these myths and the national identity are fungible, subject to manipulation, and they involve strong elements of symbolic politics. They are reflected in constitutional law and can be analyzed from an historical, sociological, legal, and political standpoint. Clearly, citizenship (like society or the economy) is subject to exogenous shocks. Immigration, as Myron Weiner and Rey Koslowski have pointed out, can change the composition of societies, alter political coalitions, and transform citizenship and the national identity. The argument therefore can be made, following Koslowski, that migration contributes to the internationalization of domestic politics and economics. Multiculturalism is the functional equivalent of multinationalism. If the rise of multinational corporations—as Milner and others have argued—con-

intensities); and (3) rights (which flow from liberal constitutions and laws); finally, a third factor is ideational, cultural, and legal (what Rogers Brubaker calls "traditions of citizenship and nationhood"). During the Cold War, liberal states were more willing to risk migration because of the bipolar nature of the international system, which prevented large scale emigration from communist states and helped to solidify rights-markets coalitions in liberal states. The end of the Cold War has radically altered the configuration of power and interests, both at the national and international level, and it has changed the dynamic of collaboration games, especially with respect to migration. States are still willing to risk trade and the institutions for maintaining stable exchange rates, specifically the IMF, are supported by a coalition of liberal states led by the U.S. There is evidence, however, that multilateralism in these areas (trade and finance) is under increasing political pressure, especially in the U.S. A new isolationism and protectionism are stirring.

The logic of cooperation is different for trade and migration. Liberal states work hard to keep trade and investment flowing in the world economy; and they work increasingly hard to keep migration, including refugees, bottled up in less developed (sending) countries. The international trade regime (WTO) is based squarely on the doctrine of comparative advantage and the principle of nondiscrimination (MFN). Free trade has come to be accepted by a wide range of states as an international public good. Ironically, following the Stolper-Samuelson theorem of factor-price equalization, trade (and FDI) are often touted as the solution to the problem of unwanted migration. According to this theorem, trade can substitute for migration in the long-term. Nevertheless, migration continues in the short-term and may actually be increased when less developed economies are exposed to the strong exogenous shocks of trade and foreign investment.

No organizing principle has emerged as a basis for international cooperation to regulate migration. The international refugee regime, based on a well founded fear of persecution, and the EU regime, based on freedom of movement for nationals of member states, are the exceptions. The primary reasons for the lack of cooperation and the absence of an international regime in the area of migration are the tremendous asymmetries between interests and power in the international system. The challenge for proponents of an international migration regime is to find (1) an organizing principle and (2) a strategy for overcoming collaboration problems in this area. In the penultimate section of this article, I suggested a principle, viz. rule of law and orderly movement of peoples, and several strategies for overcoming asymmetries of interest and building a regime. The strategies include centralization of authority to promote trust, and to provide information and enforcement mechanisms. The problem with this strategy is that it requires continuous and strong intervention by a hegemon or group of hegemonic states. A more likely strategy is suasion, which involves tactical issue link-age and international logrolls—linking unrelated issues to cooperation in controlling emigration.

The central argument in this article is that states will not continue to risk migration in the post–Cold War era without some type of international regulatory framework. If, as I and many others have argued, migration is closely linked to trade and investment, both economically (in the sense that trade and investment require factor mobility) and politically (in the sense that the same coalitions which support free trade and open investment regimes tend to support more open migration regimes), then any weakening on the part of liberal states in their commitment to support orderly move-ments of people could threaten the "new liberal world order." This argu-ment is at odds with the globalization thesis, inasmuch as I see politics and the nation-state as crucial to the stability of the global economy, especially with the end of the Cold War. Without the "continuous, centrally organized, and controlled intervention" of the most powerful liberal states, the "simple and natural liberty" of the global economy will not survive.[67] Globalization is a myth insofar as it ignores the imperatives of politics and power, which are still vested in the nation-state.

■ Notes

1. *See* KARL POLANYI, THE GREAT TRANSFORMATION: THE POLITICAL AND ECO-NOMIC ORIGINS OF OUR TIME (1957).

2. *See* CHARLES P. KINDLEBERGER, THE WORLD IN DEPRESSION, 1929–1939 (1973). Kindleberger's argument evolved into what is now called "hegemonic sta-bility theory," where in the words of Robert Keohane, "hegemonic structures of power, dominated by a single country, are most conducive to the development of strong international regimes whose rules are relatively precise and well obeyed […]. [T]he decline of hegemonic structures of power can be expected to presage a decline in the strength of corresponding international economic regimes." (quoted in ROBERT GILPIN, THE POLITICAL ECONOMY OF INTERNATIONAL RELATIONS 72(1986)).

3. MULTILATERALISM MATTERS: THE THEORY AND PRACTICE OF AN INSTITUTION-AL FORM (John Gerard Ruggie ed., 1993).

4. *See* RONALD ROGOWSKI, COMMERCE AND COALITIONS: HOW TRADE AFFECTS DOMESTIC POLITICAL ALIGNMENTS (1989); *see, e.g.*, HELEN MILNER, INTERESTS, INSTI-TUTIONS, AND INFORMATION: DOMESTIC POLITICS AND INTERNATIONAL RELATIONS (1997).

5. This is the Stolper-Samuelson theorem. Wolfgang F. Stolper & Paul A. Samuelson, *Protection and Real Wages*, 9 REV. ECON. STUD. 58, 58–73 (1941); *see also*, Robert A. Mundell, *International Trade and Factor Mobility*, 47 AM. ECON. REV. 321, 321–35 (1957).

6. *See* PHILIP L. MARTIN, TRADE AND MIGRATION: NAFTA AND AGRICULTURE (1993).

7. For a more in-depth discussion of the political economy of international migration, see JAMES F. HOLLIFIELD, IMMIGRANTS, MARKETS, AND STATES (1992) and CONTROLLING IMMIGRATION: A GLOBAL PERSPECTIVE, 6–11 (Wayne A. Cornelius et al. eds., 1994).

8. For the trends in trade, foreign direct investment, and migration, see *Foreign Direct Investment, Trade, Aid, and Migration*, Int'l Org. for Migration, UNCTAD Current Studies Series A No. 29, U.N. Doc. UNCTAD/DTCI/27 (1995); *Cf.* ROGOWSKI, *supra* note 4.

9. On the globalization thesis, see SASKIA SASSEN, THE GLOBAL CITY: NEW YORK, LONDON, TOKYO (1991), and SASKIA SASSEN, LOSING CONTROL? SOVEREIGNTY IN AN AGE OF GLOBALIZATION (1996). On migration, globalization, and the rights of foreigners, *cf.* YASEMIN SOYSAL, THE LIMITS OF CITIZENSHIP (1994); DAVID JACOBSON, RIGHTS ACROSS BORDERS: IMMIGRATION AND THE DECLINE OF CITIZENSHIP (1996).

10. NEOREALISM AND ITS CRITICS 7 (Robert O. Keohane ed., 1986).

11. KENNETH N. WALTZ, THEORY OF INTERNATIONAL POLITICS (1979).

12. *See* GUY S. GOODWIN-GILL, THE REFUGEE IN INTERNATIONAL LAW (1996).

13. *See* MYRON WEINER, THE GLOBAL MIGRATION CRISIS: CHALLENGE TO STATES AND TO HUMAN RIGHTS (1995).

14. *See* ARTHUR SCHLESINGER JR., THE DISUNITING OF AMERICA: REFLECTIONS ON A MULTICULTURAL SOCIETY (1992); Samuel P. Huntington, *The West: Unique, Not Universal*, FOREIGN AFF. (Nov.-Dec. 1996), at 45. Huntington writes, "Promoting the coherence of the West means [. . .] controlling immigration from non-Western societies, as every major European country has done and as the United States is beginning to do, and ensuring the assimilation into Western culture of the immigrants who are admitted."

15. GEORGE J. BORJAS, FRIENDS OR STRANGERS: THE IMPACT OF IMMIGRANTS ON THE U.S. ECONOMY (1990).

16. *See* JULIAN L. SIMON, THE ECONOMIC CONSEQUENCES OF IMMIGRATION (1989).

17. *See* Gary P. Freeman, *Modes of Immigration Politics in the Liberal Democratic States*, 29 INT'L MIGRATION REV. 881–97 (1995); *see also* Christian Joppke, *Why Liberal States Accept Unwanted Immigration*, 50 WORLD POLITICS 266–93 (1998).

18. For a summary of the constructivist theory of international relations and national security, see THE CULTURE OF NATIONAL SECURITY: NORMS AND IDENTITY IN WORLD POLITICS (Peter J. Katzenstein ed., 1996), especially at 1–32.

19. As Yossi Shain and Rey Koslowski have pointed out, international migration can create divided loyalties and transnational political communities. Shain stresses the rise of political diasporas, whereas Koslowski focuses on the emergence of dual nationality as a sign of the weakening of the nation-state. *Compare* YOSSI SCHAIN, THE FRONTIER OF LOYALTY: POLITICAL EXILES IN THE AGE OF THE NATION-STATE (1989) *with* Rey Koslowski, Migration, the Globalization of Domestic Politics and International Relations Theory (paper presented at the Int'l Stud. Ass'n Meeting, San Diego, Cal., 1996).

20. *See, e.g.*, MAX WEBER, THE THEORY OF SOCIAL AND ECONOMIC ORGANIZATION 158 (1977); CLAUDE LEVI-STRAUSS, THE SAVAGE MIND (1966).

21. For an interesting and pithy critique of globalization by an economist, see PAUL KRUGMAN, POP INTERNATIONALISM (1996). Krugman is particularly disturbed by globalization arguments that stress the need for nations to be more competitive, which can quickly lead into zero-sum or mercantilist thinking about trade and other forms international exchange.

22. SASSEN, THE GLOBAL CITY, *supra* note 9, at 22.

23. *See* DOUGLAS MASSEY, ET AL., RETURN TO ATZLAN (1987). For a cogent review of transnationalism and migration theory, see Alejandro Portes, *Immigration Theory for a New Century: Some Problems and Opportunities*, 31 INT'L MIGRATION REV. 799, 799–825 (1997).

24. *See* Alejandro Portes, *Transnational Communities: Their Emergence and Significance in the Contemporary World System, in* LATIN AMERICA AND THE WORLD ECONOMY (R.P. Korzeniewicz & W.C. Smith eds., 1996); *see also* A. PORTES & ROBERT L. BACH, LATIN JOURNEY: CUBAN AND MEXICAN IMMIGRANTS IN THE UNITED STATES (1985).

25. *See* SASSEN, LOSING CONTROL, *supra* note 9; *see also* WHOSE WORLD ORDER? UNEVEN GLOBALIZATION AND THE END OF THE COLD WAR (H. Holm and G. Soerensen eds., 1995). For a critique of the globalization perspective on migration, see CHALLENGE TO THE NATION-STATE: IMMIGRATION IN WESTERN EUROPE AND THE UNITED STATES (Christian Joppke ed., 1998).

26. *See* COMMISSION ON IMMIGRATION REFORM, BINATIONAL STUDY ON MIGRATION BETWEEN MEXICO AND THE UNITED STATES (1997).

27. *See* IMMANUEL WALLERSTEIN, THE MODERN WORLD SYSTEM (1974).

28. James Rosenau takes the globalization argument to its logical extreme, postulating the "individualization of the world" and the rise of "postinternational politics." *See* JAMES ROSENAU, TURBULENCE IN WORLD POLITICS: A THEORY OF CHANGE AND CONTINUITY (1990).

29. *See* SOYSAL, *supra* note 9.

30. *Id.* at 157.

31. *See* RAINER BAUBÖCK, TRANSNATIONAL CITIZENSHIP: MEMBERSHIP RIGHTS IN INTERNATIONAL MIGRATION (1994).

32. A version of the industrial reserve army argument can be found in MICHAEL J. PIORE, BIRDS OF PASSAGE: MIGRANT LABOR IN INDUSTRIAL SOCIETIES (1979). For a critique of this argument, see HOLLIFIELD, *supra* note 7, at 19.

33. *See* Wayne A. Cornelius, The Structural Embeddedness of Demand for Immigrant Labor in California and Japan (paper prepared for a meeting of the University of California Comparative Immigration and Integration Program, San Diego, February, 1998).

34. *See* ROGERS BRUBAKER, CITIZENSHIP AND NATIONHOOD IN FRANCE AND GERMANY 165 (1992).

35. A representative example of neoliberal theorizing can be found in HELEN V. MILNER, INTERESTS, INSTITUTIONS, AND INFORMATION: DOMESTIC POLITICS AND INTERNATIONAL RELATIONS 33–66 (1997).

36. *See* ROBERT O. KEOHANE & JOSEPH S. NYE, POWER AND INTERDEPENDENCE: WORLD POLITICS IN TRANSITION (1977).

37. *See* KINDLEBERGER, *supra* note 2.

38. *See* ROBERT O. KEOHANE, AFTER HEGEMONY: COOPERATION AND DISCORD IN THE WORLD ECONOMY (1984); *Cf.* JOHN GERARD RUGGIE, MULTILATERALISM MATTERS: THE THEORY AND PRACTICE OF AN INSTITUTIONAL FORM (1993) (especially the chapter by Judith Goldstein, *Creating the GATT Rules: Politics, Institutions, and American Policy* at 201–25).

39. *See* INTERNATIONALIZATION OF DOMESTIC POLITICS (Robert O. Keohane & Helen Milner, eds., 1996).

40. For an early attempt to use the IPE framework for understanding migration, see James F. Hollifield, *Migration and International Relations: Cooperation and Control in the European Community*, 26 INT'L MIGRATION REV. 568, 568–95 (1992). For a more recent and purely IPE study of migration, see Alan E. Kessler, Trade Theory, Political Incentives, and the Political Economy of American Immigration Restriction, 1875–1924 (paper presented at the annual meeting of the American Political Science Association, Washington, DC, August 1997).

41. *See* HELEN V. MILNER, RESISTING PROTECTIONISM: GLOBAL INDUSTRIES AND THE POLITICS OF INTERNATIONAL TRADE 18–44 (1988).

42. This argument, similar to Milner's, is made by MICHAEL LUSZTIG, RISKING FREE TRADE: THE POLITICS OF TRADE IN BRITAIN, CANADA, MEXICO, AND THE UNITED STATES (1996).

43. For more evidence on the relation between free trade and pro-immigration coalitions in the U.S., see James F. Hollifield & Gary Zuk, *Immigrants, Markets, and Rights, in* IMMIGRATION AND THE WELFARE STATE: GERMANY AND THE UNITED STATES IN COMPARISON 28, 28–69 (Herman Kurthen & Jurgen Fijalkowski eds., 1998); *Cf.* Kessler, *supra* note 40.

44. *See* James F. Hollifield, *Immigration and Integration in Western Europe: Comparative Analysis*, in IMMIGRATION INTO WESTERN SOCIETIES: PROBLEMS AND POLICIES 28, 28–70 (Emek M. Ucarer & Donald J. Puchala eds., 1997); *see also* JAMES F. HOLLIFIELD, IMMIGRATION ET L'ETAT NATION: A LA RECHERCHE D'UN MODELE NATIONAL (1997).

45. *See* BRUBAKER, *supra* note 34.

46. For very instructive early path-breaking works, *see* MARK J. MILLER, FOREIGN WORKERS IN WESTERN EUROPE: AN EMERGING POLITICAL FORCE (1981) and Barbara E. Schmitter, *Immigration and Citizenship in West Germany and Switzerland* (unpublished Ph.D. dissertation, University of Chicago (1979)).

47. *See* Freeman, *supra* note 17; *see also* Joppke, *supra* note 17.

48. For various country studies, see CONTROLLING IMMIGRATION, *supra* note 7.

49. For example, in the Netherlands and Sweden resident aliens have voting rights in local elections. *Compare* HOLLIFIELD, *supra* note 7, *with* SOYSAL *supra* note 9, *and* JACOBSON, *supra* note 9.

50. *See* Aristide Zolberg, *Reforming the Back Door: Perspectives Historiques wur la Reforme de la Politique Americaine d'Immigration, in* LOGIQUES D'ETAT ET IMMIGRATION (Jaqueline Costa-Lascoux and Patrick Weil eds., 1992) (one of the first to point to the "strange bedfellows" phenomenon); *see also* Daniel J. Tichenor, *The Politics of Immigration Reform in the United States*, 3 POLITY 333, 333–62 (1994).

51. On this point, see the introduction in CONTROLLING IMMIGRATION, *supra* note 7, at 9–11; *see also* James F. Hollifield, *Ideas, Institutions, and Civil Society: On the Limits of Immigration Control, in* IMMIGRATION CONTROL IN EUROPE (Tomas Hammar and Grete Brochmann eds., forthcoming 1998).

52. MULTILATERALISM MATTERS, *supra* note 3, at 3–47.

53. INTERNATIONAL REGIMES 185–205 (Stephen D. Krasner ed., 1983).

54. *See* Hollifield & Zuk, *supra* note 43.

55. *See* HOLLIFIELD, *supra* note 7, at 222; *see also* WEINER, *supra* note 13, at 112.

56. *See* BIMAL GHOSH, HUDDLED MASSES AND UNCERTAIN SHORES: INSIGHTS INTO IRREGULAR MIGRANTS AND THE SAFEGUARDING OF MIGRANT RIGHTS (1998).

57. *International Responses to Trafficking in Migrants and the Safeguarding of Migrant Rights*, International Organization for Migration (1994). See also the special issue of the International Migration Review on the UN Convention on the Rights of Migrant Workers and their Families, especially the Bosniak article. Linda S. Bosniak, *Human Rights, State Sovereignty and the Protection of Undocumented Migrants Under the International Migrant Workers Convention*. 25 INT'L MIGRATION REV. 737, 737–770 (1991).

58. *See* JAGDISH BHAGWATI, THE ECONOMICS OF PREFERENTIAL TRADE AGREEMENTS (1996).

59. *See* GHOSH, *supra* note 56, chs. 4–5; Bimal Ghosh, *Movements of People: The Search for a New International Regime, in* COMMISSION ON GLOBAL GOVERNANCE, ISSUES IN GLOBAL GOVERNANCE 405–424 (1995).

60. In the case of the British Commonwealth, for example, freedom of movement for colonial subjects was greater prior to the granting of independence. From the 1960s until the passage of the British National Act in 1981, there was a gradual restriction of immigration from the so-called New Commonwealth states. The 1981 Act effectively shut out people of color from British citizenship. *See* Zig Layton-Henry, *Britain: The Would-Be Zero Immigration Country*, *in* CONTROLLING IMMIGRATION: A GLOBAL PERSPFCTIVE 273, 273–5 (Wayne A. Cornelius, et al., eds., 1994). Certainly the same could be said of the relationship between France and its former colonies in Africa, except for the fact that the French have never completely shut former colonial subjects out of French citizenship *de jure*, although *de facto* one could argue that it is extremely difficult for North and West Africans to immigrate and naturalize. *See* James F. Hollifield, *Immigration and Republicanism in France: The Hidden Consensus*, *in* CONTROLLING IMMIGRATION: A GLOBAL PERSPECTIVE 143, 143–76 (Wayne A. Cornelius, et al., eds., 1994).

61. Judith Goldstein, *Creating the GATT Rules: Politics, Institutions, and American Policy*, *in* MULTILATERALISM MATTERS: THE THEORY AND PRACTICE OF AN INSTITUTIONAL FORM 201, 201–25 (John Gerard Ruggie ed., 1993).

62. *See* ROBERT O. KEOHANE & JOSEPH S. NYE, POWER AND INTERDEPENDENCE: WORLD POLITICS IN TRANSITION (1977); HELEN V. MILNER, RESISTING PROTECTIONISM: GLOBAL INDUSTRIES AND THE POLITICS OF INTERNATIONAL TRADE 18, 18–44 (1988).

63. *See* Lisa Martin, *The Rational State Choice of Multilateralism*, *in* MULTILATERALISM MATTERS 91, 91–121 (John Gerard Ruggie ed., 1993).

64. *Id.* at 104.

65. *Id.* at 104–06.

66. *See* Huntington, *supra* note 14.

67. *See* POLANYI, *supra* note 1.

chapter 6

The Evolution of an International Refugee Regime

6.1   *the Editors*
Introduction

The Geneva Refugee regime, like the Bretton Woods system dealing with labor migration, emerged as a response to the negative aftermath of World War II and thus overlaps the former in time, space, and norms. The Geneva Refugee regime derives from the 1951 UN Convention Relating to the Status of Refugees, signed in Geneva, and its 1967 Protocol, signed in New York. Like the Bretton Woods system, the refugee regime implies the existence of an international community informed by norms, laws, and institutions. However, unlike the Bretton Woods system, the Geneva regime is concerned with the problems of forced migration and refugees. As such, it represents a shift of emphasis away from the economic toward the political and humanitarian dimensions of migration.

The chief differences between the two systems revolve around the nature of migrants, particularly their motives, and therefore the different costs and benefits associated with them. These differences are broadly reflected in the vast chasm that divides studies of refugees and migrants. Indeed, refugee movements are too often ignored by students of migration because they are conceived of primarily as an economic phenomenon; refugee movements are generally viewed as unruly and unpredictable, and refugee flows are considered to be beyond the control of individual states. With respect to the latter assumption, the entitlements granted to refugees by an international refugee regime are viewed by some as severely circumscribing the latitude of nation-states to control the flow of refugees into their territories.

As may be concluded from Rogers and Copeland in Chapter 6.2, nowhere are the tensions between the international and domestic authorities over migration as visible as they are with regard to refugees. On one hand, the rules governing the treatment of refugees are institutionalized in international refugee and asylum law. In fact, the Geneva Convention, signed by over 100 nations, is one of the most universally revered legal international instruments as it is applied to individuals (not groups) who are "able to prove a well-founded fear of persecution for reasons of race, nationality, membership in a particular social group or political opinion." These rules are monitored by the United Nations High Commissioner for Refugees and other international agencies. They are also embedded in international human rights law, such as the International Covenant on Civil and Political Rights (1966).

On the other hand, national authority also derives its foundation from international law and, specifically, the legal principle of sovereignty, which respects the right of states to decide whom to admit into their national territory. For those privileging the significance of state control over refugee and asylum practices, there is ample evidence to suggest that the sovereignty of states to formulate refugee and asylum policies is not only sanctioned by international law but is also reflected in their domestic and constitutional policies.

First, the Convention did not guarantee that an applicant automatically would be granted asylum if he or she deserved it; rather, Article 33 more modestly stipulated the principle of *nonrefoulement,* the principle that "a person would not be returned to the frontiers of territories where his life or freedom would be threatened." Second, states create refugees, and they also take them back. Third, states fund the work of international organizations and therefore inform and shape their agendas. Fourth, even for those states that are a party to international legal or regional instruments, national laws pertaining to refugees can and do vary. In this respect, a gap often exists between the spirit of international law and its incorporation into domestic law, the distinction between signatory and ratification processes. Fifth, states influence refugee and asylum flows by how they define who is and who is not a genuine refugee. In this context, the domestic political interests in favor of or against accepting refugees may influence the way in which international legal rules are interpreted.

As many scholars have shown, the concept of refugee has evolved over time, despite only minor changes in its legal definition. The concept is largely a post–World War II construct; as defined by the United Nations, it was meant to apply primarily to the refugees of postwar Europe—not contemporary movements involving persons from the Third World. Another practical change is signaled in the rise of new types of refugees, for example, females suffering genital mutilation, persons experiencing religious

an ad hoc basis. Before the formulation of the 1967 Protocol, the UN General Assembly asked the High Commissioner for Refugees on several occasions to use his "good offices" to aid certain refugee groups excluded from his mandate because of the temporal limitation of the definition.[3] More recently, the UN General Assembly has asked UNHCR to assist persons in "refugee-like" situations.[4] On rare occasions the same mechanism has been used to assist internally displaced (as in Cyprus).

Thus, the refugee definition has not remained static over the past forty years. It has been modified both formally and on an ad hoc basis to facilitate the protection and assistance to forced migrants in need. Informal or ad hoc modifications have usually preceded formal changes. Does this mean that the international community is likely to formulate another protocol to the 1951 Convention which would adopt the broader definition as the universally recognized one? Since in the western industrialized countries asylum has generally led to permanent residence and as a rule includes the option of citizenship, it is unlikely that these countries would accept an expanded refugee definition.

Similarly, could the increasing number of ad hoc interventions on behalf of the internally displaced mean that the international community is likely to formulate a protocol to the Convention on their behalf, or perhaps a separate convention? There has definitely been a general increase of concern, including on the part of the current High Commissioner for Refugees, about the need for mechanisms to serve these populations in an efficient and predictable manner (see Clark 1989; Keely 1991; Ogata 1992a, 1992b, 1992c, 1992d). . . .

■ The Institutional Framework

Although international organizations and nongovernmental agencies are important players in international refugee protection and assistance, the governments remain the dominant actors. Governments create and take back refugees, they grant temporary or permanent asylum and resettlement, they seek regional solutions to refugee problems in cooperation with international organizations, they fund the work of international organizations and often contribute substantially to the programs of private voluntary agencies, and they intervene through various means to avert new refugee flows.

Of course, forced migrants themselves are important actors and not merely individuals or groups who are the objects of others' actions. In many instances they exercise some choice concerning when to leave and where to go. Refugees recreate their own communities in exile and invent differing modes of adaptation even when living under highly restrictive conditions. Whether in an asylum country or displaced within their own country, forced migrants frequently make the decision to return home on their own. In these returns refugees sometimes act against the desires of host or home governments or of international organizations. Many engage in secondary migration after their return. Nevertheless, refugees have generally been given few opportunities to participate in the decisionmaking process which affects them. In particular, refugee women have had little say in decisionmaking; only over the last decade have decisionmakers begun to acknowledge the specific needs of certain groups of women (for example, of female heads of households or of single women).

In states party to the international and/or regional legal instruments mentioned above, national laws often reflect closely the international principles, although this need not always be the case.[5] Furthermore, the application of similar principles may vary for different countries, times, or population groups. For example, in Pakistan in the 1980s, Afghans were acknowledged as refugees, whereas Iranian asylum seekers were not given formal recognition. At present, some Western European countries' contemplated or actual practices to deter unfounded asylum applications (such as carrier sanctions or summary dismissals of undocumented asylum seekers at a country's borders) may violate the principles of international protection.

International Organizations

The international institutional framework to assist and protect forced migrants was initially constructed under the auspices of the League of Nations. The various refugee organizations established within the League's framework had a number of features in common, which also characterized UNHCR when it was created in 1951:

- the refugees to be protected and assisted were on the European continent and outside their own countries;
- the organizations were created to be temporary; and
- they were non-operational, charged with the protection of refugees and only with the coordination—not the direct provision—of assistance activities, which had to be funded through outside contributions.

For political reasons, certain organizations with a specific mandate to aid refugees (or, more broadly, migrant populations) were established outside the League or later the UN system. . . . An early example is the 1933 nomination of a High Commissioner for Refugees Coming from Germany. This position was created outside the League in order to circumvent Germany's objections, since Germany was a member of the League (League of Nations 1933:22–29).

In anticipation of the dissolution in 1947 of the UN Relief and Rehabilitation Administration (UNRRA), the UN created in 1946 the International Refugee organization (IRO) to function relatively independently of the UN as a temporary specialized agency within the system. By then, Western countries had realized that UNRRA's acquiescence in the repatriation of nearly two million Soviet citizens in the immediate post-war months (much of which had occurred against the will of these refugees and displaced persons) had been a mistake, for many of the returnees faced persecution upon return. IRO was to be concerned mainly with "the protection and resettlement of 1,620,000 persons who were reluctant to return to their homelands either because they had lost all ties there or because of a well-founded fear of persecution" (United Nations High Commissioner for Refugees 1993b:1)

IRO was finally dissolved in 1952, after the creation of UNHCR. At the same time as the High Commissioner's office was established in the UN, Western governments at the urging of the United States also created the Intergovernmental Committee for European Migration, to be independent of the UN and thus to operate without interference from communist countries, especially the Soviet Union (Gordenker 1987:29). As of late 1992, the only group of refugees remaining outside UNHCR's mandate was the Palestinians. They are assisted by the UN Relief and Works Agency for Palestinian Refugees in the Near East (UNRWA).

Both within and outside the League and UN systems, there has been a division of labor with regard to refugees and migrants. Some organizations with broader mandates have also aided refugees. For example, for some years in the 1920s the International Labour Organisation (ILO) was active in locating employment, and thus also resettlement opportunities, for refugees (Keely and Elwell 1981:42). After World War II, the UN Relief and Rehabilitation Administration (UNRRA), established in 1942 to assist with post-war reconstruction, necessarily became involved with relief, repatriation, and resettlement of refugees. The World Food Programme (WFP), the United Nations Children's Fund (UNICEF), the United Nations Development Programme (UNDP), and other international bodies have been involved with refugees at times and some of them are taking on increasing responsibilities today.

UNHCR   The United Nations High Commissioner for Refugees was established by a General Assembly resolution in December 1950. According to the office's statute, the High Commissioner's mandate was to extend to persons considered to be refugees under various earlier international arrangements as well as to those who fit a definition similar to the one embodied in the 1951 Convention Relating to the Status of Refugees. Unlike the Convention definition, the statutory definition involved no geographical or time limitations, thus not requiring any later amendment comparable to that in the 1967 Protocol to the Convention. On the other hand, the statutory definition did not include "membership of a particular social group" as one of the reasons for fear of persecution—an important and potentially flexible category that was added in the Convention definition (for the text of the Statute, see United Nations High Commissioner for Refugees 1979:5–7).

Beginning as a small, non-operational organization, UNHCR has grown considerably in size and worldwide representation over the years. It now conducts its own operations, although most direct refugee assistance is still carried out by implementing partners. Forty years after its creation, while still existing under a temporary mandate,[6] the High Commissioner's office is more needed than ever. At the heart of UNHCR's mandate is the international protection of refugees and the search for durable solutions. Ultimately, however, it is the responsibility of states to protect recognized refugees and asylum seekers. Since its inception, UNHCR has had both to work with governments and, at times, to challenge them on behalf of refugees. While governments may cause protection problems, UNHCR depends on them for access to refugee populations, funding, and the provision of durable solutions.

Protection is as multifaceted as the needs, difficulties and dangers experienced by refugees. A refugee or asylum seeker may need protection at any stage in the process of becoming or being a recognized refugee: during flight, while in asylum in a host country, or during and after return. Protection is a legal matter: helping refugees to obtain proper documents, monitoring and commenting on governments' application of their laws pertaining to refugees, assisting in asylum adjudication, and so forth. Under some conditions, there is need to ensure the physical protection of refugees and asylum seekers from rape or attacks during flight or in refugee camps, *refoulement,* or forcible recruitment into military activities. Quite simply, protection is an eminently practical matter: ensuring that people are treated decently.

Certain activities undertaken by UNHCR and other institutions or individuals are clearly identifiable as protection activities. The behaviors of states and other actors are monitored, problems are identified, and efforts are made to ameliorate or redress them. This is the classical view of protection, and responses can range from submitting *amicus curiae* briefs in court cases that interpret the definition of refugee or otherwise affect a country's policy or practice toward refugees or asylum seekers, to training government officials in international refugee law.

At the same time the provision of protection is also inherent in the assistance activities undertaken by UNHCR, nongovernmental organizations (NGOs), and other international organizations. Emergency assistance *is* physical protection. In refugee camps, the presence of service providers from outside the refugee community functions as a protection device, discouraging infringements on the refugees' physical safety or legal rights. Indeed, such workers may be the only ones who can identify certain protection needs, as they often have unique access to particular refugee groups such as women and children.

UNHCR becomes active in refugee situations even when the countries involved are not signatories to the 1951 Convention or the 1967 Protocol. However, protection and assistance are more easily accomplished when an asylum country has acceded to the Convention or the Protocol. UNHCR can press more effectively to be involved, and the country has a greater obligation to abide by the principles established in refugee law.

An example of a government's refusal to give UNHCR access to a specific refugee population occurred in Thailand in the last decade. This is an extreme example in the sense that a new organization was created to assist the affected population. Afraid of creating a magnet effect if it freely offered fleeing Cambodians temporary asylum leading to third-country resettlement, Thailand refused refugee recognition to large numbers. The Cambodians were referred to as displaced persons and were held in camps along the Thai border, with repatriation as the only possible solution to their situation. From 1982, until the Paris Peace Settlement in 1991 led to preparations for repatriation, they were assisted by the UN Border Relief Operation (UNBRO), which, however, had no protection mandate. By the early 1990s the camp population numbered approximately 350,000. The repatriation, which took place in 1992 and 1993, was prepared and administered by UNHCR.

. . . Aside from a very limited subsidy from the regular budget of the United Nations, which is used exclusively for administrative costs, UNHCR's work is financed by voluntary contributions from governments, nongovernmental organizations, and individuals (United Nations High Commissioner for Refugees 1993b:15). The organization's yearly expenditures rose from US$ 6 million in 1967 to $ 270 million in 1979. In 1980 they jumped to $ 497 million. They reached another peak in 1989 at $ 570 million, when UNHCR experienced a considerable shortfall of funds and was forced to carry over a $ 40 million deficit into 1990. In 1991 UNHCR's expenditures rose to $ 863 million and in 1992 to $ 1,072 million.

The world refugee population has doubled between 1980 and 1992, from 8.5 million to 17 million. . . . It is evident that UNHCR's funding has not kept up with the growth in the refugee population.[7] Donor countries have become increasingly concerned about the high cost of keeping refugees in asylum for years and even decades, as well as about the mounting cost of currently ongoing humanitarian interventions when no end to these operations appears to be in sight (for example, in Bosnia as of spring 1993).[8]

UNRWA Palestinians are an important group of refugees which is outside UNHCR's mandate. Their special situation results from UN General Assembly Resolution 194 of 1948, which recognizes the right of Palestinian refugees to repatriation or compensation for their losses. Some two million out of an estimated total Palestinian population of six million persons are assisted in Syria, Jordan, Lebanon, the West Bank, and Gaza by the UN Relief and Works Agency for Palestine Refugees in the Near East (UNRWA), which was created in 1948 under a different name.[9] UNRWA's expenditure in 1990 was US$ 292.5 million (United Nations 1991b:34). It divides its assistance efforts primarily among education (over 65 percent), medical services, and welfare and relief services (United Nations 1991b:30–34). It has no protection mandate,[10] nor is it enjoined to search for durable solutions.

IOM Today the major international organization outside the UN system that specifically assists migrants and refugees is the International Organization for Migration (IOM). Created in 1951 and known until 1980 as the Intergovernmental Committee for European Migration (ICEM), its mandate has since been enlarged to serve migrant and refugee populations around the globe. Between 1980 and 1989 it was known as the Intergovernmental Committee for Migration (ICM). IOM's objective is "to ensure, throughout the world, the orderly migration of persons who are in need of international migration assistance" (International Organization for Migration 1993:1). To this end the organization performs the following functions, at the request of interested states and in coordination with international and nongovernmental organizations:

- the handling of orderly and planned migration of nationals, to meet specific needs of emigration and immigration countries;
- the transfer of qualified human resources to promote the economic, social and cultural advancement of the receiving countries;
- the organized transfer of refugees, displaced persons and other individuals compelled to leave their homeland; and
- the provision of technical assistance and advisory services.

IOM also provides "a forum to States and other partners to discuss experiences, exchange views, devise measures and promote cooperation and coordination of efforts on migration issues" (International Organization for Migration 1993:1).

In connection with the "organized transfer" of migrants and refugees, the organization is often called upon to provide language training, medical screening, and advisory services. With respect to migrants of unusual status and in unforeseen situations, such as the Asian workers leaving Kuwait and

Iraq in 1990–1991, IOM's flexible mandate allows it to respond quickly and effectively. With the end of the Cold War, IOM has been seeking to expand its membership and activities into Eastern Europe and the former Soviet Union. As of early 1993 it counted 49 member and 40 observer states (International Organization for Migration 1993:2, 6–7).

Nongovernmental Organizations (NGOs)

Historically, since before the establishment of an international refugee regime, nongovernmental organizations[11] have played an important role in aiding migrants and refugees. While they often initiate the assistance activities, NGOs must as a rule be formally invited by a country's government before they can begin to work. Today a considerable proportion of refugee assistance around the world is implemented by NGOs, on behalf of governments or of UNHCR. Other NGOs may not provide direct services to forced migrants but function as advocates for them before the sending, host and resettlement countries. Some organizations exist primarily to provide public education for issues pertaining to forced migration. The 1991 UNHCR Directory of NGOs listed 469 agencies from 78 countries with which UNHCR had established contacts. Most of these organizations were located in Europe, Canada, and the United States.

The NGO community concerned with refugees is extremely heterogeneous. Some organizations are secular, others have a religious affiliation. The organizations vary in the focus of their work (emergency assistance, development, refugee resettlement, advocacy, public education), in organizational structure, in size, and in their degree of experience. The rise of the world's refugee population in the 1980s created increased demand for services and a growth in NGO activity. Accompanying this expansion were a host of new challenges—organizational, political, and philosophical. Institutionally, agencies had to improve management systems to handle increased demand and maintain accountability.

It is difficult to measure the total contribution of NGOs to refugee assistance. Their resources include non-cash elements such as volunteers' time and in-kind contributions, which are difficult to quantify.[12] Some agencies classify refugee activities under development work. Many agencies receive some government funding to implement programs. In 1981–1982, the average contribution by the U.S. government to the total resources of the ten largest U.S. agencies involved in relief work was 64.5 percent, with a range from zero to 78 percent (Smith 1984:119).

Taken individually, NGO programs may seem small in comparison with refugees' total needs, but they constitute critical links in the network of assistance, protection, and the provision of durable solutions. NGOs are able to initiate pilot projects to test innovative designs, or they may target especially vulnerable groups. Having access to a large part of the refugee population, they can function as effective channels through which refugees can articulate their interests and concerns, and NGOs perform an important protection function.

Critics of NGOs sometimes point to a lack of coordination among agencies, inappropriate programming, nonprofessional staff and management techniques, hidden agendas (for example, proselytizing), and false advertising. Staff of some NGOs are themselves among the most vocal critics. Efforts to improve coordination have resulted in the creation of a number of umbrella groups, for example, the American Council for Voluntary International Action (InterAction) in the United States, which brings together 133 NGOs, some 45 of which are involved in refugee work (McCully 1992), the Canadian Council for Refugees, and the British Refugee Council. The International Council of Voluntary Agencies (ICVA) in Geneva has nearly 100 members from different countries. In the mid-1980s an InterAction working group undertook a two-year dialogue on the principles and practice of providing humanitarian assistance in conflict situations (Minear 1988).

■ Summary

Contrary to the expectations of the creators of the international refugee regime, the problem of forced migration has not proven to be temporary. Driven by the changing nature of refugee flows, improved understanding of the challenges of providing protection and assistance to different refugee populations, and increased sensitivity to specific concerns, the international refugee network has been continuously evolving since 1951. Today few practitioners would argue that the system is perfect, and most would acknowledge a need for certain changes while recognizing that many positive elements should be retained. . . .

■ Notes

1. Note that by contrast, Article 33, concerning *non-refoulement*, refers to the life or freedom of a refugee being threatened for one or more of five reasons, without mentioning the subjective element of a well-founded fear of persecution. A parallel distinction can be found in several national laws, including the U.S. Refugee Act of 1980.

2. The Declaration's signatories are Belize, Colombia, Costa Rica, El Salvador, Guatemala, Honduras, Mexico, Nicaragua, Panama, and Venezuela.

3. The "good offices" mechanism was first utilized in 1957 to assist persons in Hong Kong fleeing mainland China. The General Assembly also employed it for Algerians and Angolans (Goodwin-Gill 1983:7).

4. States that have written the 1951 Convention definition into their national law have encountered a similar need for parallel mechanisms. For example, asylum seekers who do not qualify for refugee status under the narrower definition may still be accepted for humanitarian reasons. A variety of statuses have been devised for such groups.

5. For example, although the United States (not a signatory to the 1951 Convention) acceded to the Protocol in 1968, the definition of refugee used in its national legislation did not conform to that embodied in the Protocol until the passage of the U.S. Refugee Act in 1980. Before 1980, refugee status in U.S. law had been restricted to persons fleeing the general area of the Middle East or a communist country. In 1980 the politically neutral definition of the Protocol was adopted, but at the same time it was expanded to include under exceptional circumstances also persons who are still within their own countries.

6. The UN General Assembly must vote to renew UNHCR's mandate every five years.

7. Of course, these numbers tell only a small part of the story: average yearly expenditures per refugee differ considerably from region to region and even from country to country within the same region.

8. A *New York Times* article reports that [in 1993] "many of [UNHCR's] biggest emergency programs are seriously underfunded. Only $178 million has been raised for the most costly effort, the $420 million it plans to spend on feeding, clothing and caring for more than three million victims of fighting and 'ethnic cleansing' in Croatia and Bosnia" (Lewis 1993).

9. There may be hundreds of thousands of other Palestinians who should be able to claim refugee status, but UNRWA assists only registered refugees living in the areas contiguous to the state of Israel. Approximately one-third of the refugees live in camps (Copeland 1990:173).

10. However, the intifada has led to UNRWA's playing a protection role in recent years, as described by Schiff (1990).

11. Nongovernmental organizations are also referred to as "PVOs" (private voluntary organizations) or as "volags" (voluntary agencies), the latter term being used most frequently to refer to domestic resettlement agencies. They must obtain at least a portion of their resources from private contributions.

12. To our knowledge there has been no study that attempts to quantify the total NGO contribution to refugee assistance. Gorman (1984) estimated that in 1980 U.S. private voluntary agencies provided development assistance in excess of US$ 1,300 million, followed by German PVOs with US$ 420.7 million, British PVOs with US$ 104.7 million, and Canadian PVOs with US$ 102 million. Typically more than half of all disbursements came from government contributions.

■ References

Clark, Lance. 1992. Written communication from Mr. Clark, Officer for Displaced Persons, United Nations Development Programme, New York, New York, to Ms. Emily A. Copeland. May 13.

Clark, Lance. 1989. "Internal Refugees–The Hidden Half." In U.S. Committee for Refugees, *World Refugee Survey, 1988 in Review*. Washington, D.C.: U.S. Committee for Refugees, 18–24.

Goodwin-Gill, Guy S. 1983. *The Refugee in International Law*. Oxford: Clarendon Press.

Gordenker, Leon. 1987. *Refugees in International Politics*. London: Croom Helm.

Gorman, Robert, ed. 1984. *Private Voluntary Organizations as Agents of Development*. Boulder, Colorado: Westview Press.

International Organization for Migration. 1993. *IOM IN FACTS*. Geneva: International Organization for Migration.

Keely, Charles B. 1991. In U.S. Committee for Refugees, *World Refugee Survey, 1991*. Washington, D.C.: U.S. Committee for Refugees, 22–27.

Keely, Charles B. with Patricia J. Elwell. 1981. *Global Refugee Policy: The Case for a Development Oriented Strategy*. New York: The Population Council. Public Issues Paper.

League of Nations. 1933. "Resolution for the Establishment of a High Commissioner for Refugees Coming from Germany." *Official Journal*, Special Supplement, no. 115:89–90.

Lewis, Paul. 1993. "U.N. Refugee Official Seeks Pledges from Donors." *The New York Times*. June 20.

Lewis, Paul. 1991. "U.N. to Centralize Its Relief Efforts: Move Comes after Criticism for Lack of Humanitarian Aid." *The New York Times*. December 18.

Marrus, Michael R. 1985. *The Unwanted: European Refugees in the Twentieth Century*. Oxford: Oxford University Press.

McCully, Timothy. 1993. Telephone communication from Mr. McCully, Program Officer, InterAction, Washington, D.C., to Ms. Rosemarie Rogers. August 26.

McCully, Timothy. 1992. Telephone communication from Mr. McCully, Program Officer, InterAction, Washington, D.C., to Ms. Emily Copeland. January 17.

Minear, Larry. 1991. *Humanitarianism under Siege: A Critical Review of Operation Lifeline Sudan*. Trenton, New Jersey: The Red Sea Press, Inc.

Minear, Larry. 1988. *Helping People in an Age of Conflict: Toward a New Professionalism in U.S. Voluntary Humanitarian Assistance*. New York: InterAction.

Ogata, Sadako. 1992a. Commencement Address, The Fletcher School of Law and Diplomacy, Tufts University, Medford, Massachusetts. May 17.

Ogata, Sadako. 1992b. "Refugees: Challenge of the 1990s." Statement by Mrs. Sadako Ogata, New School of Social Research, New York, New York. November 11.

Ogata, Sadako. 1992c. "Refugees: A Comprehensive European Strategy." Statement by Mrs. Sadako Ogata, Peace Palace, The Hague. November 24.

Ogata, Sadako. 1992d. "Refugees: A Humanitarian Strategy." Statement by Mrs. Sadako Ogata, Royal Institute for International Relations, Brussels. November 25.

Schiff, Benjamin N. 1990. "Facing New Challenges: UNRWA and the *Intifada*." In *World Refugee Survey: 1989 in Review*, Washington, D.C.: U.S. Committee for Refugees, 25–29.

Smith, Brian H. 1984. "U.S. and Canadian PVOs as Transnational Development Institutions." In Robert Gorman, ed., *Private Voluntary Organizations as Agents of Development*. Boulder, Colorado: Westview Press, 115–164.

United Nations. 1991a. "Strengthening of the Coordination of Humanitarian Emergency Assistance of the United Nations." Forty-Sixth Session, Resolution 46/182 with amendment in L.55/Corr.1, A/46/L.55. New York, New York: United Nations. December 17.

United Nations. 1991b. "United Nations Relief and Works Agency for Palestine Refugees in the Near East: Audited Financial Statements for the Year Ended 31 December 1990 and Report of the Board of Auditors." Forty-Sixth Session, Supplement No. 5C, A/46/5/Add.3: 30-34. New York, New York: United Nations.

United Nations. 1989. "Declaration and Concerted Plan of Action in Favour of Central American Refugees, Returnees and Displaced Persons." International Conference on Central American Refugees. CIREFCA/89/14. New York, New York: United Nations. May 31. Mimeo.

United Nations. 1988. "Second International Conference on Assistance to Refugees in Africa." Resolution 107, 42nd Session, December 7, 1987. In *Resolutions and Decisions Adopted by the General Assembly during Its Forty-Second Session.* New York, New York: United Nations, Volume 1, 206–207.

United Nations. 1985. "Forward Looking Strategies for the Advancement of Women." Adopted at the World Conference to Appraise the Achievement of the UN Decade for Women: Equality, Development and Peace, Nairobi, Kenya.

United Nations High Commissioner for Refugees. 1993a. "Facing the Challenge in Nicaragua: Quick Impact Projects." Managua, Nicaragua: United Nations High Commissioner for Refugees. Text in Spanish, English and French.

United Nations High Commissioner for Refugees. 1993b. "Information Paper." Geneva: United Nations High Commissioner for Refugees. March.

United Nations High Commissioner for Refugees. 1993c. "Resettlement Statistics." Washington, D.C.: United Nations High Commissioner for Refugees. July 14. Mimeo.

United Nations High Commissioner for Refugees. 1992. "Assessment of Global Resettlement Needs for Refugees in 1993." Geneva: United Nations High Commissioner for Refugees. September.

United Nations High Commissioner for Refugees. 1991a. "Guidelines on the Protection of Refugee Women." Geneva: United Nations High Commissioner for Refugees. July.

United Nations High Commissioner for Refugees. 1991b. "Note on International Protection." Report submitted by the High Commissioner to the UN General Assembly. A/AC.96/777. New York, New York: United Nations. September 9.

United Nations High Commissioner for Refugees. 1991c. "UNHCR Activities Financed by Voluntary Funds: Report for 1990–1991 and Proposed Programmes and Budget for 1992." A/AC.96/774 (Part I–VI). New York, New York: United Nations. August 29.

United Nations High Commissioner for Refugees. 1990. "UNHCR Policy on Refugee Women." Reprinted for the UN General Assembly. A/AC.96/754. New York, New York: United Nations. August 20.

United Nations High Commissioner for Refugees. 1988. "Guidelines on Refugee Children." Geneva: United Nations High Commissioner for Refugees. August.

United Nations High Commissioner for Refugees. 1985. *A Selected and Annotated Bibliography on Refugee Women.* Geneva: United Nations High Commissioner for Refugees. Revised, September 1989.

United Nations High Commissioner for Refugees. 1979. *Collection of International Instruments Concerning Refugees.* Geneva: United Nations High Commissioner for Refugees.

United Nations High Commissioner for Refugees, Regional Bureau for Europe and North America. 1992. "Statistical Tables." Geneva: United Nations High Commissioner for Refugees. June. Mimeo.

U.S. Committee for Refugees. 1993. *World Refugee Survey, 1993.* Washington, D.C.: U.S. Committee for Refugees.

U.S. Committee for Refugees. 1992. *World Refugee Survey, 1992.* Washington, D.C.: U.S. Committee for Refugees.

U.S. Committee for Refugees. 1991. *World Refugee Survey, 1991.* Washington, D.C.: U.S. Committee for Refugees.

U.S. Committee for Refugees. 1989. *World Refugee Survey, 1988 in Review.* Washington, D.C.: U.S. Committee for Refugees.

Zolberg, Aristide, Astri Suhrke and Sergio Aguayo. 1989. *Escape from Violence: Conflict and the Refugee Crisis in the Developing World.* Oxford: Oxford University Press.

David P. Forsythe

The Palestine Question: Dealing with a Long-Term Refugee Situation

Some observers of world politics may think that what the world needs least is another essay on the Palestine question by a Westerner. Be that as it may, there is reason to review this important subject. For those who have not followed the situation closely, it is important to recall the different phases that the Palestine question, with the refugee situation at its core, has passed through.

It is useful to view the Palestine refugee situation since 1947 as falling into three phases. From 1947 to 1967, diplomacy emphasized the United Nations and was, after a very brief period, directed toward the resettlement of the refugees. From 1967 more or less, and certainly after 1974, diplomacy at the United Nations focused on some form of Palestinian self-determination rather than resettlement. From 1979 to the present, Egypt, Israel, and the United States sought a breakthrough on the Palestinian question outside formal U.N. bodies through the Camp David agreement and its endorsement of Palestinian autonomy.

These phases indicate the political bankruptcy of refugee resettlement and the new consensus on recognizing in some way a Palestinian entity. Hence the refugee problem has become a problem of how to implement a people's collective right to an adequate say in determining their own future.

■ The First Phase: 1947–67

The original number of non-Jewish refugees from the first Arab-Israeli war of 1947–48 has never been authoritatively established. The range of most claims is from 500,000 to 900,000. The first U.N. survey of the problem put the figure at 711,000, but that survey did not end the controversy.[1] There has also been much acrimonious debate about the cause of the refugee problem, with many Arabs saying it was Jewish terrorism, and many Jews saying it was Arab policy, that caused the flight. Arguments over these specifics are important, but they are dwarfed by the political symbolism of the Palestinian refugees.

David P. Forsythe, "The Palestine Question: Dealing with a Long-Term Refugee Situation," *Annals of the American Academy of Political and Social Science* 467 (May 1983): 89–101.

The Palestine refugees represented from the start the key element in any attempt either to resist the establishment of a Jewish state or to construct a Palestinian state in the future. If the refugees were resettled, repatriated, or otherwise assimilated into the states of the Middle East, it would be immensely more difficult if not impossible to mount an effective effort either to contest the legitimacy of Israel or to create a new Palestine out of the Arab disaster of 1947–48. From this point of view, the exact number of original refugees does not matter.[2] They had importance as the symbolic key to future options.

From 1948, therefore, while some Palestinians found jobs and even citizenship in other Arab states, there remained a refugee problem numbering in the tens of thousands. Since the new state of Israel was supported by all of the great powers including the Soviet Union, and since these states dominated the United Nations, the main thrust of U.N. diplomacy was to get the refugees resettled in Arab states, while providing limited repatriation and a temporary relief effort. It is only slight oversimplification to say that the first phase of the refugee problem was dominated by this clash between U.N. efforts at resettlement and Arab resistance.[3]

In the autumn of 1948, the UN General Assembly adopted Resolution 194 by a vote of 40-7-4. This resolution and its famous paragraph 11 concerning the refugees became the starting point for diplomacy on the Palestine question. Paragraph 11 reads in part:

> Resolves that the refugees wishing to return to their homes and live at peace with their neighbors should be permitted to do so at the earliest practicable date, and that compensation should be paid for the property of those choosing not to return and for loss of or damage to property which, under principles of international law or in equity, should be made good by the Governments or authorities responsible.
>
> *Instructs* the Conciliation Commission to facilitate the repatriation, resettlement and economic and social rehabilitation of the refugees and the payment of compensation.[4]

This paragraph has been endorsed repeatedly by large majorities including all major powers at the General Assembly. Consequently it has become one of those U.N. norms that have special status. It may have entered into customary international law. Legal questions aside, over time paragraph 11 has apparently recorded special expectations about compliance.[5]

Under the terms of A/RES/194, a Conciliation Commission for Palestine (CCP) was created, composed of France, Turkey, and the United States, to facilitate a solution to the refugee question and hence to end the *raison d'etre* for the ad hoc program of relief extant at that time. The CCP sought to assimilate the refugees primarily through resettlement in Arab states but also through some repatriation to Israel. The Arab states directly involved—Egypt, Jordan, Lebanon, Syria—conducted secret bilateral talks with Israel on this and other issues. But no agreement was reached through either these private discussions or the formal deliberations sponsored by the CCP.[6]

By the autumn of 1949, it was clear that the refugee situation would not be eliminated quickly, so the General Assembly created the U.N. Relief and Works Agency (UNRWA) in order to improve assistance to the refugees. According to A/RES/302 creating UNRWA, "Continued assistance for the relief of the Palestine refugees is necessary to prevent conditions of starvation and distress among them."[7] But especially the United States, the most powerful actor involved in the question, was still thinking in terms of resettlement. Even in A/RES/302 there were diplomatic code words indicating a desire for something beyond relief: "Constructive measures should be undertaken at an early date with a view to the termination of international assistance for relief."[8] More clearly, one can find in the wording of the U.N. Economic Survey Mission's interim report in the autumn of 1949, the Clapp report, a coded emphasis on resettlement. In the view of this mission, dominated by the United States, the United Nations should "increase the practical alternatives available to refugees, and thereby encourage a more realistic view of the kind of future they want and the kind they can achieve."[9]

It is historically interesting that in the continuing efforts of the CCP, there was apparently some diplomatic movement on the refugee situation in 1951. Israel, at the prodding of the CCP, offered to repatriate 100,000 refugees. At the same time Jordan and Syria agreed in principle to resettle some of those remaining. Egypt seemed to suggest that it might consider some resettlement if territorial concessions were made in its favor. Whether these positions reflected real flexibility or only diplomatic posturing is not so clear. The decision had already been made in Washington to give up on direct diplomacy; the solution to the refugee problem would thenceforth be sought through de facto resettlement via UNRWA programs. Therefore, the United States made no concerted effort to follow up on the positions indicated to the CCP, the CCP itself threw in the towel concerning a negotiated settlement, and the subsequent history of the Palestine question developed into the prolonged struggle that we know.[10]

With the CCP on the back burner, the dialectic of Western and Arab views was played out for a time in UNRWA. As early as 1950, the United Nations was advertising that "Relief Works Project Aims to Solve Middle East Refugee Problem."[11] Since it was true that certain UNRWA programs directed toward getting the refugees to work and providing them with skills were designed to get them resettled in Arab states, there were Arab protests and demonstrations against this approach.

Despite these Arab views, the West continued to push slightly disguised resettlement programs through UNRWA. The Blandford Plan sought to promote economic development and especially improved water management in Arab states, in the hope that the refugees would be sucked into the vortex of economic growth. It did not happen. Increasingly in the 1950s and 1960s, UNRWA shifted as much funding as it could from relief to education and vocational training. One of the motivations for this was again to make refugees as attractive as possible to Arab societies and economies. Even though education became the largest item in UNRWA's budget, amounting to over 40 percent, and even though college scholarships and other financial assistance were provided, resettlement never affected a politically significant portion of refugees.

Superficially it seemed Arab views lacked effective power. Israel was powerful, was convinced that the solution to the refugee situation should be found through resettlement in Arab lands, and developed many arguments as to why repatriation should be rejected in principle and practice as a major solution. These views were articulated so firmly and were backed by such political power that when the Kennedy administration toyed with the idea of seeking some movement on the refugee problem in the 1960s, it got nowhere. The U.N. representative, Joseph E. Johnson, was appointed at U.S. initiative, and he did make soundings in the Middle East. But when it became clear that no change could be achieved without a major U.S. involvement in support of Johnson, the U.S. backed off and Johnson resigned.[12]

This indicated in microcosm the nature of American foreign policy toward the refugees from the early 1950s to 1967. The United States essentially drifted with the status quo, paying approximately 60 percent of UNRWA's voluntary budget, but without the commitment or power to thrust resettlement on the Arab world. Its priorities were otherwise, the refugees did not seem to be an immediate political problem, and so the refugee situation dragged on. Nothing much was changed by the 1956 Suez crisis. By the late 1960s, there were about 1.3 million refugees registered with UNRWA, over 500,000 of whom lived in UNRWA camps.

Because neither Israel nor the United States had the power to compel resettlement, the Palestinians and the Arab states were successful in resisting it. It was factually difficult to resettle unskilled workers in the Arab economies.[13] While the Arab states had discussed resettlement and repatriation with Israel and the CCP, increasingly the Arab states did not believe that Israel was offering enough for them to make the painful choice to foreclose the option of resisting Israel or of creating a Palestinian state. Regardless of how much an Arab state's specific national interests might differ from the interests of the Palestinians, each Arab state opposed resettlement. Each Arab state sought to blend its general nationalism with Palestinian nationalism, the better to win broad support in the Arab world. Moreover, every sampling of refugee attitudes showed that the refugees wanted something besides resettlement.[14]

Refugee attitudes were primarily produced by refugee experience and political socialization in the Arab host states. But they were in part the product of UNRWA education. One of the effects of that education was entirely counter to the idea of resettlement, for the schools reaffirmed and strengthened Palestinian nationalism. The overall process has been concisely and candidly described by an UNRWA official:

> One of the byproducts of the UNRWA/UNESCO education programme has been its contribution towards the preservation of the Palestinian refugees' identity with the Palestine culture and within the wider context of Arab culture. This is partly because so many of them have been able to attend schools in which almost all the children are Palestine refugees and virtually all of the teachers are also Palestinians.[15]

Thus the UNRWA decision—compelled by the host state—to use Palestinian teachers and to use textbooks and other materials approved by the respective host state contributed to the sentiment in the Arab world against resettlement. Some might even say that high UNRWA officials were coopted over time into a pro-Palestinian or pro-Arab point of view.[16]

In sum, a superficially weak Arab position was able to triumph over an apparently stronger Israeli and Western one. Control of UNRWA programs was crucial. Assistance had to be continued, resettlement blocked, and education made supportive of Palestinian and Arab views. On all counts Arab policies were successful, in part because of the commitment of the Arab host states, in part because Israel did not make concessions judged acceptable by the Arab states, and in part because the West felt a moral obligation to assist the refugees.

During this first phase, host state commitment to the Palestinians and the national interests of those states coexisted in uneasy alliance. Yasir Arafat was politically active, and Al-Fatah existed in the 1950s. The Palestine Liberation Organization (PLO) was created in 1964, and Palestinian military raids into Israel occurred with some regularity in the mid-1960s. But Palestinian politicians and organizations were carefully controlled by the various Arab states, especially Egypt. The PLO was originally an Egyptian invention, its headquarters were in Cairo, and its first head, Ahmad Shuquairy, spoke out or was silent in junction with Egyptian foreign policy.[17]

Things were to change after the 1967 war.

Palestinian people and their just requirements," years of bargaining after the framework was accepted indicated that Egypt and Israel differed as to what these words implied. If Israel had accepted the Palestinians as a people and hence entitled to certain temporary arrangements pending the final determination of their future, nevertheless it was clear in the early 1980s that Israel was not prepared to go as far as Egypt—much less other parties—wanted.[31] The Palestinians lacked enough power to compel Israel to make concessions.

As the first part of the Camp David framework was being completed in 1982 and the Sinai was turned over to Egypt, it was most unclear what could be achieved according to the second part. The Begin government continued to settle Israelis in the West Bank area in a policy condemned by most of the world. With increasing numbers of ultranationalist and ultra-religious Jews in that territory, it seemed more and more unlikely that any Israeli government would have room to maneuver on the future disposition of the area; settlements had started under Labour governments. For this and other reasons, the PLO and other so-called radicals kept up their opposition to both Israeli policies and the Camp David framework. So-called moderates like Jordan and Saudi Arabia also refused to participate in negotiations under the Camp David umbrella. But the Saudi peace plan of 1981 was rejected by Israel.

In the meantime, UNRWA continued its holding operation as best it could. UNRWA's 1981 budget was in the neighborhood of $160 million, which was about $70 million short of what the agency said it needed to maintain existing programs for the 1.8 million refugees registered— 650,000 of whom still lived in camps. Of the $104 million pledged to UNRWA, $62 million came from the United States. By 1982 the United States had contributed almost $1 billion to UNRWA. Resettlement was of course a dead letter; education was still the main focus with almost 320,000 students in schools and vocational training. As UNRWA reported blandly in 1981, "The situation today was totally different from that in which UNRWA was originally established."[32]

■ Conclusion

In 1981 the U.S. spokesman in the General Assembly addressed the Palestine question by saying that the United States regarded UNRWA as an "interim solution" to the refugee problem.[33] He was essentially correct, despite the fact that the agency had been created 32 years previously. No one looked to UNRWA as a source of solutions for the refugee dilemma, or to the CCP, which led a shadowy existence on the extreme margins of diplomatic life. The latter was kept alive by some who wished to protect A/Res/194 and its paragraph 11 on repatriation and compensation, the resolution that also created the CCP, and by some who wished to avoid blaming U.N. agencies for the deficiencies of governmental policies.

Diplomacy through the United Nations had helped transform the Palestine question and its central refugee problem into a self-determination problem. U.N. resolutions recorded sentiment and thereby created a framework for diplomacy. But because the majority at the United Nations was so antagonistic to Israel's policies if not to its existence, Israel, the United States, and finally Egypt decided to proceed outside U.N. bodies. While A/RES/194 and S/RES/242, inter alia, have importance, the future of the Palestinian dilemma is more likely to be affected by foreign policies than by institutional arrangements.

The various Palestinian fighting units and especially Al-Fatah, which greatly influenced the umbrella PLO, had employed violence to get their cause noticed in the power centers of the world. Having done so, pressures accumulated for the PLO to prove its responsibility by controlling and moderating its violence—that is, to appear as a responsible entity worthy to represent Palestinian interests, rather than as a gang of terrorists. Some observers, like Walid Khalidi, find this moderation to have occurred: "The Palestine National Council (PNC), highest PLO authority, has met 12 times since the adoption of the present Covenant in 1968. If the resolutions adopted by successive PNCs are read in sequence, a movement away from maximalism and in the direction of accommodation is unmistakable."[34]

But Israel was not convinced that the PLO, or states like Syria and Libya, had given up their maximalist objectives for the liberation of all of Palestine and were prepared to live in peace with the state of Israel. They had not accepted S/RES/242 and its norm about recognizing the political independence and territorial integrity of states in the Middle East, and they had not explicitly repudiated the PLO-revised Covenant, which called for the violent elimination of the state of Israel.

It is possible that Yasir Arafat told the *New York Times'* Anthony Lewis that Arafat would accept a Palestinian state just in the West Bank and Gaza.[35] But to many in Israel, it remains a question whether this would be a final or dangerous intermediate solution. Indeed, if one looks at the writings of a moderate member of the Palestine National Council, Edward W. Said, there may be as many questions as answers. In passages from *The Question of Palestine,* Said suggests that the dominant faction of the PLO has come to accept a state in part of Old Palestine.[36] At other places, however, Said seems to imply that Israel will ultimately be replaced by a democratic, secular state called Palestine, which is of course the main plank in the platform of the PLO. He writes that "Palestine would become the site of two societies existing together,"[37] and later that "two things are certain: the Jews of Israel will remain; the Palestinians will also remain."[38] He does not say the Israelis will remain, only the Jews of Israel.

Because of such ambiguities in the context of mutual antagonism and fear, it is difficult to be certain about the future of the Palestine question. Refugees continue to exist—frustrated, bitter, politicized, prone to violence. Israel continues to fear for its security, led at times by a Likud government perhaps bent not only on annexing Jerusalem and the Golan Heights but also on permanently controlling a renewed biblical Israel stretching across the West Bank. This seems a sure formula for further violence and misery in an area of the world that has known much of both. If annexations and settlements continue, it is unlikely that Mubarak's Egypt can long pursue a policy of accommodation, especially once it has regained the Sinai. Moreover in such a context, the more moderate Palestinians would also have great difficulty seeking accommodation. With options about the West Bank and Gaza effectively eliminated, they would probably see little choice but to pursue a policy of total confrontation.

In writing about the Palestinians, one always runs the risk of being behind fast-moving and unforeseen events. At the time of writing in early autumn 1982, the PLO had agreed to withdraw most of its armed forces from Lebanon under pressure of the Israel Defense Force. Subsequently Israel moved into West Beirut in the wake of the assassination of the Lebanese president. It was a particularly unsettled time, even by Middle Eastern standards. However, it seems to me that certain fundamentals of the Palestinians' situation remain unchanged.

The first of these fundamentals is that the Palestinian movement for self-determination continues unabated. Paradoxically, that political movement may have become stronger even as the Palestinian fighting forces were weakened by their dispersion to different countries. Israel's move into Lebanon and the Israeli destruction of some civilian lives and property led to increased empathy for the Palestinian plight. Also, in negotiating a peaceful departure, the PLO may have engaged the United States and others in pushing for real Palestinian autonomy in the West Bank. Statements by U.S. officials, in particular by President Reagan in a major speech on the Middle East,[39] seemed to suggest that the United States would not simply defer to Israeli policies but would rather insist on limits to Jewish settlements in the West Bank in order to preserve real autonomy for the Palestinians. Thus the PLO may have achieved more by leaving Beirut than by staying. In any event, the PLO's military setback did not end its Political activities.

The second of these fundamentals is that the Palestinian movement continues to have widespread support outside Israel. Upon leaving Beirut, Yasir Arafat was welcomed triumphantly in various Arab countries. He was also accorded an audience with the pope, as well as with Italian leaders. His inability to use Lebanese soil for attacks on Israel could turn into a political asset. Insofar as the PLO was led to renounce attacks on civilian targets in

Israel, it would find more acceptance in the West. It can be recalled that prior to the Israeli invasion of Lebanon, the PLO did not rocket Israel as long as Israeli planes did not fly over Beirut. Certainly the September 1982 Arab summit meeting in Fez, Morocco, showed no lessened support for Arafat and the PLO. And the Reagan administration showed at least a willingness to differ publicly with Israel on matters affecting the Palestinians. Hence the Palestinians maintained, and perhaps even increased, their backing—despite the fact that material assistance to them during the siege of Beirut was virtually nonexistent.

One could probably speculate endlessly on the future of the Palestine question. Would the Americans move finally to recognize the right of self-determination rather than just the right to a homeland and to local autonomy? What would the relationship be between Hussein of Jordan and the PLO under any scheme of federation cum autonomy? Had Israel politically weakened itself by invading Lebanon and Beirut, and by being involved at least indirectly in massacres of Palestinians after its troops entered West Beirut? In the final analysis, however, it was clear that the quest for Palestinian self-determination would continue, and that there was no turning back to trying to settle simply a refugee problem.

■ Notes

1. U.N. Doc. A/AC.24/3 (1949), p. 2.
2. It is, however, important to understand why Palestinian nationalism is felt so deeply and supported so widely. There seems general agreement that at the time of the creation of the state of Israel, the Jewish population in Palestine was about one-third of the total inhabitants. Jewish ownership of land apparently never exceeded 7 percent of Palestine. By such standards, Palestine was Arab, whatever international documents such as the U.N. partition resolution might say.
3. See David P. Forsythe, "UNRWA, the Palestine Refugees, and World Politics: 1949–1969," *International Organization,* 23(1):26–45 (Winter 1969). See also Edward H. Buehrig, *The UN and the Palestine Refugees* (Bloomington: Indiana University Press, 1971).
4. U.N. Doc. A/RES/194 (11 Dec. 1948), par. 11.
5. The process by which U.N. recommendations may become legally binding, or may become authoritative guides to what is binding, is discussed in Louis Henkin et al., *International Law: Cases and Materials* (St. Paul, MN: West, 1980), pp. 91–113. See also Kurt Rene Radley, "The Palestine Refugees: The Right to Return in International Law," *American Journal of International Law,* 72(3): 586–614 (July 1978).
6. David P. Forsythe, *United Nations Peacemaking: The Conciliation Commission for Palestine* (Baltimore: Johns Hopkins University Press, 1972), ch. 2. See also Pablo de Azcarate, *Mission in Palestine 1948–1952* (Washington, DC: Middle East Institute, 1966).
7. U.N. Doc. A/RES/302 (8 Dec. 1949), par. 5.
8. Ibid.
9. U.N. Doc. A/1106, p. 19.

10. Forsythe, *United Nations Peacemaking*, ch. 3.

11. *United Nations Bulletin,* 8(10):443 (Oct. 1950). For a discussion of the structure of UNRWA, see Buehrig, *The UN.*

12. Forsythe, *United Nations Peacemaking*, ch. 5.

13. This point is stressed by a former commissioner-general of UNRWA, John H. Davis, in *The Evasive Peace* (London: John Murray, 1968).

14. See Forsythe, "UNRWA and World Politics," p. 51; and Shaul Mishal, *West Bank/East Bank: The Palestinians in Jordan, 1949–1967* (New Haven, CT: Yale University Press, 1978), pp. 28–30.

15. George Dickerson, "Education for the Palestine Refugees: The UNRWA/ UNESCO Programme," *Journal of Palestine Studies,* 1(3): 128 (1974).

16. See, for example, Davis, *Evasive Peace.* See also Amos Perlmutter, "Patrons in the Babylonian Captivity of Clients: UNRWA and World Politics," *International Organization,* 25(2):306–8 (Spring 1971). For an excellent analysis of the political socialization that occurred in Jordan through the Baath socialist party and its impact on UNRWA teachers, see Mishal, *West Bank/East Bank.*

17. William B. Quandt et al., *The Politics of Palestinian Nationalism* (Berkeley: University of California Press, 1973), esp. p. 50.

18. U.N. Doc. S/RES/1242 (22 Nov. 1967), par. 2(b).

19. See the useful compilation of quotations in Congressional Quarterly Inc., *The Middle East,* 5th ed. (Washington, DC: Congressional Quarterly, 1981).

20. Quandt et al., *Politics of Palestinian Nationalism,* note that because of divisions within the Palestinian movement and its need for support from Arab states, Palestinian power may be able to block an undesired peace but not to make a desired one. See also William B. Quandt, *Decade of Decisions* (Berkeley: University of California Press, 1977), esp. pp. 298–99.

21. Quoted in Congressional Quarterly Inc., *The Middle East.* 4th ed. (Washington, DC: Congressional Quarterly, July 1979), p. 202.

22. U.N. Doc. A/RES/3236 (22 Nov. 1974), par. 1.

23. Mohammed K. Shadid, *The United States and the Palestinians* (New York: St. Martin's Press, 1981), p. 89. See also Quandt, *Decade,* esp. p. 257.

24. Brookings Institution, *Toward Peace in the Middle East: Report of a Study Group* (Washington, DC: Brookings, 1975).

25. Yitzhak Rabin, "On the Palestinian Problem," in *The Palestinians,* eds. Michael Curtis et al. (New Brunswick, NJ: Transaction Books, 1975), pp. 175–80. A number of Jewish circles continued to view "the Palestinians" as an artificial creation, nonexistent in history and simply a type of Jordanian national.

26. Congressional Quarterly, *The Middle East,* 5th ed.

27. The relevant documents are collected in Walter Laqueur, *The Israel-Arab Reader* (New York: Bantam Books, 1970).

28. Quandt et al., *Politics of Palestinian Nationalism,* p. 149. See also John W. Amos, *Palestinian Resistance: Organization of a National Movement* (Elmsford, NY: Pergamon Press, 1981).

29. *U.N. Chronicle,* 28(2): 10 (Feb. 1980).

30. Hermann Frederick Eilts, "Improve the Framework," *Foreign Policy,* 41:3–20 (Winter 1981).

31. For a detailed review of negotiations, see John C. Campbell, "The Middle East: A House of Containment Built on Shifting Sands," *Foreign Affairs,* 60(3):593–628 (1981). For an optimistic assessment of trends, see John Edwin Meoz, *Beyond Security* (Elmsford, NY: Pergamon Press, 1981).

32. *U.N. Chronicle,* 28(2):13 (Jan. 1981).

33. U.S. Mission to the United Nations, Press 32. *U.N. Chronicle,* 28(2): 13 (Jan. 1981). Release 142(81): 1 (3 Dec. 1981).

34. "Regiopolitics: Toward a U.S. Policy on the Palestine Problem," *Foreign Affairs,* 59(5): 1060 (Summer 1981).

35. Shadid, *United States,* p. 109, n. 72.

36. Edward W. Said, *The Question of Palestine* (New York: Vintage, 1979), esp. pp. 224, 226.

37. Ibid., p. 233.

38. Ibid., p. 235.

39. *New York Times,* 2 Sept. 1982, p. 9.

part 3

Policymaking and Politics

market and their country's traditional ties to Sweden. In contrast to the Irish, however, a large number of Finnish immigrants have considerable language difficulties after arrival, and in this respect they resemble the immigrant groups in Sweden that have more distant origins. . . .

More than three fourths of the foreign citizens in the immigration countries live in France, Germany, and Britain. Each of these countries has approximately four million resident immigrants, although the statistics are difficult to compare and in some cases are rather unreliable. Except for Liechtenstein and Luxemburg, Switzerland has the highest percentage of foreign citizens in its population (14.5 percent in 1982). If one compares statistics on the percentage of foreign workers in the project countries, they are about the same as the percentage of foreign residents (see Table 7.2.1).

These figures do not reveal that immigrants in Western Europe represent a great number of different nationalities, nor do they show how immigrants with the same nationality often settle in the same country and even the same region. Spanish and Portuguese immigrants have gone mainly to France, and to a lesser extent to Switzerland. Yugoslavs and Turks have gone mainly to Germany. Italians are an older immigrant group and have settled primarily in Switzerland and to a lesser extent in Germany and France. Immigrants from North Africa have gone to France and later to the Netherlands as well, although the bulk of immigration to the latter country has come from its former colonies in Asia and Latin America. The same is true for Britain, where almost all postwar immigration has come from former colonies in the West Indies and from India and Pakistan. The majority

Table 7.2.1   Foreign citizens residing in the European project countries in 1983 (thousands)

	All Residents		Labor Force	
	Foreign citizens	Percent of total	Foreign citizens	Percent of total
Sweden	405.5	4.9	227.7	5.2
Netherlands[1]	543.6	3.7	208.4	3.7
France[1]	4,459.0	7.2	1,436.4	6.3
Great Britain[2]	1,705.0	3.1	931.0	3.8
West Germany	4,666.9	7.6	2,037.6	9.2
Switzerland[3]	925.8	14.5	647.9	21.9

Source: OECD, *Continuous Reporting System on Migration,* SOPEMI 1983, for all countries except Great Britain.

Notes: 1. Data from 1982, and for labor force in France 1981. Based on number of residence and work permits, and therefore an overestimate of the size of the foreign population.

2. Data from 1981, Labour Force Survey.

3. Yearly average. Seasonal workers (13,400) and frontier workers (108,400) are included.

of immigration to Sweden has come from Finland and from the other Nordic countries, although there has also been a significant inflow of immigrants from Yugoslavia, Greece, and Turkey.

There are a number of possible explanations for the distribution of nationalities among the receiving countries. In many cases bilateral agreements and recruitment practices based on such agreements have led to concentrations of certain nationalities, for example, Turks and Yugoslavs in Germany or Moroccans in the Netherlands. Geographical proximity between sending and receiving countries has often had a similar effect, particularly when accompanied by a history of close relations. Geographical distance has sometimes reduced the potential for certain kinds of immigration. Since Britain and Sweden are located somewhat on the periphery of continental European migration, they have not received as many immigrants from Southern Europe and Turkey. Ex-colonies and countries with whom they have historically had close contact have provided much of the immigration to France, the Netherlands, and especially Britain. Finally, the distribution of immigrants by nationality can also be explained by "chain migration," which occurs when an initial group of immigrants settles in a country and then, by encouraging others in their home country or by providing a model for them, attract others of the same nationality to a particular receiving country.

The sources of migration to Europe have progressively moved to areas farther and farther away. While immigration from Southern Europe, initially quite extensive, has decreased in recent years, immigration from Africa, Asia, and especially the Near East has increased. The change in the sources of immigration has meant that many of the new minority groups are more highly visible, as they differ more in culture and tradition from indigenous European population than did the so-called "traditional" immigrant groups of the past. There are indications that this newer long-distance immigration will continue and increase in the future.

An important change in immigration policy occurred during the period from 1970 to 1974. For economic and other reasons the immigration countries of Western Europe heavily restricted or usually stopped recruiting foreign labor, and since then only refugees and the relatives of resident aliens are admitted. Policymakers have now come to realize, to their surprise, that many foreign workers are likely to remain as permanent residents.

This change in immigration policy, which we will call the "turning point," was the first clear break with the relatively open and unrestricted policies of the previous two decades. The change was declared in Switzerland (1970), Sweden (1972), Germany (1973), and France (1974). Though it was made with the consent of each national government, it was made without open political debate and without any formal, official decisions. It is important to note that this turning point should be thought of as a policy change towards stricter regulation but not necessarily as a "stop" for labor migration.

In Britain and the Netherlands, where most immigrants came from colonies or former colonies and usually held the citizenship of the mother country, the turning point in immigration policy did not occur at a specific time but came gradually. In Britain this process has involved the gradual elimination of the immigration rights of colonial citizens. Though this process began there in 1962 and has not yet ended, one can nevertheless say that the passage of the 1971 Immigration Act was perhaps the most significant legislation in this area. In the Netherlands there was a major reevaluation of immigration policy at the end of the 1970s. The number of new work permits issued fell sharply in 1973, but labor immigration was never formally "stopped." Not until 1980 did the government impose serious restrictions on post-colonial immigration and begin to develop a new immigrant policy.

Immigration to the six European project countries has changed during the past decade in other ways as well. While the number or single, male immigrants has decreased, mainly because of the policy change that occurred at the turning point, the immigration of refugees and the dependants of resident aliens has increased. In other words, the total amount of immigration to the project countries has not decreased substantially as a result of the "stop" in labor recruitment, but has remained constant or in some cases has actually increased. Thus, there is a relationship between the imposition of the "stop" and the change in the composition of immigrant population.

■ Immigration Policy

There are many definitions of immigration policy. They vary even within a single country. Yet when we compare a number of countries, we need a working definition that is relevant to all these countries. Thus, under our scheme, "immigration policy" will consist of two parts which are interrelated, yet distinct: (a) regulation of flows of immigration and control of aliens, and (b) immigrant policy.

Immigration Regulation and Aliens Control

Regulation of immigration is the oldest, the most obvious, and according to some people the only aspect of immigration policy. Immigration regulation refers to the rules and procedures governing the selection and admission of foreign citizens. It also includes such regulations which control foreign citizens (aliens) once they visit or take residence in the receiving country, including control of their employment. Deportation also falls under these regulations. Employers may be allowed to recruit foreign labor on their own, or labor transfer agreements may be entered into by the state and official information and recruitment bureaux be opened abroad. All this, of course, is a part of immigration regulation and must be included along with measures taken to restrict immigration or to stop it completely. The free movements of peoples, such as occur in the common labor markets of the EEC [European Economic Community] and Nordic areas, are also an aspect of immigration regulation; even though in these two cases policymakers have decided that certain kinds of immigration should *not* be regulated.

In general, all sovereign states reserve the right to determine whether foreign citizens will be permitted to enter their territory and reside there, and in all the project countries this power of the state is found in law or in administrative regulations. Most changes in immigration policy, for example the changes at what we call the "turning point," have been made by changing the application of existing aliens laws and not by changing the laws. Such laws were applied in a liberal way as long as immigration was encouraged, but later, when the goal was to limit the volume of immigration, discourage potential immigrants, and reduce the total number of foreigners in the country, the application of the same aliens laws became more strict. At the same time, however, immigration regulation was abandoned for certain groups of foreigners who were admitted without restrictions. Examples of this are, as already mentioned, the free circulation of labor in the EEC and the Nordic area and the acceptance on a permanent basis of political refugees.

Immigration regulation implies that foreign citizens remain under some kind of aliens control until they become naturalized citizens. The conditions that foreign citizens are subject to during this period of "controlled" residence vary greatly from country to country. Some countries at an early stage guarantee their foreign residents the right to remain permanently. Other countries keep them in a position of legal insecurity and uncertainty for many years. Some countries admit foreign workers for seasonal employment and require them to leave when the season ends, although they are often permitted to return again the following season. Some countries organize so-called "rotation" systems under which foreign workers are allowed to stay in the country only a maximum number of months or years, after which (in theory at least) they must depart to make room for new workers. In this way these countries hope to avoid the establishment of any new, permanent population groups whose needs and demands would be considerably greater than those of temporary "guestworkers."

Even in countries that do not apply seasonal employment or rotation systems, however, it often takes many years before foreign citizens are guaranteed that they will not be forced to leave the country against their will. By delaying "permanent status," immigration countries retain the legal right to repatriate foreign workers when desired, even those with many years of residence. The conditions attached to permanent status can thus function as a means of controlling the size or composition of immigration and must therefore also be included as a part of immigration regulation.

Compulsory repatriation of large groups of immigrants is rare. Nevertheless, it has long been a possibility which hangs over the heads of many of the foreign workers employed in Western Europe. Though seldom utilized, it nonetheless influences their living conditions and their attitudes towards residence in the host country.

Thus, the very existence of the possibility of compulsory repatriation is a factor in a country's immigrant policy. Immigration regulation may be said to foster a considerable degree of legal insecurity because decisions concerning permanent status are made by administrative authorities who have much discretion in interpreting such regulations. Such legal insecurity is made worse when foreign citizens have no right to appeal against the decisions of administrative authorities.

Immigrant Policy

Immigrant policy is the other part of immigration policy and refers to the conditions provided to resident immigrants. It comprises all issues that influence the condition of immigrants; for example, work and housing conditions, social benefits and social services, educational opportunities and language instruction, cultural amenities, leisure activities, voluntary associations, and opportunities to participate in trade union and political affairs. Immigrant policy may be either direct or indirect.

Immigrants have a number of special needs to begin with because they are different from the host population. They often speak a foreign language and represent a different culture. Immigrants also have special economic interests and ambitions for the future. All of this may sometimes prompt a country of immigration to devise special measures to improve the situation of its immigrants. Since these measures do not usually apply to the non-immigrant population, we will call them "direct" immigrant policy.

Like the non-immigrant population, immigrants are also affected by a country's general public policy, which involves economic, social, political, and other measures. These measures are not designed with only immigrants in mind; instead, they are intended to apply to all inhabitants of a country whether citizens or not. Yet they may not be applied to all inhabitants in the same way, i.e. there may be discrimination, both positive and negative, in the allocation of resources and opportunities. When general public policy affects immigrants substantially, we will talk about "indirect" immigrant policy.

Indirect immigrant policy can be termed "inequitable" or "discriminatory" when immigrants receive significantly less than others, and when they are denied opportunities to participate in society. Even when the distribution of benefits is perfectly equal, however, immigrants can still remain in an inferior position, primarily because they have recently made a new start in the host country and experience less favorable circumstances than the rest of the population. This situation can be ameliorated if immigrants are given greater benefits than other people, e.g. special language instruction, special cultural support, and so on. These measures are the tools of direct immigrant policy.

To summarize in outline form, immigration policy comprises:

1. Immigration regulation and aliens control
   (a) "strict" or "liberal" control of the admission and residence of foreign citizens
   (b) guarantees of "permanent status"; legal security versus vulnerability to arbitrary expulsion
2. Immigrant policy
   (a) indirect: immigrants' inclusion in the general allocation of benefits; "equal" versus "discriminatory" distribution
   (b) direct: special measures on behalf of immigrants; "affirmative action" and the removal of legal discrimination

Although we will in our analysis distinguish between these two parts of immigration policy, they are of course in practice at work simultaneously. What is very often not understood is the profound effect that they can have on one another. A system of rotation might, for example, leave most immigrants in a very weak legal position as residents. This may in turn impede integration and the full enjoyment of social and civil rights—both areas of concern to immigrant policy. Another example of the mutual influence between immigration regulation and immigrant policy would be when a country uses instruments of immigrant policy (e.g. housing applications, school registers, and so on) to identify and expel illegal immigrants, thus accomplishing a task of immigration regulation.

■ General Preconditions

Immigration policy should be analyzed in the context of a country's history, economy, geography, population, international relations, etc., for these are factors that affect immigration to a country, both quantitatively and qualitatively. Valid comparisons between the project countries are possible only when the general preconditions for the countries' immigration policies are analyzed.

Policymakers in each country may have tried to shape immigration policy on the basis of their own experience and their particular national needs, but the policies of all the project countries nevertheless have numerous features in common. Periods of passport exemption, rigid immigration control, and active recruitment of foreign workers have come at the same or almost the same time in every country. Thus, it seems that the shaping of immigration policy is determined in part by conditions beyond the control of policymakers in the individual countries. For example, two world wars have disrupted long-standing patterns of habitation and have forced people to flee their home countries. Economic disruptions, resulting either from the wars or from other causes, have been possibly even more unsettling than the wars themselves. The Great Depression in the 1930s affected the entire industrialized world and resulted in the widespread traumatic belief that future economic crises had to be avoided at all costs. During the following decades, Keynesian economic theory gradually provided new policy options, starting with active budget policies, which were applied to counter depressions. Of course, all countries have not been affected by war and economic crisis to the same degree, and partly because of this, there are significant differences in the immigration policies of the project countries. One might say that although they came from different parts, they are all sailing on the same heaving ocean, all exposed to the same fluctuations in weather, winds, and currents. Yet because they each set a different course and sail in a different kind of vessel, no two voyages are ever exactly alike. Similarly, no two countries' immigration policies are ever exactly alike, even though all countries are affected by and must contend with the same external conditions.

"General preconditions," as the term will be used here, are background conditions which, on the whole, remain stable for a considerable period of time and are not easily influenced or altered in the short term. For the general as well as attentive public, and also for policymakers, these conditions act as constraints on the possibilities for state action; in other words, they form a factual, concrete framework for immigration policy over a relatively long period of time.

■ Terminology

Two of the key concepts in this comparative study are immigrant and immigration. The term "immigrant" is sometimes used in the very broad sense of its root-word "migrant," a person who moves from one country to another. In common usage, however, the term "immigrant" has acquired the narrower meaning of "a person who migrates to a country with the intention of taking up permanent residence," something akin to the term "settler." The definition of immigrant that will be used in this book lies somewhere in between the broad sense of "migrant" and the narrow sense of "settler":

"Immigrant" is a person who migrates to a country and then actually resides there longer than a short period of time, i.e. for more than three months.

"Immigration" refers to the physical entrance of immigrants as here defined, either singly or as a group, into a country.

This definition thus excludes people that pay only a short visit to a country; for example, those who come on vacation or to visit relatives, or those who come on business trips or to do some specific job (a mechanic to install machinery for instance, or artists to give a performance), as long as their stay is for less than three months. On the other hand, "immigrant" does not only refer to those who plan from the beginning to stay permanently in a country. Thus, students, scholars, artists, and others who spend longer than three months as "guests" in a country are considered immigrants although they do not plan to stay permanently.

The decisive criterion is the actual length of time that a person resides in the country of immigration. People that intend to remain permanently, i.e. "settler" immigrants, are *not* included in the definition if they return home after only a couple of months; on the other hand, people that intend to remain only a couple of months but later change their mind and stay for several years are included. Obviously, the length of residence necessary for a person to be included in our definition of "immigrant" cannot be determined in any but an arbitrary fashion. Each project country allows most foreign citizens to take up residence for a limited period of time, usually three to six months, without requiring visas or residence permits, and for this reason we have set the residence criterion in our definition at three months.

Foreign citizens that remain in a country for longer than three months must usually obtain a residence permit; therefore, any foreign citizen who has such a permit is likely to become an immigrant, and is therefore considered such under our definition. But the definition also includes people who do not have residence permits, in particular illegal or "undocumented" aliens. In general, it is difficult to say with certainty that people are or are not immigrants when they arrive, although those who have applied for residence permits in advance are of course more likely to stay longer than those who have not. Under our definition, the criterion determining whether or not a foreign citizen should be considered an immigrant is if he or she stays in the country for longer than three months.

The terms "immigrant" and "immigration" are applied in a different manner in each project country, and their meanings have changed over time. The definition used here will for this reason cause more difficulties in some project countries than in others. There is an obvious relation between a country's immigration policy and its terminology. In Germany and

Switzerland immigrants are "foreign workers" (*ausländische Arbeitnehmer* in Germany and *Fremdarbeiter* in Switzerland) and they are controlled by "aliens bureaux" (*Ausländerbehörde*, or in Switzerland *Fremdenpolizei*). France has always used the terms *les immigrés* and *l'immigration*, and Sweden used similar terms (*invandrare* and *invandring*) in the 1960s when its new immigrant policy was launched. In Britain the term "immigrant" has been applied particularly to colored people, while in the Netherlands the new policy envisioned for immigrants is called a "minorities" policy.

The technical language used in each country is adjusted so that it best describes and explains the country's policy. Terminology also influences the way in which immigration policy is conceived and understood in each country; terms that should be instruments of description gradually become fixed concepts that limit flexibility and creativity. For this reason it is important that our comparative discussions use terms that are well defined.

. . .

7.3 *Sharon Stanton Russell*

Politics and Ideology in Policy Formulation: The Case of Kuwait[1]

. . . By the early 1980s, international migration for employment was estimated to involve close to 20 million people worldwide (Martin and
Richards, 1980: 4), with approximately four million migrants in the Middle
East alone (Choucri, 1983: Table 3-7). Yet, despite the magnitude of these
population movements and the fact that migration across international
boundaries invariably involves the intervention of government policies
concerning the movement and status of migrants, theoretical approaches to
international migration for employment seldom give central attention to the
role of such policies in shaping and directing the phenomenon.

With the exception of Marxist economists (*eg.* Portes 1981, Sassan-
Koob, 1980), economic approaches to international migration for employment have adopted the neoclassical economic model of internal migration
articulated by Harris and Todaro (1969; Harris and Todaro, 1970): specifically, that migration is a function of wage differentials between labor sending and receiving locations and the probability of finding employment in
the receiving location.[2] Extensions of this model have emphasized, variously, the characteristics of labor markets or of migrants, or (more recently)
the importance of migration as a risk-sharing arrangement among family
members (*cf.* Stark, Bloom, and Lucas, 1984, 1985). What all these
approaches have in common is their treatment of migration as a self-regu-
lating process which is the product of individual and household levels of
decision-making in interaction with market forces. What they do not
address is the role of government policies in mediating this process.[3]

The role of policies in migration has attracted greatest attention among
political scientists and sociologists. Weiner and Choucri have addressed
links between migration and ethnic conflicts, the structural causes and consequences of migration, and more recently the role of international migration in international relations.[4] Others have focused on the political activity
of migrants or the role of migration in bilateral relations (*eg.* Cornelius,
1976; Adler, 1975). In their work on European migration, Rogers and her

---

Sharon Stanton Russell, "Politics and Ideology in Policy Formulation: The Case of
Kuwait," *International Migration Review* 23, no. 1 (spring 1989): 24–47.

246

democracy had not been satisfied by the economic benefits conferred on their families by the Amir. Both groups within the Arab Nationalist Movement shared a commitment to the basic tenets of the regional movement: the unity of the Arab people, endorsement of Kuwait's involvement in regional issues, the free movement of Arab labor, and the extension of basic rights to resident Arabs. These views would quickly find expression in the National Assembly, established shortly after independence.

Partly in response to the emergence of the ANM, signs of a countervailing Kuwaiti nationalism had become evident by the early 1960s. This third emerging political faction found its strongest base of support among the al-Sabah family's traditional Bedouin supporters, many of whom were small business people, ordinary members of the labor force, police and defense workers, or lower-level civil servants, although members of the merchant elite and intellectuals were not absent from its ranks.[10] Kuwaiti Nationalists sought to preserve the traditional ideological bases of Kuwaiti identity: loyalty to the patriarchal leadership of the monarch and adherence to the principle that anyone who was not a member of one of the original tribes is an alien with no legitimate claims on the rights or prerogatives of tribal membership. . . .

The major policy actions toward migration taken during this first phase reflect the balance struck among these competing groups. Three bodies of law were enacted—The Aliens' Residence Law of 1959, the Nationality Law of the same year, and the Labor Law of 1964—which, together, constitute the framework for many of the future policy actions. In addition, the 1960 Law of Commercial Companies and Law No. 1 of 1962, creating the Ministry of the Interior and empowering it to enforce the Aliens' Residence Law, also had implications for migrants.

These measures reflect the four major policy objectives: First, they sought to assure the requisite economic growth by continuing to permit relatively free immigration of labor, an objective that would draw strong support from the merchant elite and both factions of the Arab Nationalists. Second, however, the policies sought to assure that government, and particularly the ruling family, maintained a measure of control of the entry, internal movement, rights and employment of aliens through a system of documentation (such as work and residence permits). Third, even in the enactment of these controls, Kuwait sought to strengthen its traditional foreign policy strategy of neutrality and reciprocity with other states, by allowing waivers of visa entry requirements for citizens of friendly Arab countries. Fourth, in measures that accorded further special privileges to merchant elites and that also took cognizance of Kuwaiti Nationalist sentiment and deeply embedded cultural traditions, the government adopted what has remained their fundamental strategy for counterbalancing the decision to permit high rates of immigration: in what may be called a "differentiation strategy," they chose to distinguish sharply between Kuwaitis and non-Kuwaitis within the society. This strategy is reflected in the Nationality Law and its amendment (State of Kuwait, 1959b), which limit the prospects that migrants might become citizens among whom government would be obliged to distribute benefits.[11] The original law allowed for only 50 naturalizations per year. Arab applicants for naturalization were required to have resided in Kuwait for eight years following the promulgation of the law; the residency requirements for non-Arabs were 15 years. In 1960, the law was amended to require that Arabs have ten years of residency (Joukadar, 1980: 65).[12] Those who have rendered special service to the country, and children of a Kuwaiti mother by a foreign father (under certain conditions) were exempted from this ceiling. . . .

1965–1966: Transition

During the second phase in the evolution of Kuwait's migration policies, 1965–1966, the new state experienced a drop in government budget surplus, a reminder that financial resources were limited. . . . The census of 1965 showed the effects of previous immigration policies: the proportion of non-Kuwaitis increased to more than 50 percent of total population. By far the largest group among the immigrants were Jordanians and Palestinians, whose numbers had risen from 14,000 in 1957 (Abu-Lughod 1983: 241) to 78,000 by 1965 (State of Kuwait 1977: 25–26, 59).

Politically, the ruling family faced new challenges to its authority as the result of the growing strength within the National Assembly of the Arab Nationalist bloc, which had succeeded in forcing dissolution of a cabinet containing six merchants—a violation of the unwritten agreement that: merchant groups would confine themselves to the commercial sphere. The cabinet crisis shifted the locus of political opposition from the merchant elite to the National Assembly (Crystal 1986: 193ff), specifically to the progressive faction of the Arab Nationalists which enjoyed broad support among the Arab immigrant population. Changes to and extensions of the Nationality and Aliens' Residence Laws enacted during this period reflected these circumstances and were directed toward two specific objectives.

The first was to preempt any tendencies toward political activism on the part of migrants by solidifying government control over the entry and employment of aliens, but without limiting immigration per se—a move that would have alienated the merchants. Accordingly, Law 26 of 1965 amended the Aliens Residence Law to stiffen the deportation provisions. Furthermore, notwithstanding the fact that it was the Ministry of Social Affairs and Labour that had nominal responsibility for regulation of employment, it was the Ministry of Interior (the body most directly concerned with protecting the ruling family) that issued new regulations under the Aliens' Residence Law (Ministerial Order No. 10 of 1965) which not only tightened entry and exit procedures, but also specified the conditions under which migrants would be permitted to work. These changes placed the Ministry of Interior at the center of control over the migration process and gave government the tools to clamp down quickly on immigration if it should choose to do so.

The second objective was to bolster the dwindling size of the Kuwaiti citizenry in a manner that would help to build support among Kuwaiti Nationalists and not add to the ranks of Arab Nationalists. Accordingly, the Nationality Law was amended again with Law No. 70 of 1966 which allowed the Minister of Interior to grant citizenship to those who had been continuous residents since 1945 or before (Farah, *et al.*, 1980: 33). More importantly, however, in 1965, government expanded its program for mass naturalization of Bedouin who could trace their attachment to Kuwait through tribal lines (Zahir, 1985: 53). Traditionally pro-government, Bedouin were viewed as a major source of support for the ruling family.

1967–1973: Security, Restriction, and Rebalance
Beginning in 1967, there was yet another shift in the context of migration policy. Economic growth continued to be both sluggish and uneven. Demographically, the most salient event was the new inflow of Palestinians following the 1967 war; more pervasive changes would become evident as this phase of policy evolved. Politically, the number one task at hand was to control not only internal unrest but, increasingly, security incidents linked to regional conflicts, which included two Arab-Israeli wars and conflicts between the PLO and King Hussein in Jordan. The second, and related, political task was to strengthen the Kuwaiti Nationalist base of support and to weaken further the domestic Arab Nationalist opposition, which had become increasingly radicalized following the 1967 war.

The migration policy objectives of this period reflected these circumstances. Faced with a rising number of security incidents, the Ministry of Interior took steps to prevent the entry of dissidents and to tighten registration requirements by implementing the provisions which had been put in place during the previous phase. As a consequence, annual rates of growth in the immigrant population slowed considerably: from a high of over ten percent prior to 1965, to a low of two percent in the early 1970s.

The second major migration-related policy objective (linked to the desire to build Kuwaiti Nationalist support) was "Kuwaitization." Estimates based on official data suggest that nearly 90,000 people had been naturalized between 1961 and 1970, a figure that represents 26 percent of the total Kuwaiti population in the latter year (State of Kuwait 1972: Table 2; 1977b: 62, Table 54; author's calculations). Unofficial estimates run as high as 200,000 (Crystal, 1986: 198). The growth in the number of Kuwaiti citizens, together with slower rates of growth in the immigrant population had two effects: demographically, it preserved the proportionate balance between Kuwaitis and non-Kuwaitis at their 1965 levels of 48 percent Kuwaiti: 52 percent non-Kuwaiti; politically, it strengthened popular demands for granting greater preference to Kuwaitis. The Labor Law already gave Kuwaitis preference in employment. Kuwaitization was intended to go further: to increase Kuwaitis' share in the labor force, their rates of participation, and their occupational mobility, especially into so-called "productive" sectors of the economy. The implications of this policy for migrants (as well as for Kuwaitis) was significantly diffused, however, by the prevailing low level of skill among the Kuwaiti citizenry—only worsened by the program to naturalize Bedouin, a significant proportion of whom were illiterate and in no position to participate in Kuwaitization.

■ 1974–1977: Liberalization

The fourth phase in Kuwait's migration policy evolution, 1974–1977, was launched by the sharp rise in oil prices. Once control of the Kuwait Oil Company passed entirely into government hands (as it did in 1975), government expenditures, channeled largely through the private sector, soon began to generate increased labor demand, at the very time Kuwait was experiencing the lowest rates of growth in its immigrant population since the 1940s. Politically, in the face of an increasingly contentious National Assembly, the first priority was to enable use of Kuwait's rapid economic growth in a way that would help to build support not only among the merchant elite, but also among other segments of the population now beginning to find political voice. The second priority was to diffuse debate concentrated in the Assembly, where liberals squared off against conservatives on a number of issues, including the role of immigrants in Kuwait, particularly the extent to which migrants' concerns should be expressed in Kuwait's political processes.

Taken together, the economic, demographic and political factors all pointed toward the same objectives for migration policy: liberalize entry, and give priority to manpower, rather than security issues.

The first step toward these ends was enactment in 1974 of a resolution by the Council of Ministers (*i.e.* Cabinet) that moved responsibility for regulation of employment activities from Interior back to the Ministry of Social Affairs and Labour, the body whose direct relationship with employers made it most responsive to commercial interests. The fact that Interior acquiesced in this move suggests an underlying political calculation: given the prevailing circumstances, regime support could best be achieved by removing the manpower constraints on economic growth through new immigration, and then distributing the benefits of that growth to Kuwaitis through extension of already liberal social welfare policies.

As the Development Plan of 1976/77–1981/82 attests, the restrictive immigration policies of the previous phase "were reversed to permit a rapid growth of industries based on employment of foreign workers, including a large number of new immigrants" (al-Moosa and McLachlan, 1985:76). There were a number of economic and structural reasons which help to explain why many of these new immigrants were Asians, and drawn from a greater number of countries than before. Asian wage rates were significantly below those acceptable to workers from traditional Arab labor-sending countries, where ambitious development programs, coupled with continuing out-migration, created new manpower bottlenecks. Massive development projects in Kuwait and elsewhere in the Gulf were let on a turn-key basis to Asian contractors who brought with them laborers perceived by many to be more disciplined than their Arab counterparts. There has been considerable speculation that what became de facto diversification of sources of labor supply was indeed an explicit policy, adopted by Kuwait and other Gulf states for political reasons. While there is no available written evidence to substantiate this contention, such a strategy (particularly one entailing the entry of Asians) is verbally acknowledged and was consistent with the political desirability of diffusing what were largely expressions of Arab migrant's concerns by changing the composition of the immigrant population. The importance to government of diffusing such concerns is reflected in the role migration politics played in the dissolution of the National Assembly in 1976.[13] Evidence of a diversification strategy was also suggested by the fact that, over the decade of the 1970s, Jordanians and Palestinians were the only group that experienced reductions in rates of immigration across all sectors. In any case, between 1976 and 1977, the number of new entry permits for work more than doubled—from 24,380 to 58,357. Asians accounted for more than one-third of new entry permits in 1977 and more than one-half the following year (State of Kuwait 1977: 1, 52).

1978–1979: Consolidation and Regulation

The fifth period of policy evolution (1978–1979) was one of consolidation and transition. In the economic sphere, a mild recession in 1978 was followed by the second oil price rise in 1979. Rapid demographic growth, particularly among the Asian population, began to generate tensions between Arab and Asian migrants, and between Kuwaitis and Arab migrants, who felt dismayed at the growing distinctions made between themselves and their fellow-Arab Kuwaitis. Politically, however, there were two other issues more salient for migration formulation. The first was civil service reform; the second was to address the tensions between the need for labor market stability on the one hand, and growing concerns over settlement of migrants on the other.

Both tasks pointed to the need for policy actions to regulate the labor market. In 1978, Labour sought to restrict immigration of new workers in sectors with "redundancies" (State of Kuwait, 1978). To enhance stability (and thus productivity) by lowering turnover, workers were required to remain with their employers for at least one year, and the validity of residence permits was increased from two to five years. At the same time, to discourage settlement and lower social costs, new limits were imposed on entry of dependents and on access to social services. In 1979, for the first time in its history, The Ministry of Social Affairs and Labour issued a comprehensive set of regulations implementing the Private Sector Labour Law (State of Kuwait, 1979). While they facilitated migration when desired, they also sought to eliminate "unnecessary immigration" and to establish a complex network of provisions for restricting, as well as controlling the inflow.

1980–1983: Political and Cultural Security

In the sixth policy phase (1980–1983), the context of migration policy again shifted. In the economic sphere, the boom ended: by 1981, worldwide recession had started, with resulting declines in both oil prices and government revenues. In 1982, Kuwait's unofficial stock market, Suq al-Manakh, collapsed, leaving more than US $90 billion in claims and counterclaims.

Demographically, the census of 1980 presented Kuwaitis with a shock: since 1975, their proportion in the total population had dropped from 47 percent to 41.6 percent. Furthermore, the proportion of Asians in the total population had grown from 9.8 percent in 1975 to 15 percent in 1980, and they now comprised nearly 26 percent of non-Kuwaitis. The census also exploded the myth that Kuwait's migrants were "temporary" in any meaningful sense of the term. Nearly a third of all non-Kuwaitis had been resident for ten years or more; nearly 16 percent had been resident for 15 years or more (State of Kuwait 1985: 51, Table 36). Politically, security-related tasks assumed a new prominence: following the Iranian revolution in 1979, there had been mass demonstrations of support by Kuwait's sizable Shia population. These, in turn, were followed in the spring and summer of 1980 by new security incidents: bombings in Kuwait and of Kuwaiti offices in London, and the highjacking of a Kuwaiti jetliner. The onset of the Iran-Iraq war in 1981 brought armed conflict to Kuwait's borders.

A second major development was the growing strength of conservative political factions, comprising traditional Bedouin tribal leaders and Islamic groups, both of which made significant gains in the 1981 elections which restored the National Assembly. Indeed, the role of "opposition" passed from Arab Nationalists to religious conservatives (Crystal, 1986: 225–226).

The objectives of migration policy measures reflected these twin concerns with security and religious issues, and signalled the onset of Kuwaitis deepening concern over their growing minority status and the increasing

expression, freer exchange of ideas and less authoritarian rule (Owen 1983: 143ff). Yet, under the immediate pressures of budget constraints, internal political dissent, and security risks, constraints on popular political participation by citizens, let alone non-citizens, have seldom been greater.[15]

The future status of migrants in the polities of the Gulf must be determined in the context of rethinking how long-range political stability and economic prosperity are best achieved. The underlying assumptions on the bases of which Gulf states chose to ensure domestic political stability and regime support by differentiating sharply between citizens and non-citizens have changed. In many places, citizens are not the majority they were when basic nationality laws were passed, nor are they as homogeneous as they once were. Both past naturalizations and rising levels of education and technical skill have introduced new subgroups, expectations and complexities among the citizenry itself. The increased sensitivity of the population to basic Islamic principles has only deepened the moral and political dilemmas inherent in differential treatment of Muslims, whether they are naturalized citizens or non-citizens of either Arab or Asian origin. Nor are migrants merely the temporary sojourners they were once expected to be. They are long-term residents who, it may be argued, have already achieved a degree of political integration in their host societies (*See*, Russell, 1987). They are, increasingly, native-born sons and daughters whose commitment to their country of birth remains an unchannelled resource for stability.

Just as ideology can be seen to shape migration policy, so may migration rock the ideological foundations of a society. As a result of past migration policies, Kuwait and other Gulf states face challenges similar to those now encountered by European countries of immigration: What are the bases of identity upon which membership in the society rests? What are the foundations of governance and sources of legitimacy in the relationship between the state and a society whose historical composition has altered substantially? These are issues of internal political and social cohesion which neither tinkering with migration policy nor even achieving "population balance" will address. The challenge for future policy lies in the realm of citizenship law. . . .

■ Notes

1. The research on which this article is based was supported in part by a grant from the Social Science Research Council with Funds from the Ford Foundation and the National Endowment for the Humanities. Earlier versions were presented to the Joint MIT-Harvard Seminar on Migration and Development, Cambridge, Massachusetts, March 5, 1987, and to the session on Politics and Ideologies of Population Issues at the Population Association of America, Annual Meeting, April 30–May 2, 1987, Chicago, Illinois.

2. This article focuses on the interaction of economic and political considera-

tions in international migration for employment and, accordingly, stresses the theoretical approaches to the subject adopted by economists and political scientists. This is not to overlook the contributions to migration theory by other disciplines. It may be argued, however, that (with some exceptions) these approaches also tend to ignore or give only passing mention to the importance of governmental actions in shaping voluntary international migration. See, for example, Clark's (1986) review of geographic treatments of migration.

3. Two recent exceptions to this characterization are Bhagwati 1984 and Papademetriou 1984. Both acknowledge that the policy context of international migration for employment has serious implications for the process; Bhagwati notes the limitations of current migration theory in view of this point.

4. See, for example, Weiner 1985a and 1985b; Choucri 1983 and 1986; and Weiner and Choucri 1986.

5. Economic and demographic data analyzed for this study were from Kuwait government and official national and international agency sources. Material for analysis of the evolution of migration policy in Kuwait was assembled from original and amended texts and notes accompanying Kuwaiti law, principally the Nationality Law (No. 15) of 1959, the Alien's Residence Law (No. 17) of 1959, and the Private Sector Labour Law (No. 64) of 1964; from government and international agency documents; published and unpublished papers, reports, and dissertations (especially Seccombe 1983); and historical sources in the Public Records Office, London. Once it was organized in chronological order, the policy material was juxtaposed with material (of which there is relatively little published) on the internal politics and foreign relations of Kuwait, derived from a wide variety of sources. Among the most useful and important of these are: Crystal 1986; Al-Ebraheem 1975 and 1984; Ismael 1982; Alessa 1981; Moubarak 1979; Khoury 1981; Joukhadar 1980; and Farah *et al.* 1980. Newspapers, periodicals, and subscription analyses (*eg.* The Economist Intelligence Unit Country Reports) covering political events of the region were also invaluable. Finally, written material was supplemented by over 150 interviews conducted during the Spring of 1985 with government, regional and international agency officials, scholars, and migrants in Kuwait, Jordan, Jerusalem and the West Bank, Egypt, Saudi Arabia, and Bahrain, as well as in New York, Washington, and Geneva.

6. *See*, for example, Richards and Martins' (1983) characterization of Middle East migration policies as "laissez-faire." The United Nations World Survey of International Migration Policies and Programs (1982, p. 54) is a notable exception to the prevailing view in that it does recognize the existence in Kuwait of formal legislation regulating employment and naturalization of immigrant workers.

7. Seccombe's work (1983, 1986) is among the few to have placed more recent Middle Eastern migration streams in any historical perspective. For a fuller discussion of other aspects of Kuwait's early history, see Crystal 1986, Ismael 1982, Al-Ebraheem 1975, and Abu-Hakima 1983.

8. British strategic interests included securing communication links between London and India, preventing Germany's establishment of a railway terminus in Kuwait, weakening the influence of the Ottoman empire in central Arabia, and relatedly, influencing events in Central Arabia by controlling the flow of arms through Kuwait to Ibn Saud.

9. Major sources for the discussion of Kuwaiti politics in this article include Crystal (1986) (who analyses the relationship between the ruling family and the merchant community in depth), Ismael 1982, Moubarak 1979, and author's interviews.

10. Prominent Kuwaiti Nationalists of the early 1960s included Merchant fam-

ily scion al-Rumi, editor of al-Yagiza; Abdul Azziz Masa id, editor of the pro-government daily al- Rai al-Am; and the intellectual Seif Shamlan.

11. One provision of the Nationality Law in particular underscores its political as distinct from its economic motivations. The law distinguishes sharply between "original" Kuwaitis and those who obtained citizenship by naturalization. All Kuwaiti citizens enjoy access to civil service employment, property ownership, retirement, education, and other socio-economic benefits. But naturalized citizens do not have the right to vote for any representative body until twenty years after the acquisition of citizenship and are ineligible for nomination or appointment to a representative body or ministerial position.

12. These provisions were further amended in 1980.

13. Several observers have linked dissolution of the Assembly to "migration politics" which laced members outspoken opposition to government on a range of issues. On the domestic front, Liberals decried the fact that educated Arabs, many born in Kuwait or long-resident there, were denied citizenship while illiterate Bedouin were being naturalized. These attacks on government also pointed to inequities in the social and economic position of migrants relative to the privileged position of at least some Kuwaitis. An even greater point of contention, however, was the assembly's call that Kuwait take a firmer stance on inter-Arab political issues of importance to migrants, including the Palestinian cause. Parliament's passage of a resolution condemning Syrian intervention in the Lebanese war was viewed by conservatives as an intrusion of migrants' political concerns into Kuwait's traditionally neutral stance toward neighboring countries of the region, and was directly linked to dissolution of the Assembly.

14. According to the Economist Intelligence Unit No. 3, 1986, Kuwait Country Report, p. 5, the residency requirement was lengthened to 30 years by action of the National Assembly in Spring 1986.

15. The suspension of Kuwait's National Assembly in July 1986 and the subsequent ouster of many leading journalists in conjunction with severe press restrictions only underscores this point. *See*, The Christian Science Monitor 1987.

■ References

Abu-Hakima, A. M.
1983 The Modern History of Kuwait. London: Luzac & Company Limited.

Abu-Lughod, J.
1983 "Social Implications of Labor Migration in the Arab World," *Arab Resources: The Transformation of a Society*. Edited by Ibrahim Ibrahim. Washington, D.C.: Center for Contemporary Arab Studies, and London: Croom Helm. Pp. 237–265.

Adler, S.
1975 *People in the Pipeline: The Political Economy of Algerian Migration to France, 1962–1974*. Unpublished Ph.D. Dissertation, Department of Political Science, Massachusetts Institute of Technology.

Alessa, S. Y.
1981 *The Manpower Problem in Kuwait*. London and Boston: Kegan Paul International.

Bhagwati, J. N.
1984 "Incentives and Disincentives: International Migration," *Weltwirtschaftliches Archiv*, Vol. 120, No. 4. Pp. 678–700.

Choucri, N.

1983 *Migration in the Middle East: Transformations, Policies, and Processes, Vol. I*. Massachusetts Institute of Technology, Technology Adaptation Program, Cambridge, Massachusetts.

1986 "Asians in the Arab World: Labor Migration and Public Policy," *Middle Eastern Studies*. 22^2:252–273, April.

Clark, W.A.V.

1986 *Human Migration*. Beverly Hills, CA: Sage Publications, Scientific Geography Series, Vol. 7.

Cornelius, W.

1976 "Mexican Migration to the United States: The View from Rural Sending Communities," Migration and Development Study Group Working Paper, Cambridge, Mass.: MIT.

Crystal, J.

1986 "Patterns of State-Building in the Arabian Gulf: Kuwait and Qatar." Unpublished Ph.D. dissertation, Department of Government, Harvard University.

Al-Ebraheem, H. A.

1975 *Kuwait: A Political Study*. Kuwait: Kuwait University.

1984 Kuwait and the Gulf, Washington, D.C.: Center for Contemporary Arab Studies, and London: Croom Helm.

Farah, T. *et al.*

1980 "Alienation and Expatriate Labor in Kuwait," *Journal of South Asian and Middle Eastern Studies*. 4^1:3–40.

Foreign Office files

Public Records Office, London: FO 371/98442, EA 1581/2; FO 371/104420/58839, EA 1624/9, EA 1626/7.

Hammar, T.

1985 *European Immigration Policy: A Comparative Study*. New York: Cambridge University Press.

Harris, J., and M. P. Todaro

1970 "Migration, Unemployment and Development: A TwoSector Analysis," *American-Economic Review*. 60 (March).

Ismael, J. S.

1982 *Kuwait: Social Change in Historical Perspective*. Syracuse, New York: Syracuse University Press.

Joukhadar, A.

1980 "Les Etrangers au Koweit," *Population*. 1 (January–February):57–82.

Khoury, N.

1981 "The Politics of Intra-Regional Migration." In *International Migration in the Arab World*. Beirut: ECVA. 2:753–776.

Kubat, D.

1979 *The Politics of Migration Policies: The First World in the 1970s*. New York: Center for Migration Studies.

Lucas, R.E.B. and O. Stark

1984 "Motivations to Remit," Cambridge, Mass.: Migration and Development Program Discussion Paper Series, No. 10.

Martin, P.L., and A. Richards

1980 "International Migration of Labor: Boon or Bane?" *Monthly Labor Review*. 103 (October):4–9.

Migdal, J.

1979 "Policy in Context: The Intended and Unintended in Migration Policy in the

members of Southern and East European "races" began to appear as early as 1880. Restrictionist campaigns were gradually legitimated by Congress and the Supreme Court. Through the campaign for literacy tests for potential immigrants, there was an attempt to reconstitute a nation that never actually existed, to obliterate the tensions of its creation (particularly the ambiguities of the place of Blacks and Native Americans), and to establish a clear line between the "in-group" and the "others." Three times Congress voted literacy restrictions on immigration that were vetoed by the president, partly because of the opposition of immigrants' associations, before being finally adopted at the eve of the entrance of the United States into World War I (Zolberg 1983, 27).

The hysteria of the 1920s, which J. Higham dubbed the "tribal years," was not without precedent (Higham 1985). Indeed, nativist local reactions appeared with each immigration wave: Irish, German, Chinese, Jewish, Italian, Mexican. On the eve of the Civil War, the xenophobic and virulently anti-Catholic "Know Nothing" party was able to attract a majority of the vote in five states. After its decline, a new anti-Catholic organization, the American Protective Association, emerged in Clinton, Iowa, in 1887, with the objective of eliminating Irish political influence. The association was eventually supported by 2.5 million members in the Midwest and the West. Later, the Ku Klux Klan (its second manifestation), created in 1917 in Georgia, became one of the most xenophobic political organizations in the country. Even today, campaigns to impose English as a national language have a similar nativist flavor.

The efforts of nativists in the 1880s to prevent foreigners from voting remained scattered and limited to certain regions. They also provoked the establishment of immigrant defense groups that were quite active during restrictionist campaigns. Moreover, nativist efforts could not counter the willingness of local parties to attract the vote of new immigrants. Until the beginning of the twentieth century, a dozen states granted voting rights to foreigners providing they made a commitment to become citizens. In 1924 Arkansas was the last state to abolish immigrant voting.

The conflict between policies of openness and exclusion is still current in the sense that it represents the continuing tension about concerns for national integration and the danger presented by foreign "races" for institutions and the American society. Racial thinking was reinforced and institutionalized by the quota system that was established after World War I, and this thinking influenced the way political institutions evolved in the twentieth century.

The process of establishing immigration policy also reinforced the structure of the national state. The federal government took over from the states the function of regulating immigration, and important new structures were established at the national level both to develop new policy (the

House and Senate immigration committees) and to implement this policy (the Bureau of Immigration). Thus, increased concern with immigration also meant increased centralization and nationalization of immigration policymaking. At the same time, the growth of administration of immigration also meant increased activity of pressure groups and political parties at all levels.

France: The Emerging Crisis of Immigration

In France, the central state has always been important in the regulation of immigration, as well as in the process of establishing policies by which immigrants would be integrated into the national community.[2] What is frequently less appreciated has been the significant role that has been played by institutions other than the central state, especially local governmental institutions, in defining, establishing, and implementing policy relevant to immigration and immigrants. Indeed, we will argue here that the 1980s was a critical period, during which the definition of the immigrant problem was tacitly changed to one of ethnicity (although the term was never used) and, at the same time, the focus of policymaking moved from the local arena to the national arena in France.

Until immigration became a nationally divisive political issue in the 1980s, local officials played a considerable role in defining public policy on immigration. Officially, the French population has been divided between Frenchmen and citizens, on one hand, and immigrants (by definition noncitizens) on the other, but in the local political arena careful public policy differences were formulated towards groups, based broadly on racial/cultural/religious (i.e., "ethnic") criteria, regardless of citizenship. For purposes of public policy, immigrants from European countries were considered different from those from Third World countries, and continental White citizens were treated differently from non-White citizens from the overseas departments and territories; Moslems from all origins were treated differently from non-Moslems.

The best-documented examples of local policymaking that depended on these criteria come from municipalities that were governed by the Left from the late 1960s to the early 1980s. This is related to the fact that a disproportionate number of non-European immigrants had settled in these municipalities during this period, but these examples of local policies can be extended to municipalities with high concentrations of Third World populations, regardless of political orientation.[3] Moreover, policymaking in the local arena involved quiet collaboration with departmental and national administrative officials. . . .

Therefore, by the time the government of the Left came to power in 1981, a great deal of policy had been made at the local level, by local elected officials (usually the initiators) in collaboration with the field services of national ministries. In general, policy decisions targeted non-Europeans, both immigrants and citizens, and focused on modes of integration for a settled rather than a migrant population. Migration policy was formulated in the national arena, but the arena for integration policy was the locality.

The constraints of the local political-administrative system tended to limit the politicization and the intensity of ethnic conflict by restricting access to decision making and by separating local decision making (administrative) from the more global considerations of the political parties of local officials. Access was limited first by the minimal political opposition at the local level that was widespread in the 1970s. Even in larger towns there was a tendency towards political consensus building that was reinforced by the electoral law in place between 1965 and 1983, a law that virtually assured that there would be no institutionalized opposition in municipal councils of larger towns.[4] Therefore, even if local decisions did come before the municipal council, a great deal of institutionalized conflict had already been precluded.

Second, local decisions about immigrants were generally dealt with through an administrative process, with local officials participating as administrators rather than as elected officials (although the former were clearly dependent on the latter). Mayors participated in the formulation of housing policy as members of the boards that governed low-income housing (OHLM); the decision to limit the number of immigrant families with children in certain areas of the Lyon region was made by the prefect of the Rhône, but with the support and even at the initiative of local political authorities.[5] While some of the important decisions concerning immigrants and integration policy did come before city councils (decisions concerning the building of mosques, for example), many did not. Because so many of these important decisions were defined as administrative, consultations with interested groups, especially immigrant groups, were restricted, or simply took place after decision had already been made.[6] This process further limited political mobilization.

However, within the local arena there were also dynamics for rapidly elevating issues to the national level, particularly when conflict could not be contained by the local system. This is more or less what happened to the issue of ethnicity and immigrant integration in the 1980s. The "emergence" of ethnicity as a national issue in French politics during the past decade is related to the inability of the local system to deal with very real problems of ethnic integration, the outbreak of urban riots, and the dynamics of the party system. But the way that the issue emerged was constrained by the formal and informal structure of center-periphery relations.

The centralized administrative system greatly facilitated the movement of issues involving education and housing, for example, from ad hoc decision making at the local level to more general policy development at the national level. In both cases, policy formulation rested on assumptions about ethnic differences and definitions of policy that had been developed at the local level. In education, problems of rising dropout rates and student failures were behind the establishment of zones of education priority (ZEP) in 1981. The designation of such zones—which meant more money, more teachers, and more experimental programs—rested upon criteria that focused on the ethnic composition of an area, and gave additional support to programs that in some cases had already been begun by local authorities.[7] . . .

Consideration by administrative authorities at the national level of problems of ethnic integration was encouraged by the perception of real problems, but was facilitated by the structural links between localities and the central state: the centralization of the administration, and the overlap between local and national political office holding (*cumul des mandats*). Over 80 percent of the deputies in the National Assembly hold local offices at the same time (about half of these are mayors), and the Senate is elected by an electoral college that consists overwhelmingly of local office holders. Thus, mayors who feel that their local problems need national help have easy access to the national arena. Marcel Houël, for example, the Communist mayor of Vénissieux in the early 1980s, was also a deputy, as were a large number of his colleagues with urban problems.

However, until the early 1980s, the focus for the formulation of integration issues and policy remained on the local level, even with increased national intervention. Restricted access to decision making in the local political-administrative system tended to limit local political mobilization and conflict around immigrant-ethnic issues. Of course, this process also mitigated the influence of opponents to the kinds of exclusionary policies that were frequently developed at the local level.

■ 2. The Dynamics of National Politics

The processes of policymaking with regard to immigration at the national level in France and the United States are quite different. The important actors are different, they appear at different historic moments, and the dynamics of their relationships are different in each country. In addition, local actors continue to play a more important role in the United States than in France, because of the dispersed way that the issue of immigration is treated in the United States. Nevertheless, given the differences between the systems, there are some surprising similarities. Both in France and in the United States the dynamics of center-periphery relations are important for policy development and implementation. While overall policy changes in both countries have been debated and processed at the national level, many of the initiatives for change have taken place at the local level and have been influenced by local problems and local political forces. In France, these local initiatives have quickly worked their way into the national political debate (indeed—have often *provoked* a national debate and moved policy considerations different from what they had been before), while in the United States, many local initiatives have been contained by the American federal system.

The United States: Federalism, Pressure Groups, and Dispersion

Since 1965, American society has had the difficult task of integrating new pieces into an already complicated ethnic mosaic. Four-fifths of new immigrants have come from the Third World, and they are quite different from one another. One approach of public policymaking has been to attempt to integrate these diverse people by creating a new kind of ethnicity, while acting as if only the gap between American society and the immigrants is important and that differences among immigrant groups do not exist. This approach, which does not clearly differentiate "immigrants" from "minorities," has influenced the range of political choices that immigrants have, as well as the way they themselves organize politically.

The federal government, in the way that it counts population, classifies students and workers, spends public aid, and develops affirmative action programs for minorities, has produced a three-part classification and has placed in the same category populations fragmented by ethnicity, race, and class. These classifications have also been adopted by local authorities and by voluntary mutual aid societies that dispense help to new immigrants, as well as by immigrant groups themselves. "Recent immigrants," notes P. Ireland, "have become conscious of the obvious tripartite division of multiethnic movements supported by the state—Black, Hispanic, and Asian—as a result of explicit approaches and categorizations [by the state] that aggregate citizens and immigrants" (Ireland 1989, 321). To have political weight, to defend their interests, Chinese, Filipinos, Vietnamese, Koreans, and others have joined together in "Asian" organizations, such as the Asian Law Caucus. This may seem peculiar, since these groups do not share the same language, and because native populations such as Native Americans have also demanded to be reclassified as "Asian." In the same way Chicanos, refugees from Central America, and the citizens from Puerto Rico (an American "commonwealth") find that it is advantageous to unite as "Hispanics" for political purposes. At the national level, the permanent or temporary political cooperation within these new categories carries considerable weight, and enables them to gain special access to the caucuses that Black, Asian, and Hispanic congressional representatives have developed into important pressure groups within the federal government.

One consequence of the imposition of these categories by the federal government, and the minority coalition building that has resulted from it, has been the magnification of the importance of immigrant issues. The alliance of minorities led by Jesse Jackson has had an important impact on the electoral registration of these groups, and, in various places, on voting turnout. In five states of the Southwest, which account for a fifth of the votes necessary for the victory of a presidential candidate, a massive "Hispanic" vote can tip the balance by 10 percent. Political parties are also conscious of the implications of multiethnic solidarity, and when no particular national group is dominant, politicians have sometimes developed a broader Asian or Hispanic image, rather than one that is more narrowly Korean or Cuban. The political benefits of this kind of minority coalition building tend to be broadly communal, and therefore extend to immigrants as well as citizens and voters.

The debates on immigration legislation also indicate the effectiveness of multiethnic lobbies. In 1986, the "Hispanics" were able to prevail on key points over the representatives of agroindustry and the trade unions. Every legal reform of immigration must, from now on, take into account "the voice" of these political participants, who are aided in the defense of their interests by powerful groups. Thus, policy has been a result of a political process that has linked the state with groups that have emerged out of society, groups whose structure and organization have been influenced by policy decisions of the state.

We find a similar relationship in policy implementation, which is defined by widespread devolution of authority for policy implementation from the national government to churches, unions, associations for the defense of the rights of immigrants and refugees, and groups of civil rights lawyers. When Congress decided to grant amnesty to undocumented immigrants in 1986, it also permitted these organizations to deal with individual cases, to act as legal advisors, and to conduct information campaigns. The unions were subsidized for giving English courses and civic instruction to candidates for naturalization. (At the same time, they socialized immigrants into the political system.) The directives came from Washington, but were carried out at the local level, in different ways in different states and cities.

Of course, this also weakens the state when it becomes the target of these partners. With the strength of legitimacy granted by the state, these groups pressure elected representatives as advocates for immigrants. They direct their attention towards problems of discrimination for which the state is responsible, towards protection for immigrants, and towards violations of human rights that are in conflict with methods of expulsion of families of undocumented aliens (separated from their children, for example), and they do not hesitate to go to court to enforce policy decisions that are slow in coming (Body-Gendrot 1990b).

These same uneasy partners, financed by the federal government, have also pressured for further reforms when political conditions were favorable, generally at the local level. One example is the creation of a bureau responsible for immigration in the office of the mayor of the city of New York; another is the decision to establish sanctuary cities under the insistent pressure of centers for the defense of immigrant and refugee rights and civil rights lawyers.

San Francisco, Oakland, Chicago, and New York are sanctuary towns, meaning that these cities do not follow the immigration policies enacted by Washington that deny political asylum to refugees from San Salvador or Guatemala. By refusing, for instance, to denounce illegal aliens to the INS, those cities are accused of disobedience and could face financial sanctions. Of course, the INS does not recognize the power of these cities to enact their own immigration policies. These grass roots organizations, in turn, have frequently found advocates within the system, since commissions for civil rights are integrated into municipal institutions by law, and because elected representatives from immigrant neighborhoods are effective advocates on the state and national levels.

Thus, in various localities, these federally financed organizations occupy a place that is more or less institutionalized (or, in more current terminology, neocorporatist). In functional terms, they have often taken the place that in other times was filled by political machines in providing everything from welfare to information on naturalization to a means of political expression for immigrants. Outside of the South, churches, unions, and immigrant defense organizations play important roles in dealing with both immigration policy and policy implementation.

This emphasis on the relationship between the national and local levels should not obscure the central fact that policy *implementation* is generally decentralized, fragmented, and tends to focus on only certain categories of immigrants. As a result, the various representatives of immigrant interests rarely question immigration laws enacted by Congress, and even less what is an often illusory "immigration policy," except at the initiative of Congress.[8] Nevertheless, the basic elements of the immigration debate in 1990 are produced by those watchful advocates of immigrant and racial minorities who are anxious to demonstrate, for example, that sanctions against employers of illegal work force have discriminatory consequences. In the case of immigration, local efforts culminate in a debate that takes place in Congress, but the dynamics of grassroots initiatives are essentially local.

Most of the issues that in France would pertain to a *national* debate under the label "immigration" and would attract the attention of politicians and media, such as voting rights and their consequences, or labor rights and illegal aliens, are processed in a decentralized manner in the United States, and are intimately linked to questions of civil rights. For instance, a 1972 amendment extended the benefits of the Voting Rights Act of 1965 to Latino and Asian citizens. Nevertheless, real change can come only from the capacity of those groups and of their advocates to engage in legal action to change electoral systems alleged to dilute the impact of their vote.

In Texas, when sixty-two cities changed districting, representation of racial minorities as council members more than doubled. In California, in 1985, the city of Los Angeles was forced by legal action by civil rights activists to modify its districts. The result was the unprecedented election of two Latinos to the city council (among fifteen members). At the county level, with a Republican majority, a 28 percent Latino population had not been represented at all because of the districting system, but because of recent legal action, mandated redistricting now seems to guarantee Latino representation (Colin 1988). In Florida, another state with a strong immigrant concentration, "Anglos" resist attempts to alter districting in Dade County, which includes Miami.

Political exclusion of minorities and immigrant groups is also facilitated by the localism of, and the weak linkages within, American political parties. Areas of the Southwest where large numbers of immigrants have settled often have strong reform traditions and nonpartisan elections, and the decentralized organization of parties tends to reflect local culture and local bias. In localities in which, in France, M. Le Pen would obtain results that would trigger a counterattack by leftist parties, the two major U.S. parties are often not present. The result is both a lack of access of immigrant groups as well as a localization of policymaking. . . .

Although, in American ethnic communities, the interests of citizens and immigrants are clearly linked both by government and the communities themselves, concentrations of immigrants within these communities have an impact on community political behavior. Thus, first-generation Asian and Latino immigrants are under severe economic pressures, and they avoid political involvement because of the distrust for politics they acquired in their native countries under the political regimes they left. Moreover, Latinos, because of the proximity of their native countries, and their desire to return, naturalize at half the rate of other immigrants. A study by the Urban Institute on the political adaptation of Latino immigrants reveals that first- and third-generation Mexican immigrants tend to concentrate on their private lives and to get less involved in politics than Anglos and Blacks. On the other hand, the second (and fourth) generations are inclined to compensate for the absence of political participation by their parents. Their experience with discrimination and their growing familiarity with the functioning of the U.S. society promotes their political involvement and their willingness to be recognized as a component of this society. Here, as everywhere else, education and socioeconomic status are also decisive determinants for participation (Goodis 1988). However, new gen-

lished Right that "the National Front poses some real questions" (the Fabius-Chirac debate in 1985), when they have been opposition; and, more generally, by alternating between a pluralist "right to difference" approach to immigrants (in December 1989) and an individualistic "right to indifference" approach (February 1989) (*Le Monde*, 11 February and 7 December 1989).

Despite the confusion, the dynamics of party competition have resulted in redefinition of the issue of immigration, from a labor market problem to a problem that touches on the structure of French society—problems of education, housing, and law and order, as well as the requirements for citizenship. A case has also been made that there is a developing consensus among the established parties of the Right and Left, if not about specific policies then about a general approach to policy, that goes back to the Fabius-Chirac debate in 1985—a policy of integration "respecting our laws, our customs and our values," that limits any substantial increase in immigrants but that also excludes recourse to forced return (Leveau 1989, 258–61).

However, within the relatively open national arena it has been difficult to arrive at a policy of integration. The National Front continues to maintain pressure on the Right, while the Socialist government is now challenged by more politicized North Africans born in France ("beurs"), who are now well organized, as well as by more assertive Moslems who are less hesitant about questioning French laws, customs, and values. Thus, the Rocard government wanted to downplay the issues of immigration when it first arrived in office. Nevertheless, it found that, because of the challenge of the "Islamic scarf" crisis in the fall of 1989, as well as the subsequent electoral victories of the National Front, it was unable to avoid the pressure that moved the issue to center stage. In the United States, a comparable crisis would have been largely contained within specific localities, and if it reached the national level at all, the route through the courts would have been long and difficult.

These incidents centered on the case of several girls who were wearing traditional Moslem scarves that covered their hair, head, and neck, were refused entry into secondary schools, and were seen by local school authorities as a challenge to the secular public school. Within days, the national press, major organizations representing immigrants (SOS-Racisme and France Plus—which sharply disagreed on both the interpretation of the issue and the proper policy that should be followed), and numerous political leaders had issued statements about the incidents, and had reinterpreted them in terms of historic conflicts over church-state relations, ethnic pluralism and integration, Islamic fundamentalism, and women's rights. Thus, this "affair" very quickly became the concern of the minister of education, as well as an issue of parliamentary debate. The minister's decision to compromise and to permit the girls to wear the scarves if they insisted was hotly debated in parliament, and eventually considered by the highest administrative court in France. The Conseil d'Etat decided to turn the decision back to local education authorities, which could decide one way or the other according to local circumstances and criteria established by the ministry. A decade earlier, such incidents might have been dealt with more quietly within the local arena, in the same way that it dealt with housing and other school problems. By 1989, however, local school problems that involved integration could no longer be contained by the local political-administrative system, and were rapidly transformed into a national political issue.

The pressures of party competition within the national arena were all played out in the spring of 1990, when the Rocard government made an attempt to develop a consensus around immigration. Using as a pretext a disturbing report by the National Consultative Committee on the Rights of Man, the prime minister called a meeting of all political leaders, except those of the National Front, to develop a program to combat racism. The opposition, however, rejected this definition of the problem and organized their own meeting the weekend preceding the meeting with the prime minister to discuss problems of immigration. When they met with the government, the opposition came armed with four propositions for changing immigration policy. They were able to extract from the Rocard government a commitment for a second meeting that would deal with their initiatives, preceding a general parliamentary debate on racism and immigration in May 1990.[13]

Thus, in the spring of 1990, the question of immigration and integration was once more on political center stage and, given the proliferation of propositions, was likely to remain there for some time. It was also likely to remain there because behind this activity was the growing pressure of the National Front, which was holding its national congress while the government and the opposition were developing their positions. The opposition groups had never come closer to agreement on a unified approach to the politics of immigration, and their propositions tentatively approached those of the National Front. The clearest statement was made by former president Valéry Giscard d'Estaing, who was quoted as saying, "The foreigners can live in France with full rights [dans le respect des droits de l'homme] but they cannot change France." Giscard promptly launched a national petition to hold a referendum to make naturalization legislation more restrictive (one of the proposals agreed to by the opposition).

What began as local initiatives in the fall of 1989 were magnified by the electoral success of the National Front, and seem to have exacerbated divisions between the government and the opposition over immigration—or rather, over how to define and treat foreigners on French soil. The far Right has benefited from growing national concern about immigration (between September 1989 and February 1990, the issue moved from seventh to second place among the concerns of French voters) but has also mediated and defined that concern within the party system. In this kind of environment, it seems unlikely that any kind of consensus will develop, despite the fact that it is frequently reported that "political leaders are convinced that the issue is too important for partisan quarrels. . . . They vie with each other to accentuate their divergences as if to mask their agreements" (*Le Monde*, 3 April 1990, 12).

Therefore, it appears that the separation of different issues of immigration between the local and national arenas in France that was still operating a decade ago, no longer exists. Both the labor market issues of immigration and issues of integration are dealt with and structured within the national arena.

Nevertheless, the local arena continues to play an important role in the development of policies related to immigrants. First, because of the structural links between the local and national arenas, through administration, political parties, and parliament, issues initiated at the local level frequently generate national politics. This was clearly the case in the Islamic scarves affair, where the decisions of local school authorities in a few localities forced a national political debate that changed the political agenda of the government and every major political party. But this case is not an exception. . . .

■ Conclusion

There are clearly many differences between the United States and France with respect to immigration policy and the process through which this policy has been developed. There are, however, two aspects of this problem that have been similar in both countries. The first is the impact of immigration on the centralization of policymaking; and the second is the definition of the problem that has slowly emerged.

In the United States, immigration was dealt with, both legally and administratively, on the state level until national political elites reformulated the problem in racial/ethnic terms at the turn of the century. In the process of dealing with what was understood as a problem of national identity and citizenship, new structures were created at the federal level that generated both political debate and new national policies. Once the major lines of policy on entry were set at the national level, however, the local arena became the focal point for policy implementation and policy development on integration.

National policy became the impetus for the organization of a multitude of interest groups, many of them linking immigrants with citizens through ethnic heritage. By the 1960s, the sons and daughters of the immigrants of the turn of the century had organized sufficiently to change the exclusionary legislation of the 1920s, but they had also changed the process through which national legislation is developed. Legislation on entry was now the product of complex group interaction, and policy on integration was now directly related to the broader politics of ethnic policy. By the 1980s, interest groups were directly involved in the implementation of national policy at the local level, and were therefore well positioned to initiate changes in that policy.

In France, policy on both entry and integration had always been formally developed at the national level. Nevertheless, the implementation of integration policy at the local level has also implied a considerable range of policy development. The emergence of immigration as a national political issue in the 1980s, and pressures to develop more exclusionary policies, have resulted from changes in the party system. Indeed, political parties have become the motor force behind the movement of policy initiation from the local to the national level. As in the United States at the turn of the century, as immigration has become increasingly politicized, the national state has become increasingly involved in both policy development and policy implementation. As in the United States, the more informal aspects of French policy on integration in the 1980s have made the traditional line between immigrants and ethnic groups less clear. As a result, immigrants and some ethnic Frenchmen have begun to organize, bringing into question the nature of French nationality and citizenship.

French commentators have frequently contended that the French model of individual integration is very different from the American model of integration through the recognition of ethnic pluralism.[14] However, the American recognition of the legitimacy of ethnic pluralism is a post–World War II phenomenon that was the result of political pressures set in motion by ethnic organization after 1924. During the period before World War II, the operating model of immigrant integration in the United States, which stressed White Protestant middle-class values, was close if not identical to the French. The symbol of "Our ancestors the Gauls" had its equivalent in the Founding Fathers for American school children[15] (Olneck 1990; Mohl 1981). The challenge to and the change in the operating model of integration was the result of a political process that has hardly begun in France, but that can be seen in the present debate over the nature of French nationality. Thus, in the American experience, if there is a lesson to be learned, it is probably the process through which well-organized immigrant/ethnic groups were able to alter the model of American national identity. Until now, immigrant pressure groups have not been able to exert comparable influence on the political process in France.[16] It is still the state that chooses its negotiating partners, and the state itself takes the initiative to generate these partners if they do not yet exist.

■ Notes

1. The "Passenger Cases" are *Smith v. Turner*, consolidated with *Norris v. City of Boston*, 48 US (1849). One previous Supreme Court decision, *Mayor, Aldermen and Commonalty of the City of New York v. Miln*, 35 US (1837), had upheld a state immigration statute against a constitutional attack based on federalism. Miln, however, was later qualified by *Holmes v. Jennison*, 39 US (1840), and has never significantly influenced subsequent Supreme Court decisions in this area. In the 1849 decision, referred to as "Passenger Cases," five of the justices held the Boston taxation unconstitutional on the ground that it usurped an exclusively federal power.

2. See, for example, the contributions of André-Clément Decouflé and Gerard Noiriel in Donald L. Horowitz and Gerard Noiriel, eds., *Immigrants in Two Democracies: French and American Experiences* (New York: NYU Press, 1992); as well as Singer-Keriel (1989).

3. By 1977, 55 percent of cities (over thirty thousand population) governed by Communist mayors had immigrant populations greater than 10 percent, compared with 23 percent for towns governed by Socialists and 21 percent of towns governed by the Center-Right. In 1977, 82 percent of the larger towns with more than 10 percent immigrant population were governed by the Left, and more than two-thirds of these were governed by the PCF (see Schain 1985).

4. A list that received a majority of the votes in the first round, or a plurality in the second round, gained all of the seats in the municipal council. The tendency for opposition in local councils to disappear is analyzed by Becquart-Leclercq 1976, 117–207.

5. The first Arreté was on 15 June 1970 (see Grillo 1985, 126).

6. This was complicated by the fact that immigrants groups could not formally organize their own associations until 1982. Thus, consultations about immigrant issues often took place with representatives of North African governments.

7. For more details on the Z.E.P.s, see Costa-Lascoux 1989, 93–95.

8. The situation is quite different in France, where immigration policy as a whole is hotly debated by interested groups (see Weil 1990).

9. For a discussion of the interplay between structures and subjects, see Body-Gendrot 1990a.

10. This term refers to inhabitants of the Caribbean islands and to those of English-speaking nations (Belize and Guyana), as well as to English-speaking inhabitants of Afro-Creole enclaves within Spanish-speaking countries of the Caribbean.

11. We are referring here to the Fontanet-Marcellin *circulaires* of 1972 (struck down by the Council of State in 1975) and the Bonnet Law of 1980. Martin Schain has elaborated on this in Schain 1985.

12. Schain has analyzed these trends in "Immigration and Changes in the French Party System," in Schain 1988. The analysis of voter volatility in this article ends in 1986, but Philippe Habert and Alain Lancelot demonstrate continuing voter volatility through the 1988 legislative elections, in Habert and Lancelot 1988.

13. The initiatives of the government and the opposition are reported in *Le Monde*, 3 and 4 April 1990.

14. Michael Wieviorka writes, for example, in a *Libération* editorial of 14 April 1990 entitled "U.S. multi-ethnicity and France": "Even in extrapolating the darkest trends, nothing indicates that French society is approaching the American model."

15. For an analysis of Americanization programs before 1924, see Maris A.

Vinovskis's chapter in Donald L. Horowitz and Gerard Noiriel, eds., *Immigrants in Two Democracies: French and American Experiences* (New York: NYU Press, 1992).

16. During the first half of 1990, Pierre Joxe, minister of the interior (responsible for the police and law and order), established an advisory council of fifteen widely respected French and foreign Moslems from the various Moslem ethnic communities. This organization will have the status that other churches have when they bargain with the state, and as a result, will diminish the impact of foreign Moslem states in French affairs.

■ **References**

Becquart-Leclercq, J. 1976. *Paradoxes du pouvoir local*. Paris: Presses de la FNSP.

Bekouchi, M. H. 1984. *Du bled a la Z.U.P. et/ou la couleur de l'avenir*. Paris: CIEM l'Harmattan.

Body-Gendrot, S. 1990a. "Migration and the Racialization of the Post-modern City in France." In M. Cross and M. Keith, eds., *Racism, the City, and the State*. London: Unwin Hyman.

———. 1990b. "Deux approches contrastées de l'immigration: la France et les Etats-Unis." *Revue Migrants-formation* (April).

Body-Gendrot, S., B. d'Hellencourt, and M. Rancoule. 1988. "Entrée interdite: la législation sur l'immigration en France, au Royaume-Uni et aux Etats-Unis." *Revue française de science politique* 39 (February).

Christopher, W., J. Corbett, and J. Stack. 1990. "Hispanic Ascendancy and Tripartite Politics in Miami." In R. Browning, et al., eds., *Racial Politics in American Cities*. New York: Longman.

Colin, M. 1988. "For Latinos, Immediate Object Is City Council Membership." *New York Times*, 4 September.

Costa-Lascoux, J. 1989. *De l'immigré au citoyen*. Paris: La Documentation Française.

Goodis, T. 1988. "The Political Adaptation of Hispanic Immigrants to the United States." Urban Institute, Policy Discussion Paper.

Grillo, R. D. 1985. *Ideologies and Institutions in Urban France*. London: Cambridge University Press.

Habert, P., and A. Lancelot. 1988. "L'emergence d'un nouvel électeur." In *Elections législatives* 1988. Paris: Le Figaro/Etudes Politiques.

Higham, J. 1985. *Strangers in the Land*. New York: Atheneum.

———. 1990. "The Pot That Didn't Melt." *New York Review of Books*, 12 April.

Ireland, P. 1989. "The State and the Political Participation of the 'New' Immigrants in France and in the U.S." *Revue française d'études américaines* 41 (July). Special issue on immigration.

Kasinitz, P. 1987. "The Minority Within: The New Black Immigrants." *New York Affairs* 10 (Winter).

Katznelson, I. 1973. *Black Men, White Cities: Race Politics and Migration in the United States, 1900–1930, and Britain, 1948–1968*. London: Oxford University Press.

Kennedy, J. F. 1964. *A Nation of Immigrants*. New York: Harper and Row.

Kepel, G. 1987. *Les Banlieues de l'Islam: naissance d'une religion en France*. Paris: Seuil.

Leveau, R. 1989. "Les partis et l'intégration des 'beurs'." In Y. Mény, ed., *Idéologies, partis politiques et groupes sociaux*. Paris: Presses de la FNSP.

Long, M. 1988. *Etre français aujourd' hui et demain.* Rapport de la Commission de la Nationalité, présenté par M. Marceau Long, président, an Premier ministre, vol. 1.

Lowi, T. 1969. *The End of Liberalism.* New York: Norton.

Les Minguettes. 1982. Rapport présenté à la Commission pour le Développement Social des Quartiers. Lyon: COURLY- Ville de Vénissieux.

Mohl, R. 1981. "Cultural Assimilation versus Cultural Pluralism." *Education Forum* (March).

Olneck, M. 1990. "Americanization and Education of Immigrants, 1900–1925: An Analysis of Symbolic Action." *American Journal of Education.*

Paine, T. 1983. *Le sens commun.* Translated by B. Vincent. Paris: Aubier.

Portes, A., and R. Rúmbaut. 1989. *Immigrant America: A Portrait.* Berkeley: University of California Press.

Schain, M. 1985. "Immigrants and Politics in France." In J. S. Ambler, ed., *The French Socialist Experiment.* Philadelphia: ISHI.

————. 1988. "Immigration and Changes in the French Party System." *European Journal of Political Research* 16.

————. 1989. "Immigration, Race, and the Crisis of Citizenship in the United States (1880–1924)." Paper delivered to the Annual Workshops of the ECPR, Paris, April.

————. 1990. "Immigration and Politics." In P. Hall, J. Hayward, and H. Machin, eds., *Developments in French Politics.* London: Macmillan.

Singer-Keriel, J. 1989. "Foreign Workers in France, 1890–1936." Paper delivered at the University of Glasgow, 15 September.

Weil, P. 1990. "La politique d'immigration: au-delà du désordre." *Regards sur l'actualité* (March).

Zolberg, A. 1983. "Contemporary Transnational Migrations in Historical Perspective: Patterns and Dilemma." In M. Kritz, ed., *U.S. Migration and Refugee Policy.* Lexington, Mass.: Lexington Books.

7.5 *Gallya Lahav*

The Rise of Nonstate Actors in Migration Regulation in the United States and Europe: Changing the Gatekeepers or Bringing Back the State?

In an era of growing anti-immigrant sentiment and heightened state efforts to curtail immigration to the developed world, Western democracies are increasingly caught between their liberal ethos and their ability to effectively control immigration. Questions are being raised concerning the form of control industrialized democracies can use to effectively manage global migration flows. How can liberal democracies reconcile efforts to control the movement of people with those that promote free borders, open markets, and liberal standards? Are national actors, as some political analysts predict, "losing control" over migration? (Sassen 1996; Cornelius, Martin, and Hollifield 1994)

This chapter addresses two main questions: How do liberal nation-states manage the administration, elaboration, and implementation of immigration policy? And, who are the gatekeepers, and to what extent do they open up new channels and opportunities for state regulation over migration? In seeking to answer these questions, I offer a comparative analysis of the policy instruments and strategies adopted by the advanced liberal democracies of Europe (particularly France) and the United States. A disaggregated institutional view of the state, I argue, helps to explain why cultural variations may lead to particular domestic and international outcomes.[1]

In line with scholars who are "bringing back the state" into their studies of migration, the analysis that follows reconceptualizes and extends theories about political aspects of migration through a focus on state regulatory modes.[2] Going beyond a monolithic view of the state, this paper highlights a devolution or transfer of functions away from the central government and the proliferation of nonstate and transnational actors in migration regulation. The term "nonstate actor" refers to a diverse group of collective actors who have the economic, social, or political resources to facilitate or curtail immigration and return.

The argument is that nonstate and third-party actors represent reinvented state forms of power and governance in a world of increasing interdependence and changing boundaries. Liberal states are resorting to older—neocorporatist—means to reconcile demands to control borders for the movement of people with demands to promote open borders for trade and goods. The strategies increasingly used to control migration make clear that states are neither losing control nor abdicating sovereignty; rather, states seek to reduce the costs of immigration and to control migration at the same time that they allow the free flow of trade and goods. European countries undertaking regional integration may have significant lessons to teach traditional immigration countries, such as the United States. They are increasingly delegating policy elaboration and implementation to third-party actors as a way to increase policy effectiveness and diminish political fallout at the national level. That the United States is also moving in this direction suggests the possible emergence of an international migration regime oriented to protectionism and exclusion in combination with free trade in capital, goods, and services.[3]

■ Theoretical and Research Frameworks

The debate on how liberal states are responding to their market and democratic-rights-based tenets, on the one hand, and political pressures and needs to limit migration, on the other, is unresolved. The school of globalization, or interdependence, posits that in an increasingly global world, in which the lines between nation-states are becoming blurred, states are seeking international solutions to domestic problems. In this view, global population movements are seen as problem areas for national welfare because they increasingly take place outside the ambit of state control (Papademetriou and Miller 1983). The traditional notion of state sovereignty has been further challenged as the state no longer has complete control over the definition of citizenship and the decision as to who will enter a country (Layton-Henry 1990; Soysal 1994; Schuck 1989). Economic interdependence, the globalization of the economy, and the emergence of global cities, it is argued, have essentially eliminated the state's role in regulating migration (Sassen 1991, 1996).

Theorists of international political economy and political sociology support such liberal outcomes stemming from national and international constraints (see Hollifield 1992; Heisler 1992; Soysal 1994; Freeman 1995; Sassen 1996). According to these theorists, domestic liberal norms are "embedded," or institutionalized, in the international state system by human rights instruments and international agreements. Theorists of embedded liberalism contend that rights expressed in the form of constitutional norms and principles act to constrain the power and autonomy of states both in their treatment of individual migrants and in their relations to other states (Hollifield 1992; Ruggie 1982; Walzer 1980; Rawls 1971). Such arguments lend support to the hypothesis that immigration policy is an area in which states may be expected to defer to international regimes (Ruggie 1982; Krasner 1982). Proponents of globalization—whether sociologists or economists—often point to a growing convergence of national legislation in industrialized countries as testament to the effects of market globalization in contracting the state. The implications are limited state control over its migration interests.

National and international structures and standards may certainly impede state efforts to regulate immigration. Indeed, despite persistent cross-national differences in immigrant rights, all advanced industrialized nations of the OECD (Organisation for Economic Co-operation and Development) have made advances in this policy area (UN 1998; OECD 1997). Yet those who herald the decline of the nation-state have not paid enough attention to actual administrative mechanisms and domestic political processes or to the limitations of rights-based norms in determining migration outcomes (see Guiraudon and Lahav 2000; Guiraudon 1997; Lahav 1997a; Chekel 1995).

Critics of interdependence and neoliberalism argue that the assumption that globalization and international instruments undermine the state's capacity to control migration fail to realize the basis from which they derive: the state itself. State-centric and realist (or neorealist) theories assume that states have the power to protect and defend territorial integrity and that they continue to regulate international migration in accordance with their "national interests" (Waltz 1979; Zolberg 1981; Weiner 1985, 1990).

The theoretical debates about the role of the state in migration have, however, tended to neglect the mechanisms that states use to effectively manage immigration policy. There has been much discussion of the challenge immigration poses to liberal democracies (Layton-Henry 1990; Lahav 1993) but little exploration of state responses to immigration. Not much has been written, for example, on the actual instruments and policy measures used to restrict and shape immigration flows. Few attempts have been made to disaggregate the state and to identify the agencies and actors involved in regulating migration. Assessments of state capacities tend to be full of generalizations and devoid of specific claims, particularly concerning the practices and modes of policy implementation in migration regulation.[4]

It is also necessary to move beyond a unitary view of the state and adopt a neo-institutional perspective in analyzing the regulation of migration. In a neo-institutional approach, both norms and institutions are intricately related to inform policy outcomes. This approach poses the question, how does the state control migration in a way that corresponds to its policy interests, with a focus on the incentives and constraints political actors face in different national contexts? (See Thelen and Steinmo 1992, 7.) Going beyond the view of the state as a unitary actor facing global and domestic constraints allows us to understand the range of responses available to national governments when they face policy constraints and the number of actors and strategies that can be incorporated and deployed. In the context of an interdependent world, in which immigration is seen as a threat emanating from the international environment, what is interesting, then, is not only that the patterns of regulation and enforcement are increasingly conforming to public policy models, which are converging in the world, but those patterns, in particular, that involve increasing enforcement, via the transfer of state functions to international, transnational, private, and local jurisdictions.

Legislative and institutional analyses reflect converging policy norms and structures in the United States and Europe. The nature of policy implementation and the changes in the character of the gatekeepers reveal a trend toward more state commitment and increasing capacities to control borders. Although it is true that liberal international and domestic norms and pluralist politics have influenced the emergence of legal modes of migration, it is becoming more difficult to support the proposition that immigration is encouraged by a rights-based embedded liberalism (Schain 1995, 11; Joppke 1997; Lahav 1997a, 1997b; Money 1999). Analysis of policy implementation reinforces what has recently been suggested of contemporary surveys of program structures: namely, that states have considerable capacities to select migrants (Freeman 1994).

The empirical findings presented in this chapter suggest that the United States and European states are responding to and using global developments to extend and rethink control over immigration politics in the 1990s. A comparative analysis of the American and French cases reveals that liberal states are adopting policy tools or lessons that may be transferable across borders. Do they represent a new era of weak states in a global economy, or instead, an extension of state control whereby "the state" has changed the gatekeepers but is still able to define and control migration norms and outcomes? What are the implications of these regulatory modes for theories of state sovereignty and for transnational migration flows?

■ Bringing Back the State and Changing the Gatekeepers: Some Empirical Data

In order to assess the extent of state control over migration and migrant groups, it is important to identify how states manage policy outcomes that respond to their policy interests and commitments in an interdependent era. We need to consider policy structures and norms—that is, the instruments and organizations that states set up to achieve their policy goals. At the state level, the main provisions governing migration are normally established by law. The legislature has the prerogative to promulgate regulations or rules through ordinances. The executive may issue circulars, and administrative officials may give instructions, which are not always made public and may be modified or revoked. Guidelines for government action are deferred to the administrative discretion of different ministries and departments, such as Justice, State, Labor, Health and Human Services, and Treasury, in addition to the president's or prime minister's staff.

Although immigration issues, political structures, and policy making vary substantially among the advanced liberal democracies, one unmistakable feature common to all is the rapid development of immigration legislation. The rate of change of immigration and asylum policy is evident from the density or flurry of legislation. In Europe, after the termination of guest-worker recruitment in 1973 (a process that did not always require legislation because it did not proceed from legislation in the first place), many countries passed little legislation for a decade, except to facilitate return migration (UNECE 1997, 168). Throughout the 1980s and early 1990s, however, nearly all European Union (EU) countries introduced restrictive legislation. From different starting points, most advanced industrialized countries have been converging toward more restrictive policies, and most have rapidly accelerated the pace of new legislative and administrative reforms to control immigration in the 1990s.

Although national legislation and immigration reforms represent the most obvious policy responses to regulate immigration, administrative decisions and policy implementation are also important. Because administrative structures and agencies have a substantial impact on policy elaboration and implementation, they are critical in analyzing state means to secure immigration and immigrant policy interests. New administrative categories (such as "temporary protection" status), for example, have been devised to accommodate authorized flows. In general, a key function of states in regulating migration is the creation of admissions and classification formulations, and this accounts for the difficulties in national comparisons (Lahav 1997b, 27). The means available to administrative agencies to create and recreate migrant categories and implement policy are considerable.

A sure sign of state efforts to adapt to migration challenges—and of a continuing state role in regulation—are the introduction of structural and institutional reforms to deal with enforcement. Some countries have adopted new institutions and commissions to deal explicitly with migration matters. Italy, for example, established the office of Extraordinary Commissioner for Immigration, who reports directly to the president of the Council of Ministers (OECD 1995, 99). More striking, however, has been the strengthening of traditional institutions dealing with migration, such as the U.S. Immigration and Naturalization Service (INS). Traditionally an agency plagued by low morale and negligible resources, in the 1990s the INS underwent a spectacular overhaul and became one of the few agencies in the government to grow.[5] The Clinton administration increased the INS budget to $3.1 billion for the 1996 fiscal, from $1.5 billion four years earlier (U.S. Department of Justice 1996). A significant proportion of the expanded budget has gone to tightening national borders, as attested by the gradual growth in the Border Patrol, scheduled to nearly double by 2001, and the adoption of new technology and automation (newly purchased computers, night-vision scopes, encrypted radios, and ground sensors).

The commitment to institutional effectiveness is perhaps nowhere better reflected than in administrative and implementation structures and norms. They are distinguished by two developments: the proliferation and diversification of third-party agents and nonstate actors and the devolution of decision making, policy elaboration, and regulation functions away from the central state. These phenomena are evident in policy making that focuses on immigrant intake as well as policies concerning the conditions of immigrants resident in the territory (Hammar 1985).

Increasingly, third-party actors define the immigration regulatory playing field as they deal with external and internal control sites, including questions of entry, stay, and exit of migrants. In terms of immigrant intake, these third-party actors include foreign states and intergovernmental groups as well as private companies such as airline carriers, transport companies, and security services. As for the control of migrants inside territories, this has increasingly become the domain of employer groups and civic actors (at both the international and local levels) dependent on nongovernmental organizations, trade unions, and even the family for regulatory intervention. Three types of actors—private, local, and international—have a role in monitoring external and internal control sites in the United States and Europe. The focus of this chapter is on the United States and France, an EU country with a substantial foreign population and anti-immigrant popular agitation,[6] and I begin with private actors.

■ Private Actors

Private actors, or independent authorities who rely on market forces, have become crucial immigration agents in extending the area of what is referred to by Aristide Zolberg as "remote control" immigration policy (1999). Before World War I, the low level of movement and modest welfare entitlement facilitated international movement free of passports and an elaborate system of controls (Torpey 1998). Since the 1920s, an elaborate system of documentation has developed, including visas for entry, work permits, and residence permits.

The initial migrant appeal to the host country typically occurs in the country of origin at embassies or consulates, through visa bureaucrats. To a significant degree, visas are a means of extending the barriers of control into the sending country, where facts about applicants can be verified in ways impossible at receiving-country ports of entry.[7]

The external site of immigration regulation became increasingly developed, complex, and diversified in the 1990s. A major thrust of recent policy efforts in many countries is interdiction, defined broadly as activity directed toward preventing the movement of people at the source (UN 1997). Interdiction initiatives take various forms, including information campaigns to deter potential migrants, visa requirements, carrier sanctions, airline training, and liaison with foreign control authorities, as well as the actual interception of persons traveling on fraudulent documents. According to its proponents, interdiction is more cost effective, humane, and efficient than enforcement action taken after the migrant has arrived in a receiving country.

A core actor in the enlarged control system at the entry level is transport or carrier companies. This is not new. Carriers have long been obliged, at their own expense, to transport inadmissible passengers back to their countries of departure. Sanctions against ships have been in force since the Passenger Act of 1902. However, since the adoption of guidelines established by the 1944 Convention on International Civil Aviation (ICAO), transport companies have increasingly been forced to assume the role of international immigration officers imposed on them by states. The standards of the convention established the airline's responsibility to ensure that passengers have the necessary travel documents. Apart from ICAO guidelines, many countries have introduced laws that increase the responsibilities of carriers and levy fines against them for noncompliance. In 1994, all EU countries, with the exception of Spain, Ireland, and Luxembourg, passed laws increasing carriers' responsibilities.

The content, interpretation, and application of laws on carriers' liabilities vary among European member states (Cruz 1994). Nonetheless, they represent an effort by states to redirect the burden of implementation away from the central government and toward the sources of control, thereby increasing national efficacy and decreasing the costs to government in the process. It is noteworthy that in all the laws on carriers' liability, there is a striking absence of any provision to fine railways. A possible reason is that most railways are state owned, and the treatment of railways as airlines are treated (that is, charging them with fines unless they can provide convincing evidence discharging them of negligence) could cause embarrassing problems between European states (Cruz 1994, 25).

The abolition of internal borders, critical to European integration, is essentially mitigated by the flurry of legislation and implementation of the carriers' liability to check passengers. Indeed, more stringent security checks at airports—of identity cards, tickets, boarding passes, baggage, and so on—have virtually offset the absence of passport controls, owing to the increasing link between international crime, terrorism, drugs, and illegal immigration (Bigo 1996). International instruments have supported and enhanced the role of carriers in border control. European Union member states cite their obligations under Article 26 of the 1990 Supplementation Agreement of the Schengen Convention in relying on carriers to serve as immigration officers.

In the United States, devolution of interstate regulation to expert bodies can be traced back to the federal government's adoption of the Interstate Commerce Act of 1887, regulating railways, and with it the creation of a regulatory body, the Interstate Commerce Commission (ICC). In passing this legislation, the Congress delegated power to regulate an important part of interstate commerce—namely, railway traffic—to an agency designed especially for the purpose. This was an important institutional innovation at the federal level (Majone 1996, 16). Although the ICC is not a private agency per se, it was set up by statute as an independent commission, a compromise to those American political leaders who rejected nationalization and sought to establish an expert authority to operate outside the line of hierarchical control or oversight by the departments of central government (Fainsod 1940, 313; Majone 1996, 15).[8] It represented the transfer of activities of state interests to semiprivate actors and technical experts and away from legislators, courts, or bureaucratic generalists. In this way, market activities may be generally regulated in areas that are considered important and in need of protection as well as control. According to Giandomenico Majone, "this mode of regulation represents a new frontier of public policy and public management in Europe" in the 1990s (1996, 15).

Although there are differences between European cases and the U.S. experience, in which business interests have been more culturally and politically dominant and state intervention in the economy is more prohibitive, the cost-benefit logic of this exchange is similar. Airlines and shipping and travel services may provide unique resources of personnel, services, and access to migrants, whereas states, by virtue of owning airspace (according to the Paris Conference of 1919), subject all these industries to national restrictions. Thus, with little training investment, these private actors may be enlisted in an enlarged control system, providing the state with the technological and resourceful means to differentiate effectively between the legal passage of travelers or economic tourists and the illegal passage of would-be overstayers or migrants (Weber 1998).

Immigration control may be equally effective in the employment sector. Increasingly, approaches to stem illegal migration at the work site have been developed to extend and redistribute the liabilities of migration control outside of the central state and to make employer groups more significant actors. In the early to middle 1970s, most advanced European countries adopted and refined employer sanctions (see Table 7.5.1).[9]

Strategies for enforcement of employer sanctions have evolved over time, involving a growing number of actors and leading to a complex web of laws. In the French case, for example, an employer who hires an illegal migrant is liable to an administrative fine from the Office of International Migrations and to judicial punishment following legal proceedings. Most citations for illegal alien employment are made by labor inspectors, but they also involve police gendarmes, judicial police, agricultural inspectors, and agents of customs, maritime affairs, and social security departments. In further removing immigration control from the central or federal government, a recent trend has been to contract out work-site enforcement to labor inspection agencies, security services, or police. In France, approximately four thousand police are qualified to enforce laws against illegal employment (Miller 1995, 23). In addition, French labor inspectors enjoy a great deal of discretion; they need not write up citations if they deem it not to be in the "public interest" to do so (Miller 1995, 23). Although the French practices and laws are controversial, there has been an unprecedented number of Special Contributions—2,498 in 1992 alone, compared with a total

Table 7.5.1   Third-Party Nonstate Actors in Immigration Regulation

Country	Transport Companies (Sanctions)	Employers (Sanctions)	Immigrants (Punishment for Illegal Entry)	Civil Society (Sanctions for Harboring Illegal Immigrants)
Belgium	Yes	Yes	Yes	Yes
Canada	Yes	Yes	Yes	Yes
Denmark	Yes	Yes	Yes	Yes
Finland	Yes	Yes	Yes	No
Germany	Yes	Yes	Yes	Yes
Italy	Yes	Yes	Yes	No
Netherlands	Yes	Yes	No	Yes
Sweden	Yes	Yes	Yes	Yes
United Kingdom	Yes	Yes	Yes	Yes
United States	Yes	Yes	Yes	Yes

Source: Author's calculations.

involve the extension of state control over migration outside and beyond its traditional boundaries.

■ Local Actors

States are increasingly relying on local actors, or decentralized bodies, for monitoring and implementation functions. Through decentralization, national governments have delegated substantial decision-making powers to local elected officials, often in a way considered to be exclusionary and detrimental to foreigners' rights. A major reason behind this kind of decentralization is that national elected officials concur and depend on local elected officials, who are under financial and political pressure to attract more funds and votes by adopting exceptionally harsh measures against immigrants.

What sort of decision-making powers have national governments delegated to local elected officials? In France, city halls now have the prerogative to inspect the veracity of marriages between nationals and foreigners. A 1993 law granted mayors the authority to refer a marriage involving an alien to the Procureur de la République (state prosecutor), who can delay the marriage for a month and then, if they see fit, prevent it. A 1996 survey revealed significant geographical diversity in the law's implementation; in some cases, it was used as a measure to arrest illegal aliens (Weil 1997).[12] Since 1982, when the Deferre laws on decentralization were passed in France, mayors have gained political powers. Mayors in urban areas and in the Southeast, where the National Front has made electoral headway, have used their new monitoring role in migration control policy to the fullest (Guiraudon and Lahav 2000, 21).

National governments have shifted other monitoring functions of immigrant stays and rights downward to local actors. Since 1993 legislation in France, foreigners living in the country illegally no longer qualify for social security (including child allowances, health insurance, old age pensions, and unemployment benefits) (UN 1997, 368), and local governments are bearing the direct costs. In the United States, Proposition 187 and the Gallegly Amendment, measures to bar the undocumented and their children from public schools and welfare programs, focused on the liabilities of local actors for implementation. These demands for more local power concur with national plans for restrictions of foreigners' rights. The 1996 Welfare Act marked the end of the sixty-one-year-old federal guarantee of cash assistance for the nation's poorest children; it revoked federal benefits like food stamps and Supplementary Security Income for noncitizen immigrants (*New York Times*, February 21, 1997, 18). This new law also gives states vast new authority to run their own welfare programs with lump sums of federal money. It thus represents renewed efforts to grant states (local actors) more control over traditionally unfunded mandates, creating a mechanism for uneven integration policies across states and regions.

Of course, as Gerald Neuman (1996) observes, in the United States, state and local governments have long regulated the movement of people across legal borders, through the use of criminal laws, vagrancy laws, quarantine laws, and registration requirements and, before 1865, through the law of slavery. In contrast to unitary states that have been decentralizing, such as France, the relation between state and federal governments in federal systems, such as the United States, has been laid out more clearly for a long time. Until the middle to late nineteenth century, states still carried a number of prerogatives in the area of migration, including the rights granted to aliens (Schuck 1998) and the bestowing of nationality (Neuman 1998). Part of the explanation stems from the fact that states with slave populations wanted control over nationality, and hence, it was not surprising that courts rescinded these state rights after the Civil War. Increasingly during the twentieth century, Supreme Court decisions emphasized the exclusive federal prerogatives in the area of immigration regulation, via the plenary power doctrine, and the dangers of state encroachment. Thus, although some argue that the devolution of immigration policy to states is a growing reality, and a legitimate one, given the handful of states that are major fiscal and political stakeholders of immigration (Spiro 1994), from a historical perspective, contemporary political demands for a state role in immigration policy is a call to turn back the clock.

In general, the delegation of immigrant policy to state and local governments is not new. However, by reinforcing the local authorities' responsibilities and autonomy in immigrant policy, federal governments have been able to effectively enlarge immigration control through burden-sharing exchanges. Still, as the legal scholar Peter Schuck (1998) has argued, it is ultimately up to the U.S. Congress to authorize states to play a role in immigration policy, as the latter did in 1996 with respect to welfare benefits. These trends have led to renewed conflicts between federal, state, and local mandates (see Neuman 1993; Olivas 1994). Thus, the 1996 Illegal Immigration Reform and Immigrant Responsibility Act, which permits the INS to train and deputize local police officers to enforce immigration laws, is likely to receive uneven political reception. The conflicts are likely to heighten contradictory goals of different arms of the state (the police, judiciary, public administration) and also to obscure the lines between national (and, in the EU case, supranational) and local mandates. The general implications of decentralization and incorporation of local actors for immigration flows are diverse local outcomes and uneven integration strategies, which often give the semblance of policy incoherence.

cies. It is also consistent with trends in other policy areas, of shifting the externalities of policy making outside of the central government. The shifts in implementation to private, local, or cooperative arrangements reflect less an abdication of state sovereignty than an experiment in which national states make rational attempts to diminish the costs of migration. The impetus to immigration reform and stricter control, it should be remembered, have come from states themselves; private and local actors face ever more restrictions, either from central governments or from international agreements. In the face of global and international pressures in the post–Cold War system, state responses may serve to neutralize the contradictions between open borders for goods, capital, and services and limited borders for the movement of people.

It is important to emphasize that these developments are not changes in state functions but shifts in modes of regulation. The processes of devolution aim to enhance the political capacity of states to regulate migration, to make states more flexible and adaptable to all types of migration pressures, to shift the focus of responsiveness, and to generate more effective state legitimacy. In practice, liberal democracies can deploy a considerable battery of policy instruments to control migration. Effectiveness must be measured not only against demographic or migration outcomes but by the means used to contain and defuse political debates and to increase state efficacy and legitimacy. Critical distinctions between policy output and policy outcomes—between stated and hidden goals and consequences of migration control—must be considered. More research on motivations, attitudes, and training of nonstate gatekeepers as they relate to broader policy or political goals is clearly required to better understand the dynamic processes of regulation I have described.

■ Notes

1. See Thelen and Steinmo (1992) for a succinct overview of the neoinstitutional literature in political science.

2. The notion of the "political" in migration analysis has not advanced much since the early 1980s, when the role of the state in migration was elaborated by Aristide Zolberg (1981). Reference here to the expression "bringing back the state" follows Max Weber's (1958) definition of the state as the legitimate owner of the means and apparatus of violence and force. It also reflects the work of Peter Evans, Dietrich Rueschemeyer, and Theda Skocpol (1985).

3. Following Stephen Krasner (1983), the term "international regime" includes principles, norms, rules, and decision-making procedures around which actor expectations converge on a given issue.

4. The United Nations Convention for the Rights of All Migrants, for example, has been commonly cited as testament to universal rights imposed on states by international human rights law. Nonetheless, considering how few states have signed or ratified the convention, its constraints become elusive. In order to make conventions or covenants relevant, states must go beyond signatory status to ratification, meaning the incorporation of legislation into national law. The approach of

the United States to the Geneva Convention, one of the most widely revered international human rights instruments, underscores how ambiguous this process may be; the United States ratified the 1951 Convention and its 1967 Protocol in 1980 with the adoption of the Refugee Act, and only in the late 1980s did it actually devise regulations for implementation.

5. In addition, in 1993, the Crime Control Act appropriated funding (almost $50 million) to implement many proposed asylum reforms, the most notable of which was the doubling of the number of INS asylum officers (OECD 1995).

6. Note again that in these comparisons, differences may also arise because of structural differences that are specific to political systems: for example, the United States is a federal system, whereas France is a decentralized unitary state.

7. The United States, for example, calls its consulates in a place like the Dominican Republic, the largest source of immigration to New York City, "the front line in the struggle against illegal immigration." In the twelve-month period ending September 30, 1996, the consulate in Santo Domingo processed 52,410 requests for immigrant visas (more than 40 percent of which were rejected) and 110,000 applications for nonimmigrant visas (*New York Times*, February 19, 1997).

8. In the United States, the tradition of regulation by independent bodies means combined legislative, judicial, and executive functions (rule making, adjudication, and enforcement, in the terminology of American administrative law). Such bodies allow public utilities and other industries deemed to affect the public interest to remain in private hands but subject to rules developed and enforced by specialized agencies or commissions (see Majone 1996, 15).

9. France decreed employer sanctions again in 1976; the United Kingdom adopted legislation prohibiting the harboring of illegal aliens, though not their employment (out of fear of fueling discrimination) in 1971; Switzerland has had antiharboring statutes since 1931 and adopted an employment statute in 1984; West Germany first prohibited the employment of clandestine aliens in 1975; the Netherlands did so in 1974, as did Austria in 1981, and Italy, Spain and Belgium have since followed suit (see Miller 1995).

10. In the United States, the number of illegal aliens deported in 1995 reached a record level of 51,600, up 15 percent from 1995 and up nearly 75 percent from 1990 (*New York Times*, December 28, 1995).

11. In Pennsylvania, a five-hundred-bed addition to York County local prison has been planned for the explicit rental to the immigration service. One county commissioner reported that the county would receive a reimbursement of fifty dollars a day per bed for what would cost only twenty-four dollars (*New York Times*, July 7, 1997).

12. The survey revealed that 41.6 percent of the marriages suspended by mayors involved an undocumented alien (Weil 1997).

13. In November, an additional requirement for airport transit visas was adopted for nationals of ten countries from which many asylum claims originated: Afghanistan, Ethiopia, Eritrea, Ghana, Iraq, Iran, Nigeria, Somalia, Sri Lanka, and Zaire.

■ References

Baldwin-Edwards, Martin. 1997. "The Emerging European Immigration Regime: Some Reflections on Implications for Southern Europe." *Journal of Common Market Studies* 35(4): 497–519.

Bigo, Didier. 1996. *Policies en Réseaux: Experience Européene.* (Police Networks: The European Experience.) Paris: Presses de la Fondation de Sciences Politiques.

———. 1998. "'Bond of Union.' Military Involvement in Internal Security." Paper presented at the annual meeting of the International Studies Association, Minneapolis, Minn. (1998).

Bunyan, Tony. 1991. "Towards an Authoritarian European State." *Race and Class* 32(3): 179–88.

Bunyan, Tony, and Frances Webber. 1995. *Intergovernmental Cooperation on Immigration and Asylum.* Brussels: Churches Commission for Migrants in Europe.

Chekel, Jeff. 1995. "International Norms and Domestic Institutions: Identity Politics in Post–Cold War Europe." Paper presented at the annual meeting of the American Political Science Association, Chicago (September 3, 1995).

Conference on Immigration and the Changing Face of America, Ames, Iowa (July 13–15, 1996).

Cornelius, Wayne, Philip Martin, and James Hollifield, eds. 1994. *Controlling Immigration.* Stanford, Calif.: Stanford University Press.

Cruz, Antonio. 1994. "Carrier Liability in the Member States of the European Union." Briefing Paper 17. Brussels: Churches Commission for Migrants in Europe.

Evans, Peter, Dietrich Rueschemeyer, and Theda Skocpol, eds. 1985. *Bringing the State Back In.* Cambridge, U.K.: Cambridge University Press.

Fainsod, Merle. 1940. "Some Reflections on the Nature of the Regulatory Process." In *Public Policy*, edited by Friedrich Mason. Cambridge, Mass.: Harvard University Press.

Faist, Thomas. 1994. "A Medieval City: Transnationalizing Labor Markets and Social Rights in Europe." ZeS-Arbeitpaper 9 (working paper 9). Bremen, Germany: Universitat Bremen Zentrum fur Sozialpolitik.

Feigenbaum, Harvey, and Jeffrey Henig. 1994. "The Political Underpinnings of Privatization: A Typology." *World Politics* 46(2): 185–208.

Freeman, Gary. 1994. "Can Liberal States Control Unwanted Migration?" *Annals of the American Academy* 534(July): 17–30.

———. 1995. "Modes of Immigration Politics in Liberal Democratic States." *International Migration Review* 29(4): 881–902.

Guiraudon, Virginie. 1997. "Avoiding the Spotlight: Explaining the Evolution of Rights of Foreigners in Germany, France, and the Netherlands, 1974–1994." Ph.D. diss., Harvard University.

Guiraudon, Virginie, and Gallya Lahav. 2000. "A Reappraisal of the State Sovereignty Debate: The Case of Migration Control." *Comparative Political Studies* 33(2): 163–95.

Hammar, Thomas. 1985. *European Immigration Policy: A Comparative Study.* Cambridge, U.K.: Cambridge University Press.

Heisler, Martin. 1992. "Migration, International Relations, and the New Europe: Theoretical Perspectives from Institutional Political Sociology." *International Migration Review* 26(2): 596–622.

Hollifield, James F. 1992. *Immigrants, Markets, and States: The Political Economy of Postwar Europe.* Cambridge, Mass.: Harvard University Press.

Joppke, Christian. 1997. "Asylum and State Sovereignty: A Comparison of the United States, Germany, and Britain." *Comparative Political Studies* 30(3): 259–98.

Keohane, Robert, and Stanley Hoffman. 1990. "Conclusions: Community Politics and Institutional Change." In *The Dynamics of European Integration*, edited by William Wallace. London: Pinter.

Krasner, Stephen. 1982. "Structural Causes and Regime Consequences: Regimes as Intervening Variables." *International Organization* 36(Spring): 379–415.

———, ed. 1983. *International Regimes*. Ithaca: Cornell University Press.

Lahav, Gallya. 1993. "Immigration, Hypernationalism, and European Security." In *The Future of European Security*, edited by J. Philip Rogers. New York: St. Martin's Press.

———. 1997a. "The Evolution of Immigration Policy in Liberal Democracies Since 1965: Changing the Gatekeepers or 'Bringing Back the State'?" Paper presented at the German-American Academic Council (GAAC) Young Scholars' Institute on Immigration, Incorporation, and Citizenship in the Advanced Industrial Democracies, Berlin, Germany (July 14–25, 1997).

———. 1997b. "International Versus National Constraints in Family Reunification Migration Policy." *Global Governance* 3(3): 349–72.

———. 1998. "Immigration and the State: The Devolution and Privatisation of Immigration Control in the European Union." *Journal of Ethnic and Migration Studies* 24(4): 675–94.

Layton-Henry, Zig, ed. 1990. *The Political Rights of Migrant Workers in Western Europe*. London: Sage.

Majone, Giandomenico. 1996. "Regulation and Its Modes." In *Regulating Europe*, edited by G. Majone. London: Routledge.

Miller, Mark. 1995. "Employer Sanctions in France: From the Campaign Against Illegal Alien Employment to the Campaign Against Illegal Work." Research paper. Washington: U.S. Commission on Immigration Reform.

Money, Jeannette. 1999. "Human Rights Norms and Immigration Control." *Journal of International Law and Foreign Affairs* 3(2): 497–525.

Münz, Rainer. 1996. "The Migrants." *The Earth Times* (February 15).

Neuman, Gerald. 1993. "The Lost Century of American Immigration Law (1776–1875)." *Columbia Law Review* (93)(8).

———. 1996. *Strangers to the Constitution: Immigrants, Borders, and Fundamental Law*. Princeton, N.J.: Princeton University Press.

———. 1998. "The Effects of Immigration on Nationality Law." Paper presented to the European Forum seminar, European University Institute, Florence, Italy (June 4–6, 1998).

Olivas, Michael. 1994. "Preempting Preemption: Foreign Affairs, State Rights, and Alienage Classifications." *Virginia Journal of International Law* (35): 217–36.

Organisation for Economic Co-operation and Development (OECD). SOPEMI. 1995. *Continuous Reporting System on Migration: Trends in International Migration*. Paris: OECD.

———. 1997. *Continuous Reporting System on Migration: Trends in International Migration*. Paris: OECD.

Papademetriou, Demetrious. 1993. "Confronting the Challenge of Transnational Migration: Domestic and International Responses." In *The Changing Course of International Migration*. Paris: OECD.

Papademetriou, Demetrious, and Mark Miller. 1983. *The Unavoidable Issue: U.S. Immigration Policy in the 1980s*. Philadelphia: Institute for the Study of Human Issues.

Pastore, Massimo. 1991. "A Historical Critical Overview of European Intergovernmental Cooperation on Matters of Immigration, Asylum, and

Internal Security." Paper presented to the Nineteenth Annual Conference of the European Group for the Study of Deviance and Social Control, Potsdam (September 4–8, 1991).

Rawls, John. 1971. *A Theory of Justice*. Cambridge, Mass.: Cambridge University Press.

Ruggie, John. 1982. "International Regimes, Transactions, and Change: Embedded Liberalism in the Postwar Economic Order." *International Organizations* 36: 379–415.

Sassen, Saskia. 1991. *The Global City: New York, London, Tokyo*. Princeton, N.J.: Princeton University Press.

———. 1996. *Losing Control?* New York: Columbia University Press.

Schain, Martin. 1995. "Policy Effectiveness and the Regulation of Immigration in Europe." Paper presented at the annual meeting of the International Studies Association (February 25, 1995).

Schuck, Peter. 1989. "Membership in the Liberal Polity: the Devaluation of American Citizenship." *Georgetown Immigration Law Journal* 3(1).

———. 1998. "The Reevaluation of American Citizenship." In *Challenge to the Nation State: Immigration in Western Europe and the United States*, edited by Christian Joppke. New York: Oxford University Press.

Soysal, Yasemin Nuhoglu. 1994. *Limits of Citizenship*. Chicago: University of Chicago Press.

Spiro, Peter. 1994. "The States and Immigration in an Era of Demi-Sovereignties." *Virginia Journal of International Law* (35): 121–78.

Thelen, Kathleen, and Sven Steinmo. 1992. "Historical Institutionalism in Comparative Politics." In *Structuring Politics: Historical Institutionalism in Comparative Analysis*, edited by Sven Steinmo, Kathleen Thelen, and Frank Longstreth. Cambridge, U.K.: Cambridge University Press.

Torpey, John. 1998. "Coming and Going: Passport Control." Paper presented at the annual meeting of the International Studies Association, Minneapolis, Minn. (March 21–24, 1998).

United Nations. 1997. *World Population Monitoring, 1997: Issues of International Migration and Development*. New York: Population Division of the Department for Social Information and Policy Analysis of the United Nations.

———. 1998. "Family Reunification Migration: Policies and Issues." In *International Migration Policies and Programmes*: A World Survey. New York: United Nations.

United Nations Economic Commission for Europe (UNECE). 1997. *International Migration and Integration Policies in the UNECE Region*. Geneva: Population Activities Unit.

U.S. Commission on Immigration Reform. 1994. *U.S. Immigration Policy: Restoring Credibility*. 1994 Report to Congress. Washington: Commission on Immigration Reform (September).

U.S. Department of Justice. 1996. Washington: U.S. Government Printing Office.

U.S. Immigration and Naturalization Service. 1994. *Statistical Yearbook of the Immigration and Naturalization Service: 1993*. Washington: U.S. Government Printing Office.

———. 1996. *Statistical Yearbook of the Immigration and Naturalization Service: 1994*. Washington: U.S. Government Printing Office.

Van Outrive, Lode. 1990. "Migration and Penal Reform: One European Policy?" Unpublished paper xviii, presented at the annual conference of the European

Group for the Study of Deviance and Social Control, Haarlem, The Netherlands (1990).

Waltz, Kenneth. 1979. *Theory of International Politics*. Reading, Mass.: Addison-Wesley.

Walzer, Michael. 1980. *Radical Principles*. New York: Basic Books.

Weber, Frank Paul. 1998. "Participation of Carriers in the Control of Migration: The Case of Germany." Paper presented to the International Studies Association, Minneapolis, Minn. (March 21–24).

Weber, Max. 1958. *From Max Weber: Essays in Sociology*, edited and translated by H. H. Gerth and C. Wright Mills. New York: Oxford University Press.

Weil, Patrick. 1997. *Mission d'étude de la législation de la nationalité et de l'immigration: Rapports au premier ministre*. Paris: La Documentation Française.

Weiner, Myron. 1985. "International migration and International relations." In *Population and Development Review* 11(September): 441–55.

———. 1990. *Security, Stability, and International Migration*. Cambridge, Mass.: MIT Center for International Studies.

Zolberg, Aristide. 1981. "International Migration in Political Perspective." In *Global Trends in Migration: Theory and Research in International Population Movements*, edited by Mary M. Kritz, Charle Keely, and S. M. Tomasi. Staten Island, N.Y.: Center for Migration Studies.

———. 1999. "Matters of State: Theorizing Immigration Policy." In *The Handbook of International Migration: The American Experience*, edited by Charles Hirschman, Philip Kasinitz, and Josh DeWind. New York: Russell Sage Foundation.

chapter 8

Economic Considerations

8.1 *the Editors*

Introduction

Most analyses of the role of economic factors in immigration policymaking involve rational-based models or cost-benefit calculations of migration. Nevertheless, experts, such as those represented in this chapter, often conflict in their judgments about migration. The reasons are usually differences in time horizons (i.e., the long-term and short-term benefits and costs of migration), bias concerning which indicators of economic health matter most or should be privileged (e.g., unemployment, inflation, growth, development, or social welfare), and perceptions of what groups are or should be the losers or winners of migration (e.g., workers, unions, business, consumers).

On the basis of the available empirical evidence, for example, Stephen Moore in Chapter 8.3 forcefully argues that the ongoing migration of a substantial number of foreign workers to advanced industrial societies has been and remains vital to the health and success of those states' economies. This line of argument readily acknowledges that the demand for foreign labor within the major immigration-receiving states is not nearly as great today as it was during the height of the great economic boom of the 1950s and 1960s. Nevertheless, four lines of evidence suggest that, whatever the route of foreign workers into the domestic economy (i.e., legal or irregular), the need for them remains significant and is not likely to wane soon.

First, despite the omnipresent threat of government sanctions, private employers are often quite ready to knowingly or unknowingly employ illegal foreign workers. The practice is commonplace throughout the Southwestern and Western United States. The demand for illegal foreign workers has also been strong in recent years in the traditional labor-exporting countries of Italy, Portugal, and Spain. Moreover, the issue of illegal labor has become increasingly thorny throughout Asia, including in Japan and Malaysia.

Second, the overall demand for immigrant labor has been and is conspicuously robust within the major immigration-receiving countries, especially in the primary and/or tertiary sectors of the economy, economic sectors in which a flexible labor force is particularly valued. Immigrant labor is especially attractive to employers at the lower end of the employment ladder for several reasons. Immigrants tend to accept low-status but nevertheless indispensable jobs that native workers reject. They are often cheaper to hire and easier to retain than native workers. Their employment can usually be terminated more easily than that of native workers, and they tend to be flexible about the conditions and the geographical location of their work. Finally, foreign labor is often a good short-term economic investment over potentially labor-saving but expensive technological innovations. Propelling the robust demand for foreign workers at the higher end of the employment ladder are labor rigidities and shortages, such as an estimated shortfall of several million information-technology technicians in Europe and North America.

Third, despite the political and social fallout that significant labor immigration typically precipitates and against the unfavorable backdrop of persistently high native unemployment, the share of foreigners in the labor force of many of the advanced industrial countries continues to expand over time. From 1986 to 1999, for example, the share of foreign labor as a percentage of the entire national workforce increased, albeit sometimes modestly, in every major immigrant-receiving country of Western Europe bar France and Sweden. In Austria, Belgium, France, Germany, Ireland, Portugal, and the United Kingdom, the percentage of foreigners in the total labor force now nearly equals or exceeds the percentage of foreigners within the general population.

Finally, in a sure sign of the embeddedness of the demand for their labor, foreign workers have penetrated nearly all sectors of the economy, with their employment in some sectors often growing faster than that of nationals. In Germany, for example, the rate of employment growth of foreigners in construction, the hotel and restaurant industries, transport and communication, public administration, and education outpaced the growth of employment of citizens between 1993 and 1997, often by a substantial margin. During this same period in Britain, the rate of growth of nonnative employment outstripped that of native employment in the wholesale and retail trade, hotels and restaurants, transport and communication, public administration, and real estate and business activities. In the aggregate, foreigners constituted more than one-fifth of all workers in mining and manufacturing in Austria, Belgium, Germany, Italy, the Netherlands, and Sweden in 1999–2000.

Weighed against the transparent economic benefits of immigrant labor, of course, are its considerable, if sometimes hidden, burdens. As George Borjas usefully reminds us in Chapter 8.2, the net returns of immigration can be rationally calculated only in the context of its considerable economic and distributional costs, including the costs of extending welfare-related services to the immigrant population as a whole and compensating the "losers" of immigration. Moreover, as the selection from the *Economist* in Chapter 8.4 points out, some kinds of immigration benefit the host countries more than others. In general, immigrant labor that complements rather than substitutes for native labor is best.

Yet, as Borjas persuasively argues, serious doubts can be raised about whether governments *can* calculate with any reasonable degree of confidence the economic and other tradeoffs inevitably associated with mass immigration. Even when they have identified most of the major costs and benefits, host governments are still severely challenged to micromanage the flow of immigration in a manner that yields predominantly favorable, let alone optimal, economic outcomes.

The New Economics of Immigration: Affluent Americans Gain, Poor Americans Lose

The United States is on the verge of another great debate over immigration. Thus far the focus of this still-inchoate debate has been on illegal immigration or welfare benefits to legal immigrants, not on the larger issue of the character and consequences of the current high levels of legal immigration. Economic factors by themselves should not and will not decide the outcome of this debate. But they will play an important role. Economics helps us to frame answerable questions about immigration:

Who gains by it? Who loses? And in light of the answers to these questions, what should U.S. immigration policy be?

There have been two major shifts in immigration policy in this century. In the twenties the United States began to limit the number of immigrants admitted and established the national-origins quota system, an allocation scheme that awarded entry visas mainly on the basis of national origin and that favored Germany and the United Kingdom. This system was repealed in 1965, and family reunification became the central goal of immigration policy, with entry visas being awarded mainly to applicants who had relatives already residing in the United States.

The social, demographic, and economic changes initiated by the 1965 legislation have been truly historic. The number of immigrants began to rise rapidly. As recently as the 1950s only about 250,000 immigrants entered the country annually; by the 1990s the United States was admitting more than 800,000 legal immigrants a year, and some 300,000 aliens entered and stayed in the country illegally. The 1965 legislation also led to a momentous shift in the ethnic composition of the population. Although people of European origin dominated the immigrant flow from the country's founding until the 1950s, only about 10 percent of those admitted in the 1980s were of European origin. It is now estimated that non-Hispanic whites may form a minority of the population soon after 2050. More troubling is that immigration has been linked to the increase in income inequal-

---

George J. Borjas, "The New Economics of Immigration: Affluent Americans Gain, Poor Americans Lose," *Atlantic Monthly* (Nov. 1996).

ity observed since the 1980s, and to an increase in the costs of maintaining the programs that make up the welfare state.

These economic and demographic changes have fueled the incipient debate over immigration policy. For the most part, the weapons of choice in this debate are statistics produced by economic research, with all sides marshaling facts and evidence that support particular policy goals. In this essay I ask a simple question: What does economic research imply about the kind of immigration policy that the United States should pursue?

■ A Formula for Admission

Every immigration policy must resolve two distinct issues: how many immigrants the country should admit, and what kinds of people they should be.

It is useful to view immigration policy as a formula that gives points to visa applicants on the basis of various characteristics and then sets a passing grade. The variables in the formula determine what kinds of people will be let into the country, and the passing grade determines how many will be let into the country. Current policy uses a formula that has one overriding variable: whether the visa applicant has a family member already residing in the United States. An applicant who has a relative in the country gets 100 points, passes the test, and is admitted. An applicant who does not gets 0 points, fails the test, and cannot immigrate legally.

Of course, this is a simplistic summary of current policy. There are a lot of bells and whistles in the immigration statutes (which are said to be only slightly less complex than the tax code). In fact the number of points a person gets may depend on whether the sponsor is a U.S. citizen or a permanent resident, and whether the family connection is a close one (such as a parent, a spouse, or a child) or a more distant one (a sibling). Such nuances help to determine the speed with which the visa is granted. A limited number of visas are given to refugees. Some are also distributed on the basis of skill characteristics, but these go to only seven percent of immigrants.

Although the United States does not officially admit to using a point system in awarding entry visas, other countries proudly display their formulas on the Internet. A comparison of these point systems reveals that the United States is exceptional in using essentially one variable. Canada, Australia, and New Zealand have more-complex formulas that include an applicant's educational background, occupation, English-language proficiency, and age along with family connections.

Sometimes a host country awards points to people who are willing to pay the visa's stated price. Canada, for example, has granted entry to virtually anyone who would invest at least $250,000 in a Canadian business.

Although this "visas-for-sale" policy is a favorite proposal of economists (if we have a market for butter, why not also a market for visas?), it is not taken very seriously in the political debate, perhaps because policymakers feel a repugnance against what may be perceived as a market for human beings. I will therefore discuss the implications of economic research only for policies in which points are awarded on the basis of socioeconomic characteristics, not exchanged for dollars.

■ What Have We Learned?

The academic literature investigating the economic impact of immigration on the United States has grown rapidly in the past decade. The assumptions that long dominated discussion of the costs and benefits of immigration were replaced during the 1980s by a number of new questions, issues, and perceptions.

Consider the received wisdom of the early 1980s. The studies available suggested that even though immigrants arrived at an economic disadvantage, their opportunities improved rapidly over time. Within a decade or two of immigrants' arrival their earnings would overtake the earnings of natives of comparable socioeconomic background. The evidence also suggested that immigrants did no harm to native employment opportunities, and were less likely to receive welfare assistance than natives. Finally, the children of immigrants were even more successful than their parents. The empirical evidence, therefore, painted a very optimistic picture of the contribution that immigrants made to the American economy.

In the past ten years this picture has altered radically. New research has established a number of points.

• The relative skills of successive immigrant waves have declined over much of the postwar period. In 1970, for example, the latest immigrant arrivals on average had 0.4 fewer years of schooling and earned 17 percent less than natives. By 1990 the most recently arrived immigrants had 1.3 fewer years of schooling and earned 32 percent less than natives.

• Because the newest immigrant waves start out at such an economic disadvantage, and because the rate of economic assimilation is not very rapid, the earnings of the newest arrivals may never reach parity with the earnings of natives. Recent arrivals will probably earn 20 percent less than natives throughout much of their working lives.

• The large-scale migration of less-skilled workers has done harm to the economic opportunities of less-skilled natives. Immigration may account for perhaps a third of the recent decline in the relative wages of less-educated native workers.

• The new immigrants are more likely to receive welfare assistance

grants pay $25–$30 billion more in taxes than they take out of the system, while other studies blame them for a fiscal burden of more than $40 billion on natives.

It is doubtful that either of these statistics accurately reflects the gap between taxes paid and the cost of services provided. Studies that claim a beneficial fiscal impact tend to assume that immigrants do not increase the cost of most government programs other than education and welfare. Even though we do not know by how much immigrants increase the cost of police protection, maintaining roads and national parks, and so forth, we do know that it costs more to provide these services to an ever larger population. However, studies that claim a large fiscal burden often overstate the costs of immigration and understate the taxes paid. As a result, estimates of the fiscal impact of immigration should be viewed with suspicion. Nevertheless, because the immigration surplus is around $7 billion, the net benefit from immigration after accounting for the fiscal impact is very small, and could conceivably be a net loss.

■ How Many and Whom Should We Admit?

In principle, we should admit immigrants whenever their economic contribution (to native well-being) will exceed the costs of providing social services to them. We are not, though, in a position to make this calculation with any reasonable degree of confidence. In fact, no mainstream study has ever attempted to suggest, purely on the basis of the empirical evidence, how many immigrants should be admitted.

This unfortunate lack of guidance from economic research has, I believe, led to sudden and remarkable swings in policy proposals. As recently as 1990 Congress legislated an increase in the number of legal immigrants of about 175,000 people annually. Last year the Commission on Immigration Reform, headed by Barbara Jordan, recommended that legal immigration be cut by about 240,000 people a year—a proposal that was immediately supported by President Clinton. (The Clinton Administration, however, successfully resisted congressional efforts to follow up on the commission's recommendations.)

Although we do not know how many immigrants to admit, simple economics and common sense suggest that the magic number should not be an immutable constant regardless of economic conditions in the United States. A good case can be made for linking immigration to the business cycle: admit more immigrants when the economy is strong and the unemployment rate is low, and cut back on immigration when the economy is weak and the unemployment rate is high.

Economic research also suggests that the United States may be better off if its policy of awarding entry visas favors skilled workers. Skilled immigrants earn more than less skilled immigrants, and hence pay more in taxes, and they are less likely to use welfare and other social services.

Depending on how the skills of immigrants compare with the skills of natives, immigrants also affect the productivity of the native work force and of native-owned companies. Skilled native workers, for example, have much to gain when less skilled workers enter the United States: they can devote all their efforts to jobs that use their skills effectively while immigrants provide cheap labor for service jobs. These gains, however, come at a cost. The jobs of less-skilled natives are now at risk, and these natives will suffer a reduction in their earnings. Nonetheless, it does not seem far-fetched to assume that the American work force, particularly in comparison with the work forces of many source countries, is composed primarily of skilled workers. Thus the typical American worker would seem to gain from unskilled immigration.

How does immigration affect companies' profits? Companies that use less-skilled workers on the production line gain from the immigration of the less skilled, who reduce the earnings of less-skilled workers in favor of increasing profits. However, other companies—perhaps even most—might be better off with skilled immigrants. Many studies in economics suggest that skilled labor is better suited to the machines that are now used widely in the production process. Most companies would therefore gain more if the immigrant flow were composed of skilled workers. Most workers prefer unskilled immigrants, whereas most companies prefer skilled immigrants. This conflict can be resolved only by measuring how much native workers gain from unskilled immigration and how much companies gain from skilled immigration, and comparing the two. Although there is a lot of uncertainty in the academic literature, we do know that the productivity of capital is very responsive to an influx of skilled workers. The large increase in the profits of the typical company, and the corresponding reduction in the cost of goods produced by skilled workers, suggest that the United States might be better off with a policy favoring skilled immigrants.

The gains from skilled immigration will be even larger if immigrants have "external effects" on the productivity of natives. One could argue, for example, that immigrants may bring knowledge, skills, and abilities that natives lack, and that natives might somehow pick up this know-how by interacting with immigrants. It seems reasonable to suspect that the value of these external effects would be greater if natives interact with highly skilled immigrants. This increase in the human capital of natives might off-set—and perhaps even reverse—the harm that immigration does to the wages of competing workers.

Although such effects now play a popular role in economic theory, there is little empirical evidence supporting their existence, let alone measuring their magnitude. I find it difficult to imagine that interaction with immigrants entering an economy as large as that of the United States could have a measurable effect. Nevertheless, if external effects exist, they reinforce the argument that the United States would gain most from skilled immigrants.

■ Efficiency Versus Distribution

Participants in the immigration debate routinely use the results of economic research to frame the discussion and to suggest policy solutions. Perhaps the most important contributions of this research are the insights that immigration entails both gains and losses for the native population, that the winners and the losers are typically different groups, and that policy parameters can be set in ways that attempt to maximize gains and minimize losses. If the objective of immigration policy is to increase the per capita income of the native population, the evidence suggests that immigration policy should encourage the entry of skilled workers. It is important to remember, however, that even though the immigration of skilled workers would be beneficial for the United States as a whole, the gains and losses would be concentrated in particular subgroups of the population.

As we have seen, the net gains from current immigration are small, so it is unlikely that these gains can play a crucial role in the policy debate. Economic research teaches a very valuable lesson: the economic impact of immigration is essentially distributional. Current immigration redistributes wealth from unskilled workers, whose wages are lowered by immigrants, to skilled workers and owners of companies that buy immigrants' services, and from taxpayers who bear the burden of paying for the social services used by immigrants to consumers who use the goods and services produced by immigrants.

Distributional issues drive the political debate over many social policies, and immigration policy is no exception. The debate over immigration policy is not a debate over whether the entire country is made better off by immigration—the gains from immigration seem much too small, and could even be outweighed by the costs of providing increased social services. Immigration changes how the economic pie is sliced up—and this fact goes a long way toward explaining why the debate over how many and what kinds of immigrants to admit is best viewed as a tug-of-war between those who gain from immigration and those who lose from it.

History has taught us that immigration policy changes rarely, but when it does, it changes drastically. Can economic research play a role in finding a better policy? I believe it can, but there are dangers ahead. Although the pendulum seems to be swinging to the restrictionist side (with ever louder calls for a complete closing of our borders), a greater danger to the national interest may be the few economic groups that gain much from immigration.

They seem indifferent to the costs that immigration imposes on other segments of society, and they have considerable financial incentives to keep the current policy in place. The harmful effects of immigration will not go away simply because some people do not wish to see them. In the short run these groups may simply delay the day of reckoning. Their potential long-run impact, however, is much more perilous: the longer the delay, the greater the chances that when immigration policy finally changes, it will undergo a seismic shift—one that, as in the twenties, may come close to shutting down the border and preventing Americans from enjoying the benefits that a well-designed immigration policy can bestow on the United States.

annual 6% of GDP. If migrants make a net contribution to taxes over their lives, they reduce that debt. But even if they do not, argues DIW's Mr. Brücker, they increase the number of future taxpayers. The same debt spread over more payers automatically reduces the individual burden of future taxpayers. In short, migration cannot prevent ageing, but it can significantly reduce its fiscal consequences.

To sum up, immigration changes both the size of a country's economy and the way the gains are shared out. Measurement is difficult, and results often disagree. But a number of broad conclusions emerge from all this.

First, migration probably raises the living standards of the rich (think of all those foreign nannies and waiters) and the returns to capital (hence the enthusiasm of employers for more flexible policies). It does not seem to increase unemployment among the native-born, although it may reduce their pay.

On balance, argued the report by America's NRC, the people whose wages immigration harms are mainly previous immigrants, for whom new immigrants are close substitutes in the job market. In addition, immigration seems to account for almost half the fall in wages of high-school drop-outs in the 1980s and early 1990s. But this is a smallish group, now less than 10% of the American workforce. Trade unions in the United States no longer argue for a ban on immigration, realizing that this is a lost cause: instead, they want to legalize the undocumented, who are much more likely to undercut their less-skilled members than are unionized legal immigrants.

The effect on jobs depends partly on whether immigrants are complements to or substitutes for native labour. Are the immigrants doing jobs that natives might have done, or would those jobs simply not exist if immigrants were not there to do them? Advertise for a cleaner in London at twice the minimum hourly wage, and you will get no response from local school drop-outs or Liverpool's unemployed. More probably, the applicants will be from Ukraine, Colombia or Poland.

Some labour economists are puzzled that immigration does not appear to have made much impact on wages or jobs. Trade economists such as Berlin's Mr. Brücker are not. They point out that an open economy may change its mix of output, leaving wages and unemployment unaltered. Indeed, in many countries, immigrants are densely concentrated in export industries such as textiles, car making and agriculture.

Immigrants also cluster in areas where the job market is tight. In Canada, half of all immigrants go to Toronto; in Britain, an even higher proportion settles in London. Harvard's Professor Borjas points out that immigrants incur much lower costs than natives in choosing to move to a particular place, because they have already decided to uproot. They gain the greatest benefit by moving to those places where their skills are in greatest demand. Not surprisingly, he finds that new immigrants are disproportionately clustered in America's high-wage states, where workers are scarcest.

That clustering helps to stop wages rising even further, and allows the entire economy to run at higher speed than might otherwise be possible. The finding has important consequences for Europe, with its lower geographical mobility and more inflexible job markets. There, the importance of immigrants as a flexible workforce is potentially even greater than in the United States.

Immigrants may boost economic growth in other ways that are harder to measure, and that depend on their skills and experience. They may bring entrepreneurial skills: almost 30% of new companies in Silicon Valley in 1995–98 were started by Chinese and Indian immigrants. Some depressed regions actively court immigrants: the chamber of commerce at Nashville, Tennessee, sees them as a source of dynamism, as does Tom Vilsack, the governor of Iowa, whose state has a meat-packing industry relying largely on Bosnian refugees. Against that, unskilled immigrants may discourage investment. Mr. Krikorian, of the Centre for Immigration Studies, argues that productivity in California's raisin industry is far lower than it could be, because of the ready supply of cheap illegal Mexicans to pick the fruit by hand. Australia, with far fewer illegals, grows grapes over trellises, which allows automated harvesting.

As far as the host country's population is concerned, then, the benefits of immigration may be modest and unevenly distributed. The NRC study estimated them at up to $10 billion a year—chickenfeed in an economy of $10 trillion. "The economic pluses and minuses are much smaller than the political and emotional salience," says Rand's Mr. Smith. In Europe, where they have been less carefully measured, they may be larger: Britain's government recently increased its underlying forecast for economic growth by a quarter of a percentage point because it now expects higher net inward migration.

■ Greatest Good for the Greatest Number

For the individual immigrants, on the other hand, the potential gains are very large. This explains why many trade economists argue that humanity as a whole benefits enormously from migration. Alan Winters of Britain's Sussex University, in a study for the Commonwealth Secretariat, has tried to quantify these gains. He concludes that, if the rich countries raised the number of foreign workers that they allowed in temporarily by the equivalent of 3% of their existing workforce, world welfare would improve by more than $150 billion a year. That is bigger, he points out, than the gains from any imaginable liberalisation of trade in goods.

Dani Rodrik, a trade economist at Harvard University, has indepen-

chapter 9

Demographic Challenges

9.1 *the Editors*

Introduction

Barring a sudden sea change, immigration will continue to perform, as it has in the past, a valuable role in boosting annual population growth within the advanced industrial societies. Numerous demographic analyses have compelled policymakers and scholars to consider the merits and practicalities of "replacement migration" to counteract the trend toward natural population decline and the negative effects of aging in the affected countries.

According to a controversial report by the United Nations, which is excerpted in Chapter 9.2, most European countries will suffer a significant loss of population during the next half century. On the basis of current patterns of fertility and immigration, Italy's population, for example, is projected to decline from 57 to 41 million during the next five decades. The UN and other national and international government agencies project similar population declines in France, Germany, the Netherlands, Portugal, Spain, and Sweden. The problem of too few children being born is not peculiar to Europe. According to the Institute of Population and Social Security Research, Japan's population of approximately 126 million will, following current trends, plummet to between 92 and 108 million by midcentury. Conspicuously exempted from this trend among the advanced industrialized countries is the United States, whose current population of 293 million, significantly swelled each year by immigration, is projected to increase to 420 million by midcentury.

In addition to the demographic time bomb of population decline are the problems of rapid aging and a concurrent rise in the dependency ratio (i.e., the number of individuals aged below 15 or above 64 divided by the number of individuals aged 15 to 64, expressed as a percentage). A rising dependency ratio concerns governments whose populations are rapidly aging because too few persons in the active labor force make it difficult for existing pension and social security systems to provide adequate resources to support a growing elderly, nonworking population. Based on current demographic trends, the dependency ratio within the first fifteen member states of the European Union (i.e., excluding the ten countries that joined the EU in 2004), for example, is expected to increase from 27.9 to 55.7 as their collective population falls by 10 percent between 2000 and 2050. The effects of aging will also afflict the United States in the coming decades, and especially Japan, where 42 percent of the population will be 60 or older by 2050, with 16 percent of these persons over 80.

Although immigration alone cannot solve the problems of population decline and demographic aging, as David Coleman forcefully argues in Chapter 9.3, there is little doubt that it can arrest these negative trends in the near term. Classic patterns of mass immigration temporarily eases the problem of population aging because most immigrants are under the age of 30. Moreover, as a less economically affluent population, many immigrant family households tend to be larger than the households of native families.

However, immigration is far from a panacea. On the basis of the afore-mentioned projections, the original EU-15, for example, would have to admit indefinitely some 1.4 million permanent immigrants annually in order to maintain the viability of their national social security systems and maintain a working-age population of 170 million. Similarly, in order to stabilize the dependency ratio at its 1990 level in the United States, immigration would have to reach 2 million per annum through 2020 and 10 million by 2080. These levels of immigration are extremely difficult to sustain politically, as we shall see in Chapter 9.2. In addition, as Coleman demonstrates empirically, at best immigration can serve as little more than a stopgap measure economically, given that immigrants inevitably age, and over time the size of immigrant families, with increasing affluence, begins to converge with that of native families.

Trends in Fertility in Europe and the Industrial World

Birth rate trends in Western Europe resemble those in the United States, only with less enthusiasm. On the whole, the postwar baby boom in Europe was later and less pronounced than in the Neo-Europes. Since the 1970s, as elsewhere in the Western industrial world, birth rates have been below replacement with one or two exceptions—a few small countries with late or incomplete demographic transitions (e.g., Iceland, Ireland and Sweden) which briefly attained replacement level fertility in the early 1990s. Underneath this ceiling of low fertility (TFR on average about 1.6 in the EU) flourishes a diversity of national characteristics. In Southern Europe the birth rate, formerly somewhat higher than average in Spain, Portugal and Greece, declined fast at the end of the 1970s to reach unprecedented low levels by the late 1980s. . . . There, the decline of the birth rate has meant that the number of deaths has, in some recent years, exceeded the number of births (since 1993 in Italy), a position not seen since the eighteenth century. So far, this decline is relatively modest and is counteracted by net immigration, which all are experiencing.

Elsewhere in the EU birth rates go up as well as down. During the 1980s, birth rates in Scandinavia and in one or two other European countries were generally rising . . . , most notably in Norway and Sweden. The increase in Sweden was particularly marked, its TFR rising to above 2.1 but has now fallen sharply to about 1.6. Other countries in northwest Europe, such as France and Germany, have had more constant (but subreplacement) fertility levels over the last 20 years. Increases, mostly small, are evident in 14 of the 18 Western European countries in 1999; preliminary figures suggest a sharp increase in TFR to 1.9 in France. In Sweden, new family support measures had the inadvertent effect of accelerating the timing of second births, provoking a transient rise of TFR to 2.1 (Sundström and Stafford 1992). A subsequent rise in unemployment, peaking at the almost unprecedented figure of 7%, is credited with the abrupt drop afterwards. Norway and Finland provide more modest and stable examples, with buoyant period fertility and little tendency for the cohort level to fall.

Is Low Fertility Inevitable?

There are reasons for being cautious about the fertility assumptions in population projections. We do not clearly understand the factors that lead couples to make decisions on the number and timing of their children, or why they decide to have children at all. Over the last decade, opinion surveys such as the Eurobarometer surveys (European Commission 1990), the World Values Surveys and the Family and Fertility Surveys consistently give desired family sizes of over two children, higher than current measured performance. These preferences must be regarded with caution, however; answers given by women who have already started families may be censored by their unwillingness to label any existing child as "unwanted" (Calhoun 1990). Low or very low fertility used to be thought inevitable because it was believed that women's workforce participation was incompatible with children. This no longer holds true in some European countries where compensation levels are high (i.e., welfare measures to compensate the financial loss occasioned to women taking time out of work and to minimize damage to careers).

Today, European countries where female workforce participation is high also have relatively high fertility. Period measures of fertility such as the TFR are low partly because the timing of first child births has been so much delayed since the 1970s. Delay depresses the magnitude of period measures based on age-specific rates. New synthetic measures of total fertility based on the probability of going on from one birth to a second, and so forth (parity progression) may give a better measure of current fertility than the TFR (Ni Bhrolcháin 1993). These parity progression-based measures avoid timing effects and recognize the extent to which the proportion of second and even third births has remained relatively high, except in countries such as Italy and Spain. Period rates calculated in this way raise TFR figures by about 0.2 higher. If the delay in childbearing eventually ceases, then further increases in contemporary birth rate may be expected.

■ Population Aging in Europe

The boundaries of European regions were redefined by the United Nations classification system in the 1990s and now includes countries suffering from various forms of economic collapse or stilt in the process of recovery. "Europe," for our purposes, comprises all of Northern and Western Europe (based on the old UN definition), as well as parts of the UN's Southern Europe, except those previously under communist control. . . .

The age structures of the major blocks of the European population are beginning to diverge. In general, countries in the northwestern region have a more "healthy" age structure than those of the Mediterranean and some Central countries. Although they have been aging for longer, the Northwestern European countries have not experienced fertility decline since the early 1970s and, in some, fertility increases have occurred. In the Mediterranean countries, on the other hand, fertility has fallen fast since the 1980s so that recent birth cohorts have fallen to unprecedented low levels. Generalizations about European population and workforce deficits must take into account these differences.

For the last decade or more, population aging in most European countries has been relatively slow, thanks to the small number of pensioner recruits entering their 60s who were born in the small birth cohorts of the

Table 9.3.3   EU 1990–2025: Some Summary Statistics

Population Category	Millions
Working age population 15–64 in 1990	219
Labor force at constant 1985 participation	145
Projected labor force decline to 2025	13
Labor force under age 25 in 1990	28
Hidden labor force in 1990	33
Unemployed in 1990	12
Unemployed under age 25 in 1990	4

Source: European Commission 1991.

source of wage or salaried employment by big companies in traditional sectors, except for high-skilled migration and inter-company transfers. For example, in Britain, managerial and professional employment has increased by 24 percent to 8.5 million, clerical and related occupations by 19.5 percent to 4.2 million, while manual work as a whole has grown slowly from 10.9 to 11.1 million—the number of unskilled general laborers has halved from 302,000 to 148,000 (Department of Employment 1991).

Within relatively small net changes in the size of the workforce major changes in broad industrial sectors are forecast (Table 9.3.4), similar in scale to those expected in France and Germany: a reduction of 24 percent in utilities and 25 percent in mining, even 15 percent in the already tiny agricultural sector. Manufacturing is expected to fall by a further one million, with 250,000 lost in mechanical engineering. Even where output is expected to rise, as in electronics, employment will fall because of productivity increases: 6 percent in electrical engineering as a whole; 33 percent in metals and minerals; 24 percent in mechanical engineering; 6 percent in electrical engineering; and 30 percent in textiles and clothing. Jobs in leisure, recreation and tourism (mostly not highly skilled) are expected to grow by 24 percent and, in health and education, by 6 percent. The highest projected growth rates are in science and engineering professions (27%); teaching, health and other professions (14–26%); other professions associated with science, engineering and health (16–21%) and among corporate managers and administrators. Clerical occupations will remain constant, skilled trades will decline by up to 10 percent and semiskilled operatives in industry and agriculture will decline by up to 19 percent (Institute for Employment Research 1991, Table 5).

Demand for highly skilled manpower did not cease through the 1980s, although over half this movement was within companies even if between countries, and forecasts suggest that future employment growth will be primarily among those with graduate or intermediate qualifications. In the

Table 9.3.4   Employment Change by Occupation in Great Britain, 1990–2000

Occupation	Percent Employment Change
Corporate managers and administrators	18
Managers/proprietors in agriculture and services	6
Science and engineering professionals	27
Health professions	14
Teachers	18
Other professionals	26
Science and engineering associated professionals	16
Health associated professionals	8
Other associated professionals	21
Clerical occupations	1
Secretarial occupations	–3
Skilled construction trades	7
Skilled engineering trades	–8
Other skilled trades	–10
Protective service occupations	15
Personal service occupations	10
Buyers, brokers and sales representatives	2
Other sales occupations	4
Industrial plant and machine operators	–17
Drivers and mobile machine operators	–7
Other occupations in agriculture	–19
Other elementary occupations	–6
All occupations	3.1

Source: Institute for Employment Research 1991.

West there is always a demand for skilled technical and professional workers in finance, medicine, science based technology, and especially information technology (IT). At the moment, the underlying demand for IT specialists is growing fast and in 2000 was being further inflated in most EU countries by preparations for the proposed launch of the Euro. In some countries, such as Britain, shortages in IT have been compounded by weakness in training and relatively low pay in science and engineering compared with (for example) finance and law. Manual workers skilled in related technologies and skilled builders are also in demand. At the bottom end of the occupational scale it can be difficult to find applicants for menial jobs in health care, catering and hotels, despite overall high unemployment rates. Regional shortages, as in the South East of England, may be due to frictional factors such as high house prices due to planning controls that inhibit internal labor mobility, rather than an absolute shortage of labor in the whole country.

There seems to be a global tendency for the rate of technical advance to outstrip the rate at which people can be trained or retrained to deal with it. For example, BIPE in France forecasts employment growth of about 20 percent in professions, technicians and corporate managers, with equivalent declines in unskilled workers, farmers and agricultural workers, a pattern echoed by the UK Institute for Employment Research. The German IAB Prognos study forecasts an increase of 3.4 million highly skilled jobs from 1985 to 2010, with a fall in 2 million unskilled jobs (European Commission 1991, Chapter 7). About 10 percent of net migration in the average EC country was estimated to be driven by labor market changes; that is, if the unemployment rate in a country rises by one percentage point, the migration rate into it drops by one tenth of a percentage point, the rest being autonomous. It was felt there was no question of a leveling of unemployment rates by migration. . . .

■ The Economic Situation in Europe

Europe's economic fortunes are somewhat mixed at the moment. Most of continental Europe spent the 1990s in a tight economic situation, partly because of the constraints on public spending required to meet the needs of the Maastricht convergence criteria for economic and monetary union. Inflation was consequently moderate, especially following the creation of the European Central Bank. In September 2000 it was still under 3 percent. Economic growth is relatively moderate (3.6% per annum in the second quarter of 2000 among the EU countries), with some exceptions (e.g., Ireland, 6%). The general outlook improved at the end of the century, although it was overshadowed by the persistent weakness of the Euro, with its threat of inflation.

In most countries unemployment is high but falling. In mid-2000 German unemployment was at about 9 percent of the workforce, in France it was 10 percent, in Italy 11 percent, and in Spain 15 percent (although many of these unemployed are believed to work in the black economy). Sweden and Switzerland, having experienced unprecedented levels of unemployment (although still modest by European levels), are now back to more modest levels (4% and 2%, respectively). Especially in the South, unemployment is strongly concentrated among women and among young people. The unemployed aged under 25 accounted for 35 percent of the EU's 18 million unemployed in the 1990s, although that position is now improved. Unemployment is particularly high among immigrants and foreigners; typically double or treble that of the native population (notably being over 40 percent among Turks and Moroccans in the Netherlands) (Table 9.3.5). Furthermore, labor force participation rates (percent of population of working age that is economically active) among immigrants tend to be low, especially among women. Because of family reunification and high fertility, dependency ratios of immigrant populations, originally lower than average in guestworker countries, are growing.

Table 9.3.5   Unemployment Rates of Foreigners in Select Countries, 1990s

Country and Year	Natives	Foreign	Turks	Moroccans	Non-EU
Belgium 1991	11.5	24.3	41.7	37.1	35.4
France 1996	11.3	24.1	—	—	32.3
Germany 1995	9.3	16.6	24.4	—	18.0
Netherlands 1996	5.8	19.0	41.0	27.0	18.0

Source: OECD 1997; 1999 (calculated from various tables).

■ The Immigration Situation in Europe

Europe has experienced a marked increase in both legal and illegal immigration since the mid-1980s. . . . The numbers of regular migrants, mostly dependants and new spouses but also labor migrants, increased substantially up to 1992. Asylum claims rose to a peak of 640,000 in 1992, although they have since declined. Overall immigration (gross inflow) reached over 2 million per year in the mid-1990s and net immigration reached about one million. If an allowance of about 350,000 illegal immigrants is added to the regular immigrants, asylum claimants and ethnic return migrants, then the total is estimated to have peaked at a gross inflow of about 2.7 million in 1992 (Widgren 1994). The cumulative effects of past immigration had given the EU countries 22.4 million foreigners in 1996, from inside and outside Europe (Eurostat 1997), of whom about 8 million were workers. According to recent estimates, foreigners comprise about 3 percent of the labor force in European countries, with higher proportions in France (6%), Germany (9%) and Switzerland (18%) (OECD 1999). This figure is net of naturalization, which has proceeded rapidly in some countries, notably France, and much slower in Germany and Switzerland. Naturalized persons of foreign birthplace would add some millions more to the total of 22.4 million given above, which include about 800,000 persons receiving temporary protection from Yugoslavia and some of the cumulative total of 6 million asylum claimants since 1980. Although most claims have been rejected as unfounded, the majority of claimants remain anyway. The stock of illegal immigrants or overstayers at the end of the 1980s was estimated to be at least one million in Italy, Spain and Greece, and up to 180,000 in Switzerland (Hoffmann-Nowotny 1990; Salt 1990).

Despite increased flows from Eastern Europe, a high proportion of immigrants to Europe come from the economically developing countries. North Africa and the Middle East are a prominent source of migration to Europe; between 37 and 45 percent of all regular immigrants to France came from that area in the 1990s. Immigrants from Turkey remain prominent in flows to Germany. Most new immigrants are dependents or new spouses; while most asylum claimants are male. A high level of pressure to emigrate to the West is generally supposed to follow an excess of population, a dearth of employment in relation to population of working age and tenfold or more disparities in income. Population growth in the developing countries is 2.5 percent per year compared with nearly zero in the advanced industrial societies. This situation is set to endure for decades. Many developing countries appear unable to create new jobs, at any level of income, to match their own natural increase. However, simple considerations of demand—pull or push—are inadequate to account for the ups and downs of immigration trends in the last few decades, not the least because most immigrants are not labor migrants, even though most may find employment. We still lack an adequate theory to account for the changes in pattern and volume of international migration, which bear no simple relationship to economic or population growth (Kritz 1998). Nonetheless, it seems reasonable to suppose that, in general, immigration pressure will last for as long as the population continues to grow fast in countries substantially poorer than the West. The population of North Africa and the Middle East is projected to almost double to 284 million people by 2025 from today's 146 million (Courbage 1998), and economic performance is not converging. South Asia, tropical Africa and much of Latin America are unlikely to converge demographically or economically with the advanced industrial societies for at least 30 years. During that time their populations will have more than doubled, while that of Europe is likely to be declining. The rights and the information revolutions (Hollifield, 1992) and political events influencing controls imposed by governments and unrest abroad seem more promising possible explanations for recent upward and downward trends (Massey 1999), which may fall more into the province of political than of economic science.

Reasons for Immigration

Since the 1970s most legal migrants to Europe have not been labor migrants (this is also true of immigration to the United States and Canada). Most are dependents, especially spouses and children, and new heads of households who are male spouses (Widgren 1994). These flows do not fit neoclassical economics models but may be regarded as an externality, deriving from obligations arising from broadly worded international conventions on human rights created in the 1950s following the end of the Second World War. . . .

The importation of marriage partners into France and other European countries is affected by pull factors from the immigrant population in France itself and from the French labor market, as well as push factors from the poor living conditions of the Maghreb. If all the marriage migrants to France were marrying into the immigrant communities (it is probably no more than half), then such network migration would account for 83 percent of legal migration in 1994. In other countries, such as the United Kingdom and the Netherlands (Coleman 1995), family reunification is being replaced by spouse migration, as the sex ratios of the maturing immigrant populations gradually become more normalized over time (Schoorl 1997). Increasingly, males enter on this pretext where previously all spouse migration was of females: in France in 1994 35 percent of Turks entering for marriage were males; male spouses made up 29 percent of Moroccan and 20 percent of Algerian and Tunisian immigrants (Tribalat 1996, 146). While Algerians in France are tending to marry someone already living in France, marriage outside the Turkish community among young immigrant Turks in France is almost unknown (Tribalat 1996, 170–191).

■ Solutions?

While the end of population growth may not be a serious problem, issues of workforce and population aging raises more serious issues, especially for very low fertility countries. What, if anything, can be done about it?

Hidden Labor Supply

The potential labor supply in many EU countries is poorly mobilized (Fuchs 1995; Fuchs and Schmidt 2000). The number of unemployed in the EU (9% in 2000) is somewhat larger than the projected reduction in the demographically defined workforce to 2025. Unemployment cannot be eliminated, of course, and its serious reduction would require structural adjustments to labor law and social protection; but given the example of some current EU countries, halving unemployment should be a realistic goal. Training of the unemployed and retraining is a favored response to skill shortages; however, 70 percent of the vacancies in employment in the EU have been filled by people who were previously economically inactive. To reduce EU unemployment from 8 to 4 percent would require at least 12 percent more jobs. Retraining is no panacea. The higher-productivity North European countries have devoted much more attention to the dilemma than the South. Two circles of development, one virtuous and one vicious, therefore seem to coexist in the EU.

Beyond unemployment, additional reserve supplies of labor in the EU remain dormant. Workforce participation is the lowest of any major trading block (about 60% in 1990, lower than 1970–63%). Comparable figures are 72 percent in the United States, 73 percent in Japan and 75 percent in non-EU Europe. Eighty percent is perhaps the highest level likely to be achieved in Western Europe, observed in some Scandinavian countries, which go to considerable lengths to enable women to work at the same time as caring for children. Of this inactive working-age population of almost 88 million people, a high proportion of the population aged 15–24 is in full-time education and early retirement of men has reduced participation rates for older married men (55–64). But most of the hidden labor force arises from the relatively low workforce participation rates of women, especially of married women in some EU countries, as low as 34 percent in Spain (EU average 59%). Assuming an irreducible "hard core" of 20 percent of inactive in each country, the hidden labor supply in the EU in 1990 was about 15 percent of the working-age population or about 33 million people, from over 20 percent in Spain and Southern Italy, Ireland, Belgium and Greece, to under 10 percent in Britain, France and most of Germany, with the lowest level in Denmark. That hidden labor supply represents 23 percent of the current labor force.

All sorts of frictional forces will prevent some of this potential being realized. Labor migration within the EU is constrained by cultural, language and social factors even though legal barriers have gone. Around 1990 there were about 600,000 intra-Community international migrants per year, a fairly modest figure. Despite the Single European Act, EU labor migration in the 1980s was lower than in the 1970s and was static or downwards, not upwards, until the end of the decade. However, some increase was apparent in the 1990s, especially among the highly skilled and professional, partly due to the growth of European institutions (Poulain 1996) and German reunification.

Demand for Migrants?

Labor demand unmet by domestic labor markets can be supplied by free movement from other EU countries, or by work permit from outside application that is open to anyone. Such migration has proceeded, little remarked, for decades. Its relatively modest scale over recent years, except to Germany, suggests a fairly modest demand. It is inevitably variable, and differs greatly by employment sector. Most of the 11 Western European countries which report work permit migration showed declines during the 1990s; Germany, Italy and the UK being important exceptions. Elsewhere it had fallen to modest levels by 1997 (15,000 to Austria; 15,000 to France; 25,000 to Switzerland). The substantial upsurge in labor demand arising from German reunification was by then much reduced; 285,000 work permits for new arrivals were issued in 1995 (mostly to Poles) compared with 409,000 in 1992 (OECD 1999, Table A2.17). However, in 2000 new schemes to recruit large numbers of IT specialists were announced in Germany, over and above the conventional work permit system, to meet a substantial reported shortage, and a similar scheme has been recently discussed in Britain. There seems to be some agreement that Italy needs further labor immigration despite its high unemployment, in view of its precarious demographic position. . . .

Immigration as Demographic Salvation?

Population aging—the growth of elderly sections of the population by comparison with the proportion of working age—is one of the most important social and demographic transformations facing Western populations. It is a permanent, irreversible consequence of the achievement of low average family size and longer expectation of life. It brings in its train a decline of the potential support ratio; that is, the ratio of the nominal working age (15–64) population to the population of (nominal) aged dependents (65 and over), from about 4 to 1 today to between 2 and 3 to 1 by mid-century. It is important to realize that there can be no "solution" to population aging and low potential support ratios—it is the future condition of the entire human population. It can be ameliorated or managed, but not solved. Immigration can stop population decline although it cannot stop the aging of populations, except at very high levels of immigration and unsustainable levels of population growth. Immigrants tend to be younger on average than the national population, but the difference is not very marked. The immigrants themselves then age and need to be replaced by more immigrants. Past levels of migration have had modest effects on population structure; for example, generating a 2.3 percent excess among males aged 40–49 in the UK but a deficit of 1.1 percent among males aged 0–9. In percentage terms, most differences are trivial (Murphy 1996).

Nonetheless, it has been suggested that immigration should be welcomed, now or in the future, to preserve population and workforce size, and to restore a favorable age structure. Whether immigration could easily maintain population or workforce numbers depends on the countries concerned. In some cases, immigration could maintain current European population levels, given current fertility trends only if record numbers of immigrants were allowed in, often double the current net immigration (Lesthaeghe, Page and Surkyn 1988). In Germany, however, although 300,000 immigrants per year are needed to maintain population size in the long run, immigration levels until 1997 were so high that the German population actually grew substantially. In the UK, however, with a higher rate of fertility, maintaining current population until at least 2035 merely requires the continuation of the status quo. However, the inevitable consequence of a population with subreplacement fertility attempting to maintain constant numbers through immigration is that the population of immigrant origin would eventually comprise the greater part of the population. Populations can only adopt this solution to stabilize the numbers at the risk of the loss of their identity.

In general, higher levels, and rather variable levels, of migration are needed to maintain the size of the working age population than to maintain the overall population, and exceptional numbers, highly variable from one period to the next, are required to preserve the support ratio, generating implausible levels of population growth. For example, to preserve a ratio of working adults to old people of 3:1 (slightly less than today's 3.5:1) by 2020, replacement fertility would be needed as well as some sharper peaks of migration; up to 180,000 per year in the case of Belgium, ten times the current gross flow (Calot 1983). That policy would itself double population and more, not the least because the migrants would themselves need migrants to balance them when they retired. . . .

In the long run, host population fertility is the crucial factor; the percentage of foreign residents of foreign origin is solely dependent on the relative fertility and mortality rates of the host and the immigrant populations and by the sex and age structure of the immigrants, not by the level of immigration. In the very long run, the minority will become the majority in a country if there remains even one region where the increase of the proportion of the minority (through immigration and higher birth rates) is not checked by integration (Feichtinger and Steinmann 1990; Kuijsten 1996; Steinmann and Jöger 1997).

The near impossibility of correcting aging through immigration is underlined by analysis of the EU countries using a common methodology. While it would only take between 500,000 and a million additional immigrants per year to avert population decline in the earlier part of the twenty-first century, to preserve the current age structure of the 15 EU countries would require 4.5 million immigrants per year by 2007 and 7 million per year by 2024 (European Commission, 1996), generating substantial population growth. An even more wide-ranging report has shown, using a common methodology, the numbers of immigrants required to maintain population size, workforce numbers, and potential support ratios over many countries and regions up to 2050 (UN 2000b). This essentially repeats in a uniform fashion what was already known about the progressive difficulty of achieving these three aims through migration. The last goal, in particular, was shown to require spectacular increases in population size through immigration, doubling the size of the EU by 2050 and in an extreme case, requiring the entire population of the world to live in Korea by that year in order to preserve its current potential support ratio. The sensational results from this adventurous projection over the unusual span of 50 years duration have been widely interpreted as policy requirements, not speculations from a hypothetical exercise (UN 2000c).

Adapting to an Aging Population

Demographic aging and the consequent reduction of the potential support ratio are a major challenge to nonfunded state pension schemes and to all other aspects of care for a growing elderly population (Daykin 1997; ILO 1989; World Bank, 1994). We have already seen that immigration can only sustain the support ratio at the cost of unsustainable levels of population growth. There is, of course, no solution to lower support ratios; the question arises whether the process can at least be moderated in other ways. In financial and actuarial circles, attention tends to be focused, in fairly optimistic terms, on fiscal, economic and workforce adjustments. What matters is that the economy can manage the changed pattern of consumption and investment and still deliver economic growth. In brief, favored approaches include the following.

1. Moderate the "support ratio." Move the average age of retirement upwards, discourage early retirement and encourage older workforce participation by removing tax disincentives for working pensioners, removing employment barriers solely on grounds of age. Encourage higher workforce participation through retraining of the unemployed, reducing obstacles to internal labor mobility, and making it easier for women to combine work with child care through a variety of measures (e.g., as developed in the Scandinavian countries).

2. Moderate the financial burden by later retirement and by resisting further increases in the value of state pension entitlement; linking it, for example, to prices not wages. Encourage alternative sources of old-age support through second and third pillar occupational and private funded pension schemes, which may have the additional advantage of improving the savings rate for investment.

3. Respond to stationary or declining workforces by increasing capital investment to improve worker productivity—a generally desirable step to improve Europe's poor international competitiveness, and one which would naturally follow from the pressure of higher wages arising from any labor shortage.

None of these by itself can offer a complete solution; none is available. For example, by 2025, additional productivity improvements would have to be about 0.8 percent per year if they were the sole means to meet the need for extra resources arising from population aging; average age at retirement would have to rise from the present average 60 to 66 (European Commission 1996, 36–39). Many countries have already begun to implement several of these measures in order to minimize problems and in the majority of European countries a multiple response appears to make them manageable. However, increased workforce participation is a one-off response—the effects of which would not last beyond about 2025. Furthermore, the extreme low-fertility countries, especially Italy, face in the long run an apparently unsustainable burden unless their birth rate increases considerably.

■ Conclusion

The level of the birth rate has the most potent effect on the level of population aging and support ratios that populations must live with in future. A TFR of more than about 2 is not to be expected, and that level would not restore support ratios to previous levels or, in countries with previously lower fertility, avert a period of population decline. But relatively high fertility (say 1.7 or over) would greatly assist the management of aging by the measures noted above. Demographic opinion is divided over how far very lower fertility is here to stay or will respond to welfare measures, whether pronatalist in intention or not (Lesthaeghe and Willems 1999). The relative buoyancy of birth rates in northwestern Europe and their apparent responsiveness to family-friendly policies suggests that it can. But before that can happen, underlying attitudes unfavorable to gender equity within the family and in society as a whole would have to change, a less predictable process (McDonald 2000).

Europe has been receiving variable but large net immigration flows, both regular and illegal, for many years now: the concept of "Fortress Europe" seems far from reality. Recent flows to most countries are little connected with labor demand. Domestic unemployment averages 9 percent and is up to 40 percent in the existing foreign populations themselves, while workforce participation rates of immigrants, especially females, are low. Demand for regular migrant labor nonetheless coexists with unemployment, partly thanks to continental labor market rigidities. This demand has been satisfied in recent decades by the free movement of labor within the EU and by the variable work permit systems that have been granted for recruitment abroad. These flows are declining in some countries, increasing in others. Much of the regular migration is of highly skilled professional or business migration, especially inter-company transfers. Exceptional demand in some sectors, notably IT, justify exceptional new measures according to some countries, such as Germany. Demand for illegal labor is strong in some sectors, exploited at low wages and with low levels of job protection in marginal areas of the economy.

As to the future, increased labor migration over and above present levels is not needed to satisfy quantitative workforce deficiencies for the next 10 or 20 years in much of Western Europe (Italy and other Southern countries are exceptions), although here the demand coexists with high structural levels of unemployment. Europe has substantial reserves of employable manpower which exceed any short-term demographic deficiencies; however, their mobilization will require structural readjustments and the effects of enhanced workforce participation to age 65 cannot extend much beyond 2025. High-level manpower movements will continue to grow as they have done for many years. While legal immigration of dependants, unavoidable immigration of asylum-seekers and illegal immigration will continue, they do not appear to be relevant to Europe's foreseeable economic needs nor helpful to the coherence of its society.

More broadly, reliance on the apparently easy option of importing labor from overseas, or to employ illegal immigrants for low wages and evade their training responsibilities, might risk exacerbating Europe's central economic problem, that of low productivity. Productivity levels in Europe are still substantially below those of their major competitors. There is no merit in perpetuating low-wage, low-output enterprises which can only survive with marginal labor, and whose services or goods can be imported instead. That impedes the modernization and capitalization of the economy.

There are no feasible migration solutions to the age-structure change and its effects on social security. It is not caused by a deficit in migration but by low fertility and increased expectation of life. In the long run, only approximately replacement level fertility can even moderate it, and even then probably not without some intervening demographic decline, not necessarily unwelcome to European opinion (Höhn 1987). Nothing will ever bring back the age structure of previous centuries. Whatever the demographic response, changes in the balance between consumption and production are inevitable. These problems appear to be manageable, though not finally soluble, in most European countries (Ermisch 1990). They point to the need for changes in pension systems and in assumptions about retirement age and workforce participation in later life. Europe has already weathered a trebling of the old age population, from 5 percent to 15 percent since 1900; a prospect which in the 1930s seemed insupportable. Some countries (Japan, U.S., UK) have already anticipated these problems by changing the rules on contributions or retirement age, although the boundaries of working life have not yet expanded in line with expectation of active life. Some forces in Europe, notably trades unions, are even arguing for still earlier retirement. . . .

In the long run perhaps we should focus attention on a more fundamental question: Why do so many of the women and couples in Europe not have the number of children that they say they would like to have? It is that mismatch that is making the population aging problem so severe in Southern European countries. This points to the need to look more closely at the conditions of family life and family formation in the low fertility areas. Instead of distracting attention with irrelevant migration solutions to demographic problems, the greatest challenge facing Europe's policy makers is to devise ways in which conditions of employment and welfare support can help to make life sufficiently tolerable for the women of Europe so that they can contemplate raising the families on which Europe's future depends, while also exercising their wish to work. To paraphrase Joshi

(1996): "perhaps Europe should take care of the people and let population decline and aging take care of itself."

■ References

Calhoun, C. 1990. "Desired and Excess Fertility in Europe and the United States: Indirect Estimates from World Fertility Survey Data." *European Journal of Population* 7: 29–57.

Calot, G. 1983. "Les perspectives démographiques françaises." *Futuribles* 67: 7–28.

Coleman, David A. 1991. "International Migrants in Europe: Adjustment and Integration Processes and Policies." Paper presented to United Nations ECE/UNFPA informal expert group meeting on International Migration, July 16–19.

Coleman, David A. 1995. "Spouse Migration from the Indian Sub-Continent to the UK: A Permanent Migration Stream?" *People and Place* 3: 1–8.

Coleman, David A. 1997. "UK Immigration Policy: 'Firm but Fair,' and Failing?" *Policy Studies* 17: 195–213.

Courbage, Y. 1998. *L'avenir démographique de la rive sud de la Méditerranée (et les pays voisins): reflexion sur les incidences socio-économiques et géopolitiques.* Turin: Fondazione Giovanni Agnelli.

Daykin, C. D. 1997. *A Crisis of Longer Life: Problems Facing Social Security Systems Worldwide and Options for Reform.* London: Government Actuary Department.

Department of Employment. 1991. *Labour Market and Skill Trends 1992–93.* Moorsfoot, Sheffield: DE Skills Unit and Skills and Enterprise Network, Employment Department Group

EC. 1990. *Eurobarometer: European Public Opinion on the Family and the Desire for Children.* Brussels, August.

EC. 1991. *Employment in Europe 1991.* Luxembourg: Office for the Official Publications of the European Communities.

EC. 1996. *The Demographic Situation in the European Union 1995.* Luxembourg: Office for the Official Publications of the European Communities.

Ermisch, J. 1990. *Fewer Babies, Longer Lives.* York: Rowntree Foundation.

Eurostat. 1988. *Demographic and Labour Force Analysis Based on Eurostat Data Banks.* Luxembourg: Office for the Official Publications of the European Communities.

Eurostat. 1991. *Demographic Statistics 1991.* Luxembourg: Office for the Official Publications of the European Communities.

Eurostat. 1996. *Demographic Statistics 1996.* Luxembourg: Office for the Official Publications of the European Communities.

Eurostat. 1997. *Demographic Statistics 1997.* Luxembourg: Office for the Official Publications of the European Communities.

Eurostat. 1999. *Demographic Statistics 1999.* Luxembourg: Office for the Official Publications of the European Communities.

Fassmann, Heinz. 1997. "Is the Austrian Labour Market Ethnically Segmented?" *European Journal of Population* 13:17–31.

Fassmann, Heinz, and Rainer Münz. 1992. "Patterns and Trends of International Migration in Western Europe." *Population and Development Review* 18: 457–481.

Feichtinger, G., and G. Steinmann. 1990. "Immigration into a Below-Replacement

Population: Reproduction by Immigration—the Case of Germany." Institut für Íkonometrie, Operations Research und Systemtheorie, Technische Universitöt Wien, Forschungsbericht Nr. 127.

Feld, S. 2000. "Active Population Growth and Immigration: Hypotheses in Western Europe." *European Journal of Population* 16: 3–40.

Foresight Aging Population Panel. 2000. *The Age-Shift: A Consultation Document.* London: Department of Trade and Industry.

Fuchs, J. 1995. "Long-term Labour Force Projections for Germany: The Concept of the Potential Labour Force." *IAB Labour Market Research Topics* 11: 28.

Fuchs, J., and D. Schmidt. 2000. "The Hidden Labour Force in the United Kingdom: A Contribution to the Quantification of Underemployment in International Comparisons." *IAB Labour Market Research Topics* 39: 23.

Ghosh, Bimal. 1998. *Huddled Masses and Uncertain Shores: Insights into Irregular Migration.* The Hague: Martinus Nijhoff.

Hoffmann-Nowotny, H-J. 1990. "Future Trends in European Migration." Paper presented to the Symposium on the Demographic Consequences of International Migration, NIAS, Wassenaar.

Höhn, C. 1987. "Population Policies in Advanced Societies: Pronatalist and Migration Strategies." *European Journal of Population* 3: 459–481.

Hollifield, James F. 1992. *Immigrants, Markets, and States: The Political Economy of Postwar Europe.* Cambridge, MA: Harvard University Press.

Institute for Employment Research. 1991. *Review of the Economy and Employment 1991.* Moorfoot, Sheffield: Employment Department.

International Labour Organisation [ILO]. 1989. *From Pyramid to Pillar: Population Change and Social Security in Europe.* Geneva: International Labour Office.

Johnson, P., C. Conrad, and D. Thomson. 1989. *Workers versus Pensioners: Intergenerational Justice in an Ageing World.* Manchester: Manchester University Press.

Joshi, H. 1996. "Projections of European Population Decline: Serious Demography or False Alarm?" In *Europe's Population in the 1990s,* ed. David A. Coleman. Oxford: Oxford University Press.

Kritz, M. M. 1998. "Investment, Population Growth and GNP as Determinants of US Immigration." *International Journal of Population Geography* 4: 243–258.

Lesthaeghe, R., H. Page, and J. Surkyn. 1988. "Are Immigrants Substitutes for Births?" Interuniversity Programme in Demography IPD Working Paper no. 1988-3. Brussels: Free University.

Lesthaeghe, R., and P. Willems. 1999. "Is Low Fertility a Temporary Phenomenon in the European Union?" *Population and Development Review* 25: 211–228.

Massey, Douglas S. 1999. "International Migration at the Dawn of the Twenty-First Century: The Role of the State." *Population and Development Review* 25: 303–322.

McDonald, P. 2000. "The 'Toolbox' of Public Policies to Impact on Fertility: A Global View." In *Low Fertility, Families and Public Policies.* European Observatory on Family Matters. Seville: Austrian Institute for Family Studies.

Murphy, M. 1996. "Population Structure and Migration: The British Case." In *Demographic Consequences of International Migration,* ed. S. Voets, J. Schoorl and B. de Bruijn. The Hague: NIDI.

Ni Bhrolchain, M. 1993. "Period Paramount: A Critique of the Cohort Approach to Fertility." In *New Perspectives on Fertility in Britain: Studies on Medical and Population Subjects No 55,* ed. M. Ni Bhrolchain. London: HMSO.

OECD. 1997. *Continuous Reporting System on Migration. SOPMEI.* Paris.

OECD. 1999. *Continuous Reporting System on Migration. SOPMEI.* Paris.

Piore, M. J. 1979. *Birds of Passage: Migrant Labor in Industrial Societies.* Cambridge, MA: Cambridge University Press.

Poulain, M. 1996. "Migration Flows between the Countries of the European Union." In *Population Migration in the European Union,* ed. P. Rees, J. Stillwell, A.Convey, and M. Kupiszewski. Chichester, NY: John Wiley.

Salt, J. 1990. *The New Wave of Migration.* Paris: OECD.

Salt, J., and J. Stein. 1997. "Migration as a Business: the Case of Trafficking." *International Migration* 35: 467–494.

Sauvy, A. 1969. *General Theory of Population.* Translated by C. Campos. London: Weidenfeld and Nicholson.

Schoorl, J. 1997. "Migration from Africa and Eastern Mediterranean Countries to Western Europe." In *Mediterranean Conference on Population, Migration and Development,* ed. Council of Europe. Strasbourg: Council of Europe.

Shaw, C., H. Cruijsen, J. de Beer, and A. de Jong. 1997. "Latest Population Projections for the European Union." *Population Trends* 90: 18–30.

Simon, J. L. 1981. *The Ultimate Resource.* Princeton: Princeton University Press.

Simon, J. L. 1989. *The Economic Consequences of Immigration.* Cambridge, England: Basil Blackwell.

Steinmann, G., and M. Jöger. 1997. "How Many Immigrants Can a Society Integrate?" Paper presented to 23rd General Conference of the IUSSP, Peking.

Stolnitz, G. J., ed. 1992. *Demographic Causes and Economic Consequences of Population Aging: Europe and North America.* New York: United Nations.

Sundström, M., and F. P. Stafford. 1992. "Female Labour Force Participation, Fertility and Public Policy in Sweden." *European Journal of Population* 8: 199–215.

Teitelbaum, M. S., and J. M. Winter. 1985. *The Fear of Population Decline.* New York: The Population Council.

Tribalat, Michèle. 1996. "Chronique de l'immigration." *Population* 51: 141–191.

United Nations. 2000a. *World Demographic Prospects as Assessed in 1998.* New York.

United Nations. 2000b. *Replacement Migration: Is It a Solution to Population Decline and Population Ageing?* New York.

United Nations. 2000c. *United Nations Expert Group Meeting on Policy Responses to Population Ageing.* New York.

Van Imhoff, E., and N. Keilman. 1996. "The Impact of Future International Migration on Household Composition and Social Security in the Netherlands." In *Demographic Consequences of International Migration,* ed. S. Voets, J. Schoorl, and B. de Bruijn. The Hague: Netherlands Interdisciplinary Demographic Institute.

Werner, H. 1996. "Temporary Migration of Foreign Workers: Illustrated with Special Regard to East-West Migrations. *IAB Labour Market Research Topics* 18: 35.

Widgren, Jonas. 1994. *The Key to Europe: A Comparative Analysis of Entry and Asylum Policies in Western Countries.* Stockholm: Fritzes.

World Bank. 1994. *Averting the Old Age Crisis: Policies to Protect the Old and Promote Growth.* Oxford: Oxford University Press.

chapter 10

The Politics
of Resentment

10.1 *the Editors*

Introduction

Two of the major trends in the domestic politics of the major immigration-receiving countries since the early 1970s or so have been the appearance and political advance of organized anti-immigrant groups, movements, and political parties. In the vanguard of the domestic actors that seek to politicize state immigration policies and issues related to the permanent settlement of new ethnic and racial minorities, anti-immigrant groups have sprung up in Australia, in the United States, and across most of Western Europe. Although their origins vary, most of these groups feed off widely held sentiments of nativism, xenophobia (i.e., the fear of strangers or foreigners), or racism within the general population.

As we shall see in this chapter, "nativist," or anti-immigrant, popular sentiment is hardly new. As Higham makes clear in Chapter 10.2, fear and suspicion of "outsiders," or foreigners or immigrants in the lexicon of contemporary public discourse, is virtually as old as human society. It is abundantly evident that within most of the major immigration-receiving societies, the political environment for these illiberal, anti-immigrant actors—in some countries represented by the "new right," or the extreme or radical populist right—has become decidedly more favorable than in the past.

Whatever the political influence of any particular anti-immigrant group, all are united by a common logic underpinned by four realities. The first is that in every major immigrant-receiving country the experience of mass immigration has eventually precipitated a nativist backlash expressed and aggregated politically by anti-immigrant groups. Second, once organized, the political fortunes of anti-immigrant groups are linked, to varying degrees, to the salience of immigration-related issues within the general population and electorate. Although some groups are more sensitive to the salience of these issues than others, all survive as anti-immigrant actors as a consequence of the general public's widespread and deep dissatisfaction with state immigration and immigrant policy. A third reality is that the salience of immigration-related issues is itself influenced by the behavior and strategies of both mainstream political parties and anti-immigrant groups. That is, regardless of the objective burden created by immigration in a given society, immigration-related issues, and particularly perceptions of threat, must first be politically framed in order for them to serve as a catalyst for the mobilization and advancement of anti-immigrant groups. Although neither mainstream political parties nor anti-immigrant groups are masters of the broad political forces that support an illiberal political environment, both can and do influence this environment. On the whole, there is no single best strategy the mainstream parties can pursue to undercut popular support for anti-immigrant groups, although neglecting immigration-related issues appears to be the worst possible approach.

Finally, the most electorally successful anti-immigrant groups, or, in Betz's phrase, those at the leading edge of the "new politics of resentment," are usually very skillful at folding their opposition to mass immigration and permanent immigrant settlement into a critique of the larger socioeconomic or sociocultural environment. According to Betz (Chapter 10.3), radical right-wing populist parties appeal especially to those who are alarmed by the increasing fragmentation of their once stable and familiar social-cultural order. They are radical in their rejection of the established political system, right-wing in their rejection of social equality and marginalized groups, and populist in their appeal to the common people.

To be sure, the popularity and the political influence of today's anti-immigrant groups and their chances of future electoral success should not be overestimated. Nowhere in the advanced industrial societies are these groups currently poised to force radical changes in state immigrant or immigration policy. None are currently on the threshold of achieving a major electoral breakthrough. Nevertheless, in most immigrant-receiving countries lacking deterring institutional barriers (i.e., electoral systems, constitutional constraints, etc.), organized, anti-immigrant forces now exercise at least a modest degree of influence over the public policy agenda. Given that the contemporary "strangers in the land" are not leaving their respective host societies anytime soon, it is reasonable to conclude that anti-immigrant groups and parties will continue to be a feature of the political landscape of the immigration-receiving countries into the indefinite future.

10.2 *John Higham*
Patterns in the Making

> Providence has been pleased to give this one connected country to one
> united people—a people descended from the same ancestors, speaking the
> same language, professing the same religion, attached to the same princi-
> ples of government, very similar in their manners and customs. . . .
>
> —*The Federalist*

Nativism has been hard for historians to define. The word is distinctively
American, a product of a specific chain of events in eastern American cities
in the late 1830's and early 1840's. Yet it has a penumbra of meaning so
broad and indefinite that sometimes it seems to refer to a perennial human
experience. Does nativism consist only of the particular complex of attitudes dominant in the anti-foreign crusade of the mid-nineteenth century?
Or does it extend to every occasion when native inhabitants of a country
turn their faces or raise their hands against strangers in their midst?

From the Garden of Eden to 1984, no age or society seems wholly free
from unfavorable opinions on outsiders. Understood in such general terms,
nativism would include every type and level of antipathy toward aliens,
their institutions, and their ideas. Its beginnings in American history would
date from the first Indian resistance to white intruders. This view, by reducing nativism to little more than a general ethnocentric habit of mind, blurs
its historical significance. On the other hand, confining nativism to the special sort of movement prominent for a couple of decades in the middle of
the nineteenth century is too narrow; the inner spirit of that movement has
taken quite different guises at other times and places. The spirit of
American nativism appeared long before the word was coined about 1840
and had its deepest impact long after the word had largely dropped out of
common parlance.

Not the nativists themselves, apparently, but rather their critics
attached the label to them. When anti-foreign parties arose in New York
and other cities after 1835 and evolved gradually into the powerful "Know-
Nothing" agitation of the 1850's, opponents denounced the movement as

John Higham, "Patterns in the Making," in Higham, *Strangers in the Land: Patterns
of American Nativism, 1860–1925* (New Brunswick, N.J.: Rutgers University Press,
1988), pp. 3–11. © 1988 by Rutgers, the State University. Reprinted by permission
of Rutgers University Press.

bigoted nativism. Its champions, however, preferred another designation. At first they called their organizations Native American parties, then simply the American party. Their philosophy they described as Americanism. "The grand work of the American party," proclaimed one of the Know-Nothing journals in 1855, "is the principle of nationality . . . we must do something to protect and vindicate it. If we do not it will be destroyed."[1]

Here was the ideological core of nativism in every form. Whether the nativist was a workingman or a Protestant evangelist, a southern conservative or a northern reformer, he stood for a certain kind of nationalism. He believed—whether he was trembling at a Catholic menace to American liberty, fearing an invasion of pauper labor, or simply rioting against the great English actor William Macready—that some influence originating abroad threatened the very life of the nation from within. Nativism, therefore, should be defined as intense opposition to an internal minority on the ground of its foreign (i.e., "un-American") connections. Specific nativistic antagonisms may, and do, vary widely in response to the changing character of minority irritants and the shifting conditions of the day; but through each separate hostility runs the connecting, energizing force of modern nationalism. While drawing on much broader cultural antipathies and ethnocentric judgments, nativism translates them into a zeal to destroy the enemies of a distinctively American way of life.

Continuous involvement in larger movements of American nationalism has meant that nativism usually rises and falls in some relation to other intense kinds of national feeling. The nationalist nexus has also meant that the nativist's most characteristic complaint runs against the loyalty of some foreign (or allegedly foreign) group. Seeing or suspecting a failure of assimilation, he fears disloyalty. Occasionally the charge of disloyalty may stand forth naked and unadorned, but usually it is colored and focused by a persistent conception about what is un-American. In other words, nativistic agitation had tended to follow certain stylized themes. Three of these themes stand out as main currents in American nativism, each with a separate history reaching back before the Civil War.

By far the oldest and—in early America—the most powerful of the anti-foreign traditions came out of the shock of the Reformation. Protestant hatred of Rome played so large a part in pre–Civil War nativist thinking that historians have sometimes regarded nativism and anti-Catholicism as more or less synonymous.[2] This identification, by oversimplifying two complex ideas, does little justice to either. Many social and religious factors, some of them nativistic only in a very indirect sense, have contributed powerfully to anti-Catholic feeling. It has drawn heavily, for example, from the very beginning of the Reformation on a conception of popery as steeped in moral depravity. Generation after generation of Protestant zealots have repeated the apocalyptic references of the early religious reformers to the

Whore of Babylon, the Scarlet Woman, the Man of Sin, to which they have added tales of lascivious priests and debauched nuns. On a rational level, too, the clash of faiths has cut deeply. One must expect some measure of tension to survive all adjustments between them, increasing or diminishing in proportion to the force with which Protestant and Catholic assert historic claims. Anti-Catholicism has become truly nativistic, however, and has reached maximum intensity, only when the Church's adherents seemed dangerously foreign agents in the national life.

Although modern nationalism was in its infancy in the sixteenth century, the Protestant revolt exhibited a vaguely patriotic tinge from the time Martin Luther first rallied the German princes against the Church of Rome. In England, particularly, hatred of Catholicism entered into an emerging national consciousness. The English in the sixteenth and seventeenth centuries were struggling more or less continuously against rival Catholic powers or their own pro-Catholic monarchs. The Roman pontiff loomed in English eyes as the great foreign tyrant, menacing the nation and its constitution; his followers had the aspect of a fifth column. By 1679 Titus Oates could plunge the whole kingdom into hysteria with crazy charges of a subversive Catholic conspiracy.

Carried across the Atlantic, the anti-Catholic heritage formed an important element in colonial loyalties and, with the rise of an American nationalism, affected that in turn. The tradition acquired a very real local significance in the New World, for the English colonies were wedged between two hostile Catholic empires, France and Spain. Consequently a militant Protestantism deeply colored the American national feeling stimulated by the French and Indian War. Then the American Revolution, accompanied by a growing religious toleration and secular democracy, largely suspended the wars of the godly.[3] But anti-Catholic xenophobia by no means disappeared. Although recessive, it remained an important counterpoise to more generous ideals of nationality.

For two principal reasons an undercurrent of Protestant nativism persisted into the new democratic America and revived in the second quarter of the nineteenth century. One reason lay in the character of American institutions. Catholic traditions continued to look dangerously un-American partly because they did not harmonize easily with the concept of individual freedom imbedded in the national culture. Americans regarded political liberty as their chief national attribute and supreme achievement. Observing the authoritarian organization of the Catholic Church and its customary association with feudal or monarchical governments, they were tempted to view American liberty and European popery as irreconcilable.

Secondly, a fresh Catholic challenge to American institutions emerged. The Catholic empires that had seemed to block national aspirations in the eighteenth century had given way; but in their place the nineteenth century brought a flood of Catholic immigrants. Nativists, charged with the Protestant evangelical fervor of the day, considered the immigrants minions of the Roman despot, dispatched here to subvert American institutions. (Indeed, the most excited patriots detected a vast European plot headed by the Pope.) Surely such creatures were unfit for citizenship. Anti-Catholic nativism, aiming at stiff naturalization laws and exclusion of Catholics and foreigners from public office, completely overshadowed every other nativist tradition.

By themselves, however, these factors were apparently not enough to make the "No-Popery" agitation a major force in national affairs. It became such only when sectional strife produced a general crisis in American society in the 1850's. With the old parties dissolving and the bonds of national unity strained to the breaking-point, the American party offered a way of championing national homogeneity. Its strength reached a climax in 1855, when it elected six governors on a platform that subordinated the foreign peril to a simple appeal for maintaining the Union by developing "a sentiment of profoundly intense American feeling."[4] But the division between North and South, which nativists endeavored to submerge, soon submerged nativism. The anti-foreign crusade could not prevail against sectional forces which were themselves evolving into overriding loyalties. Northern nativists rallied to the northern nationalism of Abraham Lincoln; southern nativists submitted to a new southern nationalism.

A second nativist tradition, much less prominent in the 1850's than anti-Catholicism, went back a half-century before. From the 1790's a fear of foreign radicals had lurked in the corners of the American mind. While agitated Protestants regarded the immigrant as yoked to religious despotism, timid conservatives sometimes found him prone to political revolution. Despite inconsistencies between the two charges of submissiveness to tyranny and abandonment to discontent, anti-Catholic and anti-radical nativism agreed in a cardinal assumption: the European's disloyalty strikes directly at republican freedom.

For a long time it was hard for Americans to view revolution in a very ominous light. Their own origins as a nation rested in it; their Declaration of Independence celebrated it. On the whole, American opinion applauded the liberal revolutions occurring in Europe and Latin America in the eighteenth and nineteenth centuries. Refugee radicals not infrequently received a hero's welcome in the home of the oppressed. Still, another attitude toward revolutionists was possible, even at an early date. In contrast to similar upheavals in other lands, the American Revolution had involved relatively little political or social transformation; its leaders aimed at perfecting an existing society, not at building a new one on its ruins.[5] In retrospect, the spirit of '76 could appear even more sober than it was, and vastly different from the temper of foreign revolutions. And since the flexibility of

American institutions has continued to discourage extreme dissent, America's most uncompromising radicals have in fact come from abroad. This persistent contrast between a generally hopeful psychology of mobility in America and the more desperate politics born in class-ridden Europe has fostered the belief that violent and sweeping opposition to the status quo is characteristically European and profoundly un-American. Thus, anti-radical movements in America, like anti-Catholic ones, have had a singular propensity to assume a nationalistic form.

Anti-radical nativism crystallized at the end of the eighteenth century under the impact of the French Revolution. In 1798 the United States faced both an internal and an external crisis comparable in some ways to the sectional split of the 1850's. Internationally the country was heading toward war with revolutionary France. At home a "factious" opposition, brandishing French slogans, was organizing against the Federalist gentlemen who had unified the new nation. Sober Federalists quailed at the ardent sympathy the Jeffersonian party showed toward French democracy; for the intellectual ties between Jeffersonian and Jacobin simply confirmed a fundamental Federalist conviction that democracy was a subversive, revolutionary idea. Furthermore, the ruling gentlemen noted grimly the internal support their opponents received from English, French, and Irish immigrants. Pessimists at heart, the Federalists concluded that Europe's disorders might swiftly overwhelm the new world.[6] In their hysterical determination to check foreign radicalism and native dissent, they proceeded to enact the notorious Alien and Sedition Acts.

By 1800 the war crisis had passed; and at home the triumph of Jeffersonian democracy largely dispelled both conservative pessimism and anti-radical nativism. The passing of Federalist gloom left the American people convinced of their invulnerability to the social ills of the Old World. For many decades confidence in the stability of American institutions and in their appeal to all mankind quieted nationalistic fears of revolution. But occasional doubts lingered in conservative circles. Perhaps people bred under oppression lack self-reliance and self-restraint; in America they may confuse equal rights with "voluptuous license." Perhaps a man discontented in his own country will have no settled principles or loyalty at all.[7] The coming of the German Forty-Eighters rekindled the flickering suspicions. These refugees from revolution, among them the founders of a Marxist movement in America, brought a whole grab-bag of unorthodox ideas. Especially in the South, where German opposition to slavery caused alarm, and in the Midwest, where German settlement concentrated, the xenophobia of the 1850's included anxiety over the threat of immigrant radicals to American institutions.[8]

The anti-radical and anti-Catholic traditions had, on the surface, a negative character that sets them apart from a third and more recent style of nativist thinking. The first two traditions declared what America was not, more clearly than what it was or should be; they aimed from the outset to define the nation's enemies rather than its essence. Racial nativism, on the other hand, began the other way around. Originally and basically, what may be called the Anglo-Saxon tradition characterized the in-group directly, the alien forces only by implication. The concept that the United States belongs in some special sense to the Anglo-Saxon "race" offered an interpretation of the source of national greatness. The idea crystallized in the early nineteenth century as a way of defining American nationality in a positive sense, not as a formula of attack on outsiders. Thus it affected American nationalism long before it became a factor in American nativism. Despite the inherently parochial bias involved in pointing to a single, limited source of nationhood, Anglo-Saxonism gave only the slightest inkling of its nativistic potentialities until the late nineteenth century.

By one of the manifold ironies of intellectual history, the Anglo-Saxon tradition began as a liberal doctrine: an idea that ended as a slogan for reaction arose as a call for freedom. By another irony, the Americans who attributed the uniqueness and distinction of their nation to the Anglo-Saxon race were simply echoing the prior claims of the English. Proud appeals to Anglo-Saxon origins and ancestors came into vogue in England in the seventeenth and eighteenth centuries among the champions of Parliament. In opposition to royal absolutism, the Parliamentarians sought precedents and roots for English liberty in the ancient institutions and temperament of the country before the Norman conquest. Relying on Tacitus' vivid picture of the Germanic barbarians and on other early texts, the Parliamentarians traced England's freedom-loving heritage to the "Goths," a collective designation for Angles, Saxons, Jutes, and the other primitive tribes that invaded the Roman Empire.

Like the parallel exaltation of Frankish and Gallic forebears in France, the Gothic vogue had little nationalistic significance until inflated by the romantic ferment of the early nineteenth century. Romantic writers and scholars, rebelling against the uniformitarian outlook of the Enlightenment, loved the diversity and the organic inwardness of all forms of life; to them a nation fulfilled itself through the endogenous forces within its own language and history. Thus the romantics sought in the mists of an early medieval (or "Gothic") past the indestructible core not only of their political institutions but of their whole national character.[9] The circle of ancestral distinction tended to narrow to the Anglo-Saxons, who emerged as the finest offshoot of the Teutonic branch of the Goths; and Englishmen discovered that they owed their national genius to this supposedly unitary racial source.

In England the fountainhead of the new racial nationalism was Sharon Turner's very popular *History of the Anglo-Saxons* (1799–1805), and in

American thought the idea received its first considerable impetus from the appearance of a Philadelphia edition of Turner's two-volume work in 1841. As the tradition passed into American hands, it preserved its early libertarian emphasis. Although it now ministered to the national ego instead of implementing a constitutional controversy, this romantic cult still stressed, as the supreme Anglo-Saxon virtue, a gift for political freedom. In the Anglo-Saxons, or perhaps the Teutons, had been implanted a unique capacity for self-government and a special mission to spread its blessings.[10]

In popular thought and emotion, this idea found an initial outlet not among nativists but among expansionists. Many an American, during the annexation of Texas and California, saw himself in the role of his conquering ancestors, executing a racial mandate to enlarge the area of freedom. The penny press roared that the Anglo-Saxon impulse would carry the American flag throughout the continent; whereas those who detested the expansionist movement, like James Russell Lowell, excoriated Anglo-Saxonism as a hypocritical mask for aggression.[11] Nativists, on the other hand, touched on this idea only very rarely and very lightly. Horace Bushnell, as early as 1837, had cautioned the Americans to protect their noble Saxon blood against the miscellaneous ride of immigration, and in the 1850's there were occasional suggestions that a Celtic flood might swamp America's distinctive Anglo-Saxon traits.[12] But on the whole, racial nationalists proclaimed an unqualified confidence in the American destiny. Sometimes they explicitly averred that the Anglo-Saxon would always retain predominance over all comers.[13]

It is significant that the very concept of race had not yet attained its later fixity and definiteness. Racial nationalism, having arisen out of political and literary speculation, not out of scientific inquiry, displayed a characteristic vagueness. In the sense in which nationalists used the word, "race" often meant little more than national character. It usually suggested some sort of innate impulse, but, despite the growing biological interests of the nineteenth century, this was understood as an ongoing spirit more than a physiological actuality. At best a minor strain in American thought before the Civil War, Anglo-Saxon nationalism then lacked both the intellectual and emotional pungency essential to a serious, nativistic appeal.

In addition to the special curbs on race-thinking, every nativist tendency in pre–Civil War America operated under powerful limitations. Only during the two great crises of the 1790's and 1850's did fear of foreign minorities strike deeply in many native hearts. Even then, wider, more inclusive ideals of nationality were stubbornly defended and ultimately victorious. In general the American people maintained a cocksure faith in themselves, in their boundless opportunities for improvement and acquisition, and in the self-perpetuating strength of their principles of freedom.

Nevertheless some of the major ideological outlines of American nativism bad been established. The anti-Catholic, anti-radical, and Anglo-Saxon traditions had opened channels through which a large part of the xenophobia of the late nineteenth and twentieth centuries would flow. The content and dynamics of that later story would come from social, economic, and intellectual changes unimagined in the days of the Know-Nothings. But the basic patterns were there.

■ Notes

1. Quoted in Sister M. Evangeline Thomas, *Nativism in the Old Northwest, 1850–1860* (Washington, 1936), 131. On terminology see Mitford M. Mathews, *A Dictionary of Americanisms on Historical Principles* (Chicago, 1951), II, 1113.

2. Popular among Catholic historians, this view was summed up most forcefully by Ray Allen Billington, *The Protestant Crusade, 1800–1860: A Study of the Origins of American Nativism* (New York, 1938).

3. Max Savelle, *Seeds of Liberty: The Genesis of the American Mind* (New York, 1948), 568–73; Sister Mary Augustina (Ray), *American Opinion of Roman Catholicism in the Eighteenth Century* (New York, 1936).

4. Reprinted in Peter G. Mode, *Source Book and Bibliographical Guide for American Church History* (Menasha, 1921), 466–69. See also W. Darrell Overdyke, *The Know-Nothing Party in the South* (Baton Rouge, 1950), 86–87; Allan Nevins, *Ordeal of the Union* (New York, 1947), II, 328–31, 398–400, 465–68.

5. Louis Hartz, "American Political Thought and the American Revolution," *American Political Science Review*, XLVI (1952), 321–42.

6. John C. Miller, *Crisis in Freedom: The Alien and Sedition Acts* (Boston, 1951).

7. "Immigration," *North American Review*, XL (1835), 461; Cephas Brainerd and Eveline Warner Brainerd, eds., *The New England Society Orations* (New York, 1901), I, 315.

8. Carl Wittke, *Refugees of Revolution: The German Forty-Eighters in America* (Philadelphia, 1952), 183–86, 215; William G. Bean, "An Aspect of Know-Nothingism—The Immigrant and Slavery," *South Atlantic Quarterly*, XXIII (1924), 328–29. See also Alfred B. Ely, *American Liberty, Its Sources, Its Dangers, and the Means of Its Preservation* (New York, 1850), 26.

9. Samuel Kliger, *The Goths in England: A Study in Seventeenth and Eighteenth Century Thought* (Cambridge, 1952); Hans Kohn, *The Idea of Nationalism: A Study in Its Origins and Background* (New York, 1944), 206–208, 518, 645–46; Arthur O. Lovejoy, "The Meaning of Romanticism for the Historian of Ideas," *Journal of the History of Ideas*, II (1941), 257–78.

10. "The Anglo-Saxon Race," *North American Review*, LXXIII (1851), 34–71; "The Anglo-Saxon Race," *American [Whig] Review*, VII (1848), 28–46; George Ripley and Charles A. Dana, eds., *The New American Cyclopaedia* (New York, 1858), I, 573–75. For a somewhat special version see George Perkins Marsh, *The Goths in New England* (Middlebury, 1843). Until Turner began to write at the turn of the century, the term Anglo-Saxon referred simply to a language, not to a race, See *Encyclopaedia; or, a Dictionary of Arts, Sciences, and Miscellaneous Literature* (Philadelphia, 1798), II, 7.

11. Albert K. Weinberg, *Manifest Destiny: A Study of Nationalist*

Expansionism in American History (Baltimore, 1935), 163, 360–61; *New York Herald*, April 6, 1850; *The Writings of James Russell Lowell* (Boston, 1890), IX, 55; Samuel J. Bayard, *A Sketch of the Life of Com. Robert F. Stockton* (New York, 1856), appendix, 83. See also the anonymous Yankee quoted in Richard Lyle Power, "A Crusade to Extend Yankee Culture, 1820–1865," *New England Quarterly*, XIII (1940), 647.

12. Horace Bushnell, "The True Wealth or Weal of Nations," Clark S. Northrup and others, eds., *Representative Phi Beta Kappa Orations* (Boston, 1915), 14; Frederick Saunders, *A Voice to America; or, The Model Republic* (New York, 1855), 83–95; Edith Abbott, *Historical Aspects of the Immigration Problem; Select Documents* (Chicago, 1926), 773.

13. "Anglo-Saxon Race," *North American Review*, LXXIII (1851), 56; "The Anglo-Saxons and the Americans: European Races in the United States," *American Whig Review*, XIV (1851), 193.

Hans-Georg Betz

The New Politics of Resentment: Radical Right-Wing Populist Parties in Western Europe

In the decades following the second world war, the liberal democracies of western Europe enjoyed a remarkable degree of social and political stability. Sustained economic growth, growing individual affluence, and the expansion and perfection of the welfare state each contributed to a social and political climate conducive to political stability while eroding support for extremist solutions on both the left and right. However, stability and consensus were only short-lived. The resurgence of ideological and political turbulence in the late 1960s, rising social conflicts in the early 1970s, and the spread of mass protest by new social movements in the 1980s were symptoms of a profound transformation of West European politics. Its contours are becoming visible in the early 1990s.

Crucial to this transformation was the political climate of the 1980s. It was marked by disenchantment with the major social and political institutions and profound distrust in their workings, the weakening and decomposition of electoral alignments, and increased political fragmentation and electoral volatility. New political issues emerged, promoted by new social actors outside and often against the established political channels. Growing awareness of environmental degradation generated rising ecological protest; advances in general welfare led to demands for social equality and greater opportunities for political participation from women and minorities.

It was expected that these conflicts would benefit the left, even if the demands of students, women, and minorities were not necessarily compatible with those of the traditional left. Indeed, the 1980s saw a significant fragmentation of the left. Distancing themselves from what they considered the growth-oriented "old politics" of socialists and social democrats, left-libertarian parties established themselves in a number of advanced West European democracies.[1] Yet despite significant electoral gains, the left-libertarian project appears to have fallen short of the expectations of both

---

Hans-Georg Betz, "The New Politics of Resentment: Radical Right-Wing Populist Parties in Western Europe," *Comparative Politics* 26, no. 4 (July 1993): 413–427. Reprinted with permission of *Comparative Politics*.

supporters and detractors. However, the stagnation and partial exhaustion of several left-libertarian parties—for example, in Germany, Sweden, Italy, and Switzerland—have not automatically benefited the traditional parties. Instead, West European party systems have increasingly come under heavy pressure from a radical populist right.

Radical right-wing populist parties are radical in their rejection of the established sociocultural and sociopolitical system and their advocacy of individual achievement, a free marketplace, and a drastic reduction of the role of the state. They are right-wing in their rejection of individual and social equality, in their opposition to the social integration of marginalized groups, and in their appeal to xenophobia, if not overt racism. They are populist in their instrumentalization of sentiments of anxiety and disenchantment and their appeal to the common man and his allegedly superior common sense. In short, they tend to combine a classic liberal position on the individual and the economy with the sociopolitical agenda of the extreme and intellectual new right, and they deliver this amalgam to those disenchanted with their individual life chances and the political system.

■ The Recent Success of the Radical Populist Right

During the past several years, radical right-wing populist parties have been able to multiply both votes and parliamentary representation. The Austrian FPÖ (Freedom Party) is a prominent example. Owing to a number of political blunders, the party had virtually ceased to exist as a relevant political force in Austrian politics in the mid 1980s. However, electoral fortune returned after the young charismatic and populist Jörg Haider was elected to the chair of the party in 1986. In the following general election the party received more than 9 percent of the vote and eighteen seats in parliament. It almost doubled its electoral support in 1990, receiving thirty-three parliamentary seats. Finally, in the 1991 regional election in Vienna the party received 22.6 percent of the vote and became the second largest party in Vienna.

Even more dramatic has been the success story of the *Lega Lombarda*. Founded in the early 1980s by Umberto Bossi, the party scored 3 percent in the 1987 national election in Lombardy. This gave Bossi a seat in the Italian senate. After that the *Lega* advanced rapidly in Lombardy. It won 8.1 percent in the European elections, followed by 18.9 percent in the 1990 regional elections. After the *Lega Lombarda* united with other leagues to form the *Lega Nord/Lega Lombardo*, the party received 24.4 percent of the vote in the 1991 local election in Brescia. The general election of April 1992 confirmed the *Lega*'s prominent position in northern Italy. With 20.5 percent in Lombardy, 17.3 percent overall in the North, and 8.7 percent nationally, it became the fourth largest party in Italy.

Similarly, the *Front National*, founded in 1972 by right-wing radicals, has established itself in the French party system. Under Jean-Marie Le Pen it emerged from virtually zero in the 1981 general election to 9.6 percent of the vote in 1988. In the presidential elections Le Pen even gained more than 14 percent of the vote. However, the regional elections of March 1992 showed that the advance of the *Front National* might have reached its limits. With 13.9 percent of the vote, the party remained considerably below its own expectations.

Impressive, if less dramatic, have been the recent developments in Switzerland, Belgium, and Sweden. In Switzerland, the *Autopartei* (Automobile Party), founded in 1985, succeeded in increasing its parliamentary representation from two seats in 1987 to ten seats in 1991. In Belgium, the *Vlaams Blok*, founded in 1978 as a Flemish regionalist party, increased its parliamentary representation from two seats in 1987 to twelve seats in 1991. Finally, in Sweden, the *Ny Demokrati* (New Democracy) party, founded in 1990, gained 6.8 percent of the vote in the 1991 general elections and twenty-five seats in parliament.

Sweden has not been the only Scandinavian democracy with a significant radical right-wing presence. In fact, the Danish and Norwegian Progress parties have been among the established radical right-wing populist parties in western democracies. Founded in the early 1970s by charismatic newcomers to politics as antitax and anti-welfare-state protest parties, they initially did rather well at the polls, yet lost much of their support in the early 1980s. However, by the end of the 1980s, the political fortunes of both parties began to improve. In the 1988 general elections, the Danish party received 9 percent of the vote, almost twice as much as in 1987. One year later the Norwegian party became, with 13 percent of the vote, Norway's third largest party.

The electoral history of the German *Republikaner* has been similar. Led by a former television talk show host, the party emerged in the early 1989 elections in Berlin, where it received 7.5 percent of the vote, followed by 7.1 percent in the European elections. However, the collapse of East Germany and quick reunification left it without much of its program or electoral support. In the first all-German elections of 1990 the *Republikaner* scored a mere 2.1 percent of the vote. After a number of leading party figures defected from the party, the *Republikaner* seemed to be at an end. However, the state election in Baden-Württemberg in April 1992, in which the *Republikaner* received almost 12 percent of the vote, showed that the party might still represent a strong challenge to the political system of unified Germany.

This short survey of the rise of radical right-wing populist parties shows the degree to which the parties have penetrated West European politics. Often led by charismatic and telegenic leaders, they have successfully mobilized a considerable portion of the West European electorate. In what follows, we will examine why radical right-wing populist parties have been able to make such significant gains at the polls. We will explore whether the rise of the radical populist right reflects merely temporary resentment and single issue protest or whether it represents a response to structural problems of advanced western democracies. An analysis of the program and social basis of these parties shows that their success depends on two factors: their ability to mobilize resentment and protest and their capability to offer a future-oriented program that confronts the challenge posed by the economic, social, and cultural transformation of advanced West European democracies.

■ Racism Revisited

It has become commonplace to attribute the growing appeal of radical right-wing populism to the recent explosion of hostility towards immigrants in much of Western Europe. According to a 1989 study on racism and xenophobia, between 11 and 14 percent of the population in the European Communities was troubled by the presence of people of other nationality, race, or religion. Among the citizens of the EC, Belgians, Germans, French, and Danes were particularly sensitive about immigrants. Overall, 5 percent of the population of the member states considered immigrants the most important problem facing their respective countries.[2] A number of reasons explains this hostility. For one, there is growing concern about the dramatic increase in the number of refugees and illegal immigrants looking for a better life in Western Europe. During the 1980s, the number of political refugees in Western Europe grew from some 75,000 in 1983 to almost 320,000 in 1989.[3] Since 1989, these numbers have dramatically increased. Switzerland alone counted 41,000 refugees in 1991, and Germany more than 250,000. In addition, Germany had to deal with a growing number of ethnic German resettlers from Eastern Europe and the former Soviet Union. As a result, the question of how to reduce, if not stop, the influx of refugees has become one of the most important political issues throughout Western Europe.

Not only the sheer numbers but also the changing composition of refugee and immigrant populations has contributed to the xenophobic upswell. Whereas in the past the large majority of foreigners in Western Europe were other West Europeans or Turks, the majority of recent arrivals comes from the Third World. As a result, in many West European countries the proportion of West European foreigners has remained fairly stable, while the non-European population has increased. One of the first to experience this trend was France. In 1968, roughly two million European immigrants lived in France, and 650,000 Africans, 95 percent of whom were from the Maghreb. By 1982, the number of Africans was almost as large (1.57 million, 90 percent from the Maghreb) as the number of Europeans (1.75 million).[4]

By the late 1980s, developments in the rest of Western Europe started to resemble those earlier in France. In Denmark, for example, between 1982 and 1991 the number of foreigners from Scandinavia and the EC countries increased slightly from 46,000 to 51,000. At the same time the number of Africans and Asians increased from 19,000 to over 45,000. In 1991, almost 50 percent of all registered foreigners in Italy and more than 40 percent of all refugees in Switzerland were from Asia and Africa.[5] As a result, West European countries are confronted with a sizable number of non-Europeans, whose physical difference makes an impression far beyond their number. This has contributed to the perception that Europe is being "invaded" by alien traditions, culture, and religion.[6]

Against the background of a growing influx and increasing visibility of non-Europeans, the success of radical right-wing populist parties marks the revival of racism in Western Europe. The success of the *Front National* in the European elections of 1984 and the growing electoral success of other radical populist right-wing parties in the late 1980s show that the growing presence of a non-European population has evoked anxiety and resentment. The radical populist right has been particularly astute in translating these sentiments into political gains without couching them in outright racist terms. Instead, they have echoed those critics of the West European refugee policy who have focused public attention on the growing financial burden that refugees impose on the host countries.[7] The central argument is that the vast majority of refugees only claim to be political refugees. In reality they are driven by economic motives. This hurts West European societies twice. Immigrants not only burden social services with new expenditures, but they also take away scarce jobs from the native unemployed.[8] Therefore, illegal immigration and "asylum tourism" should be stopped. Instead of "privileging" foreign immigrants, West European governments should give preference in regard to employment, housing, and social assistance to natives and Europeans.[9] As the German *Republikaner* put it succinctly: "Eliminate unemployment: Stop immigration!"[10]

The situation of foreign workers in advanced West European democracies shows that these claims and demands are seriously flawed. In most of these countries, the vast majority of the immigrant labor force has low levels of education and performs unskilled or semiskilled labor which the indigenous population increasingly refuses to do. In 1989 in Austria, 61 percent of foreigners and 84 percent of Turkish guest workers had no more than compulsory education, compared to 28 percent of the Austrian work force. As a result, the majority held low level positions.[11] The situation was similar in Germany and in France, where immigrant workers had lower levels of education and fewer chances to advance from unskilled to qualified positions and were considerably more at risk to lose their jobs than French workers.[12]

Not only is the degree to which immigrant workers deprive natives of job opportunities rather questionable. It is also open to discussion whether they represent a burden or rather a net gain for West European societies. Generally, immigrant workers have made significant contributions to these societies. Recruited to fill vacant positions during the period of high economic growth, they played a vital part in laying the foundation for affluence and prosperity in Western Europe. Furthermore, immigrant workers represent not only a work force but also consumers, taxpayers, and contributors to social security and pension systems.[13]

Particularly the latter aspect assumes increasing importance for Western European societies. Because of falling birth rates, much of Western Europe is experiencing a significant shift in the age pyramid. This is expected to have serious consequences both for the labor market and the social security systems. Population statistics show that in order to keep the labor force stable and to guarantee social security for a growing older generation it might be necessary to recruit more foreign labor. Thus, the French have projected that between 2000 and 2039 they might have to recruit between 165,000 and 315,000 new immigrants annually to prevent a decline in the active population.[14]

The *Front National*, the *Vlaams Blok*, and the FPÖ were among the first parties to draw a connection between falling birth rates and foreign immigration. In their propaganda pamphlets the *Front National* graphically connects rising immigration, an increase in the number of mosques, and "empty cradles" to drive home their message that there is "a great risk that we will no longer be able to pay our pensions and, above all, that we will see disappear our thousand-year old identity and the French people itself." Immigration "threatens the survival of the French nation, the security of its territory, the integrity of its patrimony, its culture, its language."[15] These words and images appeal to diffuse sentiments of anxiety and growing general insecurity over the fact that in the future western Europe's well-being might increasingly depend on non-Europeans whose growing numbers threaten its cultural and national identity. Umberto Bossi makes this quite clear when he accuses the established parties of warning to transform Italy into a "multiracial [*multirazziale*], multiethnic, and multireligious society" which "comes closer to hell than to paradise."[16]

Its success at the polls shows that the radical populist right has become the champion of growing resentment and hostility towards foreigners. Against the prospects of a future multicultural, multiethnic European society, right-wing populist parties have successfully promoted themselves as the advocates and guardians of an exclusive national culture. This culture is firmly grounded in national identity and a closely circumscribed European tradition. Xenophobia has proven to be such a powerful political issue that even the Scandinavian Progress parties have increasingly resorted to mobilizing antiforeigner sentiments in order to revive their political fortunes.[17] However, it would be wrong to attribute the appeal of the radical populist right exclusively to its anti-immigrant program. Success at the polls depends on more than the mobilization of xenophobia.

■ The Neo-Liberal Agenda

What distinguishes most radical right-wing populist parties from the established parties is not only their militant attacks on immigrants but also their pronounced neo-liberal program. Although varying in emphasis and importance, radical right-wing Populist parties have tended to hold strong anti-statist positions. They find articulation in a sharp criticism of high levels of taxation, of the bureaucratic state in general, and of welfare outlays. Some of these parties—in particular the two Progress parties—trace their origin to the tax-welfare backlash of the 1970s. Others, such as the New Democracy party, have emerged out of the more recent crisis of the welfare state. Their critique of the interventionist state fuses resentment against the state, the bureaucracy, and politicians with a populist appeal to freedom and democracy. This appeal is pronounced not only in the case of the two Progress parties, but also in those of the *Lega*, the New Democracy party, and particularly the FPÖ and the *Autopartei*, which promotes itself as the champion of "Freedom—Prosperity—Joy of Life."[18]

The resulting political program marks a revival of radical liberalism. It calls for a reduction of some taxes and the abolition of others, a drastic curtailing of the role of the state in the economy and large-scale privatization of the public sector including the state controlled media, a general deregulation of the private sector, and a restructuring and streamlining of the public sector. The main beneficiaries of these measures should be small and medium-sized enterprises which are expected to play a central role in the further development of advanced western societies, particularly since new technologies allow them to compete effectively with larger enterprises.[19]

However, the radical populist right's neo-liberal program is only secondarily an economic program. Primarily, it is a political weapon against the established political institutions and their alleged monopolization of political power which hampers economic progress and suppresses true democracy. The opponent is the bureaucratic, centralized state which is living off the work of the productive forces in society. Bossi has put this most poignantly when he declares that the political battle in Italy is between Rome and Milan, between "the capital of parasitism and clientelism, which is Rome, and the capital of the economy, which is Milan."[20] From this perspective, Le Pen's appeal to create "50 million proprietors" in a "popular capitalism" takes on an almost revolutionary spirit.[21] It would not only loosen the state's grip on power, but also guarantee that decisions are made from an economic and profit-oriented, thus efficiency-conscious perspective rather than on the basis of political and electoral considerations.

The radical populist right's hostility to the state is equaled by its hostility to the established political parties. Particularly Umberto Bossi but also Jean-Marie Le Pen and Jörg Haider have skillfully translated popular disaffection with the established parties into poignant attacks against the *palazzo*, against corruption and inefficiency, and against the "arrogance" of the *classe politique* which refuses to listen to the views of the common person. Against that Bossi boldly asserts that only with him Italy will have "honesty, cleanness, transparency, and above all TRUE DEMOCRACY." Under his guidance the Italians will recover "everything of which they have been shamefully robbed" during forty years of rule by the political establishment.[22] Similarly, Jean-Marie Le Pen charges the political establishment with having led France into a deep crisis, which threatens the country's existence, its prosperity, and its freedom.[23]

The established political parties are accused of having constructed, to the detriment of the average citizen, an all-encompassing system sustained by interventionism, clientelism, and favoritism.[24] It is against this "system" that the radical populist right goes on the offensive. Behind its strategy is the expectation that the relationship between voters and parties is profoundly changing, that voters no longer "function" according to the demands of party politics. The radical right addresses its appeal for political support to the emerging "working, sovereign citizen, who carries responsibility for family and occupation and who can judge for himself."[25]

The radical populist right's rise to political prominence has come in the wake of a profound and diffuse disaffection and disenchantment with the established political parties throughout Western Europe. According to a study from 1989, almost half of the Italian public and 35 percent of the French thought the established parties were absolutely incapable of representing them on the major issues; 33 percent of the French public thought that the political parties were most responsible for the ills affecting French society.[26] In 1991, more than half of the Italian public held the political parties incapable of resolving Italy's institutional and economic crisis; 44 percent thought political parties contributed little to facilitate participation in Italian society.[27]

Undoubtedly, the general malaise towards politics and political parties and a growing crisis of political representation has benefited radical right-wing populist parties.[28] By appealing to lingering sentiments of powerlessness, to widespread alienation from the political process, and to growing resentment against the prevailing political system, radical populist right-wing parties present themselves as the true "antiparty parties." Regional studies on the *Lega*, the *Republikaner*, and the FPÖ show that these parties successfully attracted and mobilized voters who abstained from voting in previous elections.[29] According to Italian surveys, protest against the established parties was an important motive in voting for the *Lega Lombarda*, subordinate only to the desire to express a general discontent with "Rome," symbol of the inefficiency of the Italian bureaucracy.[30] Survey data from Germany show that in 1989, at the height of support for the *Republikaner*, only 11 percent of its supporters trusted the political parties, and 26 percent the government (as compared to 73 percent of the supporters of the established center-right parties). For 80 percent of *Republikaner* supporters politics had failed in important areas.[31]

These findings suggest that an explanation of the radical populist right's success has to go beyond xenophobia. Its success can be explained in part as a protest against the established political parties and their politics. However, these populist right parties represent more than mere vehicles of protest. Behind their seemingly incoherent programs and contradictory positions stand concrete political objectives. Their anti-immigrant positions only appear to contradict their neo-liberal program. From a liberal position, unemployment problems stem not from immigrants but from too much state intervention. "Provided the proper incentives . . . immigrants invariably prove to be net contributors to an economy.[32] However, only the New Democracy party has drawn the consequences. It demands that all immigrants, including temporary foreign workers and refugees, be allowed to work in Sweden.[33]

The other parties either consider xenophobia too potent a political weapon to be sacrificed to programmatic coherence or hold it compatible with their neo-liberal program. This is only possible if their promotion of a neo-liberal program is part of a larger strategy to combat what particularly the *Front National* and the *Lega* consider the main threats to the very existence of the nation or a particular region. These threats stem not only from a loss of national or regional identity, but also from global economic competition which threatens to exacerbate domestic economic problems and to marginalize individual West European countries. The radical populist right's programmatic mixture of xenophobia and neo-liberalism might thus be seen as a response to current global changes which produce winners and losers. It is an attempt to meet the global challenge by promoting individual initiative and entrepreneurship while at the same time eliminating whatever might hamper initiative, drain resources, and thus impede competitiveness.[34] The resulting ideology might be characterized as neo-isolationism in a future "fortress Europe."[35] This might explain why radical right-wing populist parties have done particularly well in some of the most prosperous regions of western Europe (Lombardy, Flanders, Bavaria, Baden-

Württemberg), where there is growing resentment not only against immigrants but also against fellow countrymen from less advanced regions (for example, southern Italy, Wallonia, and perhaps even former East Germany), both seen as a drain on resources.

If this notion of threat partly explains the seemingly contradictory nature of the radical populist right's program, a second explanation appears equally plausible. According to this explanation, different programmatic positions appeal to different constituencies. In fact, the electoral success of the radical populist right can be attributed to the particular mixture of its program. This program combines a populist mobilization of resentment with a seemingly future-oriented response to the challenge of a profound social, cultural, and political transformation of advanced western societies. This transformation has variously been described as the coming of an information, consumer, or postindustrial society.[36] Behind these formulations is the assumption that the present accelerated process of technological modernization, particularly in the communication and information sector, has led to nothing less than revolutionary changes in the social structure of western democracies.

■ The Social Costs of Accelerated Modernization

Central to this process are two developments: on the one hand, a shift from modern mass production and mass consumption to what has been defined as a new regime of flexible accumulation, that is, the production of highly specialized, customized products through flexible manufacturing systems supervised by a highly skilled work force; on the other hand, a renewed acceleration of the shift from the secondary to the tertiary sector. As a result of both the diffusion of high tech production systems and the expansion of highly qualified jobs in organization and management, research and development, and consulting, there is a growing demand for higher levels of formal education, higher skills, and longer training. At the same time there is a marked decrease in unskilled and semiskilled jobs in production, cleaning, transportation, and sales. The result is a growing bifurcation of labor markets.

The social space of the advanced postindustrial societies is similarly characterized by the emergence of a "two-thirds society": on the one hand, an affluent, well-educated, and secure new middle class of employees, civil servants, and new professionals and a "polyvalent" blue collar work force employed in the "postfordist" factory; on the other, an increasingly marginalized sector of unskilled and semiskilled workers, young people without complete formal education and training, and the growing mass of the long-term unemployed. They represent a readily identifiable underclass of the permanently unemployed, underemployed, or marginally employed who are quickly turning into the losers of the accelerated modernization process.[37]

Finally, the cultural sphere is characterized by the dominance of consumption, the fragmentation of taste cultures, and individuality in choice and in life style, made possible by the new production regime.[38] In this view, the high standard of living and high level of social security characteristic of advanced western democracies have led to the dissipation of class distinctions and subcultural class identities. The result has been a process of "individualization" of life styles, which give rise to a new system of social diversification and stratification.[39] By rewarding individual effort, self-promotion and self-advertisement, and the ability to design one's own existence, it reinforces the trend towards social bifurcation.

Both the rise and political success of left-libertarian as well as radical right-wing populist parties have been attributed to the broad transformation of advanced West European democracies. One side has been the radical populist right as a response of modernization losers to deprivation and marginalization.[40] Others have argued that these parties represent a response to a broader transformation of the political culture of advanced democracies: the radical populist right occupies one pole on a new axis of conflict over social values. It represents a largely materialist reaction to the postmaterialist aspirations of the libertarian left and the libertarian left's promotion of environmental issues, new concepts of morality, new ways of political participation, and vision of a multicultural society. The reaction to this agenda has been an increased emphasis on "old politics": sustained economic growth, technological progress, economic stability, a tough stand on questions of law and order, and a return to traditional moral values.[41]

Neither interpretation sufficiently explains the ambiguities and paradoxes represented by the radical populist right. One of their most serious deficits is that they see the radical populist right largely as representing "reactions against change, rather than change in a new direction."[42] However, the radical populist right's central programmatic positions are only reactionary (in the sense of the desire to impede or prevent change) as far as they refer to immigrants and refugees: instead of accepting growing ethnic and cultural heterogeneity they seek to return to an ethnically and culturally homogeneous past. Their neo-liberal stance, on the other hand, explicitly anticipates, supports, and endorses radical change and thus hardly appeals to those threatened by these changes. Rather than seeking to return to the comprehensive corporatist and welfare-state-oriented policies of the past, they embrace social individualization and fragmentation as a basis for their political programs. In what follows, we will argue that one possible explanation of the ambiguities of this program is the particular social basis to which the radical populist right appeals for support: an

43. Henry Valon, Bernt Aardal, and Gunnar Vogt, *Endring og Kontinnitet, Stortingvalget* 1989 (Oslo: Central Bureau of Statistics, 1990), Table 6.7.

44. Price Plasser and Peter A. Ulram, "Abstieg oder letzte, Chance der ÖVP?" *Österreichische Monatshefte*, 7 (1990), pp. 6–15.

45. Roland Höhne, "Die Renaissance des Rechtsextremismus in Frankreich," *Politische Vierteljahresschrift*, 31 (1990), 84–85. See also Pascal Perrineau, "L'exception presidentielle et la règle léglislative," *Revue Politique et Parlementaire*, 90 (July–August 1988), 37: Nonna Mayer, "Le Front National," in *Bilan: Politique de la France* (Paris: Hachette, 1991), p. 116.

46. Mannheimer, pp. 126–129.

47. Vincenzo Cesareo, Marco Lombardi, and Giancarlo Rovati, *Localismo politico: Il caso Lega Lombarda* (Varese: Comitato Regionale Lombardo Democrazia Cristiana, 1989), p. 5.

48. Mannheimer, p. 128.

49. Dieter Roth, "Sind die Republikaner die fünfte Partei?" *Aus Politique und Zeitgeschichte*, Oct. 5, 1989, pp. 13–14; Max Kaase and Wolfgang G. Gibowski, "Die Ausgangslage für die Bundestagswahl am. 2. Dezember 1990," in Max Kaase and Hans-Dieter Klingemann, eds., *Wahlen und Wähler: Analysen aus Anlass der Bundestagwahl 1987* (Opladen: Westdeutscher Verlag, 1990), pp. 762–764; for the 1992 election, see Matthias Jung and Dieter Roth, "Der Stimmzettel als Denkzettel," *Die Zeit*, Apr. 10, 1992, p. 3.

50. Christian Vandermotten and Jean Vanlear, "Immigration et vote d'extrême-droite en Europe occidentale et en Belgique" (Brussels: mimeo, Université Libre de Bruxelles, 1991), p. 5; Larsen, p. 8.

51. *SWS-Rundschau*, 30 (1990), 570; *SWS-Rundschau*, 31 (1991), 148.

52. For France, see Desplanques and Tabard.

53. Marc Ambroise-Rend, "Le 'mal des banlieues' s'etend," *Le Monde*, Aug. 8, 1991, p. 20; François Dubet, *Immigrations: Qu'en savons-nous?* (Paris: La Documentation Française, 1989), pp. 71–72.

54. Nonna Mayer, "Le vote FN de Passy à Barbés (1984–1988)," in Nonna Mayer and Pascal Perrineau, eds. *Le Front National à découvert* (Paris: Presses de la Fondation Nationale des Sciences Politiques, 1989), pp. 249–267; François-Régis Navarre, "Clichy: Du rouge au noir," *L'Express*, Feb. 23, 1990, p. 33. For Germany, see Eike Hennig, *Die Republikaner im Schatten Deutschhlands* (Frankfurt a.M.: Suhrkamp, 1991), pp. 150–151, 214.

55. Jorgen Goul Andersen and Tor Bjorklund, "Structural Changes and New Cleavages," *Acta Sociologica*, 33 (1990), 204.

56. Ibid. p. 204.

57. Ibid. p. 207.

58. *Le Point*, Apr. 29, 1990, pp. 40–41.

59. Ilvo Diamanti, "Una tipologia dei simpatizzanti della Lega," in Mannheimer, ed., p. 169.

60. FPÖ, *Perspektive Freiheit* (Vienna: Freihitliches Bildungswek, 1991), p. 46.

61. *XXIV Rapporto Censis/1990 sulla situazione sociale del paese* (Rome: Franco Angeli, 1990), p. 125.

62. Kitschelt, p. 229.

63. For empirical evidence, see Moiloli, *Il tarlo delle leghe*, pp. 306–320.

64. Zygmunt Bauman, "Living without an Alternative," *Political Quarterly*, 62 (1991), 35–44.

chapter 11

Incorporating Immigrants

11.1 *the Editors*

Introduction

Public policies pertaining to immigrant incorporation tend to derive from historically based notions of nation-state and citizenship because, in part, as Rogers Brubaker (Chapter 11.2), Peter Schuck (Chapter 11.3), and Zeev Rosenhek (Chapter 11.5) inform us, the concept and rights of citizenship imply exclusivity. Since citizenship is a privilege enjoyed and exercised by most, but not all, persons residing within the polity and society, all others are either intentionally or by default designated as noncitizens, aliens, or denizens.

The "order-disrupting" changes that have visited the major immigration-receiving countries as a consequence of the experience of mass migration spring primarily from the challenge of incorporating the predominantly nonwhite, non-Western, and often non-Christian immigrant populations into the white and nominally Christian societies of North America and Western Europe. Governments in the West have generally responded to the policy challenges posed by mass immigration by pursuing a multipronged strategy. First, they have revamped their immigration laws. In Western Europe, for example, most of the major immigration-receiving countries had applied the brakes to unfettered immigration by the late 1970s. During the past fifteen years or so, the immigration-receiving states of Western Europe have implemented fairly similar measures to prevent or discourage the arrival of asylum seekers.

Second, as Chapter 11.4 by Anthony Messina informs us, many of the major immigration-receiving countries have attempted to accelerate the formal incorporation of immigrants into the domestic polity by extending local voting rights to immigrants, legal permanent residents (LPRs), and other noncitizens. In doing so they have altered the ideational and legal/constitutional foundations of who belongs to and may formally participate in the polity. Indeed, the incremental grant of political rights and privileges to denizens and other long-term immigrants has created a kind of informal citizenship or denizenship.

Finally, many countries have drastically revised their citizenship and nationality codes. Under the pressures of continuing immigration and permanent immigrant settlement, the immigration-receiving states have modified their nationality laws in order to facilitate the formal integration of immigrants into their societies. Access to formal citizenship has been facilitated and immigrant policy generally liberalized in recent years, including in several immigration-receiving countries where exclusionary trends had prevailed less than a decade earlier.

Children born to foreign parents in France, for example, can now more easily acquire full citizenship than previously, provided they have resided in the country between the ages of eleven and eighteen for a minimum of five years. Perhaps most notably among the ranks of recently liberalizing countries, a revised nationality law in Germany in 2000 radically compromised the long-held principle of German kinship. German citizenship, as Brubaker documents in Chapter 11.2, had historically been granted on the basis of *jus sanguinis*. Specifically, children born to non-Germans residing legally in Germany, and who experience difficulty obtaining a German passport, can exercise the right to become citizens upon reaching adulthood if they renounce the citizenship conferred on them through their parents' nationality. Moreover, provided they can pass a German-language test and demonstrate a basic knowledge of the country's constitution and democratic system, adult foreigners can naturalize or qualify for citizenship after eight years of legal residence rather than fifteen years, as was the case under the previous law.

Perhaps even more importantly as a general marker of the cross-national trend toward greater inclusiveness, immigrants are now permitted to hold dual citizenship in more than half a dozen immigration-receiving countries, a trend that has had the effect of decreasing the size of the denizen population. In the Netherlands, for example, the Dutch Nationality Act was recently amended to make it easier than before for Dutch nationals to possess dual citizenship. In Sweden the more inclusive Citizenship Act that came into effect in July 2001 also permits dual citizenship. In Germany dual citizenship, although officially discouraged, is in practice unofficially tolerated by government authorities. Indeed, approximately 41 percent of newly naturalized German citizens were allowed to keep their original citizenship in 2002 after qualifying under certain exceptions. The increasing recognition of dual nationality is a substantial deviation from the long-respected principle that citizenship implies an individual's membership in one and only one state.

More fiercely contested than the growing trend toward formal inclu-

state. The principle of self-determination, pregnant with immense disruptive potential for a dynastically organized and ethnoculturally intermixed Europe (Kedourie 1985), was invoked to justify the territorial gains of 1791–93, and even to reinterpret retrospectively the terms of the accession of Alsace to France in the seventeenth century (Soboul 1960:63; Godechot 1983:69). But the collective "self" entitled by revolutionary doctrine to self-determination was conceived in the cosmopolitan, rationalistic terms characteristic of the eighteenth, not in the Romantic terms characteristic of the nineteenth century.[24] The point of self-determination as understood by the Revolutionaries was to give expression to the universal desire for liberty and thus—how could it be otherwise?—for incorporation into France; it was emphatically not to permit the projection of ethnocultural identity onto the political plane.

Even the briefly if radically assimilationist linguistic politics of the Revolution was determined by political considerations rather than by any conception of the nation as an ethnolinguistic entity. Linguistic variety was denounced as conducive to reaction, linguistic unity advocated as indispensable to Republican citizenship.[25] This short-lived assimilationist politics was not of great consequence. Such linguistic unification as in fact occurred during the Revolutionary and Napoleonic period was due rather to the indirectly assimilationist workings of the army, the schools, and the Napoleonic administrative machine (Kohn 1967:90-93). Yet the ideological and practical importance of assimilation in the French tradition and the bad name that assimilation has acquired in the last two decades justify a more general observation. Assimilation—that is, a deliberate policy of making similar—is incompatible with all consistently "organic" conceptions of membership, according to which "natural" ethnolinguistic boundaries are prior to and determinative of national and (ideally) state boundaries. It is one thing to want to make all citizens of Utopia speak Utopian, and quite another to want to make all Utopiphones citizens of Utopia. Crudely put, the former represents the French, the latter the German model of nationhood. Whether juridical (as in naturalization) or cultural, assimilation presupposes a political conception of membership and the belief, which France took over from the Roman tradition, that the state can turn strangers into citizens, peasants—or immigrant workers—into Frenchmen.[26]

If the French nation-state was invented in 1789, French nationalism was a product of war.[27] Before the outbreak of war, nationalism existed neither as a "blind and exclusive preference for all that belongs to the nation" nor as a "demand in favor of subject nationalities."[28] Only from 1792 on, when the new order felt itself besieged by enemies within and enemies without, did there develop, superseding the ostentatious fraternal cosmopolitanism and pacifism of 1789–91,[29] and justified by the doctrine of the "patrie en danger," elements of an exclusivistic nationalism directed against foreigners inside the territory (Azimi 1988) and an expansive, aggressive nationalism directed abroad, originally missionary and crusading, later simply imperialist and triumphalist.[30] This emergent internal and external nationalism had throughout a political-ideological, not an ethnocultural, character. But it contributed to the later emergence, during the Napoleonic period, of a German counternationalism in which ethnocultural motifs came to play an important role. Revolutionary expansion, itself driven by political nationalism, thus engendered ethnocultural nationalism; the "crusade for liberty" elicited in response the myth, if not the reality, of a "holy war" of ethnonational resistance.

■ Romanticism and Reform in Germany

The German tradition of nationhood was crucially formed during the Revolutionary era by the Romantic movement, on the one hand, and the Prussian reform movement, on the other, both occurring in the shadow of French occupation of Germany (Kohn 1967). The Romantic movement, though not itself centrally concerned with nationhood, supplied patterns of thought and appraisal for the consolidation, celebration, and eventual repoliticization of the ethnocultural understanding of nationhood; while the Prussian reformers, appealing to a radically different conception of nationhood, aimed to "nationalize" the Prussian state from above and thus to regenerate the state after the catastrophic defeat of 1806.

The aesthetic and sociohistorical idiom of German Romanticism was perfectly suited to the elaboration of the ethnocultural conception of nationhood. The celebration of individuality as *Einzigkeit* or uniqueness as over against *Einzelheit* or mere oneness; of depth and inwardness as over against surface polish; of feeling as over against desiccated rationality; of unconscious, organic growth as over against conscious, artificial construction; of the vitality and integrity of traditional, rooted folk cultures as over against the soullessness and artificiality of cosmopolitan culture—all of these themes were easily transposed from the domain of aesthetics and cultural criticism to that of social philosophy. In the social and political thought of Romanticism, and in the larger and more enduring body of social and political thought permeated by its fundamental categories and values, nations are conceived as historically rooted, organically developed individualities, united by a distinctive *Volksgeist* and by its infinitely ramifying expression in language, custom, law, culture, and the state. Despite the emphasis placed on the state,[31] the Romantic understanding of nationhood is fundamentally ethnocultural. The *Volksgeist* is constitutive, the state merely expressive, of nationhood.

The social and political thought of Romanticism was completely divorced from the realities of practical politics. The Prussian reformers, conversely, were untouched by the incipient ethnocultural nationalism of the period. Awed by French triumph and Prussian collapse, they wished to create a Prussian nation in order to regenerate the Prussian state. Thus Hardenberg wrote to Friedrich Wilhelm III in 1807, "We must do from above what the French have done from below" (Pinson 1966:33). Romantics and reformers understood the relation between nation and state in completely different terms: the former in quasi-aesthetic terms, with the state as the expression of the nation and of its constitutive *Volksgeist*, the latter in strictly political terms, with the nation—the mobilized and united *Staatsvolk*—as the deliberate and artificial creation of the state.

Thus was engendered the characteristic dualism and tension between ethnonational and state-national ideologies and programs—a dualism that has haunted German politics ever since. This suggests a way of reformulating the rough contrast that supplied the point of departure for these reflections: the contrast between the French political and the German ethnocultural conception of nationhood. In fact, traditions of nationhood have political and cultural components in both countries. These components have been closely integrated in France, where political unity has been understood as constitutive, cultural unity as expressive, of nationhood. In the German tradition, in contrast, political and ethnocultural aspects of nationhood have stood in tension with one another, serving as the basis for competing conceptions of nationhood. One such conception is sharply opposed to the French conception: on this view, ethnocultural unity is constitutive, political unity expressive, of nationhood. While this ethnocultural understanding of nationhood has never had the field to itself, it took root in early-nineteenth-century Germany and has remained widely available for political exploitation ever since. No such essentially ethnocultural conception of nationhood has ever taken root in France, where cultural nationhood has been conceived as an ingredient, not a competitor, of political nationhood.

■ Nationhood and Nationalism in the Nineteenth Century

The nineteenth century saw the consolidation of the French and the construction of a German nation-state.[32] By the end of the century, there were noticeable similarities in the social structure and in the political style of the two nation-states. Nonetheless, the deeply rooted differences in the political and cultural construction of nationhood that I have sketched above remained significant, and were in certain respects reinforced.

For a hundred years from the end of the ancien régime, France experienced a succession of new regimes, the last of which, during the Boulangist crisis in the centennial year of the Revolution, seemed to be on the verge of collapsing like its predecessors before its twentieth anniversary. Chronic regime instability, however, did not impede the consolidation of the French nation-state from 1830 on. If the Bourbon regime, like the general European settlement imposed by the Congress of Vienna, was antinational, the July Monarchy was based implicitly, and all subsequent regimes explicitly, on the principle, if not the reality, of the sovereignty of the nation. Yet this formal-constitutional development represents only one aspect of the consolidation of French nation-statehood. More important was the consolidation of national memory effected in the works of historians such as Augustin Thierry, Michelet, and Ernest Lavisse; the pedagogic consolidation carried out by the schools of the Third Republic; the linguistic consolidation furthered by school and army; and the sociogeographical consolidation consequent on the development of new means of interlocal communication and transportation (Nora 1986; Weber 1976).

Nationalism, a contradictory mix of chauvinism and messianic humanism, heir to the tradition of revolutionary and Napoleonic expansion and to the principle of national self-determination, was located on the left for most of the century. After the defeat of 1870–71, it migrated to the right, with the Boulangist crisis of 1889 serving as a crucial pivot and the Dreyfus affair marking its definitive arrival (Rémond 1969:208f.; Girardet 1958). More precisely, Continental nationalism migrated to the right, while the left under Jules Ferry discovered in the 1880s a new field for the projection and reconstruction of national grandeur: a revitalized and expanded overseas empire (Girardet 1978). Ideologically and institutionally, this overseas imperialism was the heir to the Continental imperialism of the Revolutionary and Napoleonic period and, more remotely, to the Roman imperial tradition. Ideologically, it was conceived as a mission *libératrice et civilisatrice*; institutionally, it went much further than its British or German counterparts in the legal and political assimilation of metropolitan and overseas regimes, aiming at the construction of "la plus grande France." French Republicans pursued an assimilationist, civilizing, nationalizing mission inside France as well (Weber 1976:486f.); in the late 1880s, this assimilationist internal nationalism, linked to reforms of primary education and military conscription, formed the backdrop to an expansive, assimilationist reform of citizenship law whose central provisions have endured to this day (Brubaker 1992).

The newly nationalist right, despite its antiparliamentarism, shared with the old nationalist left (and with the new imperialist left) the sense of a privileged mission or vocation for France, a concern for national "grandeur," and a reverence for the army as the incarnation and instrument of this grandeur (Girardet 1958). Despite the rise of anti-Semitism toward the end of the century, the new nationalism did not abandon the traditional, essentially political, conception of nationhood for an ethnocultural conception.[33] Indeed, the question of Alsace-Lorraine led to the ideological accentuation of the subjectivist-voluntarist components of French as over against the objective-ethnocultural components of German nationhood.

The German ethnocultural conception of nationhood was a product of the distinctive political and cultural geography of central Europe. Yet a feature of that geography—the inextricable intermixture of Germans and other nationalities—made it impossible to found a German state precisely on the ethnocultural nation (Conze 1983:95; Lepsius 1985:48). None of the proposed solutions to the problem of national unification—including the "classical" Prussian-*kleindeutsch* and Austrian-*grossdeutsch* solutions—could bring into being a "perfect" nation-state: either Germans would be excluded, or non-Germans included, or both. Political considerations were dominant both in the programs of 1848 and in the later practice of Bismarck.

Unification under Bismarck, while conditioned, was not inspired by nationalism, still less by ethnocultural nationalism.[34] Nor was the constitutional structure of the unified Reich that of a nation-state. The constitution did not invoke popular sovereignty, and the imperial crown was offered to William I in Versailles by the princes, not by representatives of the people. There was no unified German citizenship: *Reichsangehörigkeit* (citizenship of the Empire) was derivative of *Landesangehörigkeit* (citizenship of the individual constituent states), and its limited political significance reflected the limited political significance of the Reichstag. The French nation-state had been constructed in polemical opposition not only to dynastic sovereignty but also to corporate and provincial privilege.[35] The German quasi nation-state challenged neither principle, even incorporating particular rights—*Reservatrechte*—into the treaties of accession of the South German states.

The Reich was nonetheless understood as a nation-state, both by those who welcomed it and by those who feared it.[36] As a nation-state, however, it was imperfect not only in its internal constitution but also in its external boundaries—indeed, doubly imperfect. As a *kleindeutsches* Reich, it was underinclusive, excluding above all millions of Austrian Germans. But it was at the same time overinclusive, including French in Alsace-Lorraine, Danes in North Schleswig, and Poles in Prussia. These were not simply linguistic but rather—especially in the last case—self-conscious national minorities. In spite of this dual imperfection, the Reich made significant progress toward consolidated nation-statehood between 1871 and 1914—chiefly through the development of new nationwide institutions and processes and through the integrative working of the state on national consciousness. At the outbreak of war, the Reich was no longer the conspicuously *unvollendete* (unfinished) nation-state of 1871 (Schieder 1961; Kocka 1985).

The Reich was heir to secular traditions of Prussian statehood and

German nationhood. To a remarkable extent, it succeeded in integrating these differing, even antagonistic traditions. Yet the old dualism survived, the old tension between statist and ethnocultural components in the German tradition of nationhood. In the context of this persisting dualism, two generations were not sufficient to create a consolidated, *selbstverständlich* (taken-for-granted), national consciousness within the frame of the new state. *Reichsnational* did not completely displace *volksnational* consciousness in Imperial Germany: the ethnocultural conception of nationhood, though in recess during the decades after the *Reichsgründung*, remained available for subsequent political exploitation. This is shown by the pan-Germanist agitation around the turn of the century (Arendt 1973:222f.), by the assumption that union with Austria would and should follow the breakup of the Habsburg Empire, and by the development of *völkisch* thought and of a *Deutschtum*-oriented politics during the Weimar Republic—to say nothing of the subsequent exploitation of *völkisch* thought by Nazi propagandists.

■ Migrants into Citizens in Late-Nineteenth-Century France

The vicissitudes of French and German traditions of nationhood in the twentieth century cannot be analyzed here. I argue elsewhere that the deeply rooted styles of national self-understanding sketched here survived the turmoil of the first half of the twentieth century, and that they continue to inform the politics of immigration and citizenship today (Brubaker 1992). But the point I want to make here is a historical one. I want to sketch in conclusion the connection between the traditions of nationhood that I have outlined and the legal definitions of citizenship in which they were embodied. For this purpose, it is unnecessary to carry the historical analysis into the twentieth century, for the rules governing the attribution of citizenship in France and Germany were fixed in very nearly their present form in 1889 and 1913 respectively. It is these rules—expansive in France, restrictive in Germany—that govern the citizenship status and chances of today's immigrants. And parliamentary debates and reports confirm the bearing of distinctive French and German traditions of nationhood on the development of these rules.

Under the 1889 law, French citizenship was attributed to all persons born in France of foreign-born parents and domiciled in France at their majority. This system, with minor modifications, remains in place today. Its effect is to automatically transform second-generation immigrants into citizens, much as happens in classical countries of immigration such as the United States and Canada.[37] Most commentators have explained the expansiveness of the law by appealing to the demographic and military interests of the French state. They suggest that French demographic stagnation, in the face of German demographic and military robustness, required the civic incorporation of second-generation immigrants. In fact, the civic incorporation of immigrants was not a military necessity (Brubaker 1992). But it did come to be defined as a *political* necessity. It was a response, first, to the "shocking inequality" that exempted even French-born foreigners from military service while Frenchmen had to serve up to five years (CD 3904; C2:594b). This exemption was especially galling now that military service had become, in theory if not yet in fact, a personal obligation of every Frenchman. By the mid-1880s, when the reform of citizenship law was being debated, it was evident that the new conscription law then in preparation would move decisively towards universal, although shorter, service. In this context, the exemption of second-generation immigrants was of scant military import; indeed, the new conscription law would saddle the military with too many, not too few, recruits. But in the context of universal service for citizens, the exemption of persons born and raised in France, yet choosing to retain their foreign citizenship, was ideologically scandalous and politically intolerable. Secondly, the civic incorporation of second-generation immigrants was a response to the incipient development of "different nations within the French nation" (C2:595a). Fears of solidary Italian ethnic communities in Southern France joined fears of "foreign" domination in Algeria, where the French barely outnumbered "foreigners" (Italians and Spaniards, for example, the vastly larger indigenous population being left out of account). Such solidary ethnic communities, real or imagined, challenged the unitarist French political formula at its core.[38]

But what made the civic incorporation of second-generation immigrants an effective and acceptable solution? Might it not be dangerous, after all, to incorporate immigrants into the army, especially now that military service was conceived in specifically national rather than statist terms, as the expression of the "nation in arms" and no longer as a "tribute exacted by an oppressive and alien state" (Monteilhet 1926:ch. 5; Challener 1965; Weber 1976:295)? How, moreover, could a formal legal transformation solve the sociopolitical problem of the nation within the nation? Would not the formal "nationalization" of the foreign population leave underlying social realities untouched? A stroke of the pen might make foreigners French from the point of view of the law—but would they be truly French?

If parliament was not susceptible to such doubts, if it did not hesitate to transform foreigners into French soldiers and French citizens, it was because of its robust confidence in the assimilatory virtues of France. Thus A. Dubost, reporting on the bill in the Chambre des Députés, called for the extension of French nationality to persons who, "having lived long on the soil on which they were born, have acquired its mores, habits and character, and are presumed to have a natural attachment for the country of their birth" (CD 2083:232b). Others echoed his sentiments. The assimilationist motif is an old one in France. But there was a new and specifically Republican tinge to the assimilationism of the 1880s. It was not mere residence or work in France that was credited with assimilatory virtue; it was participation in the newly Republicanized and nationalized institutions of the school and the army. To assimilate means to make similar: and school and army, in their Republican reincarnations, entrusted with "the mission of retempering the French soul" (Azéma and Winock 1976:149), were powerfully equipped to do just that. Their assimilatory virtues worked on persons long juridically French, reshaping their habits of thought and feeling to make them fit the wider frame of the nation. But they worked on foreigners and the newly naturalized as well. School attendance was obligatory for foreign and French children alike. And military service, after 1889, would be obligatory not only for old-stock French but for those newly defined as French by the reform of nationality law. Internal and external assimilation were sociologically identical: if school and army could turn peasants into Frenchmen,[39] they could turn native-born foreigners into Frenchmen in the same way.

■ Germany: The Citizenry as Community of Descent

Unlike French citizenship law, German citizenship law assigns no significance to birth in the territory. It thus has no mechanism for automatically transforming second- or even third-generation immigrants into citizens. Citizenship is based solely on descent.[40] When German citizenship laws were first formulated, in 1870, it was only natural that citizenship should be based on descent.[41] This was the age of nationalism, and defining the citizenry as a community of descent, following the principle of *jus sanguinis*, was self-evidently preferable to defining the citizenry as a territorial community following the principle of *jus soli*. *Jus soli* was rejected as a feudal principle that based membership on ties to the soil, *jus sanguinis* preferred as a specifically national principle, which would found the nation on ties of kinship that were more substantial and more enduring than the superficial and external ties of common birthplace (Grawert 1973:190–91, 203). There was nothing unusual about this nationalist preference for *jus sanguinis*. Similar arguments were made in France. What is unusual in the German case is that citizenship was based *exclusively* on descent. In most Continental states, the principle of descent is complemented and tempered by the principles of birthplace and prolonged residence, so as to encourage or compel second- or third-generation immigrants to join the community of citizens. Few Continental states go as far as France in imposing citizenship automatically on second-generation immigrants. But they do at least make some provision for the incorporation of second- and third-generation immigrants. German law makes none.

Why was *jus sanguinis* untempered by *jus soli* in Germany? In some respects the situation in late-nineteenth- and early-twentieth-century Germany was like that in late-nineteenth-century France. Both countries were experiencing substantial immigration, and in both countries this was a period of heightened nationalism. But the nationalisms were of different kinds. French nationalism of the 1880s, state-centered and confidently assimilationist vis-à-vis non-Francophone citizens (Weber 1976:chs. 6 and 8) and vis-à-vis immigrants permitted, even required the transformation of second-generation immigrants into citizens (Brubaker 1992). Turn-of-the-century German nationalism, on the other hand, was ethnoculturally oriented and "dissimilationist" vis-à-vis its own ethnically Polish citizens in Eastern Prussia and vis-à-vis immigrants, or rather one crucial class of immigrants: Poles and Jews in the Prussian East. That nationalism required the civic exclusion rather than the civic incorporation of these unwanted immigrants (Brubaker 1992).

Immigration was an economic necessity in the eastern provinces of Prussia in the quarter century preceding the outbreak of the First World War. But the available immigrants—Poles in particular—were undesirable from a national point of view. To a surprising extent, given the traditional distance between Prussian statism and ethnocultural nationalism, the Prussian state had made this point of view its own. The state feared that Polish immigrants would strengthen the ethnically Polish at the expense of the ethnically German element in the Prussian East. A strict naturalization policy, coupled with an immigration policy requiring migrant workers to leave the country each winter, enabled the state to prevent the settlement of ethnoculturally "unwanted elements" in its eastern borderlands. Citizenship served here as an instrument of territorial closure (Brubaker 1992). By excluding immigrants from citizenship, the state retained its freedom of action. This meant, above all, the freedom to expel immigrants from the territory. Today, long-settled immigrants in Western Europe enjoy substantial legal as well as political protection against expulsion. They enjoyed no such protection in the late nineteenth and early twentieth century. In the 1880s, Prussia had expelled 30,000 Polish and Jewish immigrants, many of them long-term residents. There had been no further mass expulsions. But in the absence of restraints on the expulsion of resident noncitizens, citizenship status mattered to the state in a way that it no longer matters today: consequently, the state retained a stronger interest in a restrictive naturalization policy than it has today. Given the strong westward migratory currents in the German-Slav borderlands of Central Europe, the labor shortages in the Prussian East that compelled the employment of migrant workers, and the cultural and political definition of Slavs and Jews as "unwanted elements," the state interest in a restrictive naturalization policy was a compelling one.

Yet if there was a compelling state interest in a restrictive naturalization policy, there was none in a system of pure *jus sanguinis*. The state had a strong interest in controlling access to citizenship (and therefore to permanent settlement) on the part of recently arrived immigrants. But it had only a highly attenuated interest in preventing the access to citizenship of someone born and raised in the territory. Such persons, in effect, had *already* been allowed to settle in the territory. The state could have prevented their settlement, but it did not. As foreigners, to be sure, such persons would remain vulnerable to future expulsion; the state would retain more leverage over them than over citizens. Having already allowed their settlement, however, the state had very little to gain from this additional leverage.

Like the French extension of *jus soli* in 1889, the German insistence on pure *jus sanguinis* in 1913 must be understood in the context of habits of national self-understanding that were deeply rooted in the national past and powerfully reinforced at a particular historical conjuncture. In France, the legal transformation of second-generation immigrants into citizens presupposed confidence in their social, cultural, and political transformation into "real" Frenchmen. The French elite possessed that confidence. Their traditionally assimilationist understanding of nationhood was reinforced by the assimilationist theory and practice of the new national institutions of universal schooling and universal military service. This made the extension of *jus soli* possible and plausible. In Germany, the vehement repudiation of every trace of *jus soli* reflected the lack of elite confidence in the social, cultural, and political transformation of immigrants into Germans. In part, this was the legacy of a traditionally less state-centered and assimilationist, more ethnocultural understanding of nationhood in Germany than in France. But this was powerfully reinforced in late Bismarckian and Wilhelmine Germany by the increasingly evident failure of attempts to assimilate ethnoculturally Polish German citizens in the Prussian East (Broszat 1972:143, 157; Blanke 1981:60; Wehler 1971:118). Having failed to win the political loyalty of Poles to the German nation-state, and having failed to assimilate them to German language and culture, Prussian-German *Polenpolitik* was increasingly "dissimilationist," treating ethnically German and ethnically Polish citizens differently in an effort to "strengthen Germandom" in frontier districts. Since the state had failed to assimilate *indigenous* Poles in the Prussian East, who had been citizens of Prussia since the late eighteenth century, there was no basis for believing that it would succeed in assimilating *immigrant* Poles. An assimilationist citizenship law, like that of France, automatically transforming second-generation immigrants into citizens, was therefore out of the question in Germany.

The French law of 1889 and the German law of 1913 established the principles that govern the attribution of citizenship even today. As a result, a substantial fraction of French postwar immigrants has (or will have) French citizenship, while only a negligible fraction of non-German immigrants to Germany has German citizenship. The French, of course, have not solved all of their problems by formally transforming immigrants into citizens. In many respects, the social, cultural, and economic situation of immigrants in the two countries is similar. Yet by transforming second-generation immigrants into citizens, France has formally recognized and guaranteed their permanent membership of state and society, and has granted them full civil, political, and social rights. When and whether the new German state will do the same is likely to be an increasingly salient question in the years to come.

■ Notes

1. An extended treatment of the issues discussed in this paper is in Rogers Brubaker, *Citizenship and Nationhood in France and Germany* (Cambridge, Mass: Harvard University Press, 1992).

2. Industrialization in Europe as elsewhere was accompanied by massive migrations, in many instances across state boundaries. Thus, while no European country is a "classical" country of immigration, Europe has considerable historical experience with international labor migration, much of it leading to settlement. I have borrowed the expression "new immigration"—used to describe the surge in Southern and Eastern European immigration to the United States in the late nineteenth century—to suggest that it is the magnitude and sources, not the mere existence, of immigration that is new in the European setting. A large and increasing proportion of European immigrants stems from Third World countries (often from ex-colonies): the Indian subcontinent and the Caribbean displaced Ireland in the 1960s as the leading source of immigration to Britain; half of the foreign population in France is now from Africa or Asia (mainly from North Africa); and Turks surpassed Italians during the 1970s as the largest group of foreign workers in Germany.

3. This section and the next draw on and amplify material that has appeared in Brubaker 1989b.

4. This schema corresponds in certain respects to T. H. Marshall's (1950:10f.) distinction of civil, political, and social components of citizenship. The norm of egalitarian membership corresponds to the civil element, that of democratic membership to the political element, and that of socially consequential membership to the social element in Marshall's model. Yet the substantive overlap is only partial. In Marshall's schema nothing corresponds to the norms of sacred, national, and unique membership.

This partial correspondence is explained by historical considerations. Marshall analyzed the specifically English form of a general European (and later global) process—the development of the civil, political, and social rights constitutive of nationwide citizenship. While his analysis was tailored in detail to English peculiarity—and has recently been criticized for its Anglocentrisin (Mann 1987)—his basic threefold distinction was modeled on the general European experience; hence the fruitful use of his schema outside the English setting (Bendix 1977; Schmid 1986; Schmitter 1979; Parsons 1965; Turner 1986). Given the integral connection, in Europe and elsewhere, between the development and institutionalization of civil, political, and social rights, and the construction of nation-statehood, the overlap between Marshall's model of citizenship and the model of nation-state membership sketched here should come as no surprise.

Nor should the incompleteness of the overlap. For the construction of citizenship in England, the basis for Marshall's model, took a peculiar form—peculiarity grounded in the geopolitical position of England, in the early coincidence of state authority and national community, in the celebrated gradualism of political development, in a continuous imperial tradition, and in the supranational character of Great Britain. England may have been the first national state, but France was the first and has remained the paradigmatic nation-state; neither England nor Britain ever became a nation-state *à la française*. The construction of citizenship in England occurred in the context of a taken-for-granted national community and thus was not bound up, as it was on the Continent, with the ideologically charged, contestatory construction of nation-statehood. Norms of membership linked specifically to the contestatory construction of nation-statehood—i.e., the principles of sacredness, uniqueness, and nationality—did not figure in the British experience and do not figure in Marshall's model.

For other general discussions of citizenship and membership, see Gallissot 1986; Balibar 1988; Leca 1983; Riedel 1972; Salmond 1901/1902; Walzer 1983:ch. 2; Walzer 1970b; Lochak 1988. And for general discussions of the nation-state with some bearing on questions of citizenship and membership, see Sayad 1984: Zolberg 1981; Young 1976:70–73; Gellner 1983:1–7, 53–58.

5. The principle of unitary citizenship, to be sure, far outstripped revolutionary practice, to which distinctions of class and gender were crucial. This does not vitiate the significance of the principle, the central place of which in the myth and mystique of the Revolution helped later to undermine the legitimacy of such distinctions.

6. The Revolution inaugurated a new style of political sacralization. The nation-state that was invented during the Revolution (and thereafter universalized as a mode of political and social organization) simultaneously *emancipated* itself from and *incorporated* the sacred. Asserting full autonomy from the sacred as a *transcendent*, external source of legitimation, it nonetheless appropriated religious emotion, transforming sacredness into an *immanent* source of legitimation.

7. To be sure, this cultural community is conceived and constructed differently in France than in Germany or—to take a very different example—in the United States.

8. The requirement of assimilation to the ethnocultural community, of course, is open to widely differing interpretations. The relevant *areas* of assimilation, as well as the *threshold* of assimilation required in a given arena, may vary considerably.

9. This principle is clearly enunciated by Rousseau. How, he asks rhetorically, can citizens be expected to love their country "if their country is no more to them than it is to foreigners, if it grants to citizens only what it can refuse to nobody"? (1755:252). The principle takes on special importance, however, only with the development of the welfare state and the proliferation of state-provided benefits that can be withheld from resident nonmembers. In principle, welfare states are closed systems, presupposing "boundaries that distinguish those who are members of a

community from those who are not" (Freeman 1986:52; see also Walzer 1983:31). In the theory of the welfare state, these boundaries are drawn between citizens and noncitizens; in practice, however, they are drawn elsewhere (Brubaker 1989d:155f).

10. For an alternative approach to internal migration as a "deviance from the prevailing norm of social organization at the world level," a norm expressed in "the model of society as a territorially based, self-reproducing cultural and political system, whose human population is assumed, tacitly or explicitly, to renew itself endogenously," see Zolberg 1981:6. For an overstated yet suggestive argument that immigration contradicts the constitutive categories of the modern social and political world, see Sayad 1984:190.

11. On the settlement process, see Piore 1979:59ff. On problems of membership, see Walzer 1983:ch. 2; Brubaker 1989b:14–22; Carens 1989.

12. These may include the renunciation of one's previous citizenship; the performance of a sacred act such as an oath of allegiance; the accomplishment of the sacred duty of military service; the manifestation of "good character," and the more or less complete assimilation to the language and customs of the national community.

13. These include special provisions for spouses of citizens or for citizens of former colonies (Brubaker 1989c: 113–15).

14. Exceptions include Brubaker 1989a; Hammar 1990; Schmitter 1979; Noiriel 1988; Wenden 1987, 1988. The following paragraphs draw on material that has appeared in Brubaker 1989:146–47.

15. Exemplary for a number of reasons—not least because of the comparable magnitude and composition of the immigrant population in the two countries and because of their fateful position at the historic center of state- and nation-building in Europe.

16. The preamble to the Grundgesetz or Basic Law, in effect the constitution of the Federal Republic, invokes the "whole German people" (*das gesamte deutsche Volk*), while Article 116 defines the legal status of "German" as follows: "everyone is a German in the eyes of the Grundgesetz . . . who holds German citizenship or who, as a refugee or expellee of German *Volkszugehörigkeit*, or as a spouse or descendant of such a person, has been admitted to the territory of the German Reich as it existed on December 31, 1937." (The criteria of German *Volkszugehörigkeit* [belonging to the German *Volk*], as specified in the 1953 Law on Expelled Persons and Refugees, include "descent, speech, upbringing, and culture.") The Germans thus defined have rights and duties virtually indistinguishable from those of German citizens. And the definition of German citizenship is itself vastly overinclusive, measured against West German territory, for it includes almost all citizens of the German Democratic Republic. There has never been a separate West German citizenship: in its citizenship law, the Federal Republic has always maintained the legal fiction of the continued existence of the German Reich, and thus of a single German citizenship. This insistence on a single German citizenship was central to the exodus of summer and autumn 1989 that set in motion the process of German unification (Brubaker 1990b).

17. By "immigrants" I mean labor migrants and their descendants, not resettlers from the German Democratic Republic or ethnic German immigrants from Eastern Europe and the Soviet Union. As one would expect, given the ethnocultural understanding of membership, these *German* immigrants to West Germany are legally defined as citizens (in the case of the East German resettlers) or quasi citizens (in the case of the ethnic German immigrants from Eastern Europe and the Soviet Union) (Brubaker 1990:359–64).

18. It is not simply that France has more liberal naturalization rules and a

political culture of naturalization that Germany lacks. For French naturalization rates, despite being four to five times higher than those of the Federal Republic of Germany, are low compared to those of the United States, Canada, or Sweden (Brubaker 1989c:117–20; 1989d:154–60). More important is the fact that there are, besides naturalization, other modes of access to French, but not to German, citizenship. Thus French citizenship is attributed at birth to a child born in France if at least one parent was also born in France—including Algeria and other colonies and territories before their independence. This means that the large majority of the roughly 400,000 children born in France since 1963 of Algerian parents are French citizens. Moreover, citizenship is acquired automatically at the age of eighteen by *all* children born in France of foreign parents, provided they have resided in France for the last five years and have not been the object of certain criminal condemnations. By this means roughly 250,000 persons have become French since 1973; and of the 1.2 million foreign residents under the age of eighteen, roughly two-thirds were born in France and are thus programmed to become French at the age of eighteen. There are no comparable provisions in the Federal Republic of Germany. Thus, while the large majority of the former *Gastarbeiter* and their families were born in the Federal Republic or have lived there for over ten years, only a minute fraction have acquired German citizenship. Of the 1.4 million Turks living in Germany, only about 1,000 are naturalized each year. Even if this number increased tenfold, to 10,000 per year, it would still be more than offset by the 25,000 to 30,000 new Turkish citizens born every year in Germany.

19. An earlier version of the next four sections appeared in Brubaker 1989a:15–27. The comparison of German and French understandings of nationhood and forms of nationalism developed here is, in its basic lines, a traditional one, going back to the early nineteenth century (Brubaker 1992:43n; Kohn 1944, 1967; Rothfels 1956; Schieder 1985; Szücs 1981). Recently, however, bipolar contrasts involving Germany, especially those pointing to a German *Sonderweg* (special road) to the modern world, have been subjected to criticism on a broad front. Such accounts, it is argued, measure German developments, minutely scrutinized for faults (in the geological and the moral sense) that might help explain the catastrophe of 1933–45, against an idealized version of "Western"—i.e., British, French, or American—developments (see especially Blackbourn and Eley 1984). Only through the doubly distorting lens of such culpabilization on the one hand, and idealization on the other, the argument continues, does the nineteenth-century German bourgeoisie appear "supine" next to its "heroic" French counterpart, the German party system deeply flawed by English standards, the "German conception of freedom" dangerously illiberal by comparison with the Anglo-American, German political culture fatally authoritarian in comparison with that of the "West" in general. Comparisons of German and French conceptions of nationhood and forms of nationalism have not escaped indictment on this count (Berdahl 1972; Breuilly 1982:65–83). To characterize French and German traditions of citizenship and nationhood in terms of such ready-made conceptual pairs as universalism and particularism, cosmopolitanism and ethnocentrism, Enlightenment rationalism and romantic irrationalism is to pass from characterization to caricature. My use here of the simplifying opposition between the French political and the German ethnocultural definitions of nationhood is intended as a pointer to, and not a substitute for, a more nuanced analysis. I have tried to recover the analytical and explanatory potency of what remains, after all, an indispensable distinction, by rescuing it from the status of the routine and complacent formula, ripe for criticism, that it had become.

20. A pejorative expression emphasizing the fragmentation of political authority in Germany.

21. The word refers to the cultivated middle classes, the bourgeoisie constituted by *Bildung* (education or cultivation) and conscious of its *ständisch* [status-based] unity.

22. Article 3 of the Declaration of Rights of August 26, 1789, located "the principle of all sovereignty" in the nation, while the Constitution of 1791 was even more categorical: "Sovereignty is one [and] indivisible. . . . It belongs to the Nation" (Title III, Article I). The "nationalization" of political authority, however, was not limited to the constitutional domain. In effect, "all that was 'royal' became . . . national: national assembly, national gendarmerie, national guard, national army, national education . . . national domains . . . national debt" (Godechot 1971:495).

23. "Il n'y d'étranger en France que les mauvais citoyens" [the only foreigners in France are the bad citizens] (quoted by Azimi 1988:702). While Tallien's remark, as Azimi notes, cannot be taken as representative of the Revolution's attitude toward *étrangers*, it can be taken as illustrative of its strictly political definition of nationhood.

24. As Meinecke notes, the right of national self-determination could be applied to nations understood in a historical-political sense, which may have a strong ethnic component, with the emphasis on the "historically developed personality of the nation," or in a rational-political sense, with the nation understood as "a subdivision of Humanity, an abstractly constructed frame without [distinctive] individual content." Meinecke registers his clear preference for the former and his criticism of the "deep weaknesses and errors" of the latter, "entirely formalistic doctrine of national sovereignty" (1919:34). This corresponds roughly to Simmel's (1950:81) distinction between the nineteenth-century conception of individuality as *Einzigkeit* (uniqueness) and the eighteenth-century conception of individuality as *Einzelheil* (oneness).

25. Thus Barère's report to the Committee of Public Safety in January 1794: "Federalism and superstition speak low Breton; emigration and hatred of the Republic speak German; the counterrevolution speaks Italian, and fanaticism speaks Basque." Only when all citizens speak the same language, according to Abbé Grégoire's "Rapport sur la nécessité et les moyens d'anéantir les patois et d'universaliser l'usage de la langue française," can all citizens "communicate their thought without hindrance" and enjoy equal access to state offices. Both reports are reprinted in de Certeau et al. 1975:291–317; the quotations are from pp. 295 and 302.

26. Weber (1976) contains a wealth of material on assimilation, but focuses on the period 1870 to 1914. On the historical roots of the stronger assimilatory tendency of French than German society, see von Thadden (1987).

27. On September 20, 1792, at Valmy, under fire from the Prussian infantry, the best-trained troops in Europe, the ragtag French army held its ground to the cry of "Vive la Nation!" Valmy itself was of no great military significance, but thanks to the celebrated phrase of Goethe, who was present at the battle—"d'aujourd'hui et de ce lieu date une ère nouvelle dans l'histoire du monde" [here and today a new era of world history begins]—the episode has come to symbolize the transformation of war through the appeal to the nation in arms (Furet and Richet 1965:175; Soboul 1960:58).

28. Godechot concludes that "it is therefore absurd to speak of French *nationalism* during the first years of the Revolution: *patriotism* is an entirely different thing" (1971:498).

29. "The French nation renounces all wars of conquest, and will never employ her force against the liberty of any people. . . . Foreigners . . . can receive successions from their parents, whether they be foreign or French. They can make con-

tracts, acquire and receive goods in France, and dispose of them, in the same way as any French citizen. . . . Their person, their goods, their industry, their religious observances are also protected by law" (Title VI, Constitution of 1791).

30. The contradictions involved in this missionary nationalism are evident: "the Grande Nation is not only the nation that, in 1789, triumphed over the monarchy; it is the nation that has triumphed over its internal and external enemies and that will deliver the oppressed patriots of all Europe. . . . The expression Grande Nation applies to the liberating, emancipating nation, the nation that propagates the 'great principles' of 1789, the nation that must aid oppressed peoples to conquer their liberty . . . but also to the nation that, despite these loudly proclaimed principles, dominates, oppresses, annexes, without regard for the will of other peoples" (Godechot 1971:499-500). On the internal nationalism, see Azimi 1988; Nora 1988; Brubaker 1992.

31. The exaltation of the state found in Romantic political thought—Adam Müller's claim, for example, that "man cannot be imagined outside the state. . . . The state is the totality of all human concerns" (quoted by Kohn 1967:189)— reflects, on the one hand, an amorphous, globalizing conception of the state and, on the other, the teleological notion that the *Volksgeist* can reach its final and perfect expression only in the state.

32. In this context, "the nineteenth century" means roughly 1830 to 1914 in France, and 1815 to 1914 in Germany.

33. Even the traditionalist "nationalisme intégrale" of Charles Maurras, it may be argued, turned, despite its anti-Semitism, on a political and not on an ethnocultural principle. Anti-Semitism, propagated by Edouard Drumont from the mid-1880s on, and uniting anticapitalist and conservative-Catholic motifs, reached a paroxysmal peak in the Dreyfus affair. Yet the affair turned not on an ethnocultural or an ethnoreligious conception of nationhood but on the ancient themes of the place of church and army in the life of the nation—themes given a new urgency by the anticlericalism of the Third Republic and by the emergence of an internationalist and pacifist left.

34. On Bismarck's distance from nationalism, see Schieder 1961:22–26. The annexation of Alsace-Lorraine, while demanded and justified in terms of the ethnocultural principle of nationhood, was in fact determined by strategic considerations (Gall 1970).

35. Thus the preamble to the Constitution of 1791: "Il n'y a plus, pour aucune partie de la Nation, ni pour aucun individu, aucun privilège, ni exception an droit commun de tous les Français."

36. In the case of Poles in the Prussian East provinces, it was not the Reich, but already the Norddeutsche Bund, that had the ominous character of a nation-state. Poles accepted membership of the nonnational Prussian state, but protested against the incorporation of the East Prussian provinces into this newly national entity. In 1871 they renewed their protest: "We want to remain under Prussian authority, but we do not want to be incorporated into the German Reich" (Polish deputies quoted in Schieder 1961:19–20).

37. There are of course important differences between French and North American citizenship law. The North American system is based on unconditional *jus soli*: citizenship is attributed to all persons born in the territory. Thus even children of undocumented immigrants are assigned U.S. citizenship if they are born in the United States. French citizenship law, by contrast, is based on *jus sanguinis*: all persons born of French parents are French citizens, regardless of birthplace. But in addition—and this is where the similarity with North American citizenship now

arises—France follows the principle of conditional *jus soli*. As a result, almost all persons born in France and residing there at majority have French citizenship.

38. Since the Revolution, the self-styled "nation une et indivisible" has been violently intolerant of anything that could be interpreted as a "nation within the nation." This unitarist attitude, at once intolerant of constituted groups and inclusive of their constituent members as individuals, is epitomized by the famous formula of the Comte de Clermont Tonnère during the Revolution: "One must refuse everything to Jews as a nation and grant everything to the Jews as individuals. . . . They must be citizens as individuals" (quoted in Schnapper and Leveau 1987:3). In the late nineteenth century, similarly, it was felt to be better that established immigrants become individually citizens than that they remain collectively foreigners, a foreign nation within the French nation and, as such, a "true peril" (CD 2083:34).

39. Weber (1976:494) stresses the "making similar": as a result of improved communications caused by roads and railroads, and a generation of Republican schooling and universal military service, "variations in language and behavior were significantly less . . . [and] the regions of France were vastly more alike in 1910 than they had been before Jules Ferry."

40. Naturalization is of course possible, but only under severely restrictive conditions (Hailbronner 1989:67–70; Brubaker 1989c:110–11).

41. The 1870 law was enacted for the North German Confederation; it was extended the following year to the German Empire.

■ Bibliography

I. French Parliamentary Materials
References are to the *Journal officiel de la République Française*. Abbreviations (CD, C) indicate the document; the page number follows.

CD 3904. Chambre des Députés, Documents Parlementaires, Session Ordinaire de 1885, Annexe no. 3904. "Proposition de loi relative à la nationalité des fils d'étrangers nés en France," présentée par M. Maxime Lecomte et al.

CD 2083. Chambre des Députés, Documents Parlementaires, Session Ordinaire de 1887, Annexe no. 2083. "Rapport fait au nom de la commission chargée d'examiner la proposition de loi, adoptée par le Sénat, sur la nationalité," par M. Antonin Dubost.

C2. Chambre des Députés, Compte Rendu, Séance du 16 mars 1889, 2e délibération sur la proposition de loi, adopté par le Sénat, relative à la nationalité.

II. Other Sources
Arendt, H. 1973. *The Origins of Totalitarianism*. New York: Harcourt Brace Jovanovich.

Azéma, J.-P., and M. Winock. 1976. *La IIIe République (1870–1940)*. Paris: Calmarm-Lévy.

Azimi, V. 1988. "L'étranger sous la Révolution." *Actes du Colloque d'Orléans, 11–13 Septembre 1986: La Révolution et l'ordre juridique privé: Rationalité ou scandale?* Paris: Presses Universitaires de France.

Balibar, E. 1984. "Sujets ou citoyens?" *Les temps modernes* 452-453-454:1726–53.

———. 1998. "Propositions sur la citoyenneté." In Wenden 1987.

Bendix, R. 1977. *Nation-Building and Citizenship*. Berkeley: University of California Press.

Berdahl, R. 1972. "New Thoughts on German Nationalism." *American Historical Review* 77:65–80.

Blackbourn, D., and G. Eley. 1984. *The Peculiarities of German History*. Oxford: Oxford University Press.

Blanke, R. 1981. *Prussian Poland in the German Empire*. Boulder, Colo.: East European Monographs.

Breuilly, J. 1982. *Nationalism and the State*. Chicago: University of Chicago Press.

Broszat, M. 1972. *Zweihundert Jahre deutsche Polenpolitik*. Frankfurt: Suhrkamp.

Brubaker, Rogers. 1992. *Citizenship and Nationhood in France and Germany*. Cambridge, Mass.: Harvard University Press.

Brubaker, W. R., ed. 1989a. *Immigration and the Politics of Citizenship in Europe and North America*. Lanham, Md.: German Marshall Fund of the United States and University Press of America.

———. 1989b. Introduction to Brubaker 1989a.

———. 1989c. "Citizenship and Naturalization: Policies and Politics." In Brubaker 1999a.

———. 1989d. "Membership without Citizenship: The Economic and Social Rights of Non-Citizens." In Brubaker 1989a.

———. 1990. "Frontier Theses: Exit, Voice, and Loyalty in East Germany." *Migration World Magazine*.

Carens, J. 1989. "Membership and Morality: Admission to Citizenship in Liberal Democratic States." In Brubaker 1989a.

Centre de Relations Internationales et de Sciences Politiques d'Amiens and Revue Pluriel-Débat. 1984. *La France au pluriel?* Paris: L'Harmattan.

Challener, R. D. 1965. *The French Theory of the Nation in Arms 1866–1939*. New York: Russell and Russell.

Commission de la Nationalité. 1988. *Etre français aujourd'hui et demain*. 2 vols. Paris: La Documentation Française.

Contamine, P. 1986. "Mourir pour la patrie." In *La Nation* vol. 3, ed. P. Nora. Paris: Gallimard.

Conze, W. 1983. "Nationsbildung durch Trennung." In *Innenpolitische Probleme des Bismarkreichs*, ed. O. Pflanze. Munich: Oldenbourg.

———. 1985. "'Deutschland' und 'deutsche Nation' als historische Begriffe." In *Die Rolle der Nation in der deutschen Geschichte und Gegenwart*, ed. O. Büsch and J. Sheehan. Berlin: Colloquium Verlag.

Costa-Lascoux, J. 1988. "Intégration et nationalité." In Wenden 1987.

de Certeau, M., D. Julia, and J. Revel. 1975. *Une politique de la langue. La Révolution française et les patois: L'enquête de Gregoire*. Paris: Gallimard.

Doorn, J. van. 1975. "The Decline of the Mass Army in the West: General Reflections." *Armed Forces and Society* 1:147–57.

Freeman, G. 1986. "Migration and the Political Economy of the Welfare State." *Annals of the American Academy of Political and Social Science* 485:51–63.

Furet, F., and D. Richet. 1965. *La Révolution française*. Paris: Hachette. (Citations are to the paperback Pluriel edition, which does not give a publication date.)

Gall, L. 1970. "Das Problem Elsass-Lothringen." In *Reichsgründung 1870/71*, ed. T. Schieder and E. Deuerlein. Stuttgart: Seewald Verlag.

Gallissot, R. 1986. "Nationalité et citoyenneté: Aperçus sur cette contradiction à travers l'evolution do nationalisme français." *Après-demain* 286:8–15.

Geertz, C. 1971. *Islam Observed: Religious Development in Morocco and Indonesia*. Chicago: University of Chicago Press.

Gellner, E. 1983. *Nations and Nationalism*. Ithaca, N.Y.: Cornell University Press.

Girardet, R. 1979. *L'Idée coloniale en France de 1871 à 1962*. Paris: Pluriel.

Godechot, J. 1971. "Nation, patrie, nationalisme et patriotisme en France au XVIIIe siècle." *Annales historiques de la Révolution française*, no. 206.

———. 1983. *La Grande Nation: L'expansion révolutionnaire de la France dans le monde de 1789 à 1799*. Paris: Aubier.

Grawert, R. 1973. *Staat und Staatsangehörigkeit*. Berlin: Duncker and Humblot.

Griotteray, A. 1984. *Les immigrés: Le choc*. Paris: Plon.

Hailbronner, K. 1989. "Citizenship and Nationhood in Germany." In Brubaker 1989a.

Hammar, T. 1989. "State, Nation, and Dual Citizenship." In Brubaker 1989a.

———. 1990. *Democracy and the Nation-State: Aliens, Denizens, and Citizens in a World of International Migration*. Aldershot: Avebury.

Kedourie, E. 1985. *Nationalism*. London: Hutchinson.

Kelly, G. A. 1979. "Who Needs a Theory of Citizenship?" *Daedalus*, Fall:21–36.

Kocka, J. 1985. "Probleme der politischen Integration der Deutschen, 1867 bis 1945." In *Die Rolle der Nation in der deutschen Geschichte und Gegenwart*, ed. O. Büsch and J. Sheehan. Berlin: Colloquium Verlag.

Kohn, H. 1944. *The Idea of Nationalism*. New York: Collier.

———. 1967. *Prelude to Nation-States: The French and German Experience, 1789–1815*. Princeton, N.J.: Van Nostrand.

Leca, J. 1983. "Questions sur la citoyenneté." *Projet* 171–72:113–25.

Lepsius, R. 1985. "The Nation and Nationalism in Germany." *Social Research* 52(1):43–64.

Lochak, D. 1988. "Etrangers et citoyens au regard du droit." In Wenden 1987.

Mann, M. 1987. "Ruling Class Strategies and Citizenship." *Sociology* 21:339–54.

Marshall, T. H. 1950. *Citizenship and Social Class and Other Essays*. Cambridge: Cambridge University Press.

Meinecke, F. 1919. *Weltbürgertum und Nationalstaat*. Munich: Oldenbourg.

Miller, M. 1986. "Policy Ad-Hocracy." *Annals of the American Academy of Political and Social Science* 485.

———. 1989. "Political Participation and Representation of Noncitizens." In Brubaker 1989a.

Minces, J. 1985. "Le piège de la société pluriculturelle." *Esprit* 102:139–42.

Monteilhet, J. 1926. *Les institutions militaires de la France (1814–1924)*. Paris: Félix Alcan.

Noiriel, G. 1988. *Le creuset français*. Paris: Seuil.

Nora, R, ed. 1986. *La nation*, 3 vols. Part 2 of *Les lieux de la mémoire*. Paris: Gallimard.

Nora, P. 1988. "Nation." In *Dictionnaire critique de la Révolution française*, ed. F. Furet and M. Ozouf. Paris: Flammarion.

Oriol, P. 1985. *Les immigrés: Métèques ou citoyens?* Paris: Syros.

Parsons, T. 1965. "Full Citizenship for the Negro American?" *Daedalus*, Fall:1009–54.

Pinson, K. 1966. *Modern Germany*. New York: Macmillan.

Piore, M. 1979. *Birds of Passage: Migrant Labor and Industrial Societies*. Cambridge: Cambridge University Press.

Rémond, R. 1969. *The Right Wing in France*. Philadelphia: University of Pennsylvania Press.

Renan, E. 1870. "Lettre à M. Strauss." *Oeuvres complètes*, vol.1. Paris: Calmarm-Lévy (undated).

Riedel, M. 1972. "Bürger, Staatsbürger, Bürgertum." In *Geschichtliche Grundbergriffe*, vol.1, ed. O. Brunner. Stuttgart.

Rothfels, H. 1956. "Die Nationsidee in westlicher und östlicher Sicht." *Osteuropa und der deutsche Osten* 1, no. 3:7–18, Cologne-Braunsfeld: Rudolf Müller.

Rousseau, J.-J. 1962 [1755]. "De l'économie politique." In *The Political Writings of Jean-Jacques Rousseau*, ed. C. E. Vaughan. Oxford: Basil Blackwell.

Salmond, J. 1901/1902. "Citizenship and Allegiance." *Law Quarterly Review* 17 (1901):270–82 and 18 (1902):49–63.

Sayad, A. 1982. "La naturalisation, ses conditions sociales et sa signification chez les immigrés Algeriens." Part 2, *Greco 13: Recherches sur les migrations internationales* 4–5:1–51.

———. 1984. "Etat, nation et immigration: L'ordre national à l'épreuve de l'immigration." *Peuples méditerranéens* 27–28:187–205.

Schieder, T. 1961. *Das deutsche Kaiserreich von 1871 als Nationalstaat*. Cologne: Westdeutscher Vertag.

———. 1985. "Typologie und Erscheinungsformen des Nationalstaats in Europa." In *Nationalismus*, ed. H. A. Winkler. Königstein/Ts: Athenäum.

Schmid, C. 1986. "Social Class, Race, and the Extension of Citizenship: The English Working Class and the Southern Civil Rights Movements." *Comparative Social Research* 9:27–46.

Schmitter, B. E. 1979. "Immigration and Citizenship in West Germany and Switzerland." Ph.D. thesis, University of Chicago.

Schnapper, D., and R. Leveau. 1987. "Religion et politique: Juifs et musulmans Maghrébins en France." Paper presented at the conference "Les musulmans dans la société française," organized by the Association Française de Science Politique (Paris, January 29–30, 1987).

Schuck, P. 1989. "Membership in the Liberal Polity: The Devaluation of American Citizenship." In Brubaker 1989a.

Schuck, P., and R. Smith. 1985. *Citizenship without Consent: Illegal Aliens in the American Polity*. New Haven, Conn.: Yale University Press.

Simmel, G. 1950. *The Sociology of Georg Simmel*, translated, edited, and with an introduction by K. H. Wolff. New York: Free Press.

Soboul, A. 1960. "De l'Ancien Régime à l'Empire: Problème national et réalités sociales." In *L'information historique*.

Szücs, J. 1981. *Nation und Geschichte*. Budapest: Corvina Kiadó.

Turner, B. 1986. *Citizenship and Capitalism: The Debate over Reformism*. London: Allen and Unwin.

von Thadden, R. 1987. "Umgang mit Minderheiten." Unpublished paper.

Walzer, M. 1970a. "The Obligation to Die for the State." In *Obligations: Essays on Disobedience, War, and Citizenship*, ed. Michael Walzer. Cambridge, Mass.: Harvard University Press.

———. 1970b. "The Problem of Citizenship." In *Obligations: Essays on Disobedience, War, and Citizenship*, ed. Michael Walzer. Cambridge, Mass.: Harvard University Press.

———. 1983. *Spheres of Justice*. New York: Basic Books.

Weber, E. 1976. *Peasants into Frenchmen*. Stanford, Calif.: Stanford University Press.

Wehler, H-U. 1971. *Sozialdermokratie und Nationalstaat*. Göttingen: Vandenhoeck & Ruprecht.

Wenden, C. de. 1987. *Citoyenneté, nationalité et immigration*. Paris: Arcantière.

Wenden, C. de, ed. 1988. *Lo citoyenneté*. Paris: Edilig/Fondation Diderot.

Young, C. 1976. *The Politics of Cultural Pluralism.* Madison: University of Wisconsin Press.

Zolberg, A. 1981. "International Migrations in Political Perspective." In *Global Trends in Migration*, ed. M. Kritz et al. New York: Center for Migration Studies.

Zolberg, A. 1983. "Contemporary Transnational Migrations in Historical Perspective." In *U.S. Immigration and Refugee Policy*, ed. M. Kritz. Lexington, Mass.: Lexington Books.

11.3 *Peter H. Schuck*

The Reevaluation of American Citizenship

. . . Citizenship talk proceeds through several different tropes. Sometimes we advance it as a powerful aspirational ideal. In this normative usage, it serves as a proxy, or placeholder, for our deepest commitments to a common life. Citizens, in this view, mutually pledge their trust and concern for each other and their full participation in shared civic and civil cultures. Sometimes—perhaps even at the same time—we also deploy citizenship as a positive concept. In this positive usage, it describes a legal-political status that some individuals enjoy, some can only aspire to, and still others have little hope of ever attaining. Here, citizenship describes a relationship between individuals and the polity in which citizens owe allegiance to their polity—they must not betray it and may have to serve it—while the polity owes its citizens the fullest measure of protection that its law affords, including (except for minors and some convicted felons) the right to vote.

These two uses of citizenship—the normative and the positive—are linked rhetorically, and perhaps even psychologically. Like the serpents on a caduceus, they are tightly intertwined. We often use the ideal of citizenship as a standard against which to evaluate the actual conduct of others, hurling the ideal as an accusation, bitterly condemning what we do not like about contemporary life and ascribing it to the defects of our fellow citizens. Whether the offense is the despoilment of public spaces in our cities, the failure to vote in our elections, the violence in our schools and neighborhoods, or the erosion of our families, we indict not only the individual perpetrators but the polity that, by debasing citizenship, has fostered or at least countenanced these wrongs. At times—and today, seems such a time—our despair may be so great that we wonder whether we remain one people dedicated to common purposes. The most disillusioned of us may conclude that citizenship should be a privilege that requires us to be better in order to claim it, a prize that can be earned only through greater rectitude.

It is precisely at these censorious moments, however, that citizenship's

---

Peter H. Schuck, "The Reevaluation of American Citizenship," in Schuck, *Citizens, Strangers and In-Betweens: Essays on Immigration and Citizenship* (Boulder, Colo.: Westview, 1998), pp. 176–206.

positive meaning can check the harsh, exclusionary impulses that its normative meaning reflexively arouses in us. When we are tempted to say (or feel) that our fellow citizens should, "shape up or ship out," or should "love our country or leave it," we may recall that our law does not view citizenship as a reward for civic virtue. . . . So the conversation goes.

In the United States today, this conversation is particularly heated. Not since the McCarthy era in the early 1950s, when many Americans aggressively questioned the loyalty of their fellow citizens, relatively few immigrants were admitted, and relatively few of those sought to become citizens, has citizenship talk been so energetic and morally charged. In Congress, at the bar of public opinion, and even in the courts, citizenship in both its normative and positive dimensions is being closely re-examined. Indeed, Congress adopted welfare reform and immigration control laws in 1996 that were intended, among other goals, to increase sharply the value of American citizenship while reducing the value of permanent legal resident status. . . .

In this essay, I explore the reasons why Americans are arguing more passionately about citizenship today, and why some of the rules that have long structured citizenship status are under vigorous assault. I shall argue that the intensity of this debate reflects the tensions that arise within and among three analytically distinct relational domains, each of which is characterized by a distinctive problematic, a wrenching conflict between competing and deeply held values.

The first domain is international law and politics. Here the nation defines the scope of its sovereignty by classifying all individuals as either insiders or outsiders. By insiders, I mean those whom the polity brings into its constitutional community by granting them legal rights against it. The American constitutional community includes citizens, legal resident aliens, and in some cases, illegal aliens. Outsiders are everybody else in the world. The United States defines its sovereignty in this international domain largely, but not exclusively, in terms of its power over territory; its constitutional community embraces virtually all individuals within its national borders and territories, as well as some who are outside them but to whom the United States has acknowledged some special political and legal relationship. The distinctive problematic in this domain is a tension between the values of national sovereignty and autonomy and the reality that many outsiders possess the power to transform themselves into insiders without the nation's consent and beyond its effective control.

The second domain is national politics. Here, public law classifies the body of insiders into different categories, defining what the polity owes to each of them and what they in turn owe to the polity. Its distinctive problematic is a tension between the values of equal treatment and communal self-definition, and the reality of limited resources. This tension is particularly delicate because it encourages the marginalization not only of outsiders but of some insiders as well. The meaning of citizenship in the national political domain is highly controversial in the United States today because it is intimately connected to bitterly divisive questions about the welfare state—its essential legitimacy, its moral character, its purposes, its programmatic scope, and its availability to citizens and to various categories of aliens.

The third domain is federalism—the structural division of the American polity into multiple, overlapping sovereignties.[1] Each individual possesses a civic status in the national polity and in a state polity. She may also live in a private enclave in which her status is regulated, often extensively, by contract. Different rights and duties attach to these diverse statuses. Federalism's distinctive problematic is a tension between the values of equality and uniformity, which the nation can promote through its power to unify the same policy throughout its territory, and the value of diversity among, and responsiveness to, the policies advanced by different states and contractual regimes. In this domain, as in that of national politics, Americans are bitterly debating the meaning of citizenship in the most divisive of contexts: a fundamental reconsideration of the welfare state. In August 1996, the United States adopted a welfare reform law—forged through a remarkable bipartisan consensus—that constitutes perhaps the most far-reaching change in American social policy since the foundations of its welfare state were established during the New Deal. . . .

■ I. Citizenship in the International Domain

In dividing up the world's population into insiders and outsiders, the United States is remarkably inclusive, at least relative to other polities. This inclusiveness takes a number of different forms. First, the United States has adopted a very liberal legal immigration policy, admitting approximately 800,000 aliens each year (the precise number fluctuates considerably) for permanent residence.[2] This annual influx probably exceeds the legal admissions totals of the rest of the world combined. Moreover, the United States has increased its legal admissions during the 1990s, a period during which other countries have been restricting them. When Congress overhauled U.S. immigration laws in 1996, it resisted intense political pressures to reduce the number of legal admissions. Hence, the post-1990 growth in the legal immigration system remains in place. Second, the United States in the 1980s and early 1990s extended legal permanent resident status to nearly 2.7 million illegal aliens through a massive amnesty, a program to legalize illegals' dependents, and more conventional immigration remedies. Third, a combination of expansive *jus sanguinis* and *jus soli* rules extends citizenship very broadly—to essentially all individuals who are born on U.S. soil, regardless of their parents' legal status, all children born abroad to two American parents, and many children born abroad to one American parent. Fourth, U.S. naturalization requirements are relatively easy—indeed, some say, too easy—to satisfy. From 1990 to 1995 the United States naturalized between 240,000 and 488,000 aliens a year; in 1996 alone, more than one million individuals were naturalized, the largest cohort in history. Propelled by welfare law changes that restrict many benefits to citizens, further increases in petitions—up to an estimated 1.8 million in 1997—are expected.[3] Fifth, dual (and even triple) citizenship is increasingly common, and the State Department no longer opposes it in principle.

Finally, more than one million aliens enter the United States illegally each year; some 250,000 to 300,000 of these individuals remain in illegal status more or less permanently, producing an illegal population now estimated at over 5 million. Simply by virtue of their presence in the United States, illegal immigrants can claim extensive procedural rights, and in some cases, substantive entitlements as well, under the Constitution, statutes, and administrative rules, although the 1996 amendments to the immigration statute severely limited some of these rights, especially for those who entered the United States illegally. Even excludable aliens stopped at the border, who possess only the most elementary constitutional rights, such as access to the courts and freedom from physical abuse, can claim many statutory rights under U.S. laws. In the international arena, the principal force reshaping Americans' conceptions of citizenship is the growing anxiety aroused by their perception that their national sovereignty is under serious challenge. Three recent developments are particularly salient: the globalization of the U.S. economy; the increase in immigration, particularly illegal immigration; and a more general diminution of American autonomy in the world.

Globalization

The integration of the world economy—its "globalization," in the already hackneyed phrase—has proceeded at an ever-quickening pace. This integration, moreover, is comprehensive, encompassing all factors of production, distribution, and communication including goods, services, capital, technology, intellectual property rules, and (most pertinent for present purposes) labor. The U.S. economy, while primarily focused on its enormous domestic market,[4] has in recent years become a nimble exporter and importer of capital and, to a lesser extent, of jobs. A number of factors strongly suggest that this trend will continue. Powerful economic and political interests are driving this trend, while enfeebled labor unions lack the bargaining-power to arrest, much less reverse, it. American producers, no longer able to count on policies protecting them from foreign competition, are rationalizing their operations by sending low-skill jobs abroad while importing high-skill technicians, managers, and professionals where needed. . . .

For present purposes, the important point is that these developments signal a growing recognition by the U.S. government that America's fate is increasingly linked to that of her neighbors, her other trading partners, and the rest of the world. These linked fates are not merely economic but are also demographic, social, and political. The United States is increasingly vulnerable to the immense migratory pressures being generated by conditions beyond her borders and her control. These "push" factors are magnified and reinforced by powerful, indeed tidal, "pull" factors: a vast and burgeoning American economy that often prefers foreign workers to domestic ones, a dynamic American culture that promises immigrants great personal freedom and mobility, and grooved pathways of kinship-based chain migration that constantly creates and replenishes immigrant and ethnic communities in the United States.

Migration
Since 1965, immigration to the United States has been transformed in virtually every vital aspect.[5] The legal immigration streams have swelled in both absolute terms and as a percentage of the overall population. Even more important than the size of those streams, the "look and feel" of American society has changed dramatically with the changing mix of the newcomers' national origins, races, and languages. All of this has occurred in a relatively short period of time, generating cultural, economic, and social anxieties among many Americans.

But it is *illegal* migration that is primarily driving the political dimension of this debate. The volume of illegal migration has grown fairly steadily during the last three decades except for the period immediately following the enactment of the employer sanctions provisions of the Immigration Reform and Control Act of 1986, when the number declined. This decline, however, proved to be brief; by 1990, the number of illegal immigrants in the United States had already returned approximately to its pre-1986 level; the permanent illegal population now exceeds 5 million. Even the growth in the resources devoted to border control during the last five years—extraordinary especially when compared to the retrenchment in other federal programs—shows no clear sign of stemming this influx (as opposed to rechanneling it). The continuing ineffectiveness of border control is a source of enormous frustration to Americans and their politicians, especially in the relatively small number of communities with high concentrations of illegals. At the same time, Americans have become more dependent on illegal workers and more aware of this dependence, which for many employers, consumers, and communities can approach an addiction. . . .

Because many Americans feel beleaguered and victimized by illegal immigration, it is profoundly affecting their political identity. These feelings are intensifying as the large number of former illegal aliens who received amnesty in the late 1980s begin to become U.S. citizens, many motivated by a desire to secure their access to welfare state benefits in the United States. Moreover, the families of these amnestied illegals are now exerting strong pressures on the *legal* immigration system, competing with the often more compelling claims of legal immigrants' relatives who wish to join their families in the United States. . . .

As the number of illegal aliens grows, their position in the American polity becomes increasingly anomalous. Americans admire the tenacity, hard work, and resourcefulness of illegal aliens (at least the majority who do not commit crimes in the United States) but at the same time, deeply resent their furtive success in penetrating U.S. territory, working in U.S. jobs, earning (and exporting) dollars, and securing legal status—even the ultimate prize, citizenship—for themselves and their families. As the data on the individuals who voted in favor of California's Proposition 187 illustrated, many legal resident aliens and recently naturalized citizens are also strongly opposed to illegal migration.[6] The fact that the United States has long countenanced illegal migrants, derived tax revenues and other economic benefits from them, and built important sectors of her economy around their continued flow arouses cognitive dissonance, but it does not really alter the fact of resentment. . . .

Diminished Autonomy

The massive breaching of American borders by illegal aliens is vivid evidence of the nation's vulnerability; "invasion" and "flood" are the metaphors that are conventionally used to describe the influx. Americans, however, are experiencing a more general sense of unease that their national destiny is moving beyond their control. This anxiety springs from many sources. I have already mentioned growing U.S. reliance on the global economy; American prosperity now depends almost as much on public and private decisions in Tokyo, Bonn, and Hong Kong as it does on those in Washington or Wall Street. But the loss of control is not confined to the economic realm. The protracted trauma of the Vietnam War convinced many Americans that the United States can no longer work its will in the world militarily. The geopolitical fragmentation encouraged by the end of the Cold War has left the United States as the sole remaining super-power, yet the American Goliath is now at the mercy of myriad ethnic rivalries and subnational conflicts that defy international intervention and order. Even threats to public health, traditionally the province of national governments, increasingly cross national borders, as the recent examples of AIDS, dengue fever, tuberculosis, and other communicable diseases suggest. Public concern with international terrorism, galvanized by several notorious bombing incidents, adds to Americans' anxieties about this loss of control.

The world has always been a dangerous place. Most Americans probably believe that it is more dangerous today than ever before, although precisely the opposite is true—at least for them but also for many others. They evidently feel growing insecurity about their jobs, marriages, safety, and personal future. People in such a state of uncertainty naturally search for safe havens from these storms. Their citizenship serves as a dependable anchorage; it gives them a secure mooring in an increasingly intrusive, turbulent, uncontrollable "worldwind." A valuable legal status, it can never be taken away. It defines who is a member of the extended political family, which, like its natural counterpart, offers some consolation in a harsh world. We imagine that we can count on the company of citizens to join us in a search for common good. Our concern for our fellow citizens is usually greater than that for the rest of humankind. Fellow citizens share our lifeboat and are in it for the long haul.

Citizenship thus imparts to the polity a special shape and expectancy—in the United States, a common claim to enjoy the "American way of life." The more perplexing and menacing we find the world and the more buffeting its gales of change, the more tenaciously we cling to our citizenship's value and insist on maintaining it. David Jacobson, drawing on the conceptions of Mircea Eliade and Benedict Anderson, suggests that this tenacity is driven by an even more profound disorientation—a crisis of what Jacobson calls the desacralization of territory.[7] . . .

■ II. Citizenship in the Domestic Domain

If citizenship provides succor to Americans in their confrontation with the outside world, it also promises them political and social standing and national identity in the domestic one. Here, citizenship crowns a hierarchy of statuses, with each one bearing a distinctive set of legal rights and obligations.[8] David Martin has suggested that this domain may be represented metaphorically by concentric circles; a community of citizens at the central core is surrounded by a series of more peripheral status categories, with ever more attenuated ties to the polity, weaker claims on it, and more limited rights against it.[9] Citizenship's normative meaning can be inferred from (among other things) the magnitude and nature of the gap between the citizens and those in the outer circles with respect to their rights and duties.

American citizenship, as Alexander Bickel famously observed, "is at best a simple idea for a simple government."[10] By this, Bickel meant that the ratification of the Fourteenth Amendment to the Constitution made membership in the American polity widely and easily available, that the legal rights and duties associated with citizenship have long ceased to be an

even to limit the family immigration rights of U.S. citizens who achieved that status only by virtue of the amnesty program enacted in 1986. If enacted, such a policy would raise novel and important constitutional questions concerning whether Congress may discriminate among U.S. citizens based on their prior immigration status.

In addition to different sponsorship rights, citizens and LPRs differ with respect to the right to remain in the United States. LPRs are subject to deportation (after the 1996 immigration control legislation, the term is "removal"); citizens (whether by birth, naturalization, or statute) are not. Deportation of a long-term resident can wreak enormous suffering upon aliens and their families and friends. Although the Supreme Court has repeatedly held that removal is not punishment and therefore does not implicate Due Process and other constitutional guarantees that surround the imposition of criminal sanctions, the fact is that, as Justice Douglas once put it, removal "may deprive a man and his family of all that makes life worthwhile."[22]

Still, it is important to place this risk in realistic context. The actual risk of removal for non-criminal LPRs living in the United States has been vanishingly small.[23] Even after the 1996 immigration control legislation, formal removal of legal aliens, especially non-criminal LPRs, remains a costly process for the INS to effectuate. Statutes, regulations, and judicial rulings require the INS to observe high standards of procedural fairness in adjudicating whether LPRs may remain in the United States. Severe administrative difficulties further limit the INS's ability to implement even the relatively few formal removal orders and the far more numerous informal departure agreements that it does manage to obtain. Except at the border, where the INS can often effectuate the "voluntary departure" of aliens, the agency has been notoriously ineffective at actually removing aliens who want to remain in the United States—even the "aggravated felons" against whom the Congress has provided special summary enforcement and removal powers.[24] As a legal and practical matter, then, a long-term, non-criminal LPR's chances of remaining in the United States if he wishes have been almost as great as those of a citizen. The 1996 law, intended to facilitate the removal of aliens who are inadmissible, commit crimes in the United States, lack credible asylum claims, or are otherwise out of status, is unlikely to increase this risk significantly.

Today the most controversial issue concerning the rights of LPRs concerns their access to public benefits to which citizens are entitled. Prior to the 1996 welfare reforms, LPRs and some other legal aliens who would likely gain LPR status sometime in the future (such as family members of amnestied aliens, refugees and asylum seekers, parolees, and Cuban-Haitian entrants) were eligible for many cash assistance, medical care, food, education, housing, and other social programs, albeit subject to some restrictions.[25] In addition, LPRs were often eligible for benefit programs, such as low tuition in state university systems. The 1996 welfare reforms significantly limit the eligibility of LPRs for all or virtually all federal cash assistance programs.[26] . . .

The Reevaluation of Citizenship

In recent years, public discourse about citizenship has returned to first principles: its nature, sources, and significance. So fundamental are these principles that the new discourse amounts to a reevaluation of American citizenship in both its normative and its positive dimensions. This reevaluation has been prompted by deep concerns about the unity and coherence of the civic culture in the United States, concerns that flow from five developments in the post-1965 era. They are the accumulation of multicultural pressures; the loss of a unifying ideology; technological change; the expansion and consolidation of the welfare state; and the devaluation of citizenship.

Multicultural Pressures

With the enactment of the 1965 immigration law, the composition of the immigration stream to the United States changed radically. Of the top source countries, only the Philippines and India sent large numbers of English-speaking immigrants. Bilingual education thus became a major issue in public education, and teaching in dozens of languages became necessary in many urban school systems. With the growing politicization of ethnicity and widespread attacks on the traditional assimilative ideal, anxieties about linguistic and cultural fragmentation increased. These anxieties have led to public referendums in California and other states establishing English as the official language. Proposals to limit affirmative action and bilingual education have been adopted or are under consideration.

Meanwhile, as genuine racial integration proved elusive, the civil rights movement took a turn towards separatism. Blacks, already severely disadvantaged, were increasingly obliged to cede political and economic influence to more recently arrived Hispanic and Asian voters. Many of the newer groups qualified for affirmative action programs, which exacerbated tensions among the groups and magnified fears that immigration and affirmative action were fragmenting American society. Certain economic sectors came to depend almost entirely upon immigrant workers, legal and illegal. Relatively parochial immigrant enclaves grew larger. These multicultural pressures caused many Americans to feel more and more like strangers in their own country.

Loss of Unifying Ideology

The end of the Cold War deprived the United States of an ideology, anticommunism, that had served for many decades as a unifying, coherent force in American political culture and as an obsessive preoccupation and goal in U.S. foreign policy. No alternative ideology has yet emerged to replace it. Only constitutionalism, our civic religion, seems potentially capable of performing the function of binding together a nation of diverse peoples.

Technological Change

Rapid changes in transportation and communication technologies have transformed a world of sovereign nations into a global web of multinational enterprises and interdependent societies. Migration has become less expensive. Immigrants no longer need to make an irrevocable commitment to their new society; they can more easily retain emotional and other ties to their countries and cultures of origin. On the other hand, there is growing concern that television tends to assimilate second-generation immigrant youths into an underclass culture rather than into the mainstream American culture.

Welfare State Expansion

In the United States, the welfare state—especially the creation of entitlements to income support, food stamps, medical care, and subsidized housing—expanded rapidly during a brief period of time, at least when compared to the more gradual, long-term evolution of European social support systems.[27] With this growth, the behavior, values, and economic progress of immigrants became matters of great fiscal significance and public policy concern. In contrast to the historical pattern, immigration no longer ebbed and flowed with the business cycle—presumably because of the growth of the social safety net. Immigration increasingly pitted citizens and aliens against one another as they competed for scarce public resources. The perennial debate over how the polity should conceive of community, affinity, and mutual obligation took on a new significance as the stakes in the outcome grew larger. Demands that Americans' obsession with legal rights be balanced by an equal concern for their social and civic responsibilities were increasingly heard in the land.[28] . . .

Devaluation of Citizenship

The egalitarian thrust of the welfare state, its nourishing of entitlement as an ideal, and the repeal of the military draft led to a progressive erosion of citizenship as a distinctive status bearing special privileges and demanding special commitments and obligations. The rights of LPRs converged with those of citizens until there was little to separate them but the franchise, citizens' greater immigration sponsorship privileges, and their eligibility for the federal civil service. Americans began to feel that U.S. citizenship had lost much of its value and that it should somehow count for more.[29]

These concerns, which have parallels in other countries,[30] have prompted calls for a revitalization of citizenship. One type of proposal, which led to the enactment in 1993 of the National Community Service Corps, looks to the creation of a spirit of public service among young people. Another approach, a centerpiece of both the 1988 and 1996 welfare reform legislation, seeks to combat the entitlement mentality by insisting that able-bodied citizens work or get training, and eventually leave welfare altogether.

A third approach, exemplified by the 1996 restrictions on immigrants' access to public benefits, is largely motivated by the desire to save scarce public resources and to favor citizens in the allocation of those resources. Its incidental effect, however, will be to increase the value of citizenship by widening the gap between the rights of citizens and aliens, thereby creating stronger incentives for the latter to naturalize. Whether this incentive is the kind of motivation for naturalization that proponents of a more robust citizenship have in mind is a question that is seldom asked.

Two other types of reform aim directly at citizenship itself. The current INS commissioner is firmly committed to enhancing the attractiveness of the naturalization process, thereby encouraging more LPRs to acquire citizenship. This effort, however, has been caught up in a congressional investigation of fraud in and partisan manipulation of the naturalization process before the 1996 elections, a review that has already produced administrative reform and may prompt changes in the naturalization law.

A more radical proposal, not at all inconsistent with encouraging naturalization, would deny citizenship to some who would otherwise obtain it automatically. This approach would alter the traditional understanding of the *jus soli* rule, embodied in the Citizenship Clause of the Fourteenth Amendment, under which one becomes a citizen merely by being born in the United States, even if the one's parents are in the country illegally or only as temporary residents. Such proposals, which have also been advanced in Canada,[31] would eliminate this type of birthright citizenship either by constitutional amendment or by statute. Advocates of such a change emphasize the importance of mutual consent—the polity's as well as the alien's—in legitimizing American citizenship. They also point to the irrationality of permitting a Mexican woman with no claims on the United States to be able to confer American citizenship on her new child simply by crossing the border and giving birth, perhaps at public expense, in an American hospital. Defenders of birthright citizenship stress the importance of avoiding the creation and perpetuation of an underclass of long-term residents who do not qualify as citizens, a condition similar to that of many guest workers and their descendants stranded in countries that reject the *jus soli* principle. . . .

■ III. Citizenship in the Federal System

Among the most striking features of contemporary geopolitics is the fragmentation of national political authority, and its devolution—through the collapse of centralized regimes, civil wars, negotiated agreements, and other decentralizing processes—to smaller, subnational, often ethnically defined groups. This devolution, of course, is still very much in flux. Indeed, as the economic, military, and political disadvantages of radical decentralization become more manifest, some recentralization is bound to occur.

Nevertheless, the rapidity and militancy with which devolution has proceeded are remarkable. This has been most apparent in the former Soviet Union, which fractured in the aftermath of the Cold War. But even before the dissolution of the Soviet Empire, the weaker states of Africa and Asia had been disintegrating into chaos. Devolution is also occurring, albeit more slowly and less dramatically, in older nation-states like Italy, Belgium, and Mexico, and in paradigmatically strong ones like the United Kingdom and France. It is even occurring in nation-states like Canada, which already has highly decentralized federal systems in place.

The United States falls into this last category. Devolution to the states is perhaps the most prominent area of policy innovation pursued by the Republican congressional majority since the 1994 elections. The programs that compose the modern welfare state are being reassessed and, in some cases, fundamentally reshaped to give the states control of central aspects of the policy process: policy design, financing, eligibility, administration, evaluation, and enforcement. The recasting of the AFDC [Aid to Families with Dependent Children] program is the most dramatic example of a fundamental curtailment of federal power and augmentation of states' authority. Although Congress has not yet overhauled the Medicaid, food stamp, and supplemental security income (SSI) programs as thoroughly as AFDC, the precise division of authority between the federal and state governments remains the subject of bitter struggle and intense negotiations. Devolution of control over social programs, along with deregulation and privatization initiatives in a number of other policy areas, reflects a significant repudiation of the New Deal and Great Society; even the Democratic Party has acceded to it. The nationalizing trajectory of American political development has not merely been interrupted; it has been reversed.

These changes are not merely ephemeral. Instead, they reflect deep and abiding forces in U.S. society[32]—and elsewhere in the world. The structures supporting national power will be almost impossible to restore once they are dismantled, for restoration would require three conditions to converge: a convulsive national crisis equivalent to the Great Depression; a renewal of public confidence in the efficacy of centralized power and of national governmental solutions; and a surrender by the states of their hard-won powers. None of these conditions, much less all three, seems likely.

In emphasizing the changing conceptions and roles of national and state citizenship, one must also take note of another institutional development—the private residential enclave—that is becoming an increasingly significant locus of civic membership and governance in the United States.[33] Whether these enclaves take the form of urban apartment condominiums, suburban homeowners' associations, or other co-operative community arrangements, these territorial organizations create new kinds of governance regimes that exercise far-reaching powers over millions of Americans. Although such enclaves are more creatures of private law than public law, and the relationship of people and activities within them are structured more by contracts than by political constitutions, they nevertheless regulate important aspects of their members' lives in ways that closely resemble the powers of government. They too devolve authority—here, from the states, which ordinarily regulate property rights and community development, to private organizations.

These reconfigurations of governance amount to a reconstruction of American citizenship. By redefining the relationships between the citizen and the nation, the citizen and the states, and the citizen and his or her community, these devolutions are fundamentally transforming the rights and duties of membership in the various layers of American polities. In doing so, they are also transforming the meanings that attach to those memberships and those polities.

An important, if relatively unremarked, aspect of this devolution-driven redefinition of citizenship is its possible effect on the status of aliens. The role of the states in defining the rights of aliens in the United States has a somewhat complex history. Until 1875, when the first federal statute restricting immigration was enacted, the states exercised broad authority over aliens' entry and legal rights. Although a Supreme Court decision in 1849 (the *Passenger Cases*) indicated that states could not regulate immigration per se but still possessed a residual constitutional responsibility for protecting the health, safety, and morals of those within their jurisdiction, including aliens. States often exercised their jurisdiction over aliens during this early period in ways that had the effect of limiting immigration, especially by aliens who were poor, ill, or otherwise considered undesirable.[34]

Even after the federal government entered and occupied the field of general immigration control and the Supreme Court invalidated some state laws regulating aliens, states continued to enforce local laws that limited aliens' rights with respect to employment, property ownership, use of public resources, eligibility for public benefits, and other matters. With some exceptions, these statutes were generally upheld by the courts until the 1970s, when the Supreme Court began to apply strict scrutiny to almost all state laws limiting aliens' rights. Relying on the federal government's exclusive, or plenary power, over immigration, the Court went so far as to invalidate even those state law discriminations that tended to reinforce federal policies against illegal aliens by disadvantaging them. In perhaps no other area of legislation has the federal government's primacy been more firmly established and the power of the states more clearly circumscribed.[35]

The plenary power doctrine is a double-edged sword. It has been criticized by many legal scholars (and I count myself among them) who find no textual warrant for it in the Constitution and who contend that the structural and policy justifications that have been used to support it, such as the need for a single voice in foreign affairs, are either weak or over-broad.[36] These scholars believe that the federal government's power over aliens, while broad, must be subject to some constitutional limitations. At the same time, these scholars have generally applauded the courts' reliance on the plenary power doctrine's federal pre-emption logic when used to constrain states' power to regulate and discriminate against aliens. Deepening this tension is the fact that differences between citizens and aliens make the main alternative doctrinal constraint on state alienage discrimination—heightened scrutiny under the Equal Protection Clause—difficult to apply.

The question, then, is how fair treatment of aliens can be assured in a federal system in which the national government possesses plenary, or at least primary, responsibility for regulating aliens while the states, which sometimes have fiscal and political incentives to discriminate against them, possess some degree of policy autonomy, especially in a devolutionary era.

Today, however, this old question has taken on a new coloration. The United States has entered a period of extraordinary constitutional ferment in which the federal government's constitutional authority—even over subjects as to which it has long played the exclusive or dominant policy-making role—is being increasingly challenged. The most dramatic example of this ferment occurred in the Supreme Court's *United States v. Lopez*[37] decision, rendered in 1995. In *Lopez*, a sharply divided Court invalidated a federal statute that prohibited the possession of firearms near schools. It did so on the ground that the federal power to regulate under the Commerce Clause of the Constitution did not extend to such a local activity. Although the decision's scope and significance remain unclear, it cast doubt on almost sixty years of jurisprudence that construed the Commerce Clause to permit virtually any regulation that Congress wished to enact. *Lopez* has already provoked new challenges to long-established laws in policy areas involving highly localized impacts—for example, environmental regulation, drug enforcement, and abortion—which had previously been considered well within the ambit of federal power.

Federal regulation of immigration, of course, would survive a constitutional challenge under *Lopez*. As noted above, more than a century of

Supreme Court decisions have emphasized the national sovereignty and foreign policy implications of immigration law, the exclusive federal prerogatives in this area, and the dangers of state encroachment. This traditional approach remains essentially sound, and it is difficult to imagine that the Court, ironically radical as some of its constitutional law conservatism is, would jettison it.

It is not the Constitution, however, that has restricted state responsibility in the immigration field. In a series of decisions invalidating state laws on federal pre-emption grounds, the Court has clearly indicated that Congress remains free as a matter of *policy* to authorize, or perhaps even require, the states to act in this area. The real impediment to a greater state role is Congress, which has long chosen to occupy the field of immigration policy through federal legislation. In recent years, Congress has prescribed only a very limited role for the states in immigration policy—to provide federally mandated social services for refugees. The recent federal court decision invalidating most of California's Proposition 187 on pre-emption grounds is only the most recent example of the limits placed on state policy discretion when it conflicts with federal policy, the state targets illegal aliens.[38]

This situation, however, could change. Nothing in the nature of immigration policy requires that it be an exclusively national responsibility. Although immigration control is a national function in all countries, subnational units in some federal systems—Canada and Germany, for example—do exercise important policy-making functions with respect to immigration. With devolution occurring in so many other areas of public policy traditionally controlled at the center, can immigration regulation remain impervious to the trend? And if the states were to assume a more significant, independent role in immigration policy, a role that Congress might encourage and that the courts might therefore sustain, how would this development alter the nature of citizenship in the American polities?

These questions are by no means academic. Some of the same economic, social, political, and ideological forces that are propelling devolution in other policy areas also affect immigration politics. Immigrants are not distributed randomly across the nation. Quite the contrary; immigration is a largely *regional* phenomenon, with the vast majority of immigrants tending to live in a handful of states and metropolitan areas. However great the economic and other benefits of immigration to the nation as a whole may be, its costs—especially those resulting from immigrants' use of schools, hospitals, prisons, and other public services—are highly concentrated in these few high-impact states and metropolitan areas, while the rest of the country need not incur immigration's costs in order to enjoy many of its benefits. For proposals like Proposition 187 have been prompted by frustration with the costs of services demanded by large immigrant concentrations. For these high-impact states, immigration is as salient as any policy area with which they deal.

That these state-level impacts also have enormous *political* significance is obvious when one considers, as politicians surely do, that the seven states with the largest immigrant populations account for two-thirds of the electoral votes needed to win the presidency.[39] This fact places immigration reform high on the *national* political agenda—and it is from the national level, principally from Congress, that devolution of power over immigration policy must ultimately issue. Signs of movement in this direction appeared in the 1995 federal law limiting unfunded national mandates on states and localities, and in the 1996 welfare reform legislation discussed earlier. One of the practices prompting the unfunded mandates law was the federal government's recent policy of admitting a growing number of refugees while at the same time reducing its funding for resettlement support, thus forcing states, localities, and non-governmental organizations to pick up the tab for the increasing deficit.[40] The 1996 welfare reform law restricts federal policy initiative even further, transmuting AFDC into block grants and leaving the states largely free to determine how to distribute those funds among U.S. citizens while barring the states from spending them on certain alien categories. State laws that impose restrictions on state-financed programs consistent with the new federal restrictions will almost certainly survive constitutional challenge in the courts.

In a recent article, Professor Peter Spiro develops a more sweeping rationale for the devolution of immigration policy to the states.[41] He argues that the interests in national uniformity and control over foreign relations, which constitute the traditional justifications for federal pre-emption in immigration policy, are no longer decisive in a "post-national world order." In that order, according to Spiro, states are the major fiscal and political stakeholders in immigration policy. They also play larger, more independent roles in their dealings with foreign nations. He attributes the more robust state role in foreign relations to the globalization of information, communications, and travel, and to the economic and cultural ties that states have increasingly forged with foreign governments and communities. "This international engagement on the states' part," Spiro writes, "has inevitably undermined the [traditional pre-emption] doctrine's more fundamental underpinning, viz., that other countries will not distinguish the states and their actions from the nation's."[42]

Spiro's argument is less important for his prescriptions, which I find quite problematic, than for his empirical claim that the federal government's monopoly of authority and influence in foreign relations and immigration is steadily (and, in his view, irrevocably) eroding, as the states and private non-governmental organizations operate more independently of Washington.[43] Assuming that he is correct about this, however, it does not follow that Congress will devolve authority over immigration policy to the states—even if it continues to do so in other policy domains. Congress may instead conclude that immigration is simply *different*, perhaps because, it believes, contrary to Spiro that immigration's foreign policy implications and the need to speak with one voice are considerations of overriding importance.

Alternatively, Congress might adopt a middle path. Congress might decide that *as a matter of national policy*, it is prepared to tolerate greater diversity among states in their treatment of aliens. By adopting an affirmative national policy that allows states to discriminate against aliens in certain areas such as welfare benefits or student loans, Congress could continue to uphold the principle of federal pre-emption while encouraging policy diversity among the states. Such a national policy might well pass constitutional muster as an exercise of Congress's plenary federal power. If so, the courts might then uphold—as consistent with and in furtherance of this federal plenary power—discriminatory state laws that would otherwise raise serious constitutional questions. They might distinguish *Graham v. Richardson*[44] and its progeny on the ground that the discriminations invalidated in those decisions were not authorized by this kind of clearly expressed congressional policy.

In the welfare reform legislation enacted in August 1996, Congress took precisely this middle path on the question of aliens' eligibility for welfare and other public benefit programs. The legislation is very complex. It creates a new legal category ("qualified aliens"); differentiates among particular programs, governmental levels, and alien categories; carves out many exceptions; contains "grandfather" clauses; and provides special transitional rules. Consequently, its specific meanings will remain uncertain for years to come. But, what is of greater interest for present purposes is this: *Congress sought to "revalue" U.S. citizenship by adopting a firm national policy favoring discrimination against LPRs (not just illegal aliens) in the distribution of public benefits and by conscripting the states in the implementation of that new policy.*

In the 1996 law, Congress defined four different policy modalities along a spectrum running from prescription to complete deference. Interestingly, these modalities do not simply track the distinction between federal and state programs (although that distinction is obviously at work in the chosen level of prescription). Moreover, Congress is somewhat prescriptive even where it is deferential.

The first modality, which deals with federal benefits (defined broadly) and is highly prescriptive, precludes any contrary state policies. It bars aliens other than LPRs, refugees and asylum-seekers, and a few other categories of immigrants from access to all federal benefits. The law also bars all *current* LPRs and other aliens with legal status, except for three favored groups,[45] from the fully federal SSI and food stamp programs.[46] Finally, it bars *new* LPRs and other legal aliens (other than those three groups) during their first five years in the United States from all federal means-tested programs such as AFDC and its successor. The law also contains a large number of exceptions including emergency Medicaid, disaster relief, child nutrition, some training, and education.

In its second modality, Congress is more deferential to the states' policies toward aliens—even relating to some federal programs. It *allows*, but does not require, states to bar aliens from three federal programs including: the block grants for temporary assistance for needy families, social services block grants, and non-emergency Medicaid. In contrast, Congress *requires* states to provide these benefits—which in the case of Medicaid benefits are very costly—to the three favored alien groups.

In its third modality, Congress adopts a prescriptive mode regarding most *state and local* benefit programs. States are prohibited from allowing any aliens other than LPRs, temporary visitors, and some other categories to receive state and local public benefits, except for certain emergency programs. States are allowed however, to make *illegal* aliens eligible for those state and local benefit programs, but only if they do so by new, specific legislation. Oddly, this empowers states to place illegal aliens in a better position than certain categories of legal aliens to whom, under the new law, the state may not provide state and local benefits. A fourth modality—deference to state programs—*allows* states to bar legal aliens, other than the three favored groups, from state programs altogether.

This crazy-quilt pattern is not accidental; it is emblematic of the complexity of U.S. policies, federal structure, and public administration. From the perspective of the polity's valuation of citizenship, however, two aspects of the new law's treatment of aliens are particularly striking. First, the federal government has now made a clear, comprehensive policy choice, albeit one that is confusing in its details, in favor of a national policy to discriminate against aliens in its federal programs, and to either require or permit the states to do so in their programs. This policy fundamentally reverses the recent law in this area. With a few exceptions, such as the wholly federal program at issue in *Mathews v. Diaz*,[47] the federal government had largely abandoned the practice of discriminating against aliens and, because Supreme Court decisions held the states to the same rules as a matter of constitutional law, the states could not discriminate either.

New York City, Florida, and other plaintiffs immediately challenged the new federal policy on equal protection grounds. A federal district court in New York, however, has upheld the statute as being rationally related to the federal government's interests in controlling program costs, encouraging aliens to naturalize and to be self-sufficient, and removing an incentive for immigration.[48]

The second noteworthy feature of this new federal mandate to discriminate is that it is part of a statute that vastly enlarges the states' discretion over most other aspects of welfare policy. This means that the new policy on alien benefits is unusual not only substantively, in that it requires discrimination that in other contexts would be unconstitutional, but also structurally, in that it presumes, contrary to the now-dominant thinking about federalism, that Washington knows best and should enforce its "one-size-fits-all" policy preferences on the states.

In general, however, the rights and obligations of individuals—U.S. citizens and aliens alike—will now depend more on state law and less on federal law than at any time since the New Deal. To the extent that Congress devolves immigration policy to the states, *state* citizenship could become more salient than in the past, and the constitutional limits on states' power to discriminate—constraints derived from state constitutions as well as from the U.S. Constitution—will become more significant. State citizenship is a status that has received little scholarly attention of late; it ceased to have much practical significance once states barred aliens from voting in their elections, American Indians received U.S. citizenship, and the Supreme Court interpreted the Constitution's Privileges and Immunities Clause to limit the states' power to discriminate against citizens of other states. . . .

If devolution thus transforms the structure of American federalism, the nature of citizenship in the American polities must also be transformed. The legal, political, and social relationships between an individual alien and the larger juridical communities that affect her relative status and well-being—the national government, state governments, and local self-governing enclaves—will in effect be redefined.

Like so much else in this new devolutionary regime, it is difficult to predict how aliens will fare under it. Some aliens will be better off than they are now, while others will be worse off. Some states and local communities already embrace legal aliens at least as warmly as the federal government does. In such states, this favorable reception is driven by enduring forces; it will probably continue even after the 1996 changes in the welfare and immigration laws are fully implemented. There, aliens are regarded as valuable economic and cultural assets, and politicians anticipate that immigrants may soon become citizens and voters and these politicians may seek support from already established ethnic communities concerned about the newcomers' welfare. State governments in Texas and New Jersey, for example, seem to view legal immigrants as beneficial to their states.[49] Even Pete Wilson, the California governor who promoted Proposition 187, has defended the welfare benefit rights of legal aliens, extending their entitlements under federally funded programs as long as possible. State and city politicians in New York and Massachusetts have welcomed even illegal aliens.[50]

Other states and communities, however, may view at least certain types of immigrants as unwanted invaders, as fiscal and political burdens that the state can hope to shift to other states. The possibility of a so-called race to the bottom, in which states seek to discourage some categories of immigration by adopting more discriminatory policies than sister states, is a powerful argument in favor of pre-empting state immigration policies in a federal system or at least for imposing limits on permissible state discrimination.[51] It is a possibility, moreover, which the 1996 welfare reform magnifies. The experience of other federal nations in dealing with this risk of immigration policy fragmentation should be of special interest to the United States in this devolutionary era.

■ IV. A Brief Note on "Post-National Citizenship"

In recent years a number of scholars have pointed to a new development in thinking about citizenship—what Yasemin Soysal and others have called the idea of "post-national citizenship." Its "main thrust," according to Soysal, "is that individual rights, historically defined on the basis of nationality, are increasingly codified into a different scheme that emphasizes universal personhood."[52] In this conception, transnational diasporic communities of individuals bearing multiple, collective identities make, and, ideally, enforce claims against states. In contrast to a traditional "national" model of citizenship, individuals—simply by virtue of their personhood—can legitimately assert claims on the basis of their universal human rights (as devolved by evolving principles of international law) whether or not they are citizens, or even residents, of those states.

In somewhat similar terms, David Jacobson notes the emergence of a "deterritorialized identity" that is transforming the nature of, and relationships among, the community, polity, and state, and he cites some judicial decisions that seem to be propelling this transformation. A new dispensation, Jacobson believes, is inevitable . . . [53] Jacobson quickly adds that this bright promise of post-national citizenship is being realized only in western Europe and North America, acknowledging that eastern Europe is experiencing the very opposite: "the territorialization of communal identity."[54]

These visions of post-national citizenship are undeniably attractive. A just state will respect and vindicate minority groups' claims to cultural diversity and autonomy. Detaching the legitimacy of these claims from their conventional territorial moorings in "normal politics"[55] and traditional citizenship law, as post-national citizenship seeks to do, may sometimes promote their recognition. Indeed, Soysal's own work on the progress of

Muslim communities in western Europe suggests this outcome.[56] Some court decisions, which have required polities to extend procedural and even substantive rights to strangers who come within their jurisdiction and claim judicial protection, also seem to point in this direction.[57]

Those decisions, however, remain exceptional and some have been overturned in the United States by the 1996 immigration and welfare reform laws. But a more important set of questions about the character and implications of post-national citizenship are raised by recent events elsewhere in the world. Bosnia, Somalia, Rwanda, Burundi, Cambodia, and all too many other areas of conflict should remind us that the ostensible goals of post-national citizenship—human rights, cultural autonomy, and full participation in a rich civil society—are tragically elusive, and that its achievements are extremely fragile.

The problem is not merely that partisans of exclusion and discrimination will oppose post-national citizenship at every turn and often succeed in establishing illiberal policies in traditional nation-states. The more fundamental problem is that post-national citizenship ultimately depends on its ability to transcend, or at least enlarge, the domains of normal politics and law. After all, if those domains would accept the post-national agenda, there would be no need to advocate it as an alternative to traditional national citizenship and hence no problem. Such a transcendence of normal politics, however, would leave post-national human rights naked and vulnerable with no firm political and institutional grounding. Without such a grounding, national courts enforcing international law principles are unlikely to provide durable, reliable protection.[58] The often feckless international human rights tribunals are even less plausible guarantors of those principles.

Soysal and Jacobson might acknowledge this point yet respond that some protection for post-national citizenship, however episodic, is better than none. But this response does little to shore up post-national citizenship, for its grounding only in adjudication would risk more than an incomplete fulfillment. The problem is not simply that courts are institutionally ill-equipped to defend their rulings in the political arena, or even, as Mr. Dooley famously put it, that the Supreme Court follows the election returns.[59] The greater risk is that the normative foundation of a post-national citizenship may be so thin and shallow that it can easily be swept away by the tides of tribalism or nationalism. As formulated by Soysal in her work on civil society, post-national citizenship, unless it includes rights already established under national laws, possesses only a limited institutional status, largely confined to some courts. Of course, if it were more fully institutionalized than this, the new ideal would be superfluous. Beyond this, Soysal argues, post-national citizenship is built on a "discourse of rights," one that explicitly renounces the Habermasian effort to fuse reason and will in pursuit of a non-coercive consensus. Instead, this discourse chooses "to focus on agendas of contestation and provide space for strategic action, rather than consensus building."[60] . . .

In reasonably democratic states—and post-national citizenship is only possible and meaningful in such states—even an imperfect constitution recognizing minority rights, and even a majoritarian politics in which groups must compete for acceptance of their communal aspirations, are likely to provide more certain guarantees of liberal human rights than a discursive ideal. This is especially true to the extent that the post-national, transnational ideal is institutionally grounded only in politically isolated courts and lends itself, because of its substantive indeterminacy, to repressive applications. A discourse whose success requires overcoming the messy exigencies of normal politics where expansive conceptions of human rights must contend for legal recognition seems destined to be either irrelevant or anti-democratic.

There is, however, a valuable role that the notion of post-national citizenship can and should fulfill. It should serve as a compelling vision of tolerance, diversity, and integration that people of good will can aspire to, that normal politics in democratic states can sometimes realize, and against which their failures can be fairly judged and condemned. This is the role that it has begun to play in the United States. To claim more for it, or to promote it as an alternative to, or as a cure for, the weaknesses of democratic politics, would ultimately discredit the humane agenda that its proponents advocate. If it can succeed in mobilizing normal politics to win that recognition in positive law, however, it will be truly transformative even as it thereby ceases, in an important sense, to be "post national."

■ Conclusion

Citizenship is a status whose meaning in any particular society depends entirely on the political commitments and understandings to which its members subscribe. In the United States, many of these commitments and understandings have always been tenuous, contestable, and contested; and some still are.[61] Of no political arrangement is this more true than the American welfare state. It was first established only sixty years ago and it only reached its current form in the 1970s and 1980s, with the rapid expansion of the food stamp, Medicaid, and social security programs.[62] In this mature form,[63] then, the welfare state is less than three decades old. During most of this period, moreover, its legitimacy has been under constant attack by much of the political and intellectual establishment; the present political struggle will determine precisely how firm its hold on the public's allegiance actually is.[64]

This feverish debate over the welfare state, which has continued and in some ways deepened since its inception in the New Deal era, has inevitably shaped Americans' conception of the meaning and incidents of citizenship. In this sense, the American debate might be seen as yet another example of what has tendentiously been called "American exceptionalism"—the notion that, for a variety of complex historical reasons, some of the patterns that have shaped the character of European democracies do not apply, or apply quite differently, to the United States. In this case, however, I believe that such a perception would be mistaken. More likely, the American debate prefigures a re-evaluation of citizenship in Europe.

Such a re-evaluation appears to be inescapable in light of a number of extremely important developments: the enlarged scope and ambition of the European Union; the migration and asylum pressures unleashed by the fall of the Iron Curtain; the social tensions created by large, unassimilated alien populations with limited access to citizenship; the recognition among many European leaders that recent budget deficits are both unsustainable and inconsistent with further monetary and political integration; and the sclerotic performance in recent years of the high-cost European economies in the intensely competitive global markets. Although this debate may resemble the American one in some respects, it will be distinctively European in many others. As the social, economic, and political conditions of Europe and the United States increasingly converge, we shall have unprecedented opportunities to learn from one another—from our triumphs as well as our mistakes.

■ Notes

1. As I note infra, I mean to include in "sovereignties" both public and private governance regimes to which individuals may be subjected.
2. The number of legal immigrants actually admitted was 915,000 in 1996, 720,000 in 1995, 804,000 in 1994, and 904,000 in 1993.
3. The Immigration and Naturalization Service (INS) rejected 200,000 petitions in 1996; 965,000 petitions were pending in March 1997.
4. The globalization phenomenon, while important, is easily exaggerated. According to a very recent study, U.S.-based firms' share of world output outside the United States actually declined from 3 percent to 2 percent between 1977 and 1993, even as the domestic U.S. economy expanded. Robert Lipsey et al., Internationalized Production in World Output, NBER Working Paper No. 5385 (1996).
5. *See* Peter H. Schuck, *The Message of 187*, Am. Prospect 85-92 (1995).
6. Some commentators maintain that the justifications for citizenship lie primarily in the international law realm; this status, they believe, has—or ought to have—little significance inside a nation's borders. *See, e.g.,* Stephen H. Legomsky, *Why Citizenship?* 35 Va J. Int'l L. 279, 300 (1994). Chapter 6 discusses Proposition 187.
7. David Jacobson, Rights Across Borders: Immigration and the Decline of Citizenship 131 (1996). I discuss, and criticize, Jacobson's conception of "postnational citizenship." *See infra* pages 202–205.

and win elective office. Moreover, following from the previous two trends, those who do win office are disproportionately affiliated with political parties of the left.

Closely related to these trends, as I will argue later, are two phenomena: (1) the degree to which post–World War II immigrants are incorporated into formal political institutions differs from one country to the next; and (2) the extent to which immigrants are politically incorporated within a given country varies, often quite significantly, from one immigrant group to another.

■ Electoral Turnout Among Immigrant Voters

The propensity of immigrants to turn out to vote in lower percentages than native citizens is a long-observed, although not universal, trend across the immigration-receiving countries. For the reasons that I will briefly outline below, Western Europe's new ethnic minorities are less inclined than natives to vote in both local and national elections. In order better to understand how well and how uniformly immigrants are incorporated into formal politics within Western Europe, it is necessary to differentiate between the participatory patterns of immigrant noncitizens, who are sometimes eligible to vote only in local elections, and those of immigrant citizens who enjoy and exercise voting rights across the board. Although fragmentary, the empirical evidence suggests that citizenship is positively correlated with higher rates of immigrant electoral participation. On the basis of this evidence, it can be argued that immigrant citizens are better incorporated than immigrant noncitizens into the electoral politics of the immigration-receiving states.

That immigrant noncitizens are significantly less inclined than so-called native citizens to vote in local elections is beyond dispute. To cite but one glaring example from the 1990s, voter turnout among noncitizens was less than half as great as that of citizens in municipal elections held in Sweden from 1991 to 2002 (Table 11.4.1). Furthermore, there is evidence from the Swedish case that immigrant noncitizens are perhaps more susceptible than natives to political disaffection and, specifically, to losing the habit of voting over time. Although voter turnout in Swedish local elections declined among all groups between 1976 and 2002, including among natives, it declined far more precipitously among noncitizens during this period.

A similar pattern of divergence between noncitizen and native citizen voter turnout was discernible in the results of the municipal elections in Denmark and the Netherlands during the 1990s (Togeby, 1999; van Heelsum, 2000). Except for Turkish voters in Amsterdam (in 1994) and

Table 11.4.1   Voter Turnout Among Foreigners in Swedish Municipal Elections, 1976–2002 (percentage)

Year	Turnout Foreigners	Turnout Swedes
1976	59.9	90.5
1979	53.4	89.0
1980[a]	53.4	75.6
1982	52.2	89.6
1985	48.1	88.0
1988	43.0	84.0
1991	41.0	84.3
1994	40.3	84.4
1998	35.0	78.6
2002	35.1	78.0

Source: Adapted from Tomas Hammar, *Democracy and the Nation State* (Aldershot, UK: Avebury, 1994), p. 156; Statistics Sweden, 1999, as cited in Lillemor Sahlberg, ed., *Excluded from Democracy? On the Political Participation of Immigrants* (Norrköping, Sweden: Integrationverkets, 2001), p. 53; Statistics Sweden, http://www.scb.se/sm/Me14SM0301_inEnglish.asp.

Note: a. A national referendum on Swedish nuclear policy in which foreign citizens were allowed to participate.

Pakistani voters in Copenhagen and Arhus and Turks in Arhus (in 1997), immigrant noncitizens were less likely to vote than native citizens in the two countries. Immigrant noncitizen turnout in the Netherlands, like that of the Dutch electorate as a whole, declined in each of five major cities and among all ethnic minority groups (except Turks in Rotterdam) between 1994 and 1998.

Patterns of electoral participation among citizens of immigrant origin, on the other hand, offer a more positive picture of immigrant voter turnout, and one that deviates somewhat from the participatory patterns of noncitizens. Although immigrant citizens too are generally less likely to vote than natives, they are distinguishable from noncitizens in two important ways.

First, immigrants who possess national citizenship are more likely to vote than noncitizens. In municipal elections held in Norway in 1999, for example, each of the country's six major ethnic minority groups voted in higher percentages than members from the same group who did not possess citizenship (Table 11.4.2). Voter turnout among immigrant citizens in the aggregate (50 percent) was 12 percent higher than that of noncitizens (38 percent).

Indeed, not only does citizenship influence voting behavior, but an immigrant's length of residence within a given country, perhaps reinforcing the participatory effects of formal citizenship, also appears to inflate immigrant voter turnout. In Sweden, for example, the longer immigrants have been settled, the more closely their political participation patterns resemble

Table 11.4.2 Voter Turnout Among Foreigners and Citizens with Immigrant Backgrounds in the 1999 Norwegian Municipal Elections (percentage)

Foreigners	Turnout	Norwegian Immigrant Citizens	Turnout
India	32	India	45
Sri Lanka	33	Sri Lanka	57
Turkey	26	Turkey	41
Pakistan	47	Pakistan	57
Yugoslavia	15	Yugoslavia	27
Morocco	15	Morocco	34
All	38	All	50

Source: Statistics Norway, "Municipal Council Elections" (Oslo: Official Statistics of Norway, 1999), p. 120.

those of Swedish natives (Sahlberg, 2001). Similarly, length of residence was positively correlated with higher rates of voter turnout among immigrant citizens in elections for the Norwegian national legislature in 2001. As Table 11.4.3 demonstrates, for each 10-year period of residence in Norway the voting turnout rate among immigrant citizens increased. Interestingly, in contrast to the modest rise of participation rates that prevailed for the previous three sets of 10-year residency terms, voter turnout among immigrant citizens with 30 or more years of residence was 25 percent greater than that among immigrants with between 20 and 29 years of residence. Overall, the gap between the voter participation rates of the most recently settled (0–9 years of residency) and the longest-settled immigrant citizens in Norway was 34 percent.

Second, although the voter turnout rates of immigrant citizens lag behind those of natives, the gap between the two groups tends to be far

Table 11.4.3 Voter Turnout Among Norwegian Citizens with Immigrant Backgrounds in General Elections by Length of Residence, 2001 (percentage)

Years of Residence	Total
0–9	41
10–19	45
20–29	50
30 or more	75
All	52

Source: Statistics Norway, available online at http://www.ssb.no/english/subjects/00/01/10/stortingsvalg_en/tab-2001-12-17-03-en.html.

smaller than that between noncitizens and natives. Indeed, in Britain, where many ethnic minorities arrived in the country possessing formal citizenship during the 1960s and 1970s, there is abundant empirical evidence that voter turnout among immigrant citizens is fairly robust and, for at least one ethnic minority group, equal to or greater than the voter turnout rates of white citizens. In his study of voter turnout across ethnic minority groups at the 1997 general election, Saggar (2001: 103) reported that voter turnout among Indian voters actually exceeded that of whites nationally, while the electoral participation of Pakistanis, Bangladeshis, and Afro-Caribbeans was more or less on a par with the participation of whites. Unfortunately, some of these gains seem to have receded during the British general election in 2001. According to the results of one survey (Electoral Commission, 2002), voter turnout among whites (59.4 percent) was approximately 13 percent higher than that of ethnic minorities taken together (47 percent), although, contrary to this general trend, Indian voters once again voted in higher percentages than whites (Travis, 2002).

Why do fewer immigrants than natives vote, even in local elections that produce political outcomes that directly affect their daily economic, social, and political environments (Koopmans and Statham, 2000; Mahnig and Wimmer, 1998)? Although it is hazardous to generalize across the cases, several reasons immediately come to the fore.

First, as suggested by the differences in voter turnout rates between immigrant citizens and noncitizens and those among groups of immigrant citizens with different terms of residence, the incentive for immigrants to vote tends to strengthen with the degree of an individual's psychological and material investment in a given society (Sahlberg, 2001: 89). Since this investment is somewhat weaker and more recently acquired among immigrants than natives, and is even more tenuous among immigrant noncitizens with an ephemeral or weak legal attachment to the domestic polity, it is hardly surprising that fewer immigrants tend to vote than natives.

Second, alienation and apathy undoubtedly play a role in depressing voter turnout among immigrants. Alienation often springs from the failure of the political system to deliver the desired symbolic and material outcomes to immigrants. Entrenched patterns of relative deprivation, social exclusion, and community segregation engender an active dislike of politics that can give the new ethnic minorities less of an apparent stake than natives in the outcome of elections (Electoral Commission, 2002: 64).

Apathy, or a sense that politics is a distant or confusing process, also depresses the incentive of immigrants to engage politically (Hammar, 1994: 146; Sahlberg, 2001: 80). This type of psychological distance can be a product of the language and cultural barriers that often unavoidably divide immigrants from mainstream politics and society. Alternatively and less benignly, it may also result from the failure of political parties and other mainstream actors or institutions to engage and embrace immigrants (Sahlberg, 2001: 89). In either event, the outcome is indifference to formal politics and electoral outcomes.

Although their effects should be recognized, alienation and apathy should not be overprivileged in the story of low immigrant voter turnout. In Britain recent evidence suggests that although ethnic minority, and especially Afro-Caribbean, voters are more politically alienated and apathetic than whites, these sentiments do not appear to pose an insuperable obstacle to engaging ethnic minorities in mainstream politics and political outcomes. Their effects on turnout, while tangible, appear to be relatively modest (Saggar, 2001: 111). In an opinion survey conducted during the 1997 British general election, 81 percent of Asian and 74.5 percent of Afro-Caribbean voters cited their "duty to vote" as the reason for voting, in contrast to 79.5 percent of whites. In the same survey 19 percent of white, 17 percent of Asian, and 24 percent of Afro-Caribbean voters professed that "caring who wins" motivated them to go to the polls (Saggar, 2001: 110).

Yet a third, subjective factor depressing immigrant voter turnout, especially in the case of immigrant noncitizens, is the proclivity of many immigrants to remain primarily focused on the politics of their country of origin (Hammar, 1994: 146). As Freeman and Ogelman (1998) argue, the strong, lingering psychological attachment of immigrants to their country of origin tends to inhibit their full integration into the institutionalized politics of their adopted country. Indeed, it is intrinsic to the nature of this homeland-immigrant relationship that not only individual immigrants but the homeland governments have a strong stake in sustaining it. According to Freeman and Ogelman, homeland governments routinely make concerted efforts to influence, control, and monitor expatriate political behavior in order to influence indirectly the host countries' policies vis-à-vis the country of origin and to diminish the potential for the activities of its expatriates to create political problems. There is suggestive evidence, for example, that the low voter turnout of Moroccans in local elections in the Netherlands in 1986 was due to the fact that the Moroccan king had urged his subjects not to vote (Sahlberg, 2001: 41).

■ Immigrant Voters and Political Parties of the Left

Whatever the turnout rate of citizen and noncitizen immigrants within a given country, a prevalent pattern among immigrant voters across the immigration-receiving states is to support and vote for socialist, left-liberal, or labor/working-class political parties. For the new ethnic and racial minorities of Western Europe, formal political representation predominantly implies representation through traditional political parties of the left.

Not surprisingly given their early arrival in the post–World War II period, the propensity of ethnic minority voters in Britain to support the left-of-center Labour Party is especially well documented. Indeed, every ethnic minority voting survey that has been conducted since the 1970s confirms that ethnic minorities favor the Labour Party by an overwhelming margin over its principal political rival, the politically right-of-center Conservative Party (Ali and Percival, 1993; Messina, 1989: 152; Electoral Commission, 2002). In each general election held since 1979, Labour has been the preferred party choice of no less than two-thirds of ethnic minority voters. Among Afro-Caribbean voters, the Labour Party vote averaged an astonishing 84 percent in the general elections from 1983 to 2001, thus making this constituency the most staunchly loyal Labour supporters within the British electorate—indeed the most solid block of voters for any one political party in the history of modern British democracy.

The strong attachment of the new ethnic and racial minorities to the Labour Party in Britain is not unusual. Ethnic minorities in Germany and in the Netherlands, too, overwhelmingly gravitate toward political parties of the left. Indeed, a 1999 survey of Turkish-born naturalized citizens conducted in Germany offers evidence that the political allegiance of this particular ethnic group to leftist political parties is almost as strong or, depending upon the yardstick employed, stronger than the ties between Labour and ethnic minority voters in Britain (Wüst, 2002). In the aforementioned survey only 12 percent of ethnic Turkish citizens expressed their intention to vote for political parties of the center or center right (Christian Democratic Union [CDU]/Christian Social Union [CSU], Free Democratic Party [FDP]) as opposed to 74 percent for parties of the left/center left (Social Democratic Party [SPD]/Greens/Party of Democratic Socialism [PDS]). The support gap of ethnic Turks for the major German party of the left, the Social Democrats, and for the major parties of the right, the Christian Democrats, was 49 percent. These results were broadly reproduced in a survey of Turkish immigrants who intended to vote in the elections for the Berlin House of Representatives in 2001. The survey showed that 89 percent of Turks intended to vote for the Socialists, Greens, or the post-Communists, whereas only 9 percent expected to support the Christian Democrats or the Liberals. Almost two-thirds (64.4 percent) of Turkish immigrants expressed their electoral preference for the Social Democratic Party (Berger, Galonska, and Koopmans, 2002).

In the Netherlands, where the national party system is fragmented among more than eight political parties, the story is quite similar. In a survey of ethnic minority voters conducted in seven major cities in 1994 and in five cities in 1998 (Tillie, 1998: 85) every ethnic minority group except one supported parties of the political left (Labour Party [PvdA], Democrats 66 [D66], Green Left Party [GroenLinks], Socialist Party [SP]) over parties of the right (Christian Democratic Appeal [CDA], People's Party for Freedom and Democracy [VVD], Political Reformed Party [SGP]). They did so by margins of between 33 and 92 percent in both elections, depending upon the group. The two political parties most favored by ethnic minority voters were the PvdA and the ecologist and socialist Green Left Party. Among Turkish, Surinamese, and Antillean immigrants the PvdA was the plurality choice; for Moroccans, the Green Left Party was the most preferred. The latter, somewhat unusual phenomenon is explained by Tillie (1998: 83) as a function of the Green Left's overt leftist political ideology and its adoption of a strong antiracist posture.

Why do immigrant voters overwhelmingly prefer political parties of the left? Somewhat surprisingly, in several countries the answer does not lie exclusively in the social class backgrounds of immigrants. Indeed, in both Britain and the Netherlands class plays a negligible role in influencing the political party preferences of immigrant voters, in contrast to native voters.

Underscoring this fact, and demonstrating the impressive strength of the political bond between ethnic minorities and the Labour Party in Britain, is the reality that the ethnic minority vote is a specific ethnic vote; social class does not predict nearly as well the political preferences of ethnic minority voters as it does those of white voters (Layton-Henry and Studlar, 1985). For example, Asian routine nonmanual (C1) voters excepted, all social classes within the ethnic minority electorate supported Labour by a ratio of more than three to one over other parties in the 1983 general election. In the 1987 general election no social class gave Labour less than 52 percent or the Conservative Party more than 33 percent of the vote. Within the lowest occupational grades (D, E), 9 out of 10 nonwhite electors in 1983 and more than 8 of 10 in 1987 voted Labour (Messina, 1989: 154). In the 1992 general election, the overall results of which allowed the Conservative Party to maintain itself in government, only 29 percent of ABC1 ethnic minority voters cast ballots for the party, in contrast to at least 43 percent of white voters. Conversely, 78 percent of C2D ethnic voters endorsed Labour in 1992, as opposed to a bare majority of whites. In the 1997 general election, the aggregate results of which ushered the Labour Party into government for the first time in eighteen years, 76 percent of ethnic minority salaried voters (as against 38 percent of whites) and 86 percent of routine, nonmanual workers (as against 44 percent of whites) voted for Labour. Overall, ethnic minority voters supported the Labour Party by 38 percent more than white voters in 1997.

As stated before, the class background of immigrant voters in the Netherlands does not predict party preferences very well either. Indeed, on the basis of an analysis of the electoral potential of all Dutch political parties to attract immigrant voters in the local elections of 1994 and 1998,

Tillie (1998: 91) concluded that "the class cleavage appears to be of no importance" in structuring the immigrant vote.

If class is not the primary driver, what factors bind immigrant voters to political parties of the left? As with explanations of why immigrants vote in fewer numbers than native citizens, it is hazardous to generalize. Specific country and ethnic group factors obviously matter; moreover, these factors naturally vary from one immigration-receiving country to the next. Nevertheless, at least two subjective variables are conspicuously prominent across the cases.

First, for reasons that I will explore in greater depth, the fact that political parties of the left are more inclined than their ideological rivals to embrace immigrants as well as the public policy issues that especially matter to this special constituency are factors whose importance should not be underestimated (Wüst, 2004). In contrast to their right-of-center political rivals, parties of the left are generally less encumbered by ideological contradictions and other complicating internal factors that prevent them from embracing immigrant voters (Messina, 1998). On the contrary, as we shall see, the peculiar history and traditionally progressive ideological orientation of the political left are powerful factors that facilitate its embrace of immigrant voters. As a consequence of this embrace, immigrant voters in turn are inclined to support the political left. Immigrants in the Netherlands, for example, predictably gravitate toward the political parties, the PvdA and the GroenLinks, that overtly appeal to them (Tillie, 1998: 23). Similarly, the well-established proclivity of the British Labour Party to identify with and actively reach out to ethnic minority voters, in stark contrast to the lackluster and inconsistent efforts of the Conservative Party to do the same, has resulted in inspiring loyalty to Labour within this special constituency (Messina, 1998). As I will argue, the Labour Party predominantly is the political party *of* Britain's ethnic minorities because it historically has been and is the party ideologically, politically, and most publicly *for* ethnic minorities.

A second factor responsible for the strong attachment of immigrants to political parties of the left is the attractiveness of such parties' policy agendas. Simply put, ethnic minority voters within the immigration-receiving countries are more inclined than not to support political parties of the left because the left's traditional policy agenda tends to dovetail with their perceived interests. Specifically, the proclivity of the left to privilege the goals of full employment, greater socioeconomic equality, universal health care, a vibrant public educational system, racial equality, and similar issues intersects with the material and subjective aspirations of immigrant voters, who generally find themselves socioeconomically disadvantaged or the objects of racial prejudice or social exclusion (Saggar, 2001: 78). As suggested by Table 11.4.4, the traditional bread-and-butter issues associated with the

Table 11.4.4   Salient Issues Among British Ethnic Minority Voters, 1987 (percentage)

Issues	Asian	Afro-Caribbean	White
Unemployment	65	70	45
Health	34	25	32
Education	17	13	19
Defense	32	18	37
Law and order	11	4	6
Pensions	6	7	9
Housing	0	21	5
Prices	10	15	7
Race	1	0	1

Source: Shamit Saggar, *Race and Representation: Electoral Politics and Ethnic Pluralism in Britain* (Manchester, UK: Manchester University Press, 2001), p. 33.

Labour Party strongly resonate with ethnic minority voters in Britain even more strongly than they do with whites. As a result, Asian voters are three times more likely to trust Labour over the Conservatives "to look after the interests of Asian people" in Britain (Saggar, 2001: 78).

However, the bond between ethnic minority voters and the Labour Party in Britain is not simply founded on instrumentally motivated, cost-benefit calculations. Rather, the pragmatic policy interests that bind ethnic minorities to Labour are reinforced by the politically left ideological orientation of Britain's ethnic minority voters, a feature that is typically a legacy of previous political allegiances of ethnic minority voters in the immigration-sending country. In the Netherlands, an affinity among immigrants with leftist ideas and policies motivates immigrant voters to gravitate toward the PvdA and GroenLinks. According to Tillie (1998: 91), "for all migrants, voting behavior and party preference can be labeled 'ideological.' That is, with respect to the national political parties in the Netherlands, migrants . . . [conform] to the dominant political discourse: left-right."

■ The Affinity of Left Parties for Immigrant Voters

In order to understand more fully the motivations and incentives inspiring the electoral choices of immigrants across Western Europe, it is necessary to underscore a simple fact: Parties of the left are more disposed than political parties of the right to advance the collective political interests of immigrant voters. As we have already seen, leftist political parties are unambiguously the parties *of* immigrant voters. What I wish to stress here is that, across countries, they are conspicuously the parties *for* immigrant voters in the sense that, to the extent immigrant voters share similar political interests, these interests are most often best articulated, promoted, and advanced by political parties of the left.

Probably the most important direct evidence indicating the special place assumed by immigrants and immigrant interests in the internal politics and the political agendas of parties of the left is the latter's advocacy of policies that target the collective social and political condition of ethnic minorities. During the 1970s, for example, social-democratic parties across Scandinavia advocated for the right to vote of long-term residents as part of a larger strategy of and commitment to immigrant incorporation (Layton-Henry, 1991: 120). Similarly, since the 1960s the British Labour Party has adopted numerous policy commitments that are transparently intended to privilege the special concerns and further the collective interests of Britain's ethnic minorities. These commitments have included the enactment of several race relations acts, the creation and empowerment of a national race relations regulatory watchdog, and the adoption of proactive procedures for selecting ethnic minority parliamentary candidates (Messina, 1989). Especially pertinent about these commitments is that they have been adopted by a political party that is more credible and inspires greater political confidence among ethnic minorities than other political parties in Britain. Indeed, in an opinion survey in 1991 Asian voters preferred the Labour Party over the ostensibly more racially progressive Liberal Democratic Party on the issue of immigration by a margin of 22 to 1 (Harris Research Centre, 1991).

What, specifically, do immigrant voters expect of political parties of the left? Numerous scholars appropriately stress that ethnic minorities are concerned with the same core issues that preoccupy natives. According to Lambert (1997: 2), North Africans have disproportionately joined or become activists within the Socialist Party (PS) in Belgium since 1994 for many of the same reasons as whites: "political ambition, economic interests (getting a job), social interests (getting council housing), and political convictions." In a similar vein, ethnic minorities in Britain consistently rank crime, education, the economy, unemployment, and housing high on their list of pressing issues (Ali and Percival, 1993).

That the aforementioned are issues of concern for both ethnic minorities and natives is no surprise; they are, after all, the core issues of contemporary domestic politics. These issues are especially salient for the lower socioeconomic classes, which include most ethnic minorities. However, the concerns of ethnic minorities are far from exhausted by these issues. On the contrary, in stark contrast to a majority of natives, ethnic minorities are concerned with a wide range of race- and immigration-related issues that indirectly or directly fall within the purview of politics. These concerns include the overall social and racial climate, the effectiveness of laws pertaining to racial discrimination, and the fair enforcement of the immigration rules (Adolino, 1998).

The British Labour Party's proclivity to adopt issue positions that are attractive to ethnic minorities is reinforced, if not mostly inspired, by the party's ideological affinity with ethnic minority political interests, especially at the national level. Consider, for example, the fairly liberal attitudes of Labour elites toward the issues of nonwhite repatriation and immigration restrictions (Messina, 1998: 61). Consider, too, the broad political and social contexts within which these progressive attitudes are held and expressed. Ethnic minorities in Britain have historically made up only a fraction of the overall national electorate. Contrary to the argument forwarded by some analysts (Ali and Percival, 1993; Community Relations Commission, 1975), ethnic minority voters have had little, if any, net positive impact on Labour's electoral fortunes in British general elections (Messina, 1989: 151–160). Ethnic minorities as a group possess only modest political resources. Few national organizations or strong political pressure groups exist to promote their collective political interests. Moreover, racial hostility toward ethnic minorities pervades British society, and from time to time such hostility finds virulent political expression (Messina, 1989: 103–125). Yet despite these powerful disincentives, Labour elites have historically advocated policies that privilege the special social position and political claims of Britain's ethnic minorities (Messina, 1989: 132, 171). Labour's historical origins as a political party of the working class and as a political champion of the socioeconomically disadvantaged, the politically vulnerable, and the socially marginalized especially disposes the party to identify with the political concerns of ethnic minorities.

The British Labour Party is certainly not unusual among political parties of the left in embracing immigrants and their political interests. In the Netherlands, for example, the Social Democrats (PvdA), Social Liberals (D66), and Greens (GroenLinks) have been in the forefront of political initiatives specifically through their advocacy of the instrument of naturalization, to better integrate immigrants into Dutch Society (Vink, 2001: 886). Indeed, on the basis of public opinion data as well as anecdotal evidence, McLaren (2001: 89) persuasively argues that what ideologically unites left-leaning voters and leftist political elites and parties across Western Europe is the proclivity of each to be more receptive toward immigrants and their interests than politically right voters and elites, especially with regard to the protection of the political rights of immigrants.

Despite the obvious electoral hazards, and especially the risk of alienating racially prejudiced, white, working-class voters, political parties of the left in Western Europe, for ideological and other reasons, have committed themselves to championing the interests of immigrants. If anything, this commitment has only deepened with time, in part, as we shall see, as a consequence of the investment of political energy and loyalty made by an entire generation of ethnic minority political activists in political parties of the left.

■ The Elevation of Ethnic Minorities to Elective Office

The primary focus of scholars concerned with ethnic minorities' political representation in Western Europe has been and continues to be their physical inclusion in local and national government. For the most part, these scholars concur on two points: Ethnic minorities are significantly underrepresented at all levels of politics and government (Togeby, 1999; van Heelsum, 2000); and their underrepresentation creates serious impediments to the achievement of ethnic political equality and, more generally, to the successful integration of ethnic minorities into West European societies (Bäck and Soininen, 1998).

There is no disputing the fact that, at every level of government, increasing numbers of ethnic minorities are winning and holding elective office across Western Europe. In London, for example, the ranks of non-white local councilors has swelled from 35 in 1978 to 79 in 1984, 179 in 1990, 213 in 1994, and 230 in 2001 (Le Lohé, 1998: 94; Improvement and Development Agency, 2001). Across England and Wales the total number of ethnic minority councilors leaped within the span of five years (1992–1997) from 342 to 662 before recently falling back to 544 (Table 11.4.5). In the Danish cities of Copenhagen, 7 of 55 representatives, and Arhus, 2 of 31 representatives were elevated to the local council in 1997 from the immigrant population (Togeby, 1999). Across France the number of Beur (French-born Arab) local councilors rose dramatically during the 1980s from 12 in 1983 to 390 in 1989 (*Economist,* 1989: 55). A more recent survey of 198 cities in France discovered that North African local councilors constitute 2.4 percent of all elected local officials (Bryant, 2002). In Belgium the number of communal councilors across the country expanded sevenfold, from 13 in 1994 to 92 in 2000 (Suffrage Universel, Undated:a). As Table 11.4.6 demonstrates, the representation of ethnic minority councilors across the Netherlands also significantly increased during the late 1990s, approximately doubling from 1994–1998 to 1998–2000. Within six of the country's largest cities the aggregate number of ethnic minority councilors more than quadrupled within a period of only a decade and a half (1986–2000).

Moreover, ethnic minority advances in attaining elective office have not been confined to the local level. In France a candidate of sub-Saharan origin was elected to the National Assembly in 1997, although no ethnic minority candidate was successful in 2002. In Britain the number of successful ethnic minority candidates for the House of Commons has incrementally increased over time: from 4 in 1987 to 6 in 1992, 9 in 1997, 12 in 2001, and 15 in 2005. Another 4 ethnic minority members represented Britain in the 1999–2004 European Parliament. In Belgium 9 of 150 deputies in the Federal Parliament and 6 of 71 senators were from the ethnic minority population in 2003. In Germany 4 ethnic minorities held seats

Table 11.4.5   Ethnic Minority Local Councilors in England and Wales, 1992–2001

Ethnic Group	Number of Councilors
Black Caribbean	97
Black African	17
Black other	21
Indian	159
Pakistani	118
Bangladeshi	32
Chinese	1
Mixed	81
Other	137
Total (1997)	662
Percentage local councilors (1997)	3.0
Total (1992)	342
Percentage local councilors (1992)	1.6
Total (2001)	544
Percentage local councilors (2001)	2.5

Source: Commission for Racial Equality, *CRE Factsheets: Ethnic Minorities in Britain* (London: Commission for Racial Equality, 1999), Table 5; Andrew Geddes, "Race Related Political Participation and Representation in the UK," *Revue Européenne des Migrations Internationales*, 14(2) (1998): 41; IDeA and EO, *National Census of Local Authority Councillors in England and Wales 2001* (London: IdeA and EO, 2003).

Table 11.4.6   Ethnic Minority Local Councilors in Six Dutch Cities, 1986–2000

City	1986–1990	1990–1994	1994–1998	1998–2000
Amsterdam	3	4	8	11
Rotterdam	1	2	2	8
Den Haag	1	3	2	6
Utrecht	0	3	4	6
Eindhoven	2	1	2	1
Zaanstad	1	1	3	3
Total	8	14	21	35
National total	—	—	74	150

Source: Anja van Heelsum, "Political Participation of Migrants in the Netherlands," paper presented to the Metropolis Conference, Vancouver, BC, Canada, November 13–20, 2000.

in the Bundestag, the lower national legislative body, while an additional 3 were members of the European Parliament in 2003. In the Netherlands, where ethnic minorities are arguably better represented than in any other national parliament in Western Europe, 11 ethnic minorities were elected to the Tweede Kamer in May 2002, an increase of 1 from the previous election in 1998 (Suffrage Universel, Undated:b).

Given the demonstrated affinity of political parties of the left for immigrants and the strong attachment of ethnic minority voters to the political left, it is hardly surprising that the vast majority of ethnic minority local and national politicians in Western Europe represent these parties. In Germany, for example, 15 of 16 of the combined ethnic minority Bundestag deputies, deputies of state parliaments, and members of the European Parliament represented either the Social Democratic Party or the Greens in 2003 (Suffrage Universel, Undated:c). The lone exception within the group, a Free Democratic Party (FDP) deputy in the lower legislative house in Hesse, defected from the Greens. In both Britain and Belgium the pattern is much the same. All but a few ethnic minority candidates elected to the British House of Commons since 1987 have represented the Labour Party. Moreover, a combined average of more than 80 percent of ethnic minority councilors across England and Wales campaigned under Labour's political banner in 1997 and 2001. In Belgium ethnic minority politicians are overwhelmingly affiliated with either the Socialist Party (PS) or the Greens (Agalev) (Suffrage Universel, Undated:a). Only the conservative liberal Liberal Reform Party (PRL)-FDP has succeeded in getting ethnic minority candidates elected to political office in significant numbers (Jacobs, Martiniello, and Rea, 2002).

In the Netherlands, too, ethnic minority politicians have mostly assumed elective office under the sponsorship of political parties of the left (van Heelsum, 2000). However, this pattern was disturbed somewhat in May 2002 when three ethnic minority candidates for the National Assembly won office under the banner of the xenophobic party, Pim Fortuyn List.

The aforementioned gains, while tangible and impressive, do not ultimately blunt the criticism that ethnic minorities are underrepresented in local and national parliaments in relation to their presence in society and the electorate. In several of the immigration-receiving countries the number of immigrant citizens holding elective office at the local level falls between 2 and 4 percent of all office holders, or approximately half or less of the percentage of ethnic minorities within the electorate. For example, although the number of Asian and Afro-Caribbean local councilors in Britain has increased by 59 percent over the past decade, at fewer than 3 percent of all local councilors in England and Wales, it is still well below the percentage of ethnic minorities within the electorate (approximately 5.5 percent). Moreover, if ethnic minorities were represented within the House of Commons in the same proportion that they are represented within the British population, the number of ethnic minority members of Parliament would be closer to 51 than the current 15.

This disparity, or "representational gap," is further reflected in the data contained in Tables 11.4.7 and 11.4.8. As Table 11.4.7 demonstrates, among five of the most significant countries of immigration within Western Europe (Belgium, Britain, France, Germany, and the Netherlands), only in

Table 11.4.7   Ethnic Minority Deputies in National Parliaments, 2002

Country	Minority Deputies	Minority Deputies as Percentage of Total Deputies	Representation Index[a]
Belgium	9	6.0	−0.32
Britain	12	1.8	−0.67
France	0	0	−1
Germany	4	0.6	−0.93
Netherlands	11	7.3	0.78

Source: Suffrage Universel, *Les Mandataires d'origine non-européenne élus en Belgique*, http://users.skynet.be/suffrage-universel/bemiel.htm (undated:a); Suffrage Universel, *Elus d'origine non-européenne aux Pays-Bas*, http://users.skynet.be/suffrage-universel/nlmiel.htm (undated:b); Suffrage Universel, *Elus allemands d'origine non-européenne*, http://users.skynet.be/suffrage-universel/demiel.htm (undated:c).
Note: a. Representation index = share of political representatives − share of the population/share of the population.

Table 11.4.8   Proportion of Immigrants Among Elected Representatives, 1979–1994, and Representation Index (RI) in Local Government, 1979 and 1992, in Sweden (percentage)

	1979	1988	1991	1994	RI 1979	RI 1992
Foreign born						
Local council	3.7	4.3	4.2	4.6	−0.54	−0.48
County council	2.5	4.0	4.0	4.4	−0.69	−0.51
Resident alien						
Local council	0.7	0.9	0.7	0.9	−0.82	−0.83
County council	0.2	0.6	0.5	0.5	−0.95	−0.91

Source: Reproduced from multiple sources in Henry Bäck and Maritta Soininen, "Immigrants in the Political Process," *Scandinavian Political Studies* 21(1) (1998): 41.

the Netherlands is the representation index positive for ethnic minority national parliamentarians. As cited earlier, there were no ethnic minority representatives within the French National Assembly in 2003, despite the growing number of Beur politicians at the local level. At only 4 of 669 deputies, there are relatively few ethnic minority members of the German Bundestag. Moreover, as Table 11.4.8 makes clear, the representation index of immigrants among elected representatives at the local level in Sweden, while improving over time, remained negative during the 1990s.

What is the ultimate significance of the underrepresentation of ethnic minority politicians? What are its implications for the representation of ethnic minority political interests? These questions are far from straightforward, in part because we have little evidence of the impact that ethnic minorities actually have had whenever they have attained elective office, but mostly because ethnic minorities are not currently well represented in West European politics and government. Indeed, because the answers to these questions are not obvious, it is not self-evident that the collective political interests of ethnic minorities across Western Europe automatically would be advanced if minorities were better represented in government. It is not clear that the election of more ethnic minority candidates, irrespective of group identification and loyalty, ideological orientation, and political party affiliation would, on balance, accelerate the progress of collective ethnic minority political concerns. In fact, if the policy preferences of natives and immigrants are broadly similar, as some scholars claim, then we can reasonably assume that the equitable inclusion of ethnic minorities in local and national government would have little, if any, practical policy advantages or consequences for ethnic minorities. Certainly, the greater physical presence of ethnic minorities in government might be important symbolically. It could, for example, encourage feelings of political efficacy and foster greater political activism among ethnic minorities.

However, it would not necessarily or automatically effect political change favorable to ethnic minorities (Norris and Lovenduski, 1995: 209–210). If, on the other hand, ethnic minorities are a fairly coherent political constituency with important, common political interests, the representative presence of ethnic minorities in government could yield substantial benefits, provided that a number of additional conditions were satisfied. First, ethnic minority politicians would have to behave as a cohesive parliamentary block, to act as agents or delegates of the larger ethnic minority constituency, and to cooperate to promote the shared interests of this constituency. Second, ethnic minority politicians would require numerous allies among white politicians. Even with much inflated numbers, ethnic minority political representatives and their collective political agenda would be dependent upon the goodwill and political support of their more numerous white colleagues. Third, and most importantly, ethnic minority politicians would need an effective means by which to achieve their collective political goals. In particular, they would require an institutionalized political vehicle to articulate, aggregate, represent, and implement their shared policy priorities. It seems reasonable to conclude that in the absence of these three conditions, the election of a "representative" number of ethnic minority politicians would probably have more symbolic value than practical political effect.

■ The Unevenness of Immigrant Political Incorporation

To this point I have more or less represented the ethnic minorities of Western Europe as a monolithic or homogeneous political constituency.

Bousetta, H. 1997. "Citizenship and Political Participation in France and the Netherlands: Reflections on Two Local Cases." *New Community* 23, no. 2 (April): 215–231.

Bryant, E. 2002. "Feature: Muslim Vote Gains Power in France." *Washington Times*, April 9.

Community Relations Commission. 1975. *Participation of Ethnic Minorities in the General Election of October 1974*. London: Community Relations Commission.

Curtice, J. 1983. "Proportional Representation and Britain's Ethnic Minorities." *Contemporary Affairs Briefing* 6, no. 2 (February). London: Centre for Contemporary Studies.

Economist. March 25, 1989, p. 55.

Electoral Commission. 2002. "Voter Engagement Among Black and Minority Ethnic Communities: Findings." http://electoralcommission.org.uk (July).

Fennema, M., and J. Tillie. 1999. "Political Participation and Political Trust in Amsterdam: Civic Communities and Ethnic Networks." *Journal of Ethnic and Migration Studies* 25, no. 4 (October): 703–726.

Freeman, G. P., and N. Ogelman. 1998. "Homeland Citizenship Policies and the Status of Third Country Nationals in the European Union." *Journal of Ethnic and Migration Studies* 24, no. 4 (October): 769–788.

Hammar, T. 1994. *Democracy and the Nation State: Aliens, Denizens and Citizens in the World of International Migration*. Aldershot, UK: Avebury.

Harris Research Centre. 1991. "Asian Poll, 1991." Richmond, England.

Heisler, B. S. 1992. "Migration to Advanced Industrial Democracies: Socioeconomic and Political Factors in the Making of Minorities in the Federal Republic of Germany." In *Ethnic and Racial Minorities in Advanced Industrial Democracies*. Eds. A. M. Messina, L. Fraga, L. Rhodebeck, and F. Wright. New York: Greenwood Press, pp. 33–48.

Hirschman, A. O. 1970. *Exit, Voice, and Loyalty*. Cambridge, MA: Harvard University Press.

Improvement and Development Agency. 2001. *National Census of Local Authorities in England and Wales 2001*. London: The Employers' Organisation for Improvement and Development Agency.

Ireland, P. 2000. "Reaping What They Sow: Institutions and Immigrant Political Participation in Europe." In *Challenging Immigration and Ethnic Relations Politics*. Eds. R. Koopmans and P. Statham. Oxford: Oxford University Press, pp. 233–282.

Jacobs, D., M. Martiniello, and A. Rea. 2002. "Changing Patterns of Political Participation of Citizens of Imigrant Origin in the Brussels Capital Region: The October 2000 Elections." *Journal of International Migration and Integration* 3, no. 2 (Spring): 201–221.

Jacobson, D. 1996. *Rights Across Borders: Immigration and the Decline of Citizenship*. Baltimore, MD: Johns Hopkins University Press.

Koopmans, R., and P. Statham. 2000. "Migrant Mobilization and Political Opportunities: An Empirical Assessment of Local and National Variation." Paper prepared for the conference Explaining Changes in Migration Policy: Debates from Different Perspectives, Geneva, October 27–28.

Lambert, P-I. 1997. "Political Participation of Belgium's Muslim Population." *Muslim Voices.* http://users.skynet.be/suffrage-universel/bemimude97.htm (September).

Layton-Henry, Z. 1991. "Citizenship and Migrant Workers in Western Europe." In

The Frontiers of Citizenship. Eds. U. Vogel and M. Moran. London: Macmillan, pp. 107–125.

Layton-Henry, Z., and D. T. Studlar. 1985. "The Political Participation of Black and Asian Britons: Integration or Alienation?" *Parliamentary Affairs* 38, no. 3 (Summer): 307–318.

Le Lohé, M. 1998. "Ethnic Minority Participation and Representation in the British Electoral System." In *Race and British Electoral Politics*. Ed. S. Saggar. London: University College London Press, pp. 73–95.

Mahnig, H., and A. Wimmer. 1998. "Zurich: Political Participation and Exclusion of Immigrants in a Direct Democracy." Paper prepared for the Third International Metropolis Conference, Israel, December.

McLaren, L. M. 2001. "Immigration and the New Politics of Inclusion and Exclusion in the European Union: The Effects of Elites and the EU on Individual-Level Opinions Regarding European and Non-European Immigrants." *European Journal of Political Research* 39, no. 1 (January): 81–108.

Messina, A. M. 1989. *Race and Party Competition in Britain.* Oxford: Oxford University Press.

———. 1998. "Ethnic Minorities and the British Party System in the 1990s and Beyond." In *Race and British Electoral Politics.* Ed. S. Saggar. London: University College London Press, pp. 47–69.

Norris, P., and J. Lovenduski. 1995. *Political Recruitment: Gender, Race and Class in the British Parliament.* Cambridge: Cambridge University Press.

Saggar, S. 2001. *Race and Representation: Electoral Politics and Ethnic Pluralism in Britain.* Manchester, UK: Manchester University Press.

Sahlberg, L. ed. 2001. *Excluded from Democracy? On the Political Participation of Immigrants.* Norrköping, Sweden: Integrationverkets.

Soininen, M., and H. Bäck. 1993. "Electoral Participation Among Immigrants in Sweden: Integration, Culture and Participation." *New Community* 20, no. 1 (October): 111–130.

Soysal, Y. N. 1994. *Limits of Citizenship: Migrants and Postnational Membership in Europe.* Chicago: University of Chicago Press.

Statistics Norway. Undated. http://www.ssb.no/english/subjects/00/01/10/stortingsvalg_en/tab-2001-12-17-06-en.html.

———. 1999. "Municipal Council Elections." Oslo: Official Statistics of Norway.

Statistics Sweden. Undated. http://www.scb.se/sm/Me14SM0301_inEnglish.asp.

Suffrage Universel. Undated:a. Les Mandataires d'origine non-européenne élus en Belgique. http://users.skynet.be/suffrage-universel/bemiel.htm.

———. Undated:b. *Elus d'origine non-européenne aux Pays-Bas.* http://users. skynet.be/suffrage-universel/nlmiel.htm.

———. Undated:c. *Elus allemands d'origine non-européenne.* http://users.skynet. be/suffrage-universel/demiel.htm.

Tillie, J. 1998. "Explaining Migrant Voting Behaviour in the Netherlands: Combining the Electoral Research and Ethnic Studies Perspective." *Revue Européenne des Migrations Internationales* 14, no. 2: 71–94.

Togeby, L. 1999. "Migrants at the Polls: An Analysis of Immigrant and Refugee Participation in Danish Local Elections." *Journal of Ethnic and Migration Studies* 25, no. 4 (October): 665–684.

Travis, A. 2002. "British Indians Show Highest Voter Turnout." *Guardian*, July 23. Available online at http://www.guardian.co.uk/guardianpolitics/story/0,,761590,00.html.

Israeli welfare state. As already noted, the judicial branch of the state has played a crucial role in the extension of rights to immigrants in Western countries (Joppke 1999a; Sassen 1998; Weil 1998). In Israel, in contrast, the courts have yet to assume any significant role in the determination of migrant workers' social rights. This is especially surprising given the activist approach adopted by the Supreme Court during the last decade with respect to other topics (Barzilai 1999). It seems that the general exclusionary regime that determines the incorporation of migrant workers in Israel and a weak constitutional basis—there is no written constitution in Israel— have so far precluded the intervention of the judicial system on behalf of the extension of social rights.

An additional actor frequently mentioned as playing a crucial role in the inclusion of migrant workers in the welfare state, especially in Western Europe, is the unions (Miller 1981). The Israeli case, again, proves to be different. Continuing its exclusionary approach towards the Palestinian workers from the occupied territories (Shalev 1992), the General Organization of Workers in Israel (*Histadrut*) has never considered the possibility of including migrant workers in its ranks or of exercising political pressure on the government to extend social rights to them. Beyond the exclusivist ideological principles dominant in the *Histadrut*, this policy is explained mainly by the fact that the migrant workers, as replacement for the Palestinian workers, were incorporated in an already deeply split labor market along national lines. Hence, they do not represent a serious threat to the Israeli workers, and the *Histadrut* has no political incentive to promote equalization of their wages and social benefits. An additional factor contributing to the passivity of the *Histadrut* is its current political and financial situation. A pivotal and powerful actor in the Israeli political-economy in the past, it is currently experiencing an extremely serious crisis that places its survival in doubt (Shalev 1998). Under these conditions, the *Histadrut* has neither the resources nor the political will to advocate for the migrant workers' rights.

Within the general framework of the Israeli migration regime, that in principle rejects the treatment of migrant workers as legitimate clients of the welfare state, the bureaucratic and professional staffs of various state agencies are the major actors in the political processes that define their access to social benefits and services. It is also between these state actors that the main conflicts have developed. These intra-state tensions appear mainly at two axes: the vertical axis, between the central and the local levels of the state apparatus; and the horizontal axis, between the professional and bureaucratic staffs of agencies charged with the provision of social services—i.e., the Ministry of Health and the Social Services Division in the Ministry of Labor and Social Affairs—and the staffs of agencies functioning mainly as carriers of the exclusionary Israeli migration regime and gatekeepers—i.e., the Ministry of Interior and the Authority for Foreign Workers in the Ministry of Labor and Social Affairs. While examining the mechanisms through which the maintenance needs of migrant workers are supposed to be satisfied, we must first distinguish between those workers with residence and work permits and those living and working in Israel without authorization. There are important differences between these populations with respect to their demographic characteristics, needs for social services and the institutional arrangements that shape their employment and living conditions. As part of the state's attempts to prevent the permanent settlement of migrant workers, it precludes the recruitment of married couples. Moreover, as these workers are not entitled to residence rights beyond the work contract period, family reunification is absolutely banned. As a consequence, the documented migrant workers population is characterized by the virtual total absence of families with children. Thus, the major maintenance needs of this workforce are related to the provision of temporary housing and health services to an adult population. In the case of the spontaneous undocumented migrants, in contrast, the state lacks the institutional capabilities to prevent the immigration of married couples, marriage of new couples in the country, and the birth of children. Therefore, among this population there are significant numbers of families and children. Due to this demographic structure, the maintenance and reproduction needs of undocumented migrants include health services for adults and children, as well as education. As we shall see below, there are significant differences in the institutional arrangements for providing these social services to documented and undocumented migrant workers.

Documented Migrant Workers

In accordance with the fundamentals of the Israeli migration regime and the non-recognition of labor migrants as prospective members of society, the basic principle guiding the state's policy on documented migrant workers is to maintain minimal direct involvement with their living conditions. A clear manifestation of this principle is the government's refusal to sign bilateral agreements with the sending countries to formalize and regulate the procedures for the recruitment and employment of foreign workers. As explained by several officials, the government has declined requests by the sending countries on that issue because such international treaties might legally define the state's responsibility for the workers' employment and living conditions, making it accountable to the governments of the sending countries, and hence imposing constraints of an international character on its policies. Moreover, such agreements might be interpreted as indicating the legitimization and formal endorsement by the state of the import of foreign workers.[4]

In line with its policy of avoiding direct involvement and accountabili-

Steinmo, Kathleen Thelen and Frank Longstreth, 90–113. Cambridge: Cambridge University Press.

1993 "Policy Paradigms, Social Learning, and the State." Comparative Politics 25:275–296.

Hall, Peter and Rosemary Taylor
1996 "Political Science and the Three New Institutionalism." Political Studies 44:936–957.

Hammar, Tomas
1990 Democracy and the Nation State—Aliens, Denizens and Citizens in a World of International Migration. Aldershot: Avebury.

Hay, Colin and Daniel Wincott
1998 "Structure, Agency and Historical Institutionalism." Political Studies 46:951–957.

Heinelt, Hubert
1993 "Immigration and the Welfare State in Germany." German Politics 2:78–96.

Hollifield, James
1992 Immigrants, Markets, and States. Cambridge: Harvard University Press.

Jacobson, David
1996 Rights Across Borders—Immigration and the Decline of Citizenship. Baltimore: The Johns Hopkins University Press.

Joppke, Christian
1999a "The Domestic Legal Sources of Immigrant Rights: The United States, Germany and the European Union." EUI Working Paper SPS No. 99/3.
1999b Immigration and the Nation-State. Oxford: Oxford University Press.

Layton-Henry, Zig
1990 "The Challenge of Political Rights." In The Political Rights of Migrant Workers in Western Europe, ed. Zig Layton-Henry, 1–26. London: Sage Publications.

Manpower Planning Authority
1999 The Labor Market in Israel During the Last Months—Statistical Data. Jerusalem: Manpower Planning Authority, The Ministry of Labor and Social Affairs (in Hebrew).

Marcelli, Enrico and David Heer
1998 "The Unauthorized Mexican Immigrant Population and Welfare in Los Angeles County: A Comparative Statistical Analysis." Sociological Perspectives 41:279–302.

March, James and Johan Olsen
1984 "The New Institutionalism: Organizational Factors in Political Life," American Political Science Review 78:734–749.

Marshall, Thomas H.
1950 "Citizenship and Social Class." In Citizenship and Social Class and other Essays, ed. Thomas H. Marshall, 1–85. Cambridge: Cambridge University Press.

Miller, Mark
1981 Foreign Workers in Western Europe—An Emerging Political Force. New York: Praeger.

Ministry of Labor
1990 "Training of Israeli Work Force to the Construction Sector." Avoda V'Revaha V'Bituach Leumi 42:5–8 (in Hebrew).

O'Connor, Julia
  1996 "From Women in the Welfare State to Gendering Welfare State Regimes." Current Sociology 44:1–124.
Quadagno, Jill
  1994 The Color of Welfare. New York: Oxford University Press.
Rosenhek, Zeev
  1998 "Policy Paradigms and the Dynamics of the Welfare State: The Israeli Welfare State and the Zionist Colonial Project." International Journal of Sociology and Social Policy 18:157–202.
Sainsbury, Diane
  1996 Gender, Equality and Welfare States. Cambridge: Cambridge University Press.
Sassen, Saskia
  1996 Losing Control? Sovereignty in an Age of Globalization. New York: Columbia University Press,
  1998 "The *de facto* Transnationalizing of Immigration Policy." In Challenge to the Nation-State—Immigration in Western Europe and the United States, ed. Christian Joppke, 49–85. Oxford: Oxford University Press.
Schmitter Heisler, Barbara
  1992 "Migration to Advanced Industrial Democracies: Socioeconomic and Political Factors in the Making of Minorities in the Federal Republic of Germany (1955–1988)." In Ethnic and Racial Minorities in Advanced Industrial Democracies, ed. Anthony Messina, Luis Fraga, Laurie Rhodebeck and Frederick Wright, 33–48. New York: Greenwood Press.
Schonwalder, Karen
  1996 "Migration, Refugees and Ethnic Plurality as Issues of Public and Political Debates in (West) Germany." In Citizenship, Nationality and Migration in Europe, ed. David Cesarani and Mary Fulbrook, 159–178. London: Routledge.
Schuck, Peter
  1987 "The Status and Rights of Undocumented Aliens in the United States." International Migration 25:125–138.
  1998a "The Legal Rights of Citizens and Aliens in the United States." In Temporary Workers or Future Citizens? Japanese and U.S. Migration Policies, ed. Myron Weiner and Tadashi Hanami, 238–290. New York: New York University Press.
  1998b "The Re-Evaluation of American Citizenship." In Challenge to the Nation-State—Immigration in Western Europe and the United States, ed. Christian Joppke, 191–230. Oxford: Oxford University Press.
Semyonov, Moshe and Noah Lewin-Epstein
  1987 Hewers of Wood and Drawers of Water. Ithaca: ILR Press.
Shafir, Gershon and Yoav Peled
  1998 "Citizenship and Stratification in an Ethnic Democracy." Ethnic and Racial Studies 21:408–427.
Shalev, Michael
  1992 Labour and the Political Economy in Israel. Oxford: Oxford University Press.
  1998 "Zionism and Liberalization: Change and Continuity in Israel's Political Economy." Humboldt Journal of Social Relations 23:219–259.
Smith, Michael and Bernadette Tarallo
  1995 "Proposition 187: Global Trend or Local Narrative? Explaining Anti-

person landing at Schipohl or Sidney airports without a valid entry visa would painfully notice. But for domestic reasons, liberal states are kept from putting this capacity to use. Not globally limited, but self-limited sovereignty explains why states accept unwanted immigrants.

Gary Freeman identified the political process in liberal democracies as one major element of self-limited sovereignty.[19] In contrast to the globalist diagnosis of vindictive yet ineffective restrictionism in Western states, Freeman starts with an opposing observation that the politics of immigration in liberal democracies is, in fact, "broadly expansionist and inclusive,"[20] for which he gives two reasons. First, the benefits of immigration (such as cheap labor or reunited families) are concentrated, while its costs (such as increased social expenses or overpopulation) are diffused. That poses a collective action dilemma, in which the easily organizable beneficiaries of concentrated benefits (such as employers or ethnic groups) will prevail over the difficult-to-organize bearers of diffused costs, that is, the majority population. Borrowing from J. Q. Wilson, Freeman argues that immigration policy in liberal states is "client politics . . . a form of bilateral influence in which small and well-organized groups intensely interested in a policy develop close working relationships with officials responsible for it."[21] Taking place out of public view and with little outside interference, the logic of client politics explains the expansiveness of liberal states vis-a-vis immigrants. Second, the universalistic idiom of liberalism prohibits the political elites in liberal states from addressing the ethnic or racial composition of migrant streams. Freeman calls that the "antipopulist norm." Its most potent expression is the principle of source country universalism in the classic settler nations, which no longer screen potential immigrants for their ethnic or racial fitness. The antipopulist norm will induce elites to seek consensus on immigration policy and to remove the issue from partisan politics.

As I shall argue, a domestic political process under the sway of client politics is one reason why liberal states accept unwanted immigration. But I suggest two modifications to Freeman's model.

First, Freeman ignores the legal process as a second source of expansiveness toward immigrants in liberal states. In fact, the political process is chronically vulnerable to populist anti-immigrant sentiments—even in the United States, as the Congressional anti-immigrant backlash in the wake of California's Proposition 187 testifies. Judges are generally shielded from such pressures, as they are only obliged to the abstract commands of statutory and constitutional law. The legal process is crucial to explaining why European states continued accepting immigrants despite explicit zero-immigration policies since the early 1970s. In open opposition to a restrictionist executive, which switched from elitist client politics to popular national interest politics, courts invoked statutory and constitutional residence and family rights for immigrants. In Europe, the legal rather than the political process explains why states accept unwanted (family) immigration.

In a second modification to Freeman's model, I suggest that there are important variations in the processing of unwanted immigration not just between the United States and Western Europe but within West European states themselves. Freeman lumps together guest-worker- and postcolonial-based immigration regimes and thus overlooks their different logics. In a guest-worker regime, such as Germany's, the state at one point actively lured (de facto) immigrants into the country, and thus is morally constrained not to dispose of them at will once it decides upon a change of course. In a postcolonial regime, such as Britain's, immigration was never actively solicited but passively tolerated for the sake of a secondary goal— the maintenance of empire. Immigration policy is thus by definition a negative control policy against immigration that at no point has been wanted. Differently developed moral obligations toward immigrants in both regimes (among other factors) help explain variations in European states' generosity or firmness toward immigrants.

Discussing the two cases of illegal immigration in the United States and family immigration in Europe,[22] I suggest that liberal states are internally, rather than externally, impaired in controlling unwanted immigration. The failure of the United States to control illegal immigration, particularly from Mexico, is due primarily to the logic of client politics and a strong antipopulist norm that feeds upon America's emphatic self-description as a universal "nation of immigrants" and upon the civil rights imperative of strict nondiscrimination. In Europe, legal and moral constraints kept states from pursuing rigorous zero immigration policies after the closing of new postcolonial and guest-worker immigration in the late 1960s and early 1970s, respectively. Juxtaposing the extreme cases of Germany and Britain, I further suggest that these constraints were most unevenly distributed across Europe, partially reflecting the different logics of guest-worker and postcolonial regimes.

■ Illegal Immigration in the United States

America's enduring incapacity to control illegal immigration is the root cause of its heated immigration debate today. Before investigating this incapacity, it is first necessary to destroy the public myth that the United States has lost control over its borders. This myth, shared by policymakers and academics alike, was powerfully established by the 1981 report of the U.S. Select Commission on Immigration and Refugee Policy, *U.S. Immigration Policy in the National Interest*. It stipulated that immigration policy was "out of control," and that the containment of illegal immigration had to be the first step in regaining control.

law is conceived in the spirit of replacing executive discretion by individual rights to be held against the executive. Foreigners now have statutory (in addition to constitutional) residence and family rights. In several respects, the law went even beyond existing administrative and legal practice. The one-year waiting period for second-generation marriages, okayed by the Constitutional Court in 1987, was abolished. In addition, spouses and children were granted their own residence rights, independent of the head of family. Finally, second—or third—generation foreigners who had temporarily returned home were given the right to return. These measures indicate the independent workings of moral obligations, not just of legal constraints. The new Foreigner Law sticks to the old premise of wrapping up a historically unique immigration episode, while perhaps containing as much liberalization as possible within the inherently limited framework of "foreigner policy."

■ Firm in Britain

In Britain also, family immigration has been subject to the two conflicting imperatives of controls and rights: closing down a historically unique immigration episode, while respecting the family rights of immigrants. But whereas in the German case the rights came to predominate over the controls imperative, in the British case the opposite happened.[61] There are at least two reasons for this outcome: the peculiar character of postcolonial immigration and the absence of a written constitution protecting individual rights.

Postcolonial immigration has been, from the start, unwanted immigration. Accordingly, its political processing can at no point be understood in terms of client politics,[62] as expressed in the widely noted (and criticized) absence of economic considerations in British immigration policy.[63] In contrast to Germany or France, the first oil crisis marks no turning point in Britain. Primary New Commonwealth immigration was effectively halted before 1973 for entirely political reasons. If Britain had acquired its colonial empire in a fit of absentmindedness, its initial approach to postcolonial immigration was strikingly similar. This immigration was at best passively tolerated by elites who stuck too long to the illusion of an empire in which the sun never sets. Until the passing of the first Commonwealth Immigrants Act in 1962, some 800 million subjects of the Crown, inhabiting one-fourth of the earth's landmass, had the right of entry and settlement in Britain. Only a hostile public, aggrieved by the most dramatic secular decline that a modern nation had ever gone through, shook the elites out of their complacency. As if to compensate for past inattention, successive Tory and Labour governments alike have since stuck to the stern imperative that New Commonwealth immigration had to be stopped. A sense of moral obligation, even guilt, has not been absent among British elites, but it has been channeled into the buildup of an elaborate race relations regime. British immigration policy has never known an active phase of recruitment; it has been from the start a negative control policy to keep immigrants out. Directed against unwanted immigration tout court, British immigration policy has been only weakly affected by moral considerations.

Nor has it been mellowed by legal-constitutional constraints, which is the second reason why the controls prevailed over the rights imperative in British family immigration policy. In Britain, which lacks a written constitution and the principle of legal review, there has been little blockading of the political branches of government by recalcitrant courts. Sovereignty is firmly and unequivocally invested in Parliament, which knows no constitutional limits to its lawmaking powers. In immigration policy, this institutional arrangement entails a dualism of extreme legislative openness and executive closure, which, in the absence of a client machine, is detrimental to the interests of immigrants. Parliamentary openness in the formulation of immigration policy keeps lawmakers within the confines of a pervasively restrictionist public opinion. Once a policy has been decided upon, there is executive closure in its implementation, with the Home Office firmly and uncontestedly in charge. In the orthodox view, Britain's "political constitution"[64] is good for democracy because it lets elected officials make decisions that, in other systems, unelected judges make. But in practice it entails executive, rather than parliamentary sovereignty, and it leaves minorities, with or without citizenship, extremely vulnerable to the whims of the majority.

The predominance of the controls over the rights imperative in British family immigration policy can be demonstrated along the fate of Section 1(5) of the 1971 Immigration Act—until its abolishment in 1988, the only family right in British immigration law. It secured for all New Commonwealth men legally settled in Britain before 1973 the right to be joined by their nuclear family from abroad, without any state interference.[65] Section 1(5) thus expressed Britain's special moral and legal obligations toward its primary immigrants. However, when it came into the way of controlling secondary immigration, Section 1(5) was simply abolished by a simple majority vote in Parliament.

The story of the slashing of Section 1(5) is a most extraordinary story because it demonstrates that for the sake of firm immigration controls the British elites have allowed the family rights not just of immigrants, but of all British citizens, to sink below the European standard. It all started with the campaign by the incoming Thatcher government against admitting the foreign husbands and fiancés of female immigrants to Britain. Such asymmetrical treatment of men and women is only a more drastic example of an immigration law shot through with sex discrimination, operating on the premise that the wife should be where the husband as head of the family was. But most importantly, husbands and fiancés were male immigrants, thus blurring the line between secondary and primary immigration. Husbands were perceived as stealth primary immigrants, crowding a strained labor market. Accordingly, the Minister of State defended his new immigration rules of 1979–80, which barred foreign husbands and fiancés from settlement in Britain: "We have a particular aim—to cut back on primary male immigration."[66]

When the European Commission on Human Rights accepted for review the cases of three British immigrant wives harmed by the husband rule, the British government responded with a prophylactic rule change in 1982–83. Whereas (in racially discriminatory intent) the old rules exempted from the husbands ban only (white) "patrial" women either born or ancestrally related to the U.K., the new rules allowed all female British citizens, irrespective of birth or ancestry, to be joined by their foreign husbands and fiancés. This could not be the end of the matter, because settled, noncitizen immigrant women still remained separated from their husbands. However, there has never been a concession in British immigration policy that was not offset by a new restriction elsewhere. Already the old immigration rules contained a number of "safeguards" applied to those patrial women who were exempted from the husband ban: most importantly, they and their spouses had to prove that the "primary purpose" of their marriage was not immigration. In the 1982–83 rules, these safeguards were tightened through shifting the burden of proof from the state to the applicant. Only now, the primary-purpose rule could unfold its venomous powers, providing the government with the perfect tool to close the loophole that had opened up at the sex equalization front.

Predictably, the European Court of Human Rights, in its *Abdulaziz, Cabales and Balkandali* landmark decision of May 1985, found that the 1980 immigration rules were discriminatory on the ground of sex. The Strasbourg rule forced the government to remove the last trace of sex discrimination from its immigration rules. As Home Minister Leon Brittan reckoned in the House of Commons, the government faced two sets of choices.[67] The first was between "narrowing" or "widening" the husbands rule: to prevent settled immigrant men from bringing in their spouses, or to permit settled immigrant wives to bring in theirs. Narrowing would imply dishonoring the government commitment to the family rights of settled immigrant men, enshrined in Section 1(5). Accordingly, the government opted for widening. But in that case, the additional annual intake of an estimated two thousand more immigrant husbands had to be offset by new safeguards. That decision predetermined the government's second choice between "abandoning" or "extending" its marriage tests. To drop the tests currently applied to husbands only "would be to go back on our firm commitment to strict immigration control." But if the tests were to be kept, the mandate of the Strasbourg rule was to apply them equally to men and women. As the home minister concluded his sharp syllogistic exercise, "[W]e cannot expect the European Court to endorse . . . the continuation of giving wives preferential treatment by not making them subject to the same requirements." While a Labour front-bencher railed against the government's "spiteful and vindictive course,"[68] one must admire the cleverness of turning a European court indictment into a means of even firmer immigration control.

As sharp as it appeared, the home minister's syllogism was faulty. The commitment to Section 1(5), which motivated his choice to widen the husband rule, was destroyed by his second choice to extend the safeguards. As long as Section 1(5) was in force, the marriage tests, including the primary-purpose rule, could not be used on immigrant men who had settled in Britain before 1973. If safeguards were to be maintained, the logic of the Strasbourg rule implied the removal of this privilege. Accordingly, even the one bit of generosity in the government's response to the Strasbourg rule was a chimera.

Because Section 1(5), which finally stood in the way of full sex equality in British policy on secondary immigration, had the status of a statutory right, it could be removed only through a change of statutory law. The 1988 Immigration Act successfully removed Section 1(5) in the first change of immigration law in seventeen years. Marked by little noise or protestation, the repeal of Section 1(5) was, nonetheless, an extraordinary event; it had been the only family right that had existed in British immigration law. Only under massive pressure, including from the House of Lords, had it been elevated from discretionary rule to statutory law in the 1971 Immigration Act. Successive governments had reaffirmed their commitment to honor this right.

But all rights are relative in British law, as the painless removal of Section 1(5) by a simple parliamentary majority epitomizes. In dropping it, the government also abandoned the one moral commitment it had undertaken vis-a-vis its primary New Commonwealth immigrants.[69] Now there was no limit to the sway of firm immigration control, affecting even ordinary Britons. Section 1(5) had so far protected white patrial men from the excruciating marriage tests. Now they were subject to them too. The immigration tail came to beat the vast nonimmigrant rest.

■ Conclusion

"Can liberal states control unwanted migration," Gary Freeman recently asked.[70] His answer was: yes, but, it depends—yes, because modern states dispose of considerable infrastructural powers that have not diminished, but increased over time; it depends, because capacity varies across states and across the type of migration subject to control. Such attention to context and detail precludes a quick and generic answer of the yes-or-no variety.

Turning Freeman's 1994 question around, this article explored why, in the cases that liberal states accept unwanted immigration, they actually do so. That liberal states do so on a large scale has been acknowledged in Cornelius, Martin, and Hollifield's "gap hypothesis," which identifies a growing gap between restrictionist policy intent and an expansionist immigration reality. A variety of globalist analyses explained this gap in reference to an externally conditioned decline of sovereignty. These analyses offered generic views of mobilized immigrants and paralyzed states, without identifying the actual mechanisms that make certain states accept certain types of unwanted immigration.

Against the diagnosis of globally limited sovereignty, this article suggested an alternative diagnosis of self-limited sovereignty, starting with Freeman's observation that the dynamics of interest group politics ("client politics") in liberal states makes them inherently expansionist vis-a-vis immigrants. But the political process is only one pillar of self-limited sovereignty, one that is fully entrenched only in a classic settler regime, like the United States. European guest-worker regimes had client politics only until the oil crisis, and a pure postcolonial regime (like Britain) never had it. Thus, other factors must be responsible if such states accept unwanted immigration. In European states, legal constraints in combination with moral obligations toward historically particular immigrant populations— not the logic of client politics—account for continuing (family) immigration despite general zero-immigration policies. But these legal and moral constraints are highly unevenly distributed across European states. Germany, with both a strong constitution celebrating human rights and the moral burdens of a negative history, is an extreme case of self-limited sovereignty, making it one of the most expansive immigrant-receiving countries in the world. Britain has managed to contain unwanted immigration more effectively than any other country in the Western world, but at the cost of trampling on the family rights of her own citizens.

At the risk of stating a tautology, accepting unwanted immigration is inherent in the liberalness of liberal states. Under the hegemony of the United States, liberalism has become the dominant Western idiom in the postwar period,[71] indicating a respect for universal human rights and the rule of law. At the same time, nationalist semantics were delegitimized because of their racist aberrations under Nazism. Only from their firm grounding in the key states of the West could the liberal principles of human rights and the rule of law triumph as "global discourse" around the world. It is therefore strange that in globalist analysis these liberal principles now reappear as external constraints on Western states that are reduced to the nationalist, sovereignty-clinching caricatures they perhaps had been a hundred years earlier, in the high noon of imperialism. Among the global factors either absent or ineffective in this discussion of the political and legal processing of unwanted immigration has been the "international human rights regime," perhaps the single most inflated construction in recent social science discourse. Of course, its absence may be the flaw of this analysis. But that has to be demonstrated.

■ Notes

1. Wayne Cornelius, Philip Martin, and James Hollifield, eds., *Controlling Immigration* (Stanford, Calif.: Stanford University Press, 1994), 3.

2. While frequently used in the literature—see, for example, Gary Freeman, "Can Liberal States Control Unwanted Migration?" *Annals of the American Academy of Political and Social Science* 534 (1994), 17–30; Cornelius, Martin, and Hollifield (fn. 1), 5—the notion of "unwanted" immigration may be criticized on analytical and normative grounds. Analytically, it reifies states as collective individuals with clear-cut preferences. Normatively, it endows a political fighting term with academic respectability. Against such objections, I wish to point out that "unwanted" is used here in a purely descriptive sense, denoting immigration that occurs despite and against explicit state policies. Qualifying illegal immigration in the United States, the first case discussed here, as "unwanted" requires no further elaboration. Family immigration in Europe, the second case, is rendered "unwanted" by uniform zero-immigration policies since the early 1970s.

3. Hannah Arendt, *The Origins of Totalitarianism* (San Diego: Harcourt Brace Jovanovich, 1973), 278.

4. David Jacobson, *Rights across Borders* (Baltimore: Johns Hopkins University Press, 1996). See Stephen Krasner, "Westphalia and All That," in Judith Goldstein and Robert Keohane, eds., *Ideas and Foreign Policy* (Ithaca, N.Y.: Cornell University Press, 1993).

5. See Janice Thomson, "State Sovereignty in International Relations," *International Studies Quarterly* 39 (1995), 213–33.

6. See Peter Evans, Dietrich Rueschemeyer, and Theda Skocpol, eds., *Bringing the State Back In* (New York: Cambridge University Press, 1985).

7. Gary Freeman, "The Decline of Sovereignty?" in Christian Joppke, *Challenge to the Nation-State: Immigration in Western Europe and the United States* (New York: Oxford University Press, 1998).

8. R. Perruchoud, "The Law of Migrants," *International Migration* 24 (1986), 699–715.

9. Luigi Ferrajoli decimates T. H. Marshall's identification of individual rights with citizenship rights, from which a new postnational "logic of personhood" is then construed as a departure. Instead, Ferrajoli shows that most individual (legal and social) rights in liberal states had never been invested in national citizenship and had always revolved around universal personhood. Ferrajoli, *From the Rights of the Citizen to Rights of the Person* (Manuscript, European Forum on Citizenship, European University Institute, Florence, 1995–96). On the logic of personhood, see Yasemin Soysal, *Limits to Citizenship* (Chicago: University of Chicago Press, 1994), chap. 8.

10. Saskia Sassen, Losing Control? *Sovereignty in an Age of Globalization* (New York: Columbia University Press, 1996), chap. 3.

11. Jacobson (fn. 4); Sassen (fn. 10), 95.

12. Sassen (fn. 10), 98.

13. Myron Weiner, *The Global Migration Crisis* (New York: HarperCollins, 1995), 80–83.

14. Janice Thomson and Stephen Krasner, "Global Transactions and the Consolidation of Sovereignty," in Ernst-Otto Czempiel and James Rosenau, eds., *Global Changes and Theoretical Challenges* (Lexington, Mass.: Lexington Books, 1989).

15. Jack Donnelly, "International Human Rights: A Regime Analysis," *International Organization* 40, no. 3 (1986).

16. Soysal (fn. 9).

17. Martha Finnemore, "Norms, Culture and World Politics: Insights from Sociology's Institutionalism," *International Organization* 50, no. 2 (1996), 339.

18. Christian Joppke, "Asylum and State Sovereignty," *Comparative Political Studies* 30, no. 3 (1997), 1.

19. Gary Freeman, "Modes of Immigration Politics in Liberal Democratic States," *International Migration Review* 29, no. 4 (1995).

20. Ibid., 881.

21. Ibid., 886. James Q. Wilson's notion of client politics is built upon Mancur Olson's theory of collective action dilemmas, which states that the organized and active interest of small groups tends to prevail over the nonorganized and nonprotected interest of large groups. The premise of this expected outcome is rational, self-interested action on part of the individual. Wilson, ed., *The Politics of Regulation* (New York: Basic Books, 1980); Olson, *The Logic of Collective Action* (Cambridge: Harvard University Press, 1965).

22. Comparing state responses to illegal immigration and family immigration may seem odd. Why not compare state responses to only one form of immigration, be it illegal or family-based? Illegal immigration in Western Europe is too recent and protean to warrant a comparison with the U.S., where it has been a recurrent stake of political debate for two decades. Family immigration in the United States is not unwanted immigration, in the sense of occurring against the backdrop of explicit zero-immigration policies. Rather, family reunification in the U.S. is the major principle of selecting wanted new quota-immigrants, having precedence even over the criterion of skills. It would have been possible to compare state responses to mass asylum-seeking, the third major source of unwanted immigration in liberal states, but it raises additional issues of refugee law and politics. I have discussed asylum policy separately; see Joppke (fn. 18).

23. Inserted in the 1952 Immigration and Nationality Act at the behest of Texan growers, the so-called Texas Proviso stated that employing illegals did not constitute the criminal act of "harboring." Accordingly, it was legal to employ illegal immigrants, although they were still subject to deportation.

24. *New York Times*, August 16, 1982, A12.

25. *New York Times*, October 5, 1983, 1.

26. Rick Swartz, interview with author, Washington, D.C., March 26, 1994.

27. William Saffire, "The Computer Tattoo," *New York Times*, September 9, 1982, A27.

28. Ellis Cose, *A Nation of Strangers* (New York: Morrow, 1992), 167.

29. Lawrence Fuchs, "The Corpse That Would Not Die: The Immigration Reform and Control Act of 1986," *Revue Européenne des Migrations Internationales* 6, vol. 1 (1990).

30. Aristide Zolberg, 1990. "The Immigration Reform and Control Act of

1986 in Historical Perspective," in Virginia Yans-McLaughlin, ed., *Immigration Reconsidered* (New York: Oxford University Press, 1990), 326–35.

31. Fuchs (fn. 29).

32. Congressman Charles Schumer, quoted in the *New York Times*, October 12, 1984, 17.

33. Swartz (fn. 26).

34. See Frank Bean, Barry Edmonston, and Jeffrey Passel, eds., *Undocumented Migration to the United States* (Washington, D.C.: The Urban Institute, 1990).

35. Demetrios Papademetriou, "Illegal Mexican Migration in the United States and U.S. Responses," *International Migration* 31, nos. 2–3 (1993), 314–48.

36. Another reason for IRCA's failure is that it does not even touch the problem of visa overstayers, which account for over 60 percent of the undocumented population. David Martin, "The Obstacles to Effective Internal Enforcement of the Immigration Laws in the United States" (Paper presented at the AAAS/GAAC Conference on German-American Migration and Refugee Policies, Cambridge, Mass., March 23–26, 1995), 3.

37. Kitty Calavita, "U.S. Immigration and Policy Responses," in Cornelius, Martin, and Hollifield (fn. 1), 71.

38. Martin (ft. 36), 6f.

39. Lamar Smith, Republican representative from Texas, used this phrase to characterize his sweeping House bill that dealt jointly with legal and illegal immigration. "House G. O. P. Moves to Cut Immigration," *New York Times,* June 22, 1995.

40. Peter Schuck, "The Meaning of 187," *The American Prospect* 85 (1995).

41. In its *Pyler v. Doe* decision (1982), the Supreme Court ruled that the children of illegal immigrants have the constitutional right to a public school education. Pyler indicates that, in addition to a political process under the sway of client politics, the legal process has bolstered the position of illegal immigrants in the U.S. For the lack of space, I cannot discuss this further here, but see Peter Schuck, "The Transformation of Immigration Law," *Columbia Law Review* 84, no. 1 (1984).

42. Barbara Jordan, "The Americanization Ideal," *New York Times*, September 11, 1995.

43. "The Strange Politics of Immigration," *New York Times*, December 31, 1995.

44. "Unlikely Allies Battle Congress over Anti-Immigration Plan," *New York Times*, October 11, 1995.

45. "Congress Plans Stiff New Curb on Immigration," *New York Times*, September 25, 1995.

46. Roy Beck, "The Pro-immigration Lobby," *New York Times*, April 30,1996.

47. "House Panel Approves Plan to Register Immigration Status," *New York Times*, November 22, 1995.

48. Quoted in "Senate Votes Bill to Reduce Influx of Illegal Aliens," *New York Times*, May 3, 1996.

49. Schuck (fn. 40), 91.

50. A second example for the absence of source-country universalism in European immigration policy is the phenomenon of ethnic-priority immigration, such as the "patrials" in Britain or the "Aussiedler" (ethnic German resettlers) in Germany, for which there is no parallel in the U.S.

51. See Thomas Faist, "How to Define a Foreigner?" *West European Politics* 17, no. 2 (1994).

52. Kay Hailbronner, "Ausländerrecht und Verfassung," *Neue Juristische Wochenschrift* 36, no. 38 (1983), 2113.

53. See Gerald L. Neuman, "Immigration and Judicial Review in the Federal Republic of Germany," *New York University Journal of International Law* 23 (1990).

54. *Decision of 26 September 1978* (1 BvR 525/77), 186.

55. Between 1973 and 1980, the number of foreign workers in West Germany fell from 2.595 million to 2.070 million; during the same period, the absolute number of foreigners increased from 3.966 million to 4.450 million. Ulrich Herbert, *A History of Foreign Labor in Germany, 1880–1980* (Ann Arbor: University of Michigan Press, 1990), 188. Because the number of asylum seekers was small before 1980, only family reunification can account for the increase.

56. Quoted in *Decision of 12 May 1987* (2 BvR 1226/83, 101, 313/84), p. 33f.

57. The German Constitutional Court thus did not go as far as the French Conseil d'Etat, which (in effect) recognized a constitutional right of family reunification in a famous 1978 decision.

58. The Court thus argued that even aliens not residing in Germany had rights under the Constitution. As Neuman (fn. 53) notes, this went far beyond the most generous rulings of the U.S. Supreme Court regarding the rights of aliens.

59. *Frankfurter Allgemeine Zeitung*, November 9, 1974.

60. Gerhard Baum (FDP), quoted in *Das Parlament* 32, no. 9 (1982).

61. This is recognized in the literature as the "exceptional" efficacy of British immigration control. Gary Freeman even argues: "The British experience demonstrates that it is possible to limit unwanted immigration." Freeman, 1994b. "Britain, the Deviant Case," in Cornelius, Martin, and Hollifield (fn. 1), 297.

62. This processing contrasts the German guest-worker policy, which followed the logic of client politics before the oil crisis and the recruitment stop of 1973.

63. See, for example, Sarah Spencer, ed., *Strangers and Citizens* (London: Rivers Oram Press, 1994).

64. J. A. G. Griffith, "The Political Constitution," *The Modern Law Review* 42, no. 1 (1979).

65. Section 1(5) of the 1971 Immigration Act stipulated: "The rules shall be so framed that Commonwealth citizens settled in the United Kingdom at the coming into force of this Act and their wives and children are not, by virtue of anything in the rules, any less free to come into and go from the United Kingdom than if this Act had not been passed."

66. Quoted in P. Thornberry, "Seven Years On: East African Asians, Immigration Rules and Human Rights," *Liverpool Law Review* 2 (1980), 146.

67. *Parliamentary Debates*, Commons, vol. 83 (1985), cols. 893–96.

68. Gerald Kaufman, quoted in ibid., col. 901.

69. Interestingly, Minister of State Timothy Renton sought to soften this break of commitment by pointing out that those who now profited from Section 1(5) had been infants in 1971: "Those who are receiving the benefit of section 1(5) are not those who were adult males at the time of the 1971 Act but the young children who had then just been born." Renton, quoted in Ibid., col. 856.

70. Freeman (fn. 2).

71. Building on John Ruggie's analysis of "embedded liberalism," James Hollifield has suggested that domestic, "rights-based liberalism" has undermined effective immigration controls in Western states. This is similar to the argument presented here. Hollifield, "Migration and International Relations," *International Migration Review* 26, no. 2 (1992).

12.3 *Jagdish Bhagwati*

Borders Beyond Control

■ A Door That Will Not Close

International migration lies close to the center of global problems that now seize the attention of politicians and intellectuals across the world. Take just a few recent examples.

• Prime Ministers Tony Blair of the United Kingdom and José Maria Aznar of Spain proposed at last year's European Council meeting in Seville that the European Union withdraw aid from countries that did not take effective steps to stem the flow of illegal emigrants to the EU. Blair's outspoken minister for development, Clare Short, described the proposal as "morally repugnant" and it died amid a storm of other protests.

• Australia received severe condemnation worldwide last summer when a special envoy of the UN high commissioner for human rights exposed the deplorable conditions in detention camps that held Afghan, Iranian, Iraqi, and Palestinian asylum seekers who had landed in Australia.

• Following the September 11 attacks in New York City and Washington, D.C., U.S. Attorney General John Ashcroft announced several new policies that rolled back protections enjoyed by immigrants. The American Civil Liberties Union (ACLU) and Human Rights Watch fought back. So did Islamic and Arab ethnic organizations. These groups employed lawsuits, public dissent, and congressional lobbying to secure a reversal of the worst excesses.

• *The Economist* ran in just six weeks two major stories describing the growing outflow of skilled citizens from less developed countries to developed countries seeking to attract such immigrants. The "brain drain" of the 1960s is striking again with enhanced vigor.

These examples and numerous others do not just underline the importance of migration issues today. More important, they show governments attempting to stem migration only to be forced into retreat and accommodation by factors such as civil-society activism and the politics of ethnicity.

Jagdish Bhagwati, "Borders Beyond Control," *Foreign Affairs* 82, no. 1 (Jan./Feb. 2003). © 2003 by the Council on Foreign Relations, Inc. Reprinted by permission of *Foreign Affairs*.

Paradoxically, the ability to control migration has shrunk as the desire to do so has increased. The reality is that borders are beyond control and little can be done to really cut down on immigration. The societies of developed countries will simply not allow it. The less developed countries also seem overwhelmed by forces propelling emigration. Thus, there must be a seismic shift in the way migration is addressed: governments must reorient their policies from attempting to curtail migration to coping and working with it to seek benefits for all.

To demonstrate effectively why and how this must be done, however, requires isolating key migration questions from the many other issues that attend the flows of humanity across national borders. Although some migrants move strictly between rich countries or between poor ones, the most compelling problems result from emigration from less developed to more developed countries. They arise in three areas. First, skilled workers are legally emigrating, temporarily or permanently, to rich countries. This phenomenon predominantly concerns the less developed countries that are losing skilled labor. Second, largely unskilled migrants are entering developed countries illegally and looking for work. Finally, there is the "involuntary" movement of people, whether skilled or unskilled, across borders to seek asylum. These latter two trends mostly concern the developed countries that want to bar illegal entry by the unskilled.

All three problems raise issues that derive from the fact that the flows cannot be effectively constrained and must instead be creatively accommodated. In designing such accommodation, it must be kept in mind that the illegal entry of asylum seekers and economic migrants often cannot be entirely separated. Frustrated economic migrants are known to turn occasionally to asylum as a way of getting in. The effective tightening of one form of immigrant entry will put pressure on another.

■ Software Engineers, Not Huddled Masses

Looking at the first problem, it appears that developed countries' appetite for skilled migrants has grown—just look at Silicon Valley's large supply of successful Indian and Taiwanese computer scientists and Venture capitalists. The enhanced appetite for such professionals reflects the shift to a globalized economy in which countries compete for markets by creating and attracting technically skilled talent. Governments also perceive these workers to be more likely to assimilate quickly into their new societies.

This heightened demand is matched by a supply that is augmented for old reasons that have intensified overtime. Less developed countries cannot offer modern professionals the economic rewards or the social conditions that they seek. Europe and the United States also offer opportunities for immigrant children's education and career prospects, that are nonexistent at home.

These asymmetries of opportunity reveal themselves not just through cinema and television, but through the immediacy of experience. Increasingly, emigration occurs after study abroad. The number of foreign students at U.S. universities, for example, has grown dramatically; so has the number who stay on. In 1990, 62 percent of engineering doctorates in the United States were given to foreign-born students, mainly Asians. The figures are almost as high in mathematics, computer science, and the physical sciences. In economics, which at the graduate level is a fairly math-intensive subject, 54 percent of the Ph.D.s awarded went to foreign students, according to a 1990 report of the American Economic Association.

Many of these students come from India, China, and South Korea. For example, India produces about 25,000 engineers annually. Of these, about 2,000 come from the Indian Institutes of Technology (IITS), which are modeled on MIT, and the California Institute of Technology. Graduates of IITS accounted for 78 percent of U.S. engineering Ph.D.s granted to Indians in 1990. And almost half of all Taiwanese awarded similar Ph.D.s in the United States had previously attended two prestigious institutions: the National Taiwan University and the National Cheng Kung University. Even more telling, 65 percent of the Korean students who received science and engineering Ph.D.s in the United States were graduates of Seoul National University. The numbers were almost as high for Beijing University and Tsinghua University, elite schools of the People's Republic of China.

These students, once graduated from American universities, often stay on in the United States. Not only is U.S. graduate education ranked highest in the world, but it also offers an easy way of immigrating. In fact, it has been estimated that more than 70 percent of newly minted, foreign-born Ph.D.s remain in the United States, many becoming citizens eventually. Less developed countries can do little to restrict the numbers of those who stay on as immigrants. They will, particularly in a situation of high demand for their skills, find ways to escape any dragnet that their home country may devise. And the same difficulty applies, only a little less starkly, to countries trying to hold on to those citizens who have only domestic training but are offered better jobs abroad.

A realistic response requires abandoning the "brain drain" approach of trying to keep the highly skilled at home. More likely to succeed is a "diaspora" model, which integrates present and past citizens into a web of rights and obligations in the extended community defined with the home country as the center. The diaspora approach is superior from a human rights viewpoint because it builds on the right to emigrate, rather than trying to restrict it. And dual loyalty is increasingly judged to be acceptable rather than reprehensible. This option is also increasingly feasible. Nearly 30 countries now offer dual citizenship. Others are inching their way to similar options. Many less developed countries, such as Mexico and India, are in the process of granting citizens living abroad hitherto denied benefits such as the right to hold property and to vote via absentee ballot.

However, the diaspora approach is incomplete unless the benefits are balanced by some obligations, such as the taxation of citizens living abroad. The United States already employs this practice. This author first recommended this approach for developing countries during the 1960s and the proposal has been revived today. Estimates made by the scholars Mihir Desai Devesh Kapur and John McHale demonstrate the reality that even a slight tax on Indian nationals abroad would substantially raise Indian government revenues. The revenue potential is vast because the aggregate income of Indian-born residents in the United States is 10 percent of India's national income, even though such residents account for just 0.1 percent of the American population.

■ Unstoppable

The more developed countries need to go through a similar dramatic shift in the way they respond to the influx of illegal economic immigrants and asylum seekers. Inducements or punishments for immigrants' countries of origin are not working to stem the flows, nor are stiffer border-control measures, sanctions on employers, or harsher penalties for the illegals themselves.

Three sets of factors are behind this. First, civil-society organizations, such as Human Rights Watch, the ACLU, and the International Rescue Committee, have proliferated and gained in prominence and influence. They provide a serious constraint on all forms of restrictive action. For example, it is impossible to incarcerate migrants caught crossing borders illegally without raising an outcry over humane treatment. So authorities generally send these people back across the border, with the result that they cross again and again until they finally get in.

More than 50 percent of illegals, however, now enter not by crossing the Rio Grande but by legal means, such as tourist visas, and then stay on illegally. Thus, enforcement has become more difficult without invading privacy through such measures as identity cards, which continue to draw strong protests from civil liberties groups. A notable example of both ineffectual policy and successful civil resistance is the 1986 Sanctuary movement that surfaced in response to evidence that U.S. authorities were returning desperate refugees from war-torn El Salvador and Guatemala to virtually certain death in their home countries. (They were turned back because they did not meet the internationally agreed upon definition for a refugee.) Sanctuary members, with the aid of hundreds of church groups, took the law into their own hands and organized an underground railroad to spirit endangered refugees to safe havens. Federal indictments and convictions followed, with five Sanctuary members given three-to-five-year sentences. Yet, in response to a public outcry and an appeal from Senator Dennis DeConcini (D-Ariz.), the trial judge merely placed the defendants on probation.

Sanctions on employers, such as fines, do not fully work either. The General Accounting Office, during the debate over the 1986 immigration legislation that introduced employer sanctions, studied how they had worked in Switzerland and Germany. The measures there failed. Judges could not bring themselves to punish severely those employers whose violation consisted solely of giving jobs to illegal workers. The US. experience with employer sanctions has not been much different.

Finally, the sociology and politics of ethnicity also undercut enforcement efforts. Ethnic groups can provide protective cover to their members and allow illegals to disappear into their midst. The ultimate constraint, however, is political and results from expanding numbers. Fellow ethnics who are U.S. citizens, legal immigrants, or amnesty beneficiaries bring to bear growing political clout that precludes tough action against illegal immigrants. Nothing matters more than the vote in democratic societies. Thus the Bush administration, anxious to gain Hispanic votes, has embraced an amnesty confined solely to Mexican illegal immigrants, thereby discarding the principle of nondiscrimination enshrined in the 1965 Immigration and Nationality Act.

■ Minding the Open Door

If it is not possible to effectively restrict illegal immigration, then governments in the developed countries must turn to policies that will integrate migrants into their new homes in ways that will minimize the social costs and maximize the economic benefits. These policies should include children's education and grants of limited civic rights such as participation in school-board elections and parent teacher associations. Governments should also assist immigrants in settling throughout a country, to avoid depressing wages in any one region. Greater development support should be extended to the illegal migrants' countries of origin to alleviate the poor economic conditions that propel emigration. And for the less developed countries, there is really no option but to shift toward a diaspora model.

Some nations will grasp this reality and creatively work with migrants and migration. Others will lag behind, still seeking restrictive measures to control and cut the level of migration. The future certainly belongs to the former. But to accelerate the progress of the laggards new institutional architecture is needed at the international level. Because immigration restrictions are the flip side of sovereignty, there is no international organization today to oversee and monitor each nation's policies toward migrants, whether inward or outward bound.

The world badly needs enlightened immigration policies and best practices to be spread and codified. A World Migration Organization would begin to do that by juxtaposing each nation's entry, exit, and residence policies toward migrants, whether legal or illegal, economic or political, skilled or unskilled. Such a project is well worth putting at the center of policymakers' concerns.

12.4 *Mark J. Miller & Boyka Stefanova*

NAFTA and the European Referent: Labor Mobility in European and North American Regional Integration

The election of Vicente Fox in Mexico and of George W. Bush in the United States led to a short-lived bilateral "honeymoon" in 2001 that waned prior to the terrorist attacks of September 11, not after them. One aspect of the honeymoon period involved recurrent allusions to a European referent for NAFTA [North American Free Trade Agreement] in US and Mexican press coverage of a possible immigration policy initiative. In several declarations, most notably President Fox's speech at the Ottawa summit of the NAFTA partners in 2001, he spoke of his vision of a border-free North America where workers enjoyed freedom of movement. The seeming European referent for NAFTA, then, was freedom of movement within the European space guaranteed European citizens under Articles 48 and 49 of the Treaty of Rome.

If President Fox and other advocates of a US-Mexico immigration policy initiative actually espouse an Article 48–like freedom of labor mobility within NAFTA, they would appear to be overlooking fundamental differences between regional integration in North America and Europe. We suggest that the Turkish-EU and Moroccan-EU relationships constitute a more appropriate European referent for NAFTA than Article 48. Turkish and Moroccan bids for membership in the EC and EU failed for many reasons, but above all because of the prospect for large-scale emigration by Turks or Moroccans to other member-states long after the end of a transition period.

■ Two Different Creatures

The history of European federalism pre-dates World War II. But the trauma of the Holocaust and the vast destruction of the two world wars convinced European leaders of a need for regional integration in order to prevent recurrence of war. Subsequent regional integration in Europe was security-

Mark J. Miller and Boyka Stefanova, "NAFTA and the European Referent: Labor Mobility in European and North American Regional Integration," Jean Monnet/Robert Shumann Paper Series 3, no. 1 (June 2003).

driven, and involved a European governance project. While Europeans differed in their approaches to regional integration, the founders of the European Coal and Steel Community (ECSC) launched a federalist project that was to evolve incrementally. A vision of freedom of worker or employee mobility already informed the creation of the ECSC.[1]

It is important to recall, however, that Italy's strategy to facilitate emigration through regional integration encountered great resistance from other member-states.[2] While the Treaty of Rome was signed in 1957, Article 48 did not become effective until 1968. In the meantime, Italy had undergone a remarkable transformation, in large part attributable to its membership in the European Community. By the time Italians possessed freedom of labor mobility, they were little inclined to exercise the right. While Italians constituted the largest group of intra-EC "community workers," such workers comprised a very tiny share of the combined workforce of the EC.[3] By 1990, the foreign resident population from other EU states had grown to over 5.5 million in a total population of 370 million, about 1.5 percent of the EU's total population.[4] The relative paucity of labor mobility between member-states of the EC and the EU contrasts strikingly with the current situation within the NAFTA area, where some eight to nine million Mexican-born individuals reside in the United States, about half illegally. In 1972, there were only 750,000 Mexicans resident in the US.

European regional integration largely involved the melding of societies at similar levels of socio-economic development. The provision of development assistance to lagging areas within the European space helped narrow socio-economic disparities, in areas like Southern Italy which, in turn, reduced incentives for emigration under Article 48. Hence, the modest propensity to migrate for employment within the European space, while often decried, in fact reflects an underlying socio-economic reality that has a counterpart in the U.S.-Canadian relationship but not yet with Mexico.

NAFTA emerged in a different historical context. It was neither security-driven nor did it involve a federalist project. Instead, it extended a free-trade area created in 1988 between Canada and the United States in response to, in retrospect, exaggerated apprehensions over the trade implications of the Single European Act. Indeed, it was these fears that gave rise to the notion of Fortress Europe, a term now inappropriately used to characterize EU-area migration policies. The origins of NAFTA can be traced to the creation of the Commission for the Study of International Migration and Cooperative Economic Development (CSIMCED) authorized by the Immigration Reform and Control Act of 1986. Essentially, CSIMCED examined alternative or complementary strategies for prevention of illegal migration to the one found in IRCA. CSIMCED commissioned scores and scores of studies including one that examined the likely effects of trade liberalization between the United States and Mexico upon the agricultural sector in Mexico and Mexican emigration. It warned that trade liberalization would adversely affect the *ejido* sector of traditional small-scale farms which employed millions of Mexicans and which sustained one third of the Mexican population.[5] Philip L. Martin would later refine his insights into a theory of a migration hump in which emigration from Mexico to the United States would increase significantly over the short to medium term before eventually declining over the long term in a scenario of trade liberalization.[6]

President Salinas of Mexico proposed NAFTA to President George Bush, Senior. The American president then referred the question to his National Security Council, which supported the proposal on the grounds that the United States and Mexico had become so interdependent, in large part due to migration, that untoward developments in Mexico would adversely affect the United States.

Hence, security concerns figured in the Bush administration's embrace of the NAFTA concept, but much less centrally than in the European regional integration context. Moreover, the NAFTA proposal involved no explicit political project as in the European context. NAFTA would deepen socio-economic interdependence between the three partner states but all three jealously guarded their sovereign prerogatives. Indeed, so sharp were differences between the United States and Mexico over illegal migration that a decision was made to exclude the "poison pill" of migration from NAFTA negotiations. Paradoxically, then, only one minor formal clause of the NAFTA treaty pertains to migration while, in fact, migration control concerns figured centrally in the diplomatic initiative. Indeed, both President Salinas and President Clinton would argue in support of signature and ratification of the NAFTA treaty that it would reduce illegal Mexican migration to the United States. To paraphrase President Salinas, either the United States would get Mexican tomatoes or Mexican workers.

A decade after the signing of the NAFTA treaty, Mexican immigration to the United States is surging. Preliminary analysis of the 2000 census suggests that the proportion of illegal entrants among Mexican migrants to the United States has increased significantly. The downward slope in the expected hump has yet to materialize although there are Mexican experts who contend that changing demographic and socio-economic realities in Mexico will result in decreasing Mexican emigration to the United States soon.

In retrospect, Article 48–like freedom of movement with the NAFTA area can at best be termed visionary. There are those who view socio-economic integration as mechanistically or inevitably leading to spillover and deeper political integration between governments involved in a regional integration process. However, it took the German Question, the resultant commitment to regional integration to prevent recurrence of war and a fed-

Turks from former Ottoman lands. Turkey is also contemplating imposition of employer sanctions and reform of its policies towards asylum seekers.[16] These proposed changes could be quite significant as Turkey has long tolerated the presence of three to four million aliens, most of whom hail from nearby countries like Iran and Iraq. If Turkey were to alter its de facto policy of toleration, and thereby more closely approximate public policies in the EU area, there could be significant repercussions upon a region already confronting politically destabilizing population movements, such as the massive inflow of Iraqis to Jordan.

Turkey's relationship to the EU somewhat parallels Mexico's to the United States, although the former involves a customs union while the latter a free trade agreement. In both instances, the legacy of past temporary foreign worker recruitment policies weighs heavily. That legacy mitigates against full membership for Turkey in the EU, turning on its head the unwarranted assumption that worker migration necessarily leads to deeper socioeconomic and political integration.

Mexico continues to seek expanded admission of its citizens as temporary workers in the US and apparently would regard a return to *bracero*-like policy as progress in the U.S.-Mexico bilateral relationship. But the *bracero* policy was terminated in 1964 for good reasons just as were guest worker policies in the 1972 to 1974 period in Western Europe. Temporary foreign worker recruitment policies in Europe and North America constituted flawed public policies that resulted in considerable unanticipated settlement and illegal migration. There is no good reason to think that expanded admissions of temporary foreign workers from Mexico to the United States is going to hasten the day that President Fox's vision of a border-free North America arrives. The track record of temporary foreign worker admissions policies contributing to harmonious bilateral or regional relations is unpromising.

Turkey, thus, may constitute a more relevant European referent for NAFTA. As long as Turkey lags far behind the EU economically and long-term prospects for high rates of Turkish emigration remain, deeper integration with the EU through fall membership will prove elusive. When guest worker policies in Western Europe were curbed or stopped in the early 1970s, several million Turks were registered for recruitment.[17] Some thirty years later, full membership for Turkey in the EU remains elusive, in part because of the perception that too many Turks would emigrate if granted freedom of labor mobility within the EU.

■ Comparing Labor Migration within NAFTA and the EU: A Research Agenda

There have been a number of efforts to compare the European and North American migratory systems, and policy-oriented transatlantic comparisons of international migration stretch back to the mid-1970s, if not earlier. Yet important misapprehensions persist as attested to by unwarranted allusions to a European referent to NAFTA in the U.S.-Mexico immigration honeymoon period. This suggests that much more work needs to be done by all concerned parties, including Americans.

Migration issues can no longer be dismissed as peripheral or esoteric. They vitally affect security, inclusive of that of migrants. The United States does not seem to appreciate fully how European security concerns are related to the prevention of "unwanted" migration. Transatlantic tensions over Iraq arise, in part, from differing perceptions of security threats. The EU wants to stabilize the Middle East, the source of so much immigration to the EU. It understands that a likely consequence of further conflict in the Middle East will be greater pressure for emigration to the EU.

The United States appears oblivious to the fears of its European allies, inclusive of Turkey. Indeed, it appears to view the war with Iraq as possibly resulting in regime change and democratization. It courts elements of the approximately four million expatriate Iraqis, out of a total population of some twenty-two million, to help bring about democratization.

Meanwhile, Arab scholars and leaders warn of a war opening the proverbial jaws of hell. Mass movement of people appears to figure centrally in this apocalyptic vision. Surely it is high time for transatlantic comparisons of immigration and migration policies to take their implications for security seriously, especially if war with Iraq increases the appeal of al-Qaida amongst Muslims in the transatlantic area, as seems predictable.

■ Notes

1. A. Geddes, *Immigration and European Integration: Towards Fortress Europe?* (Manchester and NY: Manchester University Press, 2000), p. 45.

2. F. Romero, "Migration as an Issue in European Interdependence and Integration: The Case of Italy," in A. Milward, F. Lynch, R. Ranieri, F. Romero and V. Sørenson (eds.), *The Frontier of National Sovereignty* (London: Routledge, 1993).

3. H. Werner, *Freizügigkeit der Arbeitskräfte und die Wanderungsbewegungen in den Ländern der Europäischen Gemeinschaft* (Nuremburg: Institut für Arbeitsmarkt-und Berufsforschung, 1973).

4. R. Koslowski, *Migrants and Citizens* (Ithaca, NY: Cornell University Press, 2000), p. 118.

5. P.L. Martin, *Trade and Migration: NAFTA and Agriculture* (Washington, DC: Institute for International Economics, 1993).

6. P.L Martin and J.E. Taylor, "Managing Migration: The Role of Economic Policies," in A. Zolberg and P. Benda, *Global Migrants, Global Refugees* (NY: Berghahn Books, 2001).

7. S. Ricca, *Migrations internationals en Afrique* (Paris: L'Harmattan, 1990).

8. Anderanti Andepoju, "Regional Integration, Continuity and Changing Patterns of Intra-Regional Migration in Sub-Saharan Africa," in M.A.B. Siddique,

decrease smuggling. However, if potential migrants are willing to pay the additional costs while at the same time stiffer border controls prompt more migrants to enter into the market, border controls will most likely increase the profits of human smuggling and entice new entrants into the business. Moreover, if illegal economic migrants are willing to pay higher prices and incur debts to pay smugglers, "illegal refugees" who are in fact fleeing for their lives may be even more willing to do so.

■ The Kosovo Crisis and NATO Intervention

With the NATO air strikes against Yugoslavia and the Kosovo refugee crisis, human smuggling to the EU entered a new phase that highlights the difficulties encountered by EU member states as they attempt to restrict migration and tighten border controls. As mentioned above, large numbers of Kosovo Albanians used smugglers to get into the EU and the number of cases grew during 1998 and early 1999 in conjunction with increasing Serb operations directed at villages suspected of harboring members of the Kosovo Liberation Army and sporadic massacres of civilians. Without temporary protection status, smuggled refugees who were apprehended were often held in detention or returned to transit countries.[41]

Determined to avoid opening the door to large-scale migration via temporary protection, most EU member states refused to extend temporary protection to Kosovo Albanians even after highly publicized massacres of civilians. When NATO began bombing, Serb militias and police began systematic large-scale ethnic cleansing, and Macedonia threatened to close its borders to refugees if they did not have a second country of asylum to go to, several EU member states relented and announced that they would provide temporary protection. Germany agreed to take in 40,000; Greece 5,000; Italy, the Netherlands, and Ireland several thousand each. An April 7, 1999, JHA Council meeting reaffirmed that displaced persons who were in need of protection should receive it within the region. It argued that long-term accommodation outside of the area would only consolidate displacement and help Serbian leaders achieve their objectives of cleansing Kosovo of Albanians. Finally, the council cited stress on receiving states in the region, such as Macedonia, as a justification for individual member states to offer temporary protection. By the end of April, European states allocated a total of 85,000 slots for the entry of Kosovo refugees,[42] When combined with pledges made by the United States (20,000) and Turkey (20,000), the total number of slots for refugees exceeded 125,000. Still, this was a small fraction of the 800,000 Kosovars who had already been driven from Kosovo and remained in the region, primarily in Albania and Macedonia.

The circumstances of smuggling Kosovo Albanians were transformed by the NATO military action in several ways. First, as the refugee crisis quickly melted resistance among EU member states to extend temporary protection, Kosovo Albanians could have entered the EU through regular asylum channels and should therefore not have needed the smugglers. Second, the European media image of smuggled Kosovo Albanians changed. Smuggled "illegal refugees" associated with criminal organizations suddenly were depicted as genuine refugees fleeing ethnic cleansing compared to the Holocaust. The KLA became viewed as "freedom fighters" who were legitimate representatives of the Kosovars.

Although one might think that the extension of temporary protection and the outpouring of public sympathy for Kosovo refugees should have eliminated the need for Kosovo Albanians to turn to smugglers in order to get into the EU, this was not the case. To begin with, the airlift evacuation was focused on relieving the pressure placed on Macedonia. Albania steadfastly kept its borders open and argued against removal of refugees from its territory. Hence, the option to be evacuated to the EU (or other countries) was not necessarily given to the bulk of the Kosovars who were in Albania. Moreover, although tens of thousands of refugees were flown out of Macedonia, receiving governments chose which refugees could go, and the bureaucratic red tape contributed to a situation in which some evacuation flights departed with a fifth of their seats left empty.[43]

Rather than being put out of business by the NATO intervention and the changing status of their Kosovar customers, Albanian smugglers expanded their operations. Many Kosovo refugees in Albania, who decided to leave without having to endure the application for evacuation to the EU from the camps, made their way to Vlore, the primary embarkation point for the speedboats that cross the Adriatic to Italy. Smugglers plied their services in Albanian cities and even in the refugee camps. Indeed, Albanian gangsters even posed as aid workers, approached young girls and women with fake documents, and offered to get them into "teacher training programs" in Italy. Some young women disappeared from the camps.[44] An Albanian smuggler depicted the smuggling market:

> Kosovars pay 1,000 German marks [DM] each from the border at Kukes to Italy, all inclusive. The Albanians pay DM 1,200. From here, from Vlore, the Kosovars pay DM 500 and the Albanians pay DM 700. . . . The Kosovars are already here, and there are stacks of them. Once they cross over, they get dumped wherever it is convenient to dump them, even in the sea before reaching the shore. There is no need to fix a rendezvous with the Italian taxi drivers. There is more work involved in ferrying the Albanians, and then there is the cost of the taxis.[45]

Extensions of temporary protection to Kosovo Albanians meant that smugglers could cut back on the services provided and take fewer risks on the Italian side of the Adriatic. At the same time, the number of customers grew partly because temporary protection eliminated refugees' fears of deportations in the event of capture. Once in Italy, many Kosovars make their way, with or without the assistance of smugglers, to join relatives further north in Germany and Switzerland. Even if they were stopped at or near the Italian border, they were not returned to Kosovo as had previously often been the case. For example, in the beginning of April, France granted residency permits to twenty-seven Kosovars who sneaked across the Italian-French border and President Chirac declared that France would grant asylum to Kosovars who were driven out by ethnic cleansing.[46] Finally, since Serb militia routinely seized identity documents from fleeing Kosovo Albanians, it is difficult for EU authorities who are not fluent in Albanian dialects to differentiate Kosovo Albanians from Albanian nationals, thereby enabling smugglers to take advantage of the loosening of controls prompted by the humanitarian crisis to move Albanians as well as Kosovars. Although it is not clear how many refugees have been smuggled to Italy since the bombing began, an Organization for Security and Cooperation in Europe (OSCE) observer estimated that as many as ten boatloads of forty or more left Vlore each night.[47] Aid workers in the Puglia region of Italy across the Adriatic from Albania estimated that some 1,000 per day made it to the Italian coast in the last week of April 1999.[48] It has been estimated that Albanian smugglers made DM 10 million by smuggling Kosovo refugees in the first few weeks after NATO bombing began.

These changing circumstances of the smuggling of Kosovo Albanians make it increasingly difficult for EU member states to combat human smuggling, at least of Kosovars, despite the resolve demonstrated by EU action plans and stepped-up border controls. In 1998, Kosovo Albanians were already the largest group to be smuggled into Germany, the primary target country for migrant trafficking into the EU. Hence, it is likely that in 1999 Kosovo Albanians will constitute an even greater share of the customers of those who smuggle migrants into the EU.

With Serbian withdrawal from Kosovo, it would appear that Kosovo Albanians would no longer need the services of the smugglers. Despite the massive and rapid return of the refugees from Albania and Macedonia to Kosovo, the widespread destruction of homes and uncertain security future of Kosovo may lead a significant portion of the refugees, especially those in the EU, to think twice about returning.[49] Moreover, the EU quickly announced a reconstruction fund for Kosovo to the tune of $500 million per year for three years. However, much of the money for rebuilding Kosovar homes will most likely come from where it has in the recent past, Kosovo Albanians working abroad. According to a 1998 International Monetary Fund (IMF) estimate, Albanian migrant workers—many of whom are in the EU illegally—sent home remittances to the tune of $1 million per day.[50]

Moreover, given that Britain and other EU member states stated their refusal to provide funds to rebuild Serbia as long as Milosevic is in power, it is anticipated that "hundreds of thousands" of Serbs will go abroad in search of work.[51] Displaced Kosovo Serbs have joined displaced Kosovo Albanians among the destitute and desperate to whom the smugglers market their services. For example, in July 1999 the number of asylum seekers in Germany from Yugoslavia who were not ethnic Albanians was nearly twice as much as that of July 1998.[52] If EU member states do not provide rapid and sufficient financial assistance to Kosovo and Serbia, there will be pressure for Kosovo Albanian and Serb families to institute their own foreign aid programs by sending one or more family members abroad. EU member states may choose to tolerate such illegal migration for the sake of lowering the need for official foreign aid (as the United States did for Central Americans in the aftermath of Hurricane Mitch). If not, one can be sure that smugglers will be waiting for the migrants.

EU cooperation to toughen asylum policies led asylum seekers into the arms of smugglers and prompted the EU to step up efforts to combat the smuggling of "illegal refugees." Although the EU has increased cooperation to combat smuggling of such "illegal refugees," *refugee* crises that trigger humanitarian intervention can quickly neutralize such efforts by reclassifying certain unwanted "illegal refugees" into bona fide refugees who are greeted at the EU's external border with offers of shelter and assistance. Moreover, once temporary protection is offered to those refugees who use smugglers to get to the EU, it reduces the number of services provided by smugglers necessary for successful entry. By offering refugees a greater probability of entry at a discounted price, smugglers can take advantage of refugee crises to expand their operations at the expense of EU efforts to control clandestine migration.

■ State Power and Dueling Nonstate Actors: Hired Smugglers Versus the State's Deputies

While increasingly effective EU cooperation to restrict unwanted migration prompts human smuggling, and refugee crises become opportunities for smugglers to poke holes in, increasingly restrictive asylum policies, the expansion of the human smuggling business may counter European states' outsourcing of migration control functions to private-sector actors such as airlines. By means of imposing fines on airlines that transport people without proper documentation, states have compelled airlines to essentially extend border controls to the check-in counters and gates of airports in sending and transit countries.[53] Document checks by airline employees may have stopped many would-be migrants from ever getting close to an airplane, but human smugglers are changing the equation by shifting routes and providing fraudulent documents to the migrants that states are trying to keep out.

As Salt and Stein point out, as the trafficking business expands, the smugglers, rather than the migrants and asylum seekers, make more decisions regarding where their customers actually go.[54] Part of the smugglers' success in getting migrants across borders is the smugglers' ability to change routes and destinations in order to overcome obstacles that states have placed in their way. In a sense, the traffickers gather and process information about the weak links in terms of transportation systems, border controls, and liberal visa and asylum policies, and then they provide it to their customers. Therefore, shifts in the flows of illegal migration via air travel have accelerated and those flows move to where it is easiest to gain entry using false documents.

Smugglers may actually provide false documents to clandestine migrants as part of a "package deal," much like a tour operator. For example, Kurds pay $6,000 in Istanbul for passage and a fraudulent passport that will get them to Italy via Albania. There are similar packages available from Albania offered by a smuggler known as Shaqir. While the poor pay $600 for a speedboat to Italy, those who can pay $4,000 can purchase a "luxury' package that includes airfare (to Paris even), a passport with a valid visa, and bribes for officials at the airport. With the $2,000 "standard" package to Italy, the passport must be returned upon arrival to one of the smugglers who ride along. Shaqir uses a passport with a valid visa three to four times by replacing the photo until the damage becomes noticeable.[55]

Smugglers may also simply inform the would-be clandestine migrant as to where he or she may purchase false documents, much as a travel agent may provide information to tourists about where and how to get visas. The smuggler is an intermediary who has both the information that the migrant needs as well as the access to the counterfeiters' target market. In this way, counterfeiters can more effectively (and perhaps more quietly) market their products than if they attempted to reach the pool of would-be clandestine migrants directly by themselves. The division of labor enables expert counterfeiters to devote more resources and time to making better false documents. Smugglers, therefore, help to increase demand for counterfeit documents among clandestine migrants who might not otherwise have used them. They also provide expert counterfeiters easier (and potentially safer) access to the illegal migrant market, thereby encouraging production of more fraudulent travel documents.

The EU is developing a new European passport, which will include state-of-the-art features such as an optical reading zone, holograms, and special textured topographical printing. Nevertheless, "The most secure document in the world can be counterfeited or altered. The true test of the security of a document is how difficult it is for a forger to simulate successfully the genuine to the point that it can fool those tasked with inspecting it."[56] Document security is a function of the quality of the document, whether or not that document is attached to a database and the quality of inspection. While the growing smuggling business has prompted the development of higher quality counterfeits, increasing reliance on nonstate personnel to inspect travel documents has increased the opportunity for successful evasion of border controls.

Countering document fraud with high technology has its limits. Counterfeiters need only acquire the same computer technology as the state.

> (D)ocuments are effectively counterfeited using many of the same techniques that are used to create the corresponding genuine documents. . . . A scanned image of a genuine security document can be then endlessly manipulated using software, e.g. Corel or Adobe Photoshop. The computer savvy manipulator can also duplicate bar codes, magnetic stripes, background printings, and special fonts. These images can then be printed or sent around the world as email attachments.[57]

Ironically, documents produced using new computer technologies are often easier to counterfeit than less sophisticated documents produced with handcrafted plates. Moreover, known defects in authentic documents produced by lower tech means are often signifiers of authenticity—in other words, defect-free counterfeits may be "too good" in some cases. Finally, it is unlikely that high technology will substitute for the inspection of documents by humans, especially in all places that the documents might be used.[58]

Application of new technologies often only increases the price of reproducing a document rather than making it foolproof. In the face of such increasing costs of counterfeiting, the growing market and influx of cash from human smuggling has subsidized the research and development of the counterfeit document business and increased its sophistication. It is also important to remember that even though it might cost a great deal to produce the first high-quality counterfeit of a new more secure document and discourage its production, the next copy costs much less and the profits on subsequent copies help amortize the initial investment to produce the first.[59] In this way, counterfeiters, working in conjunction with smugglers, counter one technological advance in document production after the other.

As the expansion of the human smuggling business promotes migrant use of ever better fraudulent documents, it calls into question the effectiveness of states' extension of migration controls through document checks by airline personnel. In general, the more that document inspection and verification is devolved to nonexpert personnel, the greater the chances that fraudulent documents will not be detected and the greater the likelihood that migrants using them will be successful in evading migration controls. It is important to remember that fraudulent documents often only need to be good enough to board aircraft. Migrants may destroy fraudulent documents and flush them down the toilet and then apply for asylum once they arrive in the target country. Indeed, migrants have even boarded planes using identity and travel documents with the names of countries such as British Honduras, Burma, Rhodesia, South Vietnam, and Zanzibar. The production and purchase of such documents is perfectly legal since the purported issuing authorities no longer exist as states.

Receiving countries may require airlines to take such migrants back to the country of embarkation. However, the airline may find itself in a catch-22 situation because that country may not accept a returnee without an established identity and travel documents. Since it is well known that when confronted with such situations, many receiving countries with liberal asylum procedures have, in the end, allowed asylum seekers to remain until their cases are adjudicated, the false document that got the migrant past an airline employee often also gets the migrant into the target country. Although the stay may only be as long as the asylum application, appeals, and deportation processes last, these processes can take up to several years in many countries. Moreover, if the smuggled asylum seeker is not detained until deportation, he or she may simply vanish into the underground economy.

Given that virtually any document can be reproduced for the right price, the only secure document is one that is linked to a database and that document is only as secure as the database to which it is linked. Document fraud could be virtually eliminated by identity document systems in which a biometric identifier (e.g., hand geometry or facial recognition) that is stored in a database can be called up by a border guard and compared to a scan of the bearer of a document. A future EU passport with biometric identifiers has been envisioned. The problem, of course, is that however much continental Europeans may accept registration with state authorities and use of national identity cards, European norms regarding personal data protection militate against building such a database of biometric identifiers, let alone establishing a requirement that travel documents include fingerprints. Moreover, for the delegation of document inspection to carriers to be effective in using such secure document systems, the biometric databases maintained by the government would have to be opened to private corporations—an unimaginable proposal given existing norms and laws governing personal data protection.

■ Conclusions

EU member states have taken cooperation on migration beyond that of any other group of states in the world. This cooperation and the integration of member state migration policymaking into supranational institutional frameworks can be viewed as one more issue area in which member state sovereignty is being transformed in the context of policy formation at the European level. EU cooperation can also be a means through which member states more effectively control their territorial borders and thereby reassert sovereignty with respect to "unwanted" migration. Hence, a member state may actually sacrifice its sovereignty vis-à-vis the states with which it is cooperating in order to exercise sovereignty over its borders.[60]

The collective exertion of state power by EU member states to restrict illegal migration and non-bona-fide asylum seeking has further implications for member state sovereignty. On the one hand, if the recent EU activity to combat human smuggling is any indication, the policy discourse in the EU linking integration of migration policy to public concerns with personal security facilitates the formation of a political dynamic that may make major future transfers of sovereignty to the EU increasingly possible.[61] On the other hand, human smuggling, particularly of asylum seekers and in the context of humanitarian intervention, calls into question the effectiveness of the redeployment of state power to the EU and nonstate actors.

Gallya Lahav argues that the transfer of policymaking to the EU by member states does not indicate that "states are 'losing control' or abdicating sovereignty. European states are increasingly delegating policy elaboration and implementation to third party actors—especially the European Union itself—as a means to increase policy effectiveness."[62] Lahav is correct: the delegation of border control functions to the EU and nonstate actors is not necessarily a sign of the decline of state capacity, and enlisting nonstate personnel to assist in border control may simply be thought of as a redeployment of state power. This argument depends, however, on whether the lifting of internal border controls while fortifying common external borders is truly effective when smugglers are able to shift flows of illegal migrants to the most permeable points along that external border. It also depends on whether nonstate actors such as deputized carriers are actually effective. If such redeployment of state power amounts to increasing reliance on non-expert document examiners to detect increasingly sophisticated document fraud, it may be more a matter of dereliction of duty on the part of the state rather than an efficacious redeployment of power that increases state capacity.

Although the practice of human smuggling is age-old, the study of its policy implications is in its infancy. The EU systematically gathers and reports asylum-seeker statistics, but EU-wide statistics on illegal migration or apprehensions of the smuggled and smugglers along the common external border have yet to appear. Declining numbers of asylum applications demonstrate the effectiveness of EU cooperation on asylum policy to reduce one form of "unwanted" migration. Until better evidence can be generated, we can only point to the redeployment of state power to combat illegal migration. Whether or not this redeployment is effective or merely symbolic is not clear. Whether or not cooperation within the EU enables member states to more effectively control their borders and thereby reassert one dimension of their sovereignty through such cooperation also remains an open question.

▪ Notes

1. For supporting the revision of this chapter, I thank the Center of International Studies at Princeton University.

2. Wayne A. Cornelius, Philip L. Martin, and James F. Hollifield, *Controlling Immigration: A Global Perspective* (Stanford: Stanford University Press, 1994).

3. Brinley Thomas, *Migration and Economic Growth* (Cambridge: Cambridge University Press, 1973); Sidney Weintraub and Chandler Stolp, "The Implications of Growing Economic Interdependence," in *The Future of Migration* (Paris: OECD, 1987); Richard Layard, Oliver Blanchard, Rudiger Dornbusch, and Paul Kingman, *East-West Migration: The Alternatives* (Cambridge, Mass.: The MIT Press, 1992); Douglas Massey et al., *Worlds in Motion* (Oxford: Clarendon, 1998).

4. Yasemin Nuhoglu Soysal, *Limits of Citizenship: Migrants and Postnational Membership in Europe* (Chicago: University of Chicago Press, 1994); David Jacobson, *Rights Across Borders: Immigration and the Decline of Citizenship* (Baltimore: Johns Hopkins University Press, 1996).

5. Gary P. Freeman, "Can Liberal States Control Unwanted Migration?" in Mark J. Miller, ed., *Strategies for Immigration Control, Annals of the American Academy of Political and Social Science*, vol. 534 (May 1994): 17–30.

6. Gallya Lahav and Virginie Guiraudon, "The Devolution of Immigration Regimes in Europe," presented at the European Community Studies Association Meeting, Seattle, Washington, May 29–June 1, 1997; Gallya Lahav, "Immigration and the State: The Devolution and Privatization of Immigration Control in the EU," *Journal of Ethnic and Migration Studies,* vol. 24, no. 1 (1998): 675–694.

7. Myself included: Rey Koslowski, "EU Migration Regimes: Established and Emergent," in Christian Joppke, ed., *Challenge to the Nation-State: Immigration in Western Europe and the United States* (Oxford: Oxford University Press, 1998).

8. See, for example, Douglas Massey et al., "Theories of International Migration," *Population and Development Review*, vol. 19, no. 3 (1993): 431–466.

9. Lahav, "Immigration and the State," 680.

10. John Salt and Jeremy Stein, "Migration as a Business: The Case of Trafficking," *International Migration,* vol. 35, no. 4, (1997): 467–494; Bimal Ghosh, *Huddled Masses and Uncertain Shores: Insights into Irregular Migration* (Doredrecht: Klwer Law International, 1998).

11. IOM, "Trafficking in Migrants: IOM Policy and Activities," at: www.iom.ch/lOM/ Trafficking/lOM_Policy.html.

12. IOM, "Organized Crime Moves into Migrant Trafficking," *Trafficking in Migrants, Quarterly Bulletin*, no. 11 (June 1996).

13. Jonas Widgren, "Multilateral Co-Operation to Combat Trafficking in Migrants and the Role of International Organizations" (Vienna: International Centre

for Migration and Policy Development, 1994).

14. Mario Kaiser, "Spediteure des Elends," *Die Zeit,* September 9, 1999.

15. IOM, "Organized Crime Moves into Migrant Trafficking," *Trafficking in Migrants, Quarterly Bulletin,* no. 11 (June 1996); IOM, *Trafficking in Migrants, Quarterly Bulletin,* no. 17 (January 1998); Global Survival Network, *Crime and Servitude: An Expose of the Traffic in Women for Prostitution from the Newly Independent States* (Washington, D.C., 1997).

16. "More Human Smuggling Across the Eastern Border," *Migration News Sheet,* no. 186/98-09 (September 1998): 5; Karin Dalka, "Smuggling of Human Beings Experiencing Up-swing," *Frankfurter Runaschau,* March 12, 1999.

17. IOM, "Organized Crime Moves into Migrant Trafficking," *Trafficking in Migrants, Quarterly Bulletin,* no. 11 (June 1996).

18. "Interior Minister Reports Crime Rise in 1997," *PAP Polish Press Agency,* February 18, 1998; "Conference on Border Control," MTI Hungarian News Agency, April 22, 1998.

19. IOM, *Trafficking and Prostitution: The Growing Exploitation of Migrant Women from Central and Eastern Europe* (Geneva: IOM, 1995); Global Survival Network, *Crime and Servitude.*

20. IOM, *Trafficking in Migrants, Quarterly Bulletin,* no. 17 (January 1998).

21. "Germany Cannot Receive Kosovo Albanians," *Migration News Sheet,* no. 186/98-09 (September 1998): 12; "No Temporary Protection for Kosovo Albanians," *Migration News Sheet,* no. 186/98-09 (September 1998): 10.

22. "More Human Smuggling Across the Eastern Border," *Migration News Sheet,* no. 186/98-09 (September 1998): 5; "Large Smuggling Ring Broken Up," *Migration News Sheet,* no. 186/98-09 (September 1998): 6.

23. Dalka, "Smuggling of Human Beings Experiencing Upswing."

24. "Increasing Number of Persons Arrested for Clandestine Entry," *Migration News Sheet,* no. 197/99-08 (August 1999): 6.

25. Kaiser, "Spediteure des Elends," author's translation.

26. Kaiser, "Spediteure des Elends."

27. Diego Pistacchi, "PKK Leaders Sentenced for Smuggling Illegal Immigrants," *Il Giornale* (Milan), January 4, 1999.

28. Frederika Randall, "Italy and Its Immigrants: Refugees from the Balkan Peninsula," *The Nation,* May 31, 1999.

29. Roger Boyes and Eske Wright, "Drugs Money Linked to the Kosovo Rebels," *The Times* (London), March 24, 1999.

30. Justice and Home Affairs, Council of the European Union, "Recommendation on Trafficking in Human Beings," Council Press Release 10550/93 of November 9 and 30, 1993.

31. Justice and Home Affairs, Joint Action 96/700/JHA at: europa.eu. intlcomm/sg/scadplus/leg/.

32. "Conference of Ministers on the Prevention of Illegal Migration," *Migration News Sheet,* no. 177/97-12 (December 1997): 3–6.

33. "Influx of Kurds Prompts Adoption of a 46-Point Action Plan," *Migration News Sheet,* no. 179/98-2 (February 1998): 4–6.

34. "Jusfice and Home Affairs: EU Struggles to Define CEEC Strategy," *European Report,* no. 2288, February 4, 1998.

35. Quoted in "Influx: of Kurds Prompts Adoption of a 46-Point Action Plan," *Migration News Sheet,* no. 179/98-02 (February 1998): 4.

36. "Influx of Kurds Prompts Adoption of a 46-Point Action Plan," 4–6.

37. Paul J. Smith, "Smuggling People into Rich Countries is a Growth Industry," *International Herald Tribune,* June 28, 1996.

Belgium, the Federal Republic of Germany, Sweden and the Netherlands had been experiencing positive net inflows of persons from developing countries, whereas they had tended to record either lower or even negative net migration of persons from developed countries (their own citizens included). It is with that background in mind that one must assess the contribution made by female migration and particularly that of women from developing countries to overall migration trends.

■ South-to-North Female Migration in Selected Developed Countries

Data on international migration by sex often are not readily available, especially when the goal is to analyze the role of gender in relation to other characteristics of migrants. In particular, detailed tabulations of data on migration flows by both sex and place of origin that would permit the identification of migrants originating in developing countries are generally not published. Partly because of such data constraints and partly because the nature of female migration has varied considerably from one country to another, this article focuses only on the experience of four countries: Belgium, the Federal Republic of Germany, the United Kingdom and the United States. Those countries were chosen because they all gather and publish data on migration flows and because they represent a variety of migration experiences.

The United States is the country admitting the largest number of immigrants in the world, and with its long tradition as a country of immigration, it had the perhaps unique experience of admitting more women than men as immigrants during 1930–1980 (Houston *et al.*, 1984). The Federal Republic of Germany has been one of the major migrant-receiving countries of Europe, and during the past 30 years it has adopted a variety of strategies to mold migration that have had important effects on the female component of it. The United Kingdom is both an important country of emigration and a receiver of migrants from its former colonies. The relative participation of women in those flows sheds light on whether cultural barriers militate against the international migration of women. Lastly, Belgium, as one of the former labor-importing countries of Europe, provides a basis for comparison with the migration experience of the Federal Republic of Germany. . . .

■ Conclusion

This article has documented the extent of female migration in various contexts, especially in connection with the growing relevance of migration from developing to developed countries. In the European context, in particular, female migration has been a major component of the generally reduced net migration flows originating in developing countries after the discontinuation of temporary labor migration in 1974. The evidence does not support, however, the generalized view that female immigration to the former labor-importing countries of Europe has predominated over male immigration since that time. Instead, women have outnumbered men only in terms of net migration, which remained at relatively low levels during 1975–1984. In contrast with European countries, immigration to the United States has been characterized by including more women than men over most of the postwar period.

With respect to region of origin, there are certain patterns of sex selectivity that show some consistency between receiving countries. In general, the proportion of women in gross immigration is lower when flows originate in developing than in developed countries. For immigrants originating in the different developing regions, high proportions of women are more likely among those from Latin America and from East and Southeast Asia (denominated "Other Asia" in the presentation) than among those from either Southern Asia or West Asia and North Africa. Cases in which such differentials do not hold indicate that special factors are in operation, such as selective admission policies in the countries of destination or a particular stage in the migration history of expatriate populations.

Although the data discussed here do not provide information on the causes of the sex selectivity of migration and its changes over time, they indicate that women's participation in international migration flows is comparable to that of men and that it evinces distinct traits worthy of further consideration. Unfortunately, as long as data on international migration by sex and on the different characteristics of male and female migrants remain scarce or difficult to obtain, further advances in the understanding of the dynamics of female migration are unlikely. Today, when international migration and its consequences are increasingly the objects of public attention, it is especially important to underscore the role of women as migrants and to ensure that they become visible both in terms of statistics and as major actors in the migration process. . . .

■ References

Boyd, M.
1995 "Migration Regulations and Sex Selective Outcomes in Developed Countries." In *International Migration Policies and the Status of Female Migrants*. Proceedings of the United Nations Expert Group Meeting on International Migration Policies and the Status of Female Migrants, San Miniato, Italy, March 1990. New York: United Nations.

Donato, K. M.
1989 "Why Some Countries Send Women and Others Send Men: Cross-National Variation in the Sex Composition of U.S. Immigrants." Paper presented at the 1989 Meeting of the American Sociological Association. Mimeo.

Federal Republic of Germany Statistisches Bundesamt
1991 *Statistisches Jahrbuch 1991 für das Vereinte Deutschland.* Wiesbaden: Metzler-Poeschel.
1974 *Statistisches Jahrbuch 1974 für die Bundesrepublik Deutschland.* Wiesbaden: W. Kohlhammer.
France, Institut National de la Statistique et des Etudes Démographiques
1992 *Recensement de In Population de 1990*: *Nationalitiés, Résultats du Sondage au Vingtième.* Paris: INSEE.
Houston, M. F., R. G. Kramer, and J. M. Barrett
1984 "Female Predominance of Immigration to the United States since 1930: A First Look," *International Migration Review* 18(4):908–963.
International Labour Organization (ILO)
1989 *Statistical Report 1989.* Bangkok: Regional Office for Asia and the Pacific.
Organisation for Economic Cooperation and Development (OECD)
1992 *SOPEMI*: *Trends in International Migration*, Paris.
Potts, L.
1990 *The World Labor Market: A History of Migration.* New Jersey: Zed Books Ltd.
Rees, T.
1993 "United Kingdom I: Inheriting Empire's People." In *The Politics of Migration Policies.* Ed. D. Kubat. New York: Center for Migration Studies. Pp. 87–107.
Sweden, Statistika Centralbyran
1986 *Statistisk Arsbok for Sverige 1986.* Stockholm: Statistika Centralbyran.
Tribalat, M.
1989 "Rapport Francais." Paper presented at the Meeting on the Working Group on International Migration of the European Association for Population Studies, Paris.
United Kingdom, General Register Office
1966 *Census 1961*: *Great Britain, Summary Tables.* London: Her Majesty's Stationery Office.
United Nations
1989 *World Migrant Populations*: *The Foreign-Born.* Sales No. E.89.XII.7A.
1985 *World Population Trends, Population and Development Interrelations and Population Policies: 1983 World Monitoring Report.* Sales No. E.84.XII.10.
United Nations Secretariat
1995 "Measuring the Extent of Female International Migration." In *International Migration Policies and the Status of Female Migrants.* Proceedings of the United Nations Expert Group Meeting on International Migration Policies and the Status of Female Migrants, San Miniato, Italy, March 1990. New York: United Nations.
Vellinga, M.
1993 "The Benelux Countries: Divergent Paths toward Restrictive Immigration." In *The Politics of Migration Policies.* Ed. D. Kubat. New York: Center for Migration Studies. Pp.141–163.
Zlotnik, H.
1992a "Le Migrazione di Donne," *Politica Internazionale*, 19(5): 31–40. Sept.-Oct.
1992b "Empirical Identification of International Migration Systems." In *International Migration Systems*: *A Global Approach.* Ed. M. M. Kritz, L. L. Lim, and H. Zlotnik. Oxford: Clarendon Press.
1991 "South-to-North Migration: The View from the North," *Population Bulletin of the United Nations*, pp. 17–37.

13.4 *Saskia Sassen*

Foreign Investment: A Neglected Variable

There is considerable evidence both on international labor migrations and on the internationalization of production. But they are mostly two separate bodies of scholarship. Analytically these two processes have been constructed into unrelated categories. As socioeconomic givens, there are certain locations where one can identify the presence of both. Our question then becomes whether there is an articulation between these two processes and, if so, how we can capture this analytically. Furthermore, the notion of the internationalization of production needs to be elaborated in order to incorporate more of its central components. Theoretical and empirical studies of this process have focused largely on one particular component: the massive shift of jobs to Third World countries through direct foreign investment, resulting in the development of an off-shore manufacturing sector.

The question about the articulation of these two processes stems from both a broader theoretical argument on the nature of the world economy and from the concrete details of the new migrations to the U.S. Similarly, the need to elaborate the notion of the internationalization of production stems from that broader theoretical argument as well as from the concrete details of the U.S. economy over the last twenty years. In this . . . [essay] I briefly review the main conceptual and empirical lines of analysis that bring these various concerns together.

The new Asian and Caribbean Basin immigration to the U.S. reveals patterns that escape prevailing explanations of why migrations occur. Two of these patterns are of interest here. One concerns the timing, magnitude and origins of the new immigration. Why did the new immigration take place at a time of high unemployment in the U.S., including major job losses in sectors traditionally employing immigrants, and of high growth rates in the major immigrant sending countries? There are two separate issues worth considering here, to wit, the initiation of a new migration flow and its continuation at ever higher levels. Understanding why a migration began entails an examination of conditions promoting outmigration in countries

Saskia Sassen, "Foreign Investment: A Neglected Variable," in Saskia Sassen, *The Mobility of Labor and Capital: A Study in International Investment and Labor Flow* (Cambridge: Cambridge University Press, 1990), pp. 12–25.

of origin and the formation of objective and subjective linkages with receiving countries that make such migration feasible. Understanding why a migration flow continues and sustains high levels invites an examination of demand conditions in the receiving country. This brings up the second pattern, the continuing concentration of the new immigration in several major cities which are global centers for highly specialized service and headquarters activities, an economic base we do not usually associate with immigrant labor. The questions raised by these patterns in the new immigration become particularly acute when we consider that the major immigrant-sending countries are among the leading recipients of the jobs lost in the U.S. and of U.S. direct foreign investment in labor-intensive manufacturing and service activities. If anything, this combination of conditions should have been a deterrent to the emergence of new migrations or at least a disincentive to their continuation at growing levels. Why is it that the rapidly industrializing countries of South-East Asia, typically seen as the success stories of the Third World, are the leading senders of the new immigrants? I will briefly examine each of these patterns.

Immigrant entry levels since the late 1960s are among the highest in U.S. immigration history. Legally admitted immigrants numbered 265,000 in 1960. By 1970 such entries reached half a million, a level sustained since then with a gradual tendency to increase over the years. The overall estimate now is that the combination of all different types of entry had reached about 1 million a year by 1980 (see INS, 1978; Teitelbaum, 1985). The highest numbers of immigrants from 1970 to 1980 came from Mexico, the Philippines, and South Korea, followed by China (Taiwan and People's Republic), India, the Dominican Republic, Jamaica, Colombia, and several Caribbean Basin countries. New entries and natural growth resulted in the pronounced expansion of the Asian and Hispanic populations in the U.S. From 1970 to 1980, the Asian population increased by 100 percent and the Hispanic by 62 percent (U.S. Bureau of the Census, 1981). These growth rates were surpassed by some nationalities, notably the 412 percent increase of South Koreans.

The new Caribbean Basin and South-East Asian immigration, by far the largest share in the current immigration, is heavily concentrated in cities with high job losses in older industries, and job growth in high-technology industries and specialized services. Asians have gone largely to Los Angeles, San Francisco, and New York City; these have the three largest concentrations of Asians. West Indians and the new Hispanics (excluding Mexicans and Cubans) have gone largely to New York City. What conditions in the economies of these cities have facilitated the absorption of such massive immigrant flows and induced their continuation at ever higher levels? The fact that these are traditional destinations and contain large immigrant communities goes a way towards answering the question. And so does the fact that declining sectors of the economy need cheap labor for survival. But the magnitude and new origins of the immigrant influx, its continuation at ever higher levels and the extent of job losses in sectors historically employing immigrants point to the need for additional explanations.

The increase in immigration took place at a time of rather high economic growth in most countries of origin. For example, annual GNP growth in the decade of the seventies hovered around 5 to 9 percent for most of these countries. Growth rates in manufacturing employment were even higher. Massive increases in direct foreign investment, mostly from the U.S. but also from Japan and Europe, contributed to these growth rates.

While U.S. direct foreign investment generally accelerated from 1965 to 1980 and continues to go to Europe and Canada, it quintupled in the less developed countries. This is a noteworthy trend, since much of it goes to a few select countries in the Caribbean Basin and South-East Asia. The average annual growth rate of U.S. direct foreign investment from 1950 to 1966 was 11.7 percent for developed countries and 6.2 percent for developing countries; from 1966 to 1973 these rates were, respectively, 10.7 percent and 9.7 percent, and, from 1973 to 1980, 11.8 percent and 14.2 percent (these figures exclude the petroleum industry). There has also been a massive increase of Western European direct foreign investment during the 1970s, mostly in these same countries. Given the particular conceptualization of the migration impact of such investment . . . , briefly described later in this . . . [essay], this increase of European and Japanese investment in countries sending migrants to the U.S. is also significant. The average annual growth rates of direct foreign investment in developing countries by all major industrial countries were 7 percent from 1960 to 1968; 9.2 percent from 1968 to 1973, and 19.4 percent from 1973 to 1978.

Furthermore, a growing share of direct foreign investment in developing countries over the last two decades has gone into production for export, mostly to the U.S. As I will discuss later, export manufacturing and export-agriculture tend to be highly labor-intensive kinds of production which have mobilized new segments of the population into waged-labor and into regional migrations. The main migrant-sending countries to the U.S. over the last fifteen years all have received large export-oriented foreign investment. This would seem to go against a central proposition in the development literature, to wit, since foreign investment creates jobs it should act as a deterrent to emigration; this deterrent should be particularly strong in countries with high levels of export-oriented investment because of its labor-intensive nature.

Using Export Processing Zones (EPZs) as an indicator of export oriented direct foreign investment, a distinct pattern emerges. These zones, all built in the last fifteen years, tend to be concentrated in a few countries,

and (b) the shrinking of traditional manufacturing industries and their replacement with a downgraded manufacturing sector and high technology industries, in both of which sweatshops are mushrooming. The evidence shows that the result is an expansion of very high-income professional and technical jobs, a shrinking of middle income blue- and white-collar jobs, and a vast expansion of low-wage jobs. The expansion of the low-wage job supply is in good part a function of growth sectors and only secondarily of declining industries in need of cheap labor for survival. It is in this expansion of the low-wage job supply that we find the conditions for the absorption of the immigrant influx.

Immigration can be seen as providing labor for (1) low-wage service jobs, including those that service (a) the expanding, highly specialized, export-oriented service sector and (b) the high-income lifestyles of the growing top level professional workforce employed in that sector; (2) the expanding downgraded manufacturing sector, including but not exclusively, declining industries in need of cheap labor for survival, as well as dynamic electronics sectors, some of which can actually be seen as part of the downgraded sector. A third source of jobs for immigrants is the immigrant community itself (Light, 1972; Chaney, 1976; Portes and Bach, 1980). These jobs include not only those that are a temporary arrangement until a job in the mainstream society can be found. They include also a large array of professional and technical jobs that service the expanding and increasingly income-stratified immigrant communities in the city (Cohen and Sassen-Koob, 1982). And they include jobs that produce services and goods for the subsistence of members of the community, and therewith contribute to lower the costs of survival—both for themselves and, ultimately, for their employers.

The redeployment of manufacturing and the associated international trade in specialized services contain new business opportunities for major urban centers. There has been a sharp rise in the national and international demand for specialized services, induced both by the dispersion of manufacturing and clerical work and by the technological transformation of work. Thus this growth rests in part on the crisis of traditional manufacturing. While a city like Detroit just loses factories, New York and Los Angeles find new business opportunities in their own and Detroit's factory losses. Furthermore, unlike what is the case with other kinds of services, production of specialized services does not tend to follow population patterns. On the contrary, they are subject to agglomeration economics and hence tend towards strong locational concentration and production for export nationally and internationally. Since the highly specialized service sector is the most dynamic in the U.S. economy, its concentration in major cities also entails that these come to contain a disproportionate component of national economic growth.

. . . .The timing, magnitude and destination of the new immigration become particularly noteworthy when juxtaposed with the pronounced changes in the job supply in major urban centers. I [am] particularly interested in examining the generation of low-wage jobs in major growth sectors, the advanced services and the downgraded manufacturing sector. I use the term downgraded manufacturing sector to refer to both the downgrading of old industries, e.g., replacing unionized shops with sweatshops and industrial homework, and to the prevalence of low-wage, dead-end production jobs in new industries, particularly in the field of high technology. What is notable is that even the most dynamic and technologically developed sectors of the economy, such as the advanced services and high technology industries generate a considerable supply of low-wage jobs with few skill and language proficiency requirements.

Two analytical distinctions important to my argument are (a) the distinction between job characteristics and sector characteristics, and (b) the distinction between sector characteristics and growth status. Thus, backward jobs can be part of the most modern sector of the economy and backward sectors can be part of major growth trends in the economy. Use of these two kinds of distinctions allows me to explain the presence of immigrants in technologically developed sectors of the economy and it allows me to posit that the downgraded manufacturing sector—also an important employer of immigrants—is part of major growth trends. Furthermore, these distinctions also lead me to a partial reconceptualization of what is often referred to as the informal sector. As Portes (1983) has discussed, the informal sector represents a survival strategy for the people involved and a mechanism to transfer surplus to the formal sector of the economy. I . . . argue further that the development of informal sectors in major cities in the U.S. (and Western Europe) is in good part a function of the characteristics of growth sectors in such cities; the existence of immigrant communities facilitates the development of an informal sector but does not cause it, for example, via importation of survival strategies typical of the Third World. Changes in the organization of production, particularly the growing importance of highly customized goods and services, promote the desirability and viability of small scales of production and labor-intensive work processes. These are conditions that will tend to induce informalization. And informalization can easily lead to a demand for immigrant workers. . . .

■ References

Bach, Robert L., 1978. "Mexican immigration and the American state," *International Migration Review* 12 (Winter): 536–558.

Bailey, Tom and Marcia Freedman, 1981. "The restaurant industry in New York City." New York: Conservation of Human Resources, Columbia University.

Project on Newcomers to New York City (Conservation of Human Resources), Working Paper No. 2.

Centro de Estudios Puertorriqueños, 1979. *Labor Migration Under Capitalism: The Puerto Rican Experience*. History Task Force. New York: Monthly Review Press.

Chaney, Elsa, 1976. *Columbian Migration to the United States* (Part 2). Occasional Monograph Series, Smithsonian Institution, Interdisciplinary Communications Program, vol. 2, no. 5.

Cohen, S. and Saskia Sassen-Koob, 1982. "Survey of six immigrant groups in Queens." Department of Sociology, Queens College, City University of New York.

Cornelius, Wayne A., 1981. *Mexican Migration to the United States: The Limits of Government Intervention. Working Papers*, No. 5. Center for U.S.-Mexican Studies, University of California, San Diego.

Fernandez Kelly, Maria Patricia, 1983. *For We Are Sold, I and My People: Women and Industry in Mexico's Frontier*. Albany: SUNY Press.

Grossman, Rachael, 1979. "Women's place in the integrated circuit," *Southeast Asia Chronicle 66-Pacific Research* 9 (Joint Issue): 2–17.

INS [Immigration and Naturalization Service], 1978. *Annual Report*. Washington, D.C.: U.S. Government Printing Office.

Keely, Charles B. 1979. *U.S. Immigration: A Policy Analysis*. New York: The Population Council.

Light, Ivan, 1972. *Ethnic Enterprise in America*. Berkeley: University of California Press.

Lim, L.Y.C., 1980. "Women workers in multinational corporations: the case of the electronics industry in Malaysia and Singapore," in Krishna Kumar, *Transnational Enterprises: Their Impact on Thrid World Societies and Cultures*. Boulder, CO: Westview Press.

Piore, Michael P., 1979. *Birds of Passage: Migrant Labor and Industrial Societies*. Cambridge University Press.

Portes, Alejandro, 1983. "The informal sector: Definition, controversy, and relation to national development," *Review* 7 (Summer): 151–174.

Portes, Alejandro and R.L. Bach, 1980. "Immigrant earnings: Cuban and Mexican immigrants in the United States," *International Migration Review* 14: 315–341.

Portes, Alejandro and John Walton, 1981. *Labor, Class and the International System*. New York: Academic Press.

Reimers, David M., 1983. "An unintended reform: the 1965 Immigration Act and Third World immigration to the U.S.," *Journal of American Ethnic History* 3 (Fall): 9–28.

Reubens, E.P., 1981. "Interpreting migration: current models and a new integration." Paper presented at the New York Research Program in Inter-American Affairs at New York University on Hispanic Migration to New York City: Global Trends and Neighborhood Change (December).

Ricketts, Erol R., 1983. "Periphery to Core Migration: Specifying a Model." Unpublished Ph.D. dissertation, University of Chicago, Department of Sociology.

Safa, Helen I., 1981. "Runaway shops and female employment: the search for cheap labor," *Signs* 7 (2; Winter): 418–433.

Sassen-Koob, Saskia, 1979. "Colombians and Dominicans in New York City," *Internatioonal Migration Review* 13 (Summer): 314–331.

———. 1980. "Immigrant and minority workers in the organization of the labor process," *Journal of Ethnic Studies* 8 (Spring).

Teitelbaum, Michael S., 1985. *Latin Migration North: The Problem for U.S. Foreign Policy*. New York: Council on Foreign Relations.

UNIDO [United Nations Industrial Development Organization], 1980. *Export Processing Zones in Developing Countries*. Working Papers on Structural Change No. 19. New York: UNIDO.

United States Department of Commerce, Bureau of the Census, 1981a. *1980 Census of Population, Supplementary Report*. Washington D.C.: U.S. Government Printing Office.

———. 1981b. *1980 Census of Population and Housing: Advance Report*. Washington D.C.: U.S. Government Printing Office.

Wilson, Kenneth L. and Alejandro Portes, 1980. "Immigrant enclaves: an analysis of the labor market experiences of Cubans in Miami," *American Journal of Sociology* 86: 295–319 (Sept.).

Wong, A.K. 1980. *Economic Development and Women's Place: Women in Singapore. International Reports: Women and Society*. London: Change.

not only include the study of anti-immigrant violence but also the rhetoric of regular immigration politics. The second task is to extend our knowledge not only about the import viz. export of conflicts through international migration but more virtuous cycles of transnationalization such as the diffusion of human rights and democratic principles with the help of emigres, migrants and refugees. This would constitute one modest step towards removing fuzzy fantasies about "the migrant" as a security threat. This also implies a redirection of the study of the politics of international migration. At first sight the events of September 11 have dealt another devastating blow to the Kantian utopia of perpetual peace. Yet, the age of globalization demands to renew Kant's vision. Immanuel Kant argued that perpetual peace is possible in a system of republics, which we would now call liberal democracies, governed by the rule of law.[8] He wrote about a federation of states as one guarantor of peace. Nowadays this vision has to be supplemented by an empirical analysis of how transnationalizing civil societies may underpin the diffusion of human, civil and political rights. Sometimes, international migrants actively voice ideas and interests in this transnational realm.

■ Notes

1. The original French version was published in 1997 by *J'ai In* (*Littérature Générale*).

2. Terrorism is a difficult term, fraught with many ambiguities and often not used in historically specific ways. It is itself part of a semantic war. For example, in the 1970s the USA spoke of Moscow as the source of terrorism, in 2001 the networks of *Al Qu'aida* around Osama bin Laden have become the center of attention.

3. Cambridge, MA: Harvard University Press, 1999.

4. On the terminology of exit and voice, see Albert O. Hirschman, *Exit, Voice, and Loyalty: Responses to Decline in Firms, Organizations, and States*. Cambridge, MA: Harvard University Press, 1970.

5. Harold Lasswell, *World Politics and Personal Insecurity*. New York: Whittlesey, 1935.

6. Thomas Faist, How to Define a Foreigner? The Symbolic Politics of Immigration in German Partisan Discourse, 1978–1993, *West European Politics* No. 17, 1994, pp. 50–71.

7. Two of many examples are: Josef Joffe, Das Weltgericht der Hundert Tage. Der 11. September, der Krieg gegen den Fanatismus und die Wiedercrudeckung des Besten am Westen (The World Judgement of 100 Days: 11 September, the War against Fanaticism and the Redisocovery of the Best in the West), *Die Zeit*, 27 December 200 1, p.1; Der Glaube der Ungläubigen. Welche Werte hat der Westen? (The Belief of the Non-Believers. Which Belief has the West?), *Der Spiegel*, No. 52, 2001, pp. 50–66.

8. Immanuel Kant: Perpetual Peace: A Philosophical Sketch, in: *Political Writings*, ed. By H.S. Reiss. Cambridge: Cambridge University Press, 1970 (reprinted in 2000), pp. 93–130.

question of whether contemporary state immigration policy is ethically circumscribed, every contributor in this chapter agrees that it is and, moreover, that it should be. Where the authors conspicuously part company, however, is on the question of how and to what extent contemporary states, and especially the advanced industrial democracies, can keep their borders open to significant numbers of refugees and immigrants.

In Chapter 14.2, Joseph Carens makes the most forceful case for a liberal immigration regime when he argues that from the perspective of every stream of contemporary political theory—Rawlsian, Nozickean, utilitarian, and even communitarian—borders should be open and "people should normally be free" to settle in any country of their choosing "subject only to the sorts of constraints that bind current citizens." For Carens, immigration restrictions of any kind cannot be justified in a liberal society. Although free immigration may not be immediately achievable, it is nevertheless "a goal toward which we should strive."

In Chapter 14.3 Teitelbaum, on the other hand, rejects the notion that completely open borders are desirable or practical. According to Teitelbaum, the only "humane and sustainable" immigration and refugee policy is one that closely reflects the U.S. national interest and humanitarian values; moreover, it is one that "protects the civil liberties and rights of citizens and immigrants alike, and recognizes the importance of trade and foreign assistance policies for developing countries." Such a policy should be not be founded on any predetermined or "correct" number of refugees and immigrants who are allowed to enter the United States annually but instead should be guided by a system of "periodic flexibility" informed by national political and economic conditions and humanitarian circumstances in the international arena during any given period.

Christina Boswell in Chapter 14.4 agrees with Teitelbaum that a humane refugee and immigration policy is possible only if it is politically sustainable. The starting point of Boswell's answer to the question of how to make such a policy politically sustainable is to deny the universal validity of "liberal universalism" and to offer a new interpretation that liberates liberal universalism from what she sees as its practical unfeasibility and conceptual rigidity. This interpretation abandons the universalist foundations of liberalism and allows that liberal responses to refugees can evolve from a "tradition of western thought that is constitutive of the group identity and culture of most European nations." According to Boswell, "a generous attitude to helping outsiders can affirm group identities." In so doing, it can lay the foundation for solving the "liberal dilemma in the ethics of refugee policy in liberal democratic states."

14.2 *Joseph H. Carens*
Aliens and Citizens:
The Case for Open Borders

Many poor and oppressed people wish to leave their countries of origin in the third world to come to affluent Western societies. This essay argues that there is little justification for keeping them out. The essay draws on three contemporary approaches to political theory—the Rawlsian, the Nozickean, and the utilitarian—to construct arguments for open borders. The fact that all three theories converge upon the same results on this issue, despite their significant disagreements on others, strengthens the case for open borders and reveals its roots in our deep commitment to respect all human beings as free and equal moral persons. The final part of the essay considers communitarian objections to this conclusion, especially those of Michael Walzer.

Borders have guards and the guards have guns. This is an obvious fact of political life but one that is easily hidden from view—at least from the view of those of us who are citizens of affluent Western democracies. To Haitians in small, leaky boats confronted by armed Coast Guard cutters, to Salvadorans dying from heat and lack of air after being smuggled into the Arizona desert, to Guatemalans crawling through rat-infested sewer pipes from Mexico to California—to these people the borders, guards and guns are all too apparent. What justifies the use of force against such people? Perhaps borders and guards can be justified as a way of keeping out criminals, subversives, or armed invaders. But most of those trying to get in are not like that. They are ordinary, peaceful people, seeking only the opportunity to build decent, secure lives for themselves and their families. On what moral grounds can these sorts of people be kept out? What gives anyone the right to point guns at *them*?

To most people the answer to this question will seem obvious. The power to admit or exclude aliens is inherent in sovereignty and essential for any political community. Every state has the legal and moral right to exercise that power in pursuit of its own national interest, even if that means denying entry to peaceful, needy foreigners. States may choose to be generous in admitting immigrants, but they are under no obligation to do so.[1]

Joseph H. Carens, "Aliens and Citizens: The Case for Open Borders," *Review of Politics* 49, no. 2 (spring 1987): 251–273.

I want to challenge that view. In this essay I will argue that borders should generally be open and that people should normally be free to leave their country of origin and settle in another, subject only to the sorts of constraints that bind current citizens in their new country. The argument is strongest, I believe, when applied to the migration of people from third world countries to those of the first world. Citizenship in Western liberal democracies is the modern equivalent of feudal privilege—an inherited status that greatly enhances one's life chances. Like feudal birthright privileges, restrictive citizenship is hard to justify when one thinks about it closely.

In developing this argument I will draw upon three contemporary approaches to political theory: first that of Robert Nozick; second that of John Rawls; third that of the utilitarians. Of the three, I find Rawls the most illuminating, and I will spend the most time on the arguments that flow from his theory. But I do not want to tie my case too closely to his particular formulations (which I will modify in any event). My strategy is to take advantage of three well-articulated theoretical approaches that many people find persuasive to construct a variety of arguments for (relatively) open borders. I will argue that all three approaches lead to the same basic conclusion: there is little justification for restricting immigration. Each of these theories begins with some kind of assumption about the equal moral worth of individuals. In one way or another, each treats the individual as prior to the community. These foundations provide little basis for drawing fundamental distinctions between citizens and aliens who seek to become citizens. The fact that all three theories converge upon the same basic result with regard to immigration despite their significant differences in other areas strengthens the case for open borders. In the final part of the essay I will consider communitarian objections to my argument, especially those of Michael Walzer, the best contemporary defender of the view I am challenging.

■ Aliens and Property Rights

One popular position on immigration goes something like this: "It's our country. We can let in or keep out whomever we want." This could be interpreted as a claim that the right to exclude aliens is based on property rights, perhaps collective or national property rights. Would this sort of claim receive support from theories in which property rights play a central role? I think not, because those theories emphasize *individual* property rights and the concept of collective or national property rights would undermine the individual rights that these theories wish to protect.

Consider Robert Nozick as a contemporary representative of the property rights tradition. Following Locke, Nozick assumes that individuals in the state of nature have rights, including the right to acquire and use property. All individuals have the same natural rights—that is the assumption about moral equality that underlies this tradition—although the exercise of those rights leads to material inequalities. The "inconveniences" of the state of nature justify the creation of a minimal state whose sole task is to protect people within a given territory against violations of their rights.[2]

Would this minimal state be justified in restricting immigration? Nozick never answers this question directly, but his argument at a number of points suggests not. According to Nozick the state has no right to do anything other than enforce the rights which individuals already enjoy in the state of nature. Citizenship gives rise to no distinctive claim. The state is obliged to protect the rights of citizens and noncitizens equally because it enjoys a *de facto* monopoly over the enforcement of rights within its territory. Individuals have the right to enter into voluntary exchanges with other individuals. They possess this right as individuals, not as citizens. The state may not interfere with such exchanges so long as they do not violate someone else's rights.[3]

Note what this implies for immigration. Suppose a farmer from the United States wanted to hire workers from Mexico. The government would have no right to prohibit him from doing this. To prevent the Mexicans from coming would violate the rights of both the American farmer and the Mexican workers to engage in voluntary transactions. Of course, American workers might be disadvantaged by this competition with foreign workers. But Nozick explicitly denies that anyone has a right to be protected against competitive disadvantage. (To count that sort of thing as a harm would undermine the foundations of *individual* property rights.) Even if the Mexicans did not have job offers from an American, a Nozickean government would have no grounds for preventing them from entering the country. So long as they were peaceful and did not steal, trespass on private property, or otherwise violate the rights of other individuals, their entry and their actions would be none of the state's business.

Does this mean that Nozick's theory provides no basis for the exclusion of aliens? Not exactly. It means rather that it provides no basis for the *state* to exclude aliens and no basis for individuals to exclude aliens that could not be used to exclude citizens as well.

Poor aliens could not afford to live in affluent suburbs (except in the servants' quarters), but that would be true of poor citizens too. Individual property owners could refuse to hire aliens, to rent them houses, to sell them food, and so on, but in a Nozickean world they could do the same things to their fellow citizens. In other words, individuals may do what they like with their own personal property. They may normally exclude whomever they want from land they own. But they have this right to exclude as individuals, not as members of a collective. They cannot prevent

which Rawls's use of the original position and the "veil of ignorance" depends upon a particular understanding of moral personality that is characteristic of modern democratic societies but may not be shared by other societies.[11] Let us grant the objection and ask whether it really matters.

The understanding of moral personality in question is essentially the view that all people are free and equal moral persons. Even if this view of moral personality is not shared by people in other societies, it is not a view that applies only to people who share it. Many members of our own society do not share it, as illustrated by the recent demonstrations by white racists in Forsythe County, Georgia. We criticize the racists and reject their views but do not deprive them of their status as free and equal citizens because of their beliefs. Nor is our belief in moral equality limited to members of our own society. Indeed our commitment to civic equality is derived from our convictions about moral equality, not vice versa. So, whatever we think about the justice of borders and the limitations of the claims of aliens, our views must be compatible with a respect for all other human beings as moral persons.

A related objection emphasizes the "constructivist" nature of Rawls's theory, particularly in its later formulations.[12] The theory only makes sense, it is said, in a situation where people already share liberal-democratic values. But if we presuppose a context of shared values, what need have we for a "veil of ignorance"? Why not move directly from the shared values to an agreement on principles of justice and corresponding institutions? The "veil of ignorance" offers a way of thinking about principles of justice in a context where people have deep, unresolvable disagreements about matters of fundamental importance and yet still want to find a way to live together in peaceful cooperation on terms that are fair to all. That seems to be just as appropriate a context for considering the problem of worldwide justice as it is considering the problem of domestic justice.

To read Rawls's theory only as a constructive interpretation of existing social values is to undermine its potential as a constructive critique of those values. For example, racism has deep roots in American public culture, and in the not-too-distant past people like those in Forsythe County constituted a majority in the United States. If we think the racists are wrong and Rawls is right about our obligation to treat all members of our society as free and equal moral persons, it is surely not just because the public culture has changed and the racists are now in the minority. I gladly concede that I am using the original position in a way that Rawls himself does not intend, but I think that this extension is warranted by the nature of the questions I am addressing and the virtues of Rawls's approach as a general method of moral reasoning.

Let us therefore assume a global view of the original position. Those in the original position would be prevented by the "veil of ignorance" from knowing their place of birth or whether they were members of one particular society rather than another. They would presumably choose the same two principles of justice. (I will simply assume that Rawls's argument for the two principles is correct, though the point is disputed.) These principles would apply globally, and the next task would be to design institutions to implement the principles—still from the perspective of the original position. Would these institutions include sovereign states as they currently exist? In ideal theory, where we can assume away historical obstacles and the dangers of injustice, some of the reasons for defending the integrity of existing states disappear. But ideal theory does not require the elimination of all linguistic, cultural, and historical differences. Let us assume that a general case for decentralization of power to respect these sorts of factors would justify the existence of autonomous political communities comparable to modern states.[13] That does not mean that all the existing features of state sovereignty would be justified. State sovereignty would be (morally) constrained by the principles of justice. For example, no state could restrict religious freedom and inequalities among states would be restricted by an international difference principle.

What about freedom of movement among states? Would it be regarded as a basic liberty in a global system of equal liberties, or would states have the right to limit entry and exit? Even in an ideal world people might have powerful reasons to want to migrate from one state to another. Economic opportunities for particular individuals might vary greatly from one state to another even if economic inequalities among states were reduced by an international difference principle. One might fall in love with a citizen from another land, one might belong to a religion which has few followers in one's native land and many in another, one might seek cultural opportunities that are only available in another society. More generally, one has only to ask whether the right to migrate freely within a given society is an important liberty. The same sorts of considerations make migration across state boundaries important.[14]

Behind the "veil of ignorance," in considering possible restrictions on freedom, one adopts the perspective of the one who would be most disadvantaged by the restrictions, in this case the perspective of the alien who wants to immigrate. In the original position, then, one would insist that the right to migrate be included in the system of basic liberties for the same reasons that one would insist that the right to religious freedom be included: it might prove essential to one's plan of life. Once the "veil of ignorance" is lifted, of course, one might not make use of the right, but that is true of other rights and liberties as well. So, the basic agreement among those in the original position would be to permit no restrictions on migration (whether emigration or immigration).

There is one important qualification to this. According to Rawls, liberty may be restricted for the sake of liberty even in ideal theory and all liberties depend on the existence of public order and security.[15] (Let us call this the public order restriction.) Suppose that unrestricted immigration would lead to chaos and the breakdown of order. Then all would be worse off in terms of their basic liberties. Even adopting the perspective of the worst-off and recognizing the priority of liberty, those in the original position would endorse restrictions on immigration in such circumstances. This would be a case of restricting liberty for the sake of liberty and every individual would agree to such restrictions even though, once the "veil of ignorance" was lifted, one might find that it was one's own freedom to immigrate which had been curtailed.

Rawls warns against any attempt to use this sort of public order argument in an expansive fashion or as an excuse for restrictions on liberty undertaken for other reasons. The hypothetical possibility of a threat to public order is not enough. Restrictions would be justified only if there were a "reasonable expectation" that unlimited immigration would damage the public order and this expectation would have to be based on "evidence and ways of reasoning acceptable to all."[16] Moreover, restrictions would be justified only to the extent necessary to preserve public order. A need for some restrictions would not justify any level of restrictions whatsoever. Finally, the threat to public order posed by unlimited immigration could not be the product of antagonistic reactions (*e.g.*, riots) from current citizens. This discussion takes place in the context of ideal theory and in this context it is assumed that people try to act justly. Rioting to prevent others from exercising legitimate freedoms would not be just. So, the threat to public order would have to be one that emerged as the unintended cumulative effect of individually just actions.

In ideal theory we face a world of just states with an international difference principle. Under such conditions, the likelihood of mass migrations threatening to the public order of any particular state seems small. So, there is little room for restrictions on immigration in ideal theory. But what about nonideal theory, where one takes into account both historical contingencies and the unjust actions of others?

In the nonideal, real world there are vast economic inequalities among nations (presumably much larger than would exist under an international difference principle). Moreover, people disagree about the nature of justice and often fail to live up to whatever principles they profess. Most states consider it necessary to protect themselves against the possibility of armed invasion or covert subversion. And many states deprive their own citizens of basic rights and liberties. How does all this affect what justice requires with regard to migration?

First, the conditions of the real world greatly strengthen the case for state sovereignty, especially in those states that have relatively just domestic institutions. National security is a crucial form of public order. So, states are clearly entitled to prevent the entry of people (whether armed invaders or subversives) whose goal is the overthrow of just institutions. On the other hand, the strictures against an expansive use of the public order argument also apply to claims about national security.

A related concern is the claim that immigrants from societies where liberal democratic values are weak or absent would pose a threat to the maintenance of a just public order. Again the distinction between reasonable expectations and hypothetical speculations is crucial. These sorts of arguments were used during the nineteenth century against Catholics and Jews from Europe and against all Asians and Africans. If we judge those arguments to have been proven wrong (not to say ignorant and bigoted) by history, we should be wary of resurrecting them in another guise.

A more realistic concern is the sheer size of the potential demand. If a rich country like the United States were simply to open its doors, the number of people from poor countries seeking to immigrate might truly be overwhelming, even if their goals and beliefs posed no threat to national security or liberal democratic values.[17] Under these conditions, it seems likely that some restrictions on immigration would be justified under the public order principle. But it is important to recall all the qualifications that apply to this. In particular, the need for some restriction would not justify any level of restriction whatsoever or restrictions for other reasons, but only that level of restriction essential to maintain public order. This would surely imply a much less restrictive policy than the one currently in force which is shaped by so many other considerations besides the need to maintain public order.

Rawls asserts that the priority accorded to liberty normally holds under nonideal conditions as well. This suggests that, if there are restrictions on immigration for public order reasons, priority should be given to those seeking to immigrate because they have been denied basic liberties over those seeking to immigrate simply for economic opportunities. There is a further complication, however. The priority of liberty holds absolutely only in the long run. Under nonideal conditions it can sometimes be justifiable to restrict liberty for the sake of economic gains, if that will improve the position of the worst-off and speed the creation of conditions in which all will enjoy equal and full liberties. Would it be justifiable to restrict immigration for the sake of the worst-off?

We have to be wary of hypocritical uses of this sort of argument. If rich states are really concerned with the worst-off in poor states, they can presumably help more by transferring resources and reforming international economic institutions than by restricting immigration. Indeed, there is rea-

alism.[28] The extension of the right to immigrate reflects the same logic: equal treatment of individuals in the public sphere.

As I noted at the beginning of this section, Walzer asserts that the political community is constrained by principles of justice from admitting permanent guest workers without giving them the opportunity to become citizens. There is some ambiguity about whether this claim is intended to apply to all political communities or only to ones like ours. If states have a right to self-determination, broadly conceived, they must have a right to choose political forms and political practices different from those of liberal democracies. That presumably includes the right to establish categories of second-class citizens (or, at least, temporary guest workers) and also the right to determine other aspects of admissions policy in accordance with their own principles.[29] But if the question is what *our* society (or one with the same basic values) ought to do, then the matter is different both for guest workers and for other aliens. It is right to assert that *our* society ought to admit guest workers to full citizenship. Anything else is incompatible with our liberal democratic principles. But so is a restrictive policy on immigration.

Any approach like Walzer's that seeks its ground in the tradition and culture of *our* community must confront, as a methodological paradox, the fact that liberalism is a central part of our culture. The enormous intellectual popularity of Rawls and Nozick and the enduring influence of utilitarianism attest to their ability to communicate contemporary understandings and shared meanings in a language that has legitimacy and power in our culture. These theories would not make such sense to a Buddhist monk in medieval Japan. But their individualistic assumptions and their language of universal, ahistorical reason makes sense to us because of *our* tradition, *our* culture, *our* community. For people in a different moral tradition, one that assumed fundamental moral differences between those inside the society and those outside, restrictions on immigration might be easy to justify. Those who are *other* simply might not count, or at least not count as much. But we cannot dismiss the aliens on the ground that they are other, because *we* are the products of a liberal culture.

The point goes still deeper. To take *our* community as a starting point is to take a community that expresses its moral views in terms of universal principles. Walzer's own arguments reflect this. When he asserts that states may not expel existing inhabitants whom the majority or the new government regards as alien, he is making a claim about what is right and wrong for *any* state not just our own or one that shares our basic values. He develops the argument by drawing on Hobbes. That is an argument from a particular tradition, one that may not be shared by new states that want to expel some of their inhabitants. Nonetheless, Walzer makes a universal claim (and one I consider correct). He makes the same sort of argument when he insists that states may not legitimately restrict emigration.[30] This applies to all political communities not just those that share our understanding of the relation of individual and collective.

Recognition of the particularity of our own culture should not prevent us from making these sorts of claims. We should not try to force others to accept our views, and we should be ready to listen to others and learn from them. But respect for the diversity of communities does not require us to abandon all claims about what other states ought to do. If my arguments are correct, the general case for open borders is deeply rooted in the fundamental values of our tradition. No moral argument will seem acceptable to *us*, if it directly challenges the assumption of the equal moral worth of all individuals. If restrictions on immigration are to be justified, they have to be based on arguments that respect that principle. Walzer's theory has many virtues that I have not explored here, but it does not supply an adequate argument for the state's right to exclude.

■ Conclusion

Free migration may not be immediately achievable, but it is a goal toward which we should strive. And we have an obligation to open our borders much more fully than we do now. The current restrictions on immigration in Western democracies—even in the most open ones like Canada and the United States—are not justifiable. Like feudal barriers to mobility, they protect unjust privilege.

Does it follow that there is *no* room for distinctions between aliens and citizens, no theory of citizenship, no boundaries for the community? Not at all. To say that membership is open to all who wish to join is not to say that there is no distinction between members and nonmembers. Those who choose to cooperate together in the state have special rights and obligations not shared by noncitizens. Respecting the particular choices and commitments that individuals make flows naturally from a commitment to the idea of equal moral worth. (Indeed, consent as a justification for political obligation is least problematic in the case of immigrants.) What is *not* readily compatible with the idea of equal moral worth is the exclusion of those who want to join. If people want to sign the social contract, they should be permitted to do so.

Open borders would threaten the distinctive character of different political communities only because we assume that so many people would move if they could. If the migrants were few, it would not matter. A few immigrants could always be absorbed without changing the character of the community. And, as Walzer observes, most human beings do not love to move.[31] They normally feel attached to their native land and to the particular language, culture, and community in which they grew up and in which

out most of human history, national boundaries (where they existed) were far more permeable to the temporary ebb and flow or permanent movement of peoples than they are today.

The second is the rapid increase in the size of human populations, which has magnified greatly the potential for mass movements across borders, and led to the exhaustion of relatively open spaces for new occupation. In the post–World War II period the rapid rise of population in the developing countries has greatly outstripped the rates of increase that prevailed in Europe during its most rapid period of growth and migration (chiefly to America).[2]

A further new factor is the revolution in international communication and transportation. Modern communications have brought the relative attractiveness of life in the developed world to the attention of quite remote populations in the developing world, and the speed and availability of international travel have sharply reduced the barriers to international movement. The same modern communications have brought vividly before the world's conscience the suffering of refugees on the high seas or in hastily erected encampments, suffering of which most of us would have been unaware in the past.

In addition to these broad historical trends, there is general agreement that the world of the 1980s is a less stable place, both in political and in economic terms, than it has been for much of the postwar period. Domestic or international conflicts may produce real or only pyrrhic victors, but they always produce refugees. Increasing strife, coupled with populations that are today more than twice as large as those of 1950, portends burgeoning numbers of refugees seeking asylum in the coming decades.

The United States is a nation of immigrants, and most of us look with pride upon the invigoration and pluralism that immigrants continue to provide. We have not fully lived up to the poem inscribed on the Statue of Liberty, but the concept of a melting pot of many national origins, however lumpy we know it to be in practice, is still an American ideal. Today, however, the U.S. situation is unique both in world terms and in terms of our own history, by reason of five central facts—and one near-certain projection—that are not always widely grasped:

1. This country is by far the world's largest receiver of refugees and immigrants for permanent settlement; indeed it accepts on the order of twice as many as the rest of the world combined.

2. Immigration and refugee flows to the United States in the late 1970s were at or near the highest levels ever experienced, including the period before immigration was first broadly restricted in the 1920s.

3. There is much dispute as to the numbers of illegal immigrants in the United States, but no responsible group believes there are fewer than sever-

al million, and the consensus range is from four to six million as of the mid-1970s. Of these, about 50–60 percent are thought to be from Mexico, with many other countries providing the rest.

4. While immigration reforms since 1965 have had the laudable intent of eliminating discrimination and promoting diversity among immigrants, the reality has turned out differently. The actual working of the law and the sharp increase in illegal entry have produced an unprecedented concentration among a single linguistic group—Spanish-speakers.

5. There is every indication that the pressures of unemployment, poverty and political instability in much of the developing world will increase greatly in the 1980s and 1990s, and despite conspicuous possible exceptions will tend toward an even greater concentration of immigrants in the groups already dominating current flows.

6. Enforcement of American immigration law by the Immigration and Naturalization Service (INS) is remarkably poor; under present circumstances the chances are very low of even detecting, much less apprehending, violators who show a little persistence.

. . . The remainder of this article therefore seeks to review available evidence on the costs and benefits of large-scale immigration as objectively as possible, with full attention paid to the limits and ambiguities of our knowledge, and to suggest at least the outlines of alternative policy approaches.

■ V

We begin by emphasizing that today's heated debate is concerned solely with *large-scale* immigration and refugee flows, of the magnitudes that have been experienced in the United States during the past several years, i.e., numbers on the order of a million or more legal and illegal immigrants and refugees per year, or nearly half of total population growth. Similar disputes do not arise regarding moderate levels of legal immigration such as those of the 1950s, which averaged about 250,000 per year and 10 percent of population growth, or those of the 1960s, which averaged about 330,000 per year and just over 15 percent of population growth. . . .

Historically, a primary motivation for a policy permitting or encouraging large-scale immigration into the United States has been the need for labor in a burgeoning continental nation with a rapidly expanding economy. For the immigrants, a prominent attraction of the United States (in addition to political and religious freedom) was the easy availability of jobs providing high remuneration by the standards of the sending countries.[3]

The question in 1980 is whether the contribution of large-scale immigration to the U.S. labor force continues to be as important and productive as in the nineteenth and early twentieth centuries, or whether in changed economic and technological conditions it no longer contributes substantially to the economy. A related question is whether large-scale immigration benefits some groups but has high costs for others, and if so how to balance these interests.

There can be little doubt that the millions of guest workers who migrated to some Western and Northern European countries in the 1950s and 1960s were an important factor in the economic miracle experienced by those countries in that period. In the face of a shortage of labor to staff the rapidly expanding economic structure, primarily in the Federal Republic of Germany, France and Switzerland, many governments chose to import temporary workers from labor-surplus countries such as Italy, Greece, Yugoslavia, Turkey, Spain, Portugal and Algeria, with the view that these workers would stay for only a year or two and then return to their home countries with accumulated savings and know-how that would make them more productive there. In the meantime, the intention was to encourage automation and higher productivity in the sectors employing such foreign labor so that it would not be required in the future.

As is well known, this "temporary" migration grew to be far more permanent than intended; at the present time, there are five million guest-workers and seven million dependents in Western and Northern Europe,[4] in spite of an almost universal policy shift in 1973 seeking to avoid recourse to foreign labor and to encourage return migration by those already present. The underlying reason for this policy shift in Western Europe was the increasing social costs of the guest-worker program that became visible in the late 1960s and early 1970s, although the proximate explanation given was fear of recession after the 1973 oil embargo and quadrupling of oil prices. There were also domestic political backlashes (including racial or ethnic antagonisms in France, Germany, and the Netherlands, and a national anti-immigration referendum in Switzerland that failed only narrowly). . . .

Similar economic forces led to sharp downward revisions in immigration quotas at about the same time in most other Western countries receiving large numbers of immigrants, e.g., Canada, Australia and New Zealand. The only exception to this pattern in the Western world has been that of the United States, in which the number of legal immigrants has actually increased substantially over the 1970s, as apparently has the number of illegal or undocumented immigrants.

A major question for future U.S. policy therefore arises: What are the impacts of current and prospective patterns of immigration on the U.S. labor market and economic system? Opinions on this subject range widely among labor economists and other experts. The predominant view is that while continuation of a significant flow of immigrants with scarce skills can represent an important contribution by filling gaps in the American labor force, there is no longer economic justification for large numbers of relatively unskilled and ill-educated immigrant workers and their dependents. In this view, the U.S. economy is now a highly advanced one in which relatively high or specialized levels of education and work skills are virtual necessities for productive employment. While jobs can be found by unskilled workers willing to accept low pay and poor conditions of employment (a maid in El Paso is said to earn \$30–\$40 per week, with no limits on hours worked and no social security or other benefits), a large pool of such workers contributes little to productivity. Indeed, in this view the fact that most illegal aliens are employed in low-skill occupations represents a self-fulfilling prophecy: the large number of compliant workers generates market demand for such labor by retarding the upgrading of wage and working conditions that would make the same jobs attractive to Americans and encourage investment in labor-saving technologies.

As to the future, projections of the balance of demand and supply of labor are clouded in uncertainty. It seems clear that the fertility decline in the United States since the 1960s will mean a tapering off of the rate of growth of indigenous young labor force entrants in the coming decades: specifically, the labor force is projected to still be growing by about 1.2 million per year in the mid-1980s, down from the recent annual increase of 1.5 million. However, if labor force participation of women continues to increase more rapidly than previously anticipated, as has been the case over the past decade, and if political and economic forces lead to a gradual increase in the average age of retirement, as seems likely, the native-born labor force of the United States may well expand more rapidly than projected.

On the other side of the supply-demand equation, there is consensus that it is quite impossible to predict the demand for labor in the U.S. economy beyond the next few years. Fundamentally this is true because no one is able to predict the future of the American economy as a whole, with uncertainties about energy, inflation and capital formation looming large. Moreover, the demand for labor is itself closely related to the supply. For example, if unskilled labor were to become relatively scarce, then its price would rise in relative terms, thereby encouraging mechanization of tasks otherwise performed by unskilled laborers, and also stimulating labor force participation by potential workers who under previous wage conditions found little work incentive as compared to other sources of support available to them.[5]

Under these circumstances of simultaneous uncertainty about both supply and demand, it appears to be beyond the realm of our capacity to predict accurately the tightness or looseness of U.S. labor markets very far into the future. Undaunted, some have tried nonetheless, and on the basis of their results have argued that much-expanded immigration is a necessity for future American economic growth.[6] Such efforts notwithstanding, there is no supportable evidence that U.S. labor markets require large-scale immigration now or in the coming decades, although periodic and objective reassessments must be made as conditions change.

A different view—essentially a different philosophical stance—is taken by a minority of labor economists and other commentators, who hold that there exists a "dual economy" in modern industrial societies, which requires a substantial and growing number of low-paid and unskilled workers in the "secondary labor market." In this view, these jobs will continue to be necessary but so undesirable that they cannot attract enough members of the domestic labor force, no matter what their wages and conditions, and unskilled labor from abroad must therefore be imported to fill them.[7] Hence they see large-scale immigration of unskilled workers as a structural requirement of industrialized capitalist states.

A subsidiary issue is whether immigrants contribute to the productivity of the U.S. economy because they are more hard-working and energetic than are citizens of the United States. The legal immigrants in the 1950s and early 1960s were relatively well educated and highly skilled, and appear to have done well as measured by income, eventually surpassing the average income levels of members of the domestic population with equal educational attainment; the one exceptional group that did not do well economically was immigrants from Mexico, who were predominantly unskilled.[8] Unfortunately, there is no comparable evidence on the considerably different legal immigration flows of the late 1960s and the 1970s, as these must await data from the 1980 Census. . . .

To summarize, it is apparent that immigration can contribute substantially to economic welfare under conditions of rapid economic growth and low unemployment, as in the United States in the nineteenth and early twentieth centuries and in Europe in the 1950s and 1960s. Such benefits are far less likely to have occurred under the conditions that have prevailed in the United States since the early 1970s: low economic growth and high unemployment, especially among those with the lowest educational and skill levels. The predominant expert view, therefore, is that large-scale immigration of low-skill workers cannot be expected to contribute to overall economic well-being over the foreseeable future, though there is economic evidence favoring continued openness to persons with needed skills.
. . .

As indicated above, a related economic question is whether large-scale immigration, whatever might be its contribution to aggregate economic performance, may contribute differentially to the economic well-being of different social groups. Here there seems to be a general consensus among economists that to the extent that there are beneficiaries of immigration, they are the immigrants themselves and the employers and middle-class consumers who tend to benefit from cheap labor in the industrial, agricultural, service and domestic sectors. The possible losers appear to be the lower-income groups of the U.S. population—relatively disadvantaged citizens and recent immigrants who are affected by a growing population of energetic and sometimes even desperate foreign workers willing to work under wage and working conditions that to domestic workers are unattractive but for the immigrants far exceed anything they have experienced.[9]

Despite emotional claims to the contrary, there is general agreement that only moderate direct displacement of labor occurs through one-on-one competition between citizen and immigrant for a particular job, since most citizens are unwilling even to apply for jobs with poor wages and working conditions. However, it is also generally agreed that large-scale inflows of unskilled and compliant labor tend to depress (or to retard improvement of) the wage and benefit conditions of the jobs that are the only ones available to many domestic labor force entrants, especially minorities, youth, women and recent immigrants.[10] Hence the pattern is predominantly one of indirect effects, through relative distortion downward as wages and working conditions in affected markets do not change while those in other jobs continue to improve.[11]

■ VI

There has been much discussion regarding the use by immigrants, legal and illegal, of expensive social services, with consequent effects upon the budgetary problems of federal, state and local governments. Here there have been especially extreme claims on both sides. Those seeking to minimize the impact of migrants claim that there is little or no utilization of such services, especially by illegal immigrants who are said to be fearful of applying for benefits. Those who seek to maximize the perceived impacts of immigration in these sectors appeal to the widespread dismay among the American public regarding the rapid growth of governmental spending, and of welfare, health and education spending in particular, and seek to blame these expansions very largely on immigrants.

A calmer statement of what we know would look something like this. Immigrants, legal and illegal, do make use of social and educational services at levels varying from high to low. Legal immigrants (and especially refugees) initially make substantial use of many such services, though most appear to become productive labor force participants within several years of arrival.[12] With regard to illegal immigrants, the available evidence (admittedly from record systems not designed to record legal status) suggests that publicly financed health services (especially emergency, obstetric and pediatric services) are widely employed; educational (especially remedial and bilingual) services used substantially; unemployment insurance used but not disproportionately; welfare less so; and social security retirement benefits very little. At the same time, immigrants both legal and illegal do pay taxes to support such services, though in the case of the low-paid workers who apparently predominate among illegal immigrants, such taxes are of course very low. [13]

Each of these social service sectors is clouded in controversy and litigation. . . . While some argue that recent immigrant workers are subsidizing the social security retirement system because they have payments withheld but draw little in retirement benefits, others note that this is apparently due primarily to the youthful nature of the immigrant population, and that in the future lower paid immigrants who retire in the United States are likely to become net beneficiaries of the Social Security system.[14]

To summarize the state of knowledge regarding social service costs, immigrants both legal and illegal cannot be blamed for the rapid increase in governmental expenditure on such services, but their impact also cannot be dismissed as trivial. Use of such benefits by immigrants ranges from high to low, depending upon the benefit examined and the characteristics of the immigrant population.

Marginal or incremental costs may be quite high in some areas of health care, remedial education and bilingual education, and in overall educational expenditures in areas with rapidly growing enrollments (e.g., Texas, California), while simultaneously quite low in long-term medical care and in school districts with declining enrollments and hence surplus capacity (e.g., New York City). In all discussions of this set of issues, due attention must be paid to the average age and income of immigrants insofar as these affect their present and future demands on health services, social security, and other age- and income-related services.

■ VII

The controversies about large-scale immigration and refugee flows extend well beyond economic cost/benefit calculations to weighty issues concerning the distribution of political power and the size, composition and coherence of the American populace. One such controversy surrounded by uncharted political and jurisprudential shoals is that currently under review by the federal courts—whether persons present illegally in the United States are constitutionally entitled to full congressional representation and, ultimately, even to the vote. This extraordinary issue was joined in the buildup to the 1980 Census, when the Census Bureau decided to make intensive efforts to enumerate undocumented aliens. This stimulated a law suit (by an advocacy group, several members of Congress, and several states) seeking to enjoin the Census Bureau from including persons illegally present in the United States in congressional reapportionment calculations, on the ground that citizens and legal residents of states with few illegal residents would lose congressional seats to which they were entitled. In its defense brief, the Justice Department argued not only that illegal aliens are constitutionally entitled to be counted for purposes of receiving full representation in the U.S. House of Representatives, but also that "nothing in the Constitution forbids a state from permitting even illegal aliens from voting for Representatives."[15] The case is presently before the U.S. Court of Appeals for the District of Columbia.

The demographic implications of immigration have been exaggerated in opposing ways, with assertions by some that the U.S. population can never cease growing unless illegal immigration is stopped and legal immigration is severely curtailed, and others arguing that current immigration flows represent a miniscule percentage of the U.S. population and are relatively lower than in preceding periods this century.[16]

In this area one is closer to ascertainable fact and reliable projection. If total net immigration into the United States, legal and illegal, is over one million per year at the present time (it surely will be much higher in 1980, as indicated above), then immigration today is contributing at least 40–50 percent of population increase. In addition to this crude estimate, one must add the indirect future effects of the immigrants' fertility behavior, which is likely to be somewhat higher than that of the domestic population since a high percentage of U.S. immigrants are now coming from high-fertility countries. If U.S. fertility rates stay at current low levels, then the proportionate contribution of immigration to total population increase will rise rapidly, although the size of the total increase itself could be declining.[17] Authoritative demographic analyses[18] have shown that substantial net immigration—400,000 per year, or about the level of legal immigration in the early 1970s—is consistent with an eventual stabilizing of the U.S. population well into the next century, if domestic fertility averages slightly below two children per woman.[19]

A further demographic fact is that the Hispanic population is the most rapidly growing subgroup of the U.S. population, due to the unintended predominance of Spanish-speaking immigrants described earlier, coupled with higher than average fertility among some Hispanic groups. Many politically active members of this growing minority group (which is normally defined so as to include many Spanish-speaking U.S. citizens from Puerto Rico) are outspoken in describing their common language as a symbol of cultural pride and a force for ethnic unity and power, and therefore have pressed strongly for bilingual educational, legal, police, fire and other governmental services.[20]

These trends in turn have engendered growing concern about increasing bilingualism and political polarization along linguistic lines.

Labour and Conservative governments in Britain since 1968, and a nation-wide referendum in Switzerland that failed narrowly but would have had the effect of expelling many foreign workers.)

The second broad option is effective enforcement of existing law. While it might seem surprising at first glance that this would face vocal opposition, this is the case and has much to do with the present lax enforcement situation. Under existing law, it is unlawful to enter the United States without permission, to overstay the terms of temporary visas, or to obtain employment under such visas unless authorization to work has also been granted. Hence enforcement of existing law would require effective policing of entry points, adequate follow-up of legal visitors to assure that they depart promptly, and sufficient enforcement of employment prohibitions to make it reasonably difficult to violate them. . . .

A third option is a thoroughgoing revision of present law and practice regarding immigration and refugee policy. Such was the intent of congressional action in 1978 establishing the commission now chaired by Father Hesburgh of the University of Notre Dame. Entitled the Select Commission on Immigration and Refugee Policy, it was charged under Public Law 95-412 with the evaluation of all existing laws, policies and procedures governing the admission of immigrants and refugees and the preparation of legislative and administrative recommendations to the President and Congress. The Commission, due to report in early 1981, has a distinguished membership consisting of four members each of the House and Senate Judiciary Committees, including Chairmen Rodino and Kennedy, four Cabinet officers (Justice, State, Labor, and Health and Human Services), and four public members including its Chairman. A commission of this high quality and political influence ordinarily could be expected to carry considerable weight. Unfortunately, the Select Commission has been plagued from its inception with serious staff problems that are now widely known, and it will require strong efforts by the Commissioners themselves to build internal consensus and external support for the Select Commission's recommendations when they are put forward.

Ultimately, any reforms will depend upon the Congress, which historically has exercised its prerogatives strongly in the immigration and refugee field.[25] The congressional process will, in turn, depend upon a complex and virtually unpredictable confluence of domestic and international political considerations, economic circumstances, and the increasingly Byzantine internal politics of the Congress itself and of its various committees. Despite such uncertainties, the broad outlines of alternative reforms are reasonably clear, and much can be gained by stepping back from the ongoing fray for a dispassionate assessment of the trade-offs that must be made among conflicting values and interests.

require that the sponsor's income and assets be counted in considering a newly arrived alien's application for Supplemental Security Income (SSI), a quasi-welfare benefit for which only low-income persons who are over 65, disabled, or blind are eligible.

13. Advocates of continued illegal immigration have been impressed by data from David S. North and Marion F. Houstoun, *The Characteristics and Role of Illegal Aliens in the U.S. Labor Market: An Exploratory Study*, U.S. Department of Labor, Washington, 1976, showing that 73.2 percent of apprehended illegal aliens report having had income taxes withheld from their pay. It is worth noting, however, that the relatively low wages paid most illegal immigrants mean that any income taxes withheld are small. For example, a single person earning the minimum wage would pay less than $500 a year in federal income tax, if the person is married, with one child, the tax would be $4 a year. Such a worker would of course pay modest Social Security contributions and local taxes as well.

14. Social security retirement benefits are deliberately redistributive, with higher relative payments going to lower paid workers. Hence to the extent legal and illegal immigrants are concentrated among the lower paid, eventual social security payments will be redistributive in their favor. This fact renders implausible arguments by some that social security deficits can be eliminated by increasing immigration flows of young, unskilled workers.

15. Department of Justice Memorandum submitted in *Federation for American Immigration Reform (FAIR) et al. v. Klutznick et al.*, unreported, Federal District Court for the District of Columbia, Case No. 79-3269, February 26, 1980, p. 10.

16. See, for example, the paper by staff members of the Select Commission on Immigration and Refugee Policy entitled "Immigration How Many?," p. 2 and the same Commission's *Newsletter*, No. 4 (Feb., 1980), p. 8.

17. The "proportion of population growth" calculation can be misleading if growth is near zero, since even a small number of net immigrants would then account for nearly 100 percent of population growth. However, under the assumptions specified here, U.S. population growth would not approach zero until the middle of the next century.

18. Ansley J. Coale, "Alternative Paths to a Stationary Population," Commission on Population Growth and the American Future, *Demographic and Social Aspects of Population Growth*, edited by Charles F. Westoff and Robert Parke, Jr., Washington GPO, 1972, pp. 589–603. There is of course no national consensus as to the desirability of a non-growing U.S. population.

19. Note that the above fertility assumptions are qualified by "if." Some reputable demographers expect a continuation of recent record-low fertility (e.g., Charles F. Westoff, "Marriage and Fertility in the Developed Countries," *Scientific American, 239* (6), December 1978, while others anticipate a new baby boom (e.g., Richard A. Easterlin, *Birth and Fortune*, New York: Basic Books, 1980).

20. The bilingual debate is usually discussed in terms of a multiplicity of first languages other than English, but in fact bilingual services are provided overwhelmingly to Spanish-speaking residents of the United States. For example, while federally supported bilingual education is provided in fully 72 languages, 70–75 percent of the students participating are Spanish-speaking. See National Center for Education Statistics, Bulletin 78B-5, August 22, 1978.

21. A Mexican government official is quoted as stating recently that "twelve million rural Mexicans were undernourished, fourteen million lacked drinking

water, half earned less than 435 U.S. dollars a year, and 44 percent of those who had work could only find it for three months in the year. A study by the Mexican National Bank of Rural Credit suggested that "of the seven and a quarter million *campesinos* of working age some five million were unemployed or underemployed." The Mexican national unemployment rate is estimated at 35 percent, with an income distribution that leaves 50 percent of the population with less than 17 percent of national income. See Peter Cleaves, Michael Redclift and Nanneke Redclift, "Mexican Development Problems of an Oil-Rich Neighbor" (Ms, The Ford Foundation, Mexico City, 1980).

22. Cited in Otis L. Graham, Jr., "Illegal Immigration and the New Reform Movement," Immigration paper II, Federation for American Immigration Reform, Washington, D.C., February 1980, p. 11.

23. Smith, *op. cit.*, footnote 13, p. 26.

24. The apparent currency of such arguments in some State Department circles is suggested by a devastating Herblock cartoon in *The Washington Post* (December 15, 1978) showing four foreign policy experts in a situation room before a map of the Mexico-U.S. border, with one exclaiming in a flash of insight, "What if we asked each illegal alien to roll a barrel of oil in with him?"

25. The 1952 McCarran-Walter Act was passed by Congress over President Truman's veto—the only postwar case of a Democratic Congress overriding a Democratic President until the rejection of President Carter's "oil conservation tax" in June 1980. Conversely, President Carter's 1977 initiative on illegal immigration sank without a trace in Congress.

26. The policies of the American Civil Liberties Union are instructive ACLU opposition is expressed toward sanctions against employers hiring aliens unlawfully in the United States (Board Policy No. 327), use of a social security card or any other governmentally issued document as a condition of employment (*ibid.*), deportation of any minors illegally in the United States (No. 329), raids on workplaces suspected of employing illegal aliens (*Ramos v. Anderson* suit in Texas), and so on.

27. Some INS limitations have an Alice in Wonderland quality. Two examples: first, INS investigators who receive reliable but confidential information from informants about places of work or residence harboring large numbers of illegal aliens are prohibited by Justice Department directives from inspecting these premises. Second, due to budget problems, Border Patrol stations in Texas suffered a 60–70 percent cut in their gasoline allocations for at least one month of 1980, leading to a ration of 4–6 gallons per (gas-guzzling) patrol vehicle for each eight-hour shift in one important border sector.

28. International City Management Association, *Municipal Yearbook 1980*, Washington, 1979, p. 120.

29. In this respect, recent policies of the U.S. government—both permitting dramatically increased refugee flows and curtailing law enforcement against illegal immigration during a period of severe economic stresses—must be adjudged to be lacking in prudence by long-sighted supporters of continued openness in immigration policy.

30. Since 1952, as former Attorney General Griffin Bell has noted, the present "parole" authority of the Attorney General has frequently been exercised in circumstances not envisaged by the Congress. The problem has recently been highlighted by the widely criticized handling of the so-called freedom flotilla from Cuba.

31. To this end, the immigration policies of Canada and other leading countries of immigration would appear to be worthy of our careful examination. The

practice of many states and additional emphasis on protecting IDPs and human rights monitoring in places of origin. But the critique remains relevant and questions the impartial liberal universalist ethical credentials of the international refugee regime.

The challenge from the other side is arguably more serious, and it is the main focus of this paper: the claim that the Geneva Convention imposes unfeasible obligations on states. It established a cumbersome legal procedure for examining individual applications, with a bias toward permanent exile rather than repatriation. These provisions were feasible in the postwar years, but given the increased numbers of refugees and would-be migrants, so the argument runs, the convention now places excessive obligations on receiving states. Arguments about the outdatedness of the Geneva Convention were used to justify the introduction of temporary protection schemes as a more limited form of protection for those fleeing civil conflict or generalized violence. But temporary protection has raised its own set of dilemmas about integration and repatriation, and in any case has not solved the problem of the continued numbers of asylum seekers and irregular migrants seeking to enter European states.

This feasibility challenge to the post–World War II refugee regime needs to be taken seriously. It has already precipitated the erosion of protection standards in European states through the introduction of restrictions on entry, accelerated procedures, declining standards of assistance for asylum seekers, and more restrictive interpretations of the definition of *refugee*. It has been used to justify calls for a more radical revision of the Geneva Convention, threatening to undermine the liberal universalist principles codified in international refugee law.

How can liberal universalists best defend their conception of refugee rights against the attack? Before considering possible responses, it is important to examine the substance and force of rival arguments based on notions of nationalism and the national interest.

■ Nationalist Justifications for Restriction

Nationalism in its broadest sense is a doctrine or theory asserting the special claims of members of a particular national group. The rise of nationalism and theories of the moral relevance of nations was closely bound up with the process of state formation and consolidation in Europe. Notions of a shared national character or identity began to emerge around the fifteenth century as a number of European states gradually consolidated and centralized control over the population of clearly demarcated national territories. This consolidation was achieved partly through the centralization of administration, improved education, and the imposition of a national language (Gellner, 1983). Notions of the moral and political relevance of nationalism were also actively mobilized to ensure support for taxation and military recruitment for defense and international wars (Hobsbawm, 1990). A more populist form of nationalism exemplified in Rousseau's concept of the "general will" was meanwhile given impetus by the French Revolution, which identified national self-determination with democratic popular resistance against monarchical rule. Notions of nationalism were given a more particularist slant in nineteenth-century romantic theories of nationalism, which were also used to justify and generate support for claims to self-determination, national unification (in the cases of Italy and Germany), colonialism, and territorial expansion.

The relevance of national membership became more decisive with the expansion of suffrage and development of the welfare state. Citizenship now carried not only civil and political rights but also a range of socioeconomic entitlements. In the context of refugee and migration policy, this expansion gave rise to what I term *welfare nationalism,* the claim of nationals to a privileged standard of socioeconomic welfare. This form of nationalism has characterized left-wing and trade union arguments for restricting migration on the grounds that it would undermine wages, threaten job security, or lead to a decline in the level of welfare support. Such welfare nationalist arguments were evident in the interwar debate in France, the United Kingdom, and the Netherlands on accepting refugees from Germany, Italy, and Spain (Marrus, 1985). These arguments reemerged from the 1970s onward in the face of rising unemployment and subsequent programs in many countries to liberalize labor markets and reduce social benefits. These arguments have taken on increased force as political parties have competed to mobilize electoral support with guarantees to protect the labor and welfare rights of nationals from outsiders.

A second form of nationalism, what I term *ethnocentric nationalism,* was built on the more romantic or culturalist strands of nineteenth-century thought.[8] Here the relevance of nationality has more to do with shared culture, language, and norms than with privileged access to welfare. Although racist forms of ethnocentric nationalism have been widely discredited, they continue to crop up more or less explicitly in the rhetoric of far-right parties. More common, though, is the idea of preserving the cultural identity of national communities, which is evident in the discourse of center-right and Christian democratic parties in many European states.

Both welfare and ethnonationalism arguments have been drawn on in the political debate to challenge the relevance and feasibility of liberal universalist approaches to refugees. Over the past two decades they have come to the fore in the context of the "renationalizing" discourse on migration and refugee issues, justifying states' prerogative to restrict migration. In explaining this tendency, a number of theorists have stressed the impact of globalization, which has generated anxieties about the changing role and functions of the state, and especially its capacity to protect citizens' socio-economic stability and cultural identity (Heisler and Henry, 1993: 196; Huysmans, 1998: 242; Schmidtke, 1999: 87). Other scholars have stressed the significance of the end of the Cold War, which demoted refugee policy from high politics to a subject of domestic electoral politics (Chimni, 1998; Gibney, 2000). Both of these developments generated a revival of national-ist arguments. From the welfare nationalist perspective, socioeconomic insecurity is channeled into antiforeigner sentiment, with immigrants and asylum seekers blamed for unemployment or perceived as receiving overly generous welfare support. An ethnonationalist perspective would attribute anxieties about identity to the damaging impact of immigration on the shared norms and values of the receiving community.

Since both varieties of the nationalist argument privilege the interests of nationals over those of immigrants and refugees, it is difficult to see how they are reconcilable with the liberal universalist position. Certainly in philosophical terms, they seem entirely incompatible. Universalism, as we saw, is grounded in the moral equality of all individuals, regardless of nationality, ethnic group, or other ethically arbitrary characteristics. Nationalism, on the other hand, emphasizes the particular characteristics of members of national communities. It is these special, shared characteristics that are morally relevant: They establish special duties and ties between members of the community that justify a privileged status relative to non-members. From this perspective, duties based on universal characteristics take second place, and communities are morally justified in prioritizing the claims of members over those of outsiders. The two positions also appear to be irreconcilable in their practical prescriptions, lending support to opposing policies on asylum and migration.

Why should this dichotomy between the two positions be of serious concern to liberal universalists? According to one line of reasoning, com-munitarian nationalist arguments are simply a "rationalisation of selfish-ness" and should not be given any credibility or moral weight in the debate (Barry, 1987: 106). But this judgment seems too hasty. Such arguments do express an important and deep-seated notion of the ethical relevance of community ties, shared values, and norms. Moreover, from a pragmatic perspective, defenders of refugee rights simply cannot afford to ignore these arguments. Over the past two decades nationalist arguments have dominated the populist discourse on refugee policy in many European states.[9] Despite the growing electoral significance of ethnic minorities, such arguments for restriction are accepted by almost all mainstream par-ties. Center-left and moderate right parties have continued to pay lip ser-vice to international obligations to refugees, but in practice, as we saw, they have introduced various legislative reforms that have made it almost impossible for refugees to seek asylum in European states. By contrast, the practical demands of liberal universalist refugee law appear to have become politically unacceptable, generating a risk that they will come to be seen as increasingly irrelevant to the refugee policy debate. By advancing such stringent conceptions of duties, liberal universalism may be effectively relegating itself to the margins of political discussion.

If one accepts the fact that liberal refugee policies are being marginalized, it may make sense to look for some sort of compromise between the demands of universalism and nationalism. But liberal universalism faces a second (related) problem in responding to this threat of marginalization, stemming from its structural rigidity. The fundamental commitment to equal rights makes it difficult to find ways to combine a commitment to universal duties with recognition of the ethical relevance of local communities. If people's claims to protection are grounded in their universally shared characteristics, a consistent universalist cannot accept that special duties to fellow nationals could ever override the obligation to help nonmembers whose need is greater. As such, liberal universalist theories have problems accounting for the significance of membership in particular sates or communities. Starting from a premise of the moral equality of all individuals, pure universalist theories view the claims of national membership as ethically irrelevant. The various philosophical attempts to combine universalist positions with a commitment to "special ties" reveal the problems inherent in mixing the two ethical positions. Such hybrid theories tend to result in an incoherent jumble of different types of justification based on conflicting premises (e.g., Miller, 1995). Alternatively, they may be based on implausible empirical premises about the limited level of refugee flows, denying that such a conflict between the two accounts need arise at all (Singer, 1979; Walzer, 1990; Habermas, 1992; Rawls, 1999).

It could be countered that this conceptual rigidity is limited to the theoretical level and that in practice liberal universalists have been able to recognize and integrate both universalist and communitarian or nationalist claims. But it is my contention that the lack of a coherent conceptual basis for defending this type of hybrid position gives liberal universalist arguments rather shaky foundations. It has made it difficult for advocates of refugee rights to adopt consistent and well-reasoned positions on which sorts of policies are ethically acceptable and which are not. Hence the confused debate surrounding the legitimacy of policies such as reception in the region, voluntary repatriation, temporary protection, and dispersal of asylum seekers, to name but a few. Most liberal universalists have acknowledged the potential legitimacy of such responses under certain conditions, mainly for pragmatic reasons or because they intuitively accept at least limited claims of states to keep down the costs of asylum. But in each case, liberal universalists have found it difficult to agree on where to draw the appropriate balance between recognizing the claims of receiving states and ensuring protection for displaced persons (for a selection of critiques, see Nicholson and Twomey, 1999; Barutciski, 1996; Hathaway, 1995).

It is important to consider whether liberal universalists can find a more helpful conceptual basis for defining possible responses to declining protection standards. Is there an alternative ethical position that could help realize refugee rights while being more politically acceptable? Although the commitment to the moral equality of human beings seems to make any compromise in this direction extremely difficult philosophically, perhaps there are possibilities for bridging the dichotomy between nationalist and universalist positions. I shall consider four possibilities in the final section.

■ Overcoming the Impasse?

Deny Any Practical Conflict Between the Two Agendas
The first approach denies that there is any real conflict in the prescriptions of the two ethical positions. Rather, one should stress the potential for practical convergence of the demands of these two ethical positions. This position draws on evidence of the emerging proimmigration agenda in many European countries. We saw earlier that until the 1970s the two ethical positions did not significantly conflict in practice. The two philosophies came into clear political conflict only in the 1970s because of growing political resistance to receiving more migrants and refugees. Yet over the past two years many European countries have been once more acknowledging the need for more liberal migration policies to fill gaps in labor markets or offset the welfare costs of aging populations. In principle, the economic need for migration could imply a convergence of liberal universalist arguments for more open migration policies and arguments for protecting the socioeconomic interests of nationals. Clearly, this economic argument for migration would not allay the concerns of ethnonationalists, whose objection to immigration is based on cultural rather than economic concerns. But it could arguably win over welfare nationalists, insofar as immigration is seen as benefiting the economy and funding the rising costs of pensions. As such, it could render the conflict between universalism and nationalism largely academic.

Attractive as this thesis may be, the demand for labor migrants is unlikely to resolve the conflict over refugee and asylum issues. The demand for labor is—at least at present—restricted to particular sectors and hence will only target those with the relevant skills (e.g., information technology specialists, medical staff, and caterers). Not all asylum seekers will have the relevant qualifications or professional experience. Moreover, the favored channels for recruiting labor in, for example, the UK or Germany are through green-card or points systems. It is unlikely that European states will draw on the pool of asylum seekers as a channel for recruitment: The asylum system is expensive and difficult to manage, and recruiting through this channel would be seen as a possible "pull" factor for potential asylum seekers. So the notion that the demands of universalism and welfare nationalism will converge around this agenda appears overly optimistic.

Reach Consensus Through Dialogue

The second possibility is to accept that there is a conflict between the two but to try to win over nationalists through constructive engagement and dialogue. This approach implies that liberal universalists should adopt a pragmatic position, continuing to push for refugee protection standards but accepting that they will have to compromise with nationalist positions where these standards are not feasible. The underlying assumption is that policymakers and European publics are in principle open to arguments about refugee rights and can be influenced to make at least moderate concessions to ensure refugee protection. Although the dominant policy discourse may be nationalist, there is nonetheless a continued recognition by many of the moral claims of liberal universalism. This is the approach that has been more or less adopted by UNHCR and human rights and refugee lobby groups. It is a strategy that may have helped stop an even more radical erosion of refugee law, but it has certainly not succeeded in preventing a serious decline in protection standards. It may become more difficult to make this case in the aftermath of the terrorist attacks of September 11, 2001, which are being used by politicians to justify a range of measures to restrict the rights of asylum seekers. As long as governments continue to rely on electoral support through playing the national protectionist card, and as long as they can make a convincing ethical case for prioritizing the interests of nationals over international protection obligations, liberal universalist arguments are unlikely to prevent the emergence of these restrictionist agendas.

Explore Alternative Strands
in Liberal Universalist Thought

A third option is to explore alternative strands of liberal universalist thought that might provide a better basis for developing more politically acceptable solutions. There is limited space here to explore the possibilities in detail, but one approach that has been particularly favoured in literature on international ethics is social contract theories.[10] In principle, social contract theories could offer a route for reconciling commitments to universal duties with a recognition of the special claims of national membership. Such arguments tend to run as follows: All human beings have equal rights, but these rights are best realized through membership in particular states. Thus, rather than focusing on responding to the symptoms of breakdown of national protection in problematic states through offering asylum to refugees, the onus should be on measures to ensure that people are better protected in countries of origin. This approach provides an ethical justification for investing more resources in so-called alternative solutions to refugee problems, such as reinforced human rights monitoring, protection of internally displaced persons, protection in the region, prevention, and so on—the list is familiar.

However, this approach is difficult to sustain where national protection has effectively broken down. Refugee flows are an outcome precisely of the failure of this division of responsibility for protection between different states. It is of limited help to treat the phenomenon of refugees as an unfortunate aberration from the norm: It is a widespread and ongoing problem that requires robust rules to address it. Perhaps there should be more emphasis on addressing the causes of flight and finding solutions to refugee problems in countries of origin. But such forms of intervention have a patchy record and will certainly not eliminate the need for asylum in industrialized states.

Reground Liberal Universalist Ethics

So what options remain? A fourth possible approach—and the one I advocate here—is to challenge the very foundations of this supposed dichotomy between liberal universalism and nationalism. The divergence between the two appeared to be particularly intractable because of the very different ethical premises upon which they are grounded. According to liberal universalism, adopting an ethical perspective involves abstracting different people or groups from their special ethnic or religious characteristics and according them all equal rights based on their shared humanity. On this basis, what is ethically relevant about people are certain universally shared attributes—a capacity for reason, autonomy, or certain basic needs. From this claim, liberal universalists proceed to justify universally valid ethical norms that should trump other values and practices. By contrast, nationalism puts the ethical weight on precisely those special, nonuniversal characteristics that are common to members of particular communities. It does not accept that there is one universally shared set of characteristics that grounds universally valid norms. Instead each community or nation develops its own set of ethical norms and practices, which define and shape the beliefs, interests, and identity of its members.[11]

The liberal universalist perspective has increasingly come under fire from critics claiming that liberal values have no special claim to universal validity. Instead, it is argued, liberal universalism is just one tradition of moral and political thought, particular to Western liberal democracies. This type of liberal universalism emerged in Western states because of a specific configuration of socioeconomic, political, and cultural conditions.[12] It may

be a particularly tenacious tradition of thought, but it is nonetheless historically contingent and has no special claim to universal truth.

Recognizing the historical contingency of liberal universalist ideas
does not have to undermine their force. These values are deeply constitutive of the identity of those socialized in liberal democracies and are not
something we can simply choose to opt into or out of. Moreover, the appeal
of these ideas has spread well beyond liberal democratic states, mainly
because of the hugely successful record of this model of governance in
bringing about economic prosperity and political stability. Human rights
discourse has also proved to be highly effective in mobilizing resistance to
authoritarian regimes as well as struggles for socioeconomic equality. This
effectiveness suggests that despite the rejection of the foundational claims
of liberal universalism—the notion that these values are somehow universally valid or transcendental—they do nonetheless have a particularly
enduring and pervasive influence.

This denial of the universal validity of liberal universalism might
appear to be a rather counterproductive move for an advocate of more liberal refugee policies. But by abandoning these claims, one can arguably offer
a more effective route for mobilizing commitment to refugee rights. We
saw that nationalist arguments appeal to shared values and culture to justify
closure to outsiders. But there is also a central strand of European and
Christian culture that advocates extending rights to all human beings. Such
values need not be juxtaposed with nationalist ideas but should be seen as
an important element of shared norms in liberal democratic states. Refugee
campaigners need to emphasize that liberal responses to refugees are not an
external imposition of international law, which will necessarily conflict
with local cultures. Rather, they embody a tradition of Western thought that
is constitutive of the group identity and culture of most European nations.
By articulating a commitment to these liberal goals, communities can also
celebrate and reinforce their shared norms. A generous attitude toward
helping outsiders can reaffirm group identities.[13]

I have perhaps stated the argument too forcefully, and there are of
course risks in abandoning the universalist foundations of liberalism.
However, there appears to be more mileage to be gotten out of mobilizing
support by appealing to shared liberal traditions. It helps undermine the
notion of a necessary dichotomy between group values and universal
norms, locating a commitment to universal values in the culture of receiving communities. This approach offers a means of overcoming some of the
constraints of liberal universalism discussed in the last section. It provides
conceptual scope for combining a commitment to universal rights with a
recognition of the relevance of community ties. And, arguably, it offers a
better strategy for mobilizing support for more generous refugee policies
through emphasizing a group's pride in affirming a shared liberal tradition.

It is an approach that could be further explored by advocates of refugee rights.

■ Conclusion

Ethical norms play an important role in justifying different policy responses to refugees. Equally, the shortcomings of these ideas can constrain the debate on legitimate policies. I have argued that the practical unfeasibility and conceptual rigidity of liberal universalism is currently imposing this sort of constraint on the debate on refugee policy. Its philosophical grounding and practical prescriptions seem to conflict irreconcilably with nationalist or communitarian notions of the privileged claims of nationals vis-à-vis outsiders. My suggested response was to reject the foundational claims of liberal universalism to the status of universal validity. Instead these values should be located in a distinctive tradition of Western liberal thought. Although this shift may at first sight appear to undermine their validity, I argued that this move would both overcome the supposed dichotomy between liberal and nationalist ethical claims and provide an alternative route for mobilizing support for more generous refugee policies. Arguably, this change could help solve the liberal dilemma of the ethics of refugee policy in liberal democratic states.

But where does this leave us in relation to the other liberal dilemma? Does this discussion inform responses to the tension between economic liberalism and political closure? There are several parallels between the two debates. As with ethical liberalism and nationalism, the economic liberal paradox reflects a conflict between claims for free movement and the politics of closure and exclusion. But although economic liberalism is also opposed by nationalists, it does not risk the same type of marginalization as ethical liberal universalism. With strong backing from business interests and most center and liberal parties, the economic liberal case has enough powerful supporters to ensure that it remains firmly on the political agenda. Thus, economic liberalism does not need salvaging in the same way that ethical liberalism does. It has more robust political backing from an influential constituency. This may, however, be of little consolation to ethical liberal universalists. As we saw in the last section, the two positions will not always coincide in their prescriptions for refugee policy. Economic liberalism favors free movement of workers to maximize the efficiency and competitiveness of markets. Its rationale is economic rather than ethical, and as such it is not committed to defending refugee rights except insofar as these may help liberalize the free movement of labor.

This divergence in the practical prescriptions of economic and ethical liberalism has two important consequences. The first is that it leaves the future direction of European migration policies highly uncertain.

Economic-liberal calls for more generous migration policies may in some cases coincide with the agenda of ethical universalists, especially if they imply admitting those in need of protection. Such policies may also potentially win over welfare nationalists if it can be shown that immigration of highly skilled laborers could boost economic production, create jobs, or contribute to pensions. But the case for more liberal migration policies will be most strongly resisted by ethnonationalists, keen to protect the values and culture of receiving communities. Even these right-wing groups, however, will find it increasingly difficult to resist pressure from the business community. So the outcome of the policy debate will depend in large part on the specific constellation of interest groups, political parties, electoral systems, and policy discourse in each country. Far from being a clear dichotomy between two distinct sets of interests, the coalitions appear to be highly fluid and show varying patterns in different states (Boswell, 2003).

The second point to stress is that insofar as policies to liberalize migration do prevail in some countries, these policies will not necessarily have a positive impact on refugees and asylum seekers. On the contrary, the current tendency seems to point in the other direction. Proponents of economic liberalism appear all too willing to draw a sharp distinction in their treatment of economically desirable labor migrants and burdensome asylum seekers and illegal migrants. On a pessimistic projection, political parties will be keen to channel public ill feeling about the costs of immigration into anti–asylum seeker sentiment rather than letting it undermine their business-friendly migration agenda. Under this scenario, ethical liberal universalism will need to be more resourceful than ever in mobilizing a commitment to protecting the rights and welfare of those migrants in categories not deemed to be economically beneficial. I have suggested one way in which ethical liberal universalism could be refashioned to generate more support for this cause. But even this move will have limited impact in the absence of support from political parties and business interests. So one can conclude with a third liberal paradox: The economic liberal agenda for increased labor migration could be just as undermining to ethical liberal refugee policies as that of nationalism.

■ Notes

1. As Favell puts it, they represent "the palette of ideas that exist as reference-points in political debates and justifications." Favell goes on to stress, however, that an analysis of traditions of political thought cannot provide a full explanation for the emergence of particular policy responses—a point I would agree with. Favell (1998), 334. See also Favell (1999: 211–216) for a more general critique of purely normative theory approaches.

2. This section will draw on an argument developed in Boswell (2000).

3. The most influential theories to have emerged so far are the political econ-

omy model of Gary Freeman and neoinstitutional approaches offered by writers such as Joppke (1999), James Hollifield (1992), and Guiraudon (2003).

4. There are a few notable exceptions. A number of political philosophers have analyzed the question of duties to refugees, including Matthew Gibney (2004) and collections by Barry and Goodin (1992) and Mark Gibney (1989); see also Singer (1979) and Carens (1987) and brief comments in the theories of Ackerman (1980), Walzer (1983), Habermas (1992), and Rawls (1999).

5. See, for example, Defoe's pamphlet justifying English generosity toward Protestant refugees from Germany in the early eighteenth century (Defoe, 1709). Marrus provides fascinating accounts of the debate on reception of political exiles in nineteenth-century Europe (Marrus, 1985).

6. These concerns were voiced by delegates from France, Germany, Italy, and the Netherlands—despite the fact that the convention was originally limited to Europe.

7. See Hathaway (1997) for a defense of the narrow definition against this attack. Interestingly, he justifies his defense on grounds of feasibility.

8. This typology of "ethno-" and "welfare" nationalism draws on the account of Michael Mann, although he does not use these terms (Mann, 1995; 1999). Rogers Brubaker also adopts a similar distinction between "political" and "ethnocultural" nationalism (Brubaker, 1992).

9. Schmidtke even questions whether liberal states' migration policies "can still be considered to be within the framework of liberal politics" (1999: 90).

10. Rawls applies his contract theory to the international level in Rawls (1999); the account owes much to Kant's classic argument in his "Law of Nations"—see Kant (1977). For alternative applications of Rawlsian theory to the international sphere, see Beitz (1979) and Pogge (1989).

11. For classic accounts of this conception of community, see Sandel (1982), MacIntyre (1988), Taylor (1989), and Honneth (1995).

12. For histories of liberal thought, see Shapiro (1986), MacIntyre (1988), Taylor (1989), or, for an intelligent Marxist account, MacPherson's classic (1962).

13. Taylor makes this point about the motivating force of articulating shared values (1989: 518). There are two main risks. The first is that denying the universal validity of liberal universalism will undermine its general legitimacy. The second related risk is that it implies that liberal universalist values are valid only for members of communities with a tradition of this type of thought. The first concern is debatable—indeed, I argue here that it is precisely a recognition of these values as rooted in communities that can give them more appeal. The second argument needs to be taken seriously, although is not a concern for liberal democratic societies where there is a historical tradition of this kind. Arguably, most societies also have some set of norms justifying hospitality or assistance to nonmembers, which could provide a local basis for mobilizing support for refugee protection.

■ References

Ackerman, Bruce. 1980. *Social Justice in the Liberal State*. New Haven, CT: Yale University Press.

Barry, Brian. 1987. "Can States be Moral? International Morality and the Compliance Problem." In *International Ethics in the Nuclear Age*. Ed. Robert J. Myers. Lanham, MD, and London: University Press of America, pp. 85–110.

Barry, Brian, and Robert E. Goodin, eds. 1992. *Free Movement: Ethical Issues in the Transnational Migration of People and of Money*. Hemel Hempstead: Harvester Wheatsheaf.

Barutciski, Mikhael. 1996. "The Reinforcement of Non-Admission Policies and the Subversion of UNHCR." *International Journal of Refugee Law* 8, no.1/2: 49–110.

Beitz, Charles. 1979. *Political Theory and International Relations*. Princeton, NJ: Princeton University Press.

Boswell, Christina. 2000. "European Values and the Asylum Crisis." *International Affairs* 76, no. 3: 537–557.

———. 2003. *European Migration Policies in Flux: Changing Patterns of Inclusion and Exclusion*. Oxford: Blackwell and RIIA.

Brubaker, Rogers. 1992. *Citizenship and Nationhood in France and Germany*. Cambridge, MA: Harvard University Press.

Carens, Joseph H. 1987. "Aliens and Citizens: The Case for Open Borders." *Review of Politics* 49, no. 2: 251–273.

Chimni, B. S. 1998. "The Geopolitics of Refugee Studies: A View from the South." *Journal of Refugee Studies* 11, no. 4: 350–374.

Coles, Gervase. 1990. "Approaching the Refugee Problem Today." In *Refugees and International Relations*. Eds. Gil Loescher and Laila Monahan. Oxford: Clarendon Press, pp. 373–410.

Defoe, Daniel. 1709. *A Brief History of the Poor Palatine Refugees, Lately Arriv'd in England*. London.

d'Entreves, A. Passerin. 1970. *Natural Law*. London: Hutchinson.

Favell, Adrian. 1998. "Multicultural Race Relations in Britain: Problems of Interpretation and Explanation." In *Challenge to the Nation-State: Immigration in Western Europe and the United States*. Ed. Christian Joppke. Oxford and New York: Oxford University Press, pp. 319–349.

———. 1999. "To Belong or Not to Belong: The Postnational Question." In *The Politics of Belonging: Migrants and Minorities in Contemporary Europe*. Eds. Andrew Geddes and Adrian Favell. Aldershot, UK: Ashgate, pp. 209–227.

Freeman, Gary P. 1995. "Modes of Immigration Politics in Liberal Democratic States." *International Migration Review* 24, no. 4: 881–902.

———. 1998. "The Decline of Sovereignty? Politics and Immigration Restriction in Liberal States." In *Challenge to the Nation-State: Immigration in Western Europe and the United States*. Ed. Christian Joppke. Oxford and New York: Oxford University Press, pp. 86–108.

Gellner, Ernest. 1983. *Nations and Nationalism, New Perspectives on the Past*. Oxford: Blackwell.

Gibney, Mark, ed. 1989. *Open Borders? Closed Societies? The Ethical and Political Issues*. New York and London: Greenwood.

Gibney, Matthew J. 2000. "The State of Asylum: Democratization, Judicialization and Evolution of Refugee Policy in Europe." *New Issues in Refugee Research*, Working Paper no. 50. Geneva: UNHCR.

———. 2004. *The Ethics and Politics of Asylum*. Cambridge: Cambridge University Press.

Guiraudon, Virginie. 2003. "The Constitution of a European Immigration Policy Domain: A Political Sociology Approach." *Journal of European Public Policy* 10, no. 2: 263–282.

Habermas, Jürgen. 1992. "Citizenship and National Identity: Some Reflections on the Future of Europe." *Praxis International* 12, no. 1: 1–19.

Hathaway, James C. 1995. "New Directions to Avoid Hard Problems: The

Distortion of the Palliative Role of International Protection." *Journal of Refugee Studies* 8, no. 3: 288–300.

———. 1997. "Is Refugee Status Really Elitist?" In *Europe and Refugees: A Challenge?* Eds. Jean-Yves Carlier and Dirk Vanheule. The Hague: Kluwer Law International, pp. 79–88.

Heisler, Martin O., and Zig Layton Henry. 1993. "Migration and the Links Between Social and Societal Security." In *Identity, Migration and the New Security Agenda in Europe.* Eds. Ole Weaver, Barry Buzan, Morten Kelstip, and Pierre Lemiare. London: Pinter Publishers, pp. 148–166.

Hobsbawm, Eric J. 1990. *Nations and Nationalism Since 1780: Programme, Myth, Reality.* Cambridge: Cambridge University Press.

Hollifield, James F. 1992. *Immigrants, Markets and States: The Political Economy of Postwar Europe.* Cambridge, MA: Harvard University Press.

———. 2000. "The Politics of International Migration: How Can We 'Bring the State Back In'?" In *Migration Theory: Talking Across Disciplines.* Eds. Carline B. Brettell and James F. Hollifield. New York and London: Routledge, pp. 137–185.

Honneth, Axel. 1995. "The Limits of Liberalism: On the Political-Ethical Discussion Concerning Communitarianism." *The Fragmented World of the Social: Essays in Social and Political Philosophy.* New York: State University of New York Press, pp. 231–246.

Huysmans, Jef. 1998. "Security! What Do You Mean? From Concept to Thick Signifier." *European Journal of International Relations* 4, no. 2: 226–255.

Jacobson, David. 1996. *Rights Across Borders: Immigration and the Decline of Citizenship.* Baltimore and London: Johns Hopkins University Press.

Joppke, Christian. 1998. "Immigration Challenges to the Nation-State." In *Challenge to the Nation-State: Immigration in Western Europe and the United States.* Ed. Christian Joppke. Oxford and New York: Oxford University Press, pp. 5–46.

———. 1999. *Immigration and the Nation-State.* Oxford and New York: Oxford University Press.

Kant, Immanuel. 1977. *Kant's Political Writings.* Ed. Hans Reiss. Cambridge: Cambridge University Press.

MacIntyre, Alasdair. 1988. *Whose Justice? Which Rationality?* London: Duckworth.

MacPherson, C. B. 1962. *The Political Theory of Possessive Individualism: Hobbes to Locke.* Oxford and New York: Oxford University Press.

Mann, Michael. 1995. "A Political Theory of Nationalism and Its Excesses." In *Notions of Nationalism.* Ed. Sukumar Periwal. Budapest: Central European University Press, pp. 44–64.

———. 1999. "The Dark Side of Democracy: The Modern Tradition of Ethnic and Political Cleansing." *New Left Review* 235: 18–45.

Marrus, Michael. 1985. *The Unwanted: European Refugees in the 20th Century.* New York: Oxford University Press.

Miller, David. 1995. *On Nationality.* Oxford: Oxford University Press.

Nicholson, Frances, and Patrick Twomey, eds. 1999. *Refugee Rights and Realities.* Cambridge: Cambridge University Press.

Pogge, Thomas W. 1989. *Realizing Rawls.* Ithaca, NY, and London: Cornell University Press.

Rawls, John. 1999. *The Law of Peoples.* Cambridge, MA, and London: Harvard University Press.

Sandel, Michael J. 1982. *Liberalism and the Limits of Justice*. Cambridge: Cambridge University Press.
Sassen, Saskia. 1996. *Losing Control? Sovereignty in an Age of Globalization*. New York: Columbia University Press.
———. 1998. "The De Facto Transnationalizing of Immigration Policy." In *Challenge to the Nation-State: Immigration in Western Europe and the United States*. Ed. Christian Joppke. Oxford and New York: Oxford University Press, pp. 49–85.
Schmidtke, Oliver. 1999. "Illiberal Policies in Liberal Societies: Some Remarks on Hollifield's Thesis of the Immigration Dilemma in Liberal Societies." In *International Migration and Liberal Democracies*. Eds. Axel Schulte and Dietrich Thränhardt. Münster: Lit Verlag, pp. 87–100.
Shapiro, Ian. 1986. *The Evolution of Rights in Liberal Theory*. Cambridge: Cambridge University Press.
Singer, Peter. 1979. "Insiders and Outsiders." In *Practical Ethics*. Ed. Peter Singer. Cambridge and New York: Cambridge University Press, pp. 247–163.
Soysal, Yasemin Nuhoglu. 1994. *Limits of Citizenship: Migrants and Postnational Membership in Europe*. Chicago and London: University of Chicago Press.
Straw, Jack. 2000. "Towards a Common Asylum Procedure." Speech by the British Home Secretary to the European Conference on Asylum, Lisbon, June 16.
Taylor, Charles. 1989. *Sources of the Self: The Making of Modern Identity*. Cambridge, MA: Harvard University Press.
Tuck, Richard. 1979. *Natural Rights Theories: Their Origin and Development*. Cambridge: Cambridge University Press.
Tuitt, Patricia. 1999. "Rethinking the Refugee Definition." In *Refugee Rights and Realities*. Ed. Frances Nicholson and Patrick Twomey. Cambridge: Cambridge University Press, pp. 106–118.
Walzer, Michael. 1983. *Spheres of Justice: A Defence of Pluralism and Equality*. New York: Basic Books.
———. 1990. "The Communitarian Critique of Liberalism." *Political Theory* 18, no. 1: 6–23.
Weiner, Myron. 1993. "Introduction: Security, Stability and International Migration." In *International Migration and Security*. Ed. Myron Weiner. Boulder, CO: Westview Press, pp. 1–35.
Weis, Paul. 1994. *The Refugee Convention, 1951: The Travaux Preparatoires Analysed*. Cambridge: Cambridge University Press.

Index

About the Book

The Migration Reader introduces the key articles and documents that analyze the complex phenomenon of transnational migration and the challenges it poses for contemporary societies, states, and international relations.

Enhanced by the editors' commentary, the selections identify concepts and trends in international migration, review the historical origins of contemporary migration and refugee regimes, consider immigration politics and policies, and explore migration in a global context. The result is an intellectual window through which students can better understand the changes occurring in the international environment and in state-society relations within both affluent and less-developed countries.

Anthony M. Messina is associate professor of political science at the University of Notre Dame. His most recent book is *The Logic and Politics of Postwar Migration to Western Europe*. **Gallya Lahav** is associate professor of political science at the State University of New York at Stony Brook. She is author of *Immigration and Politics in the New Europe: Reinventing Borders*.